Human Rights
Under African Constitutions

Pennsylvania Studies in Human Rights

Bert B. Lockwood, Jr., Series Editor

A complete list of books in the series is available from the publisher.

Human Rights Under African Constitutions

Realizing the Promise for Ourselves

Edited by Abdullahi Ahmed An-Naʿim

PENN

University of Pennsylvania Press

Philadelphia

10 9 8 7 6 5 4 3 2 1

Published by
University of Pennsylvania Press
Philadelphia, Pennsylvania 19104-4011

Library of Congress Cataloging-in-Publication Data

Human rights under African constitutions : realizing the promise for ourselves / edited
by Abdullahi Ahmed An-Na'im.
p. cm. — (Pennsylvania studies in human rights)
Includes bibliographical references and index.
ISBN 0-8122-3677-7 (cloth : alk. paper)
1. Human rights—Africa. 2. Rule of law—Africa. 3. Africa—Politics and government.
I. Na'im, 'Abd Allah Ahmad, 1946– II. Series.

JC599.A36 H88 2003
323'.096—dc21   2002074030

Contents

Preface

All the country studies in this book were prepared for a major project on the legal protection of human rights in African countries co-organized by the International Centre for the Legal Protection of Human Rights (Interights), based in London, and the Inter-African Network for Human Rights and Development (Afronet), based in Lusaka, Zambia. The project was generously supported by grants from the British Council, the Ford Foundation, GTZ (Germany), Norwegian Church Aid, and the Swedish NGO Foundation for Human Rights.

As emphasized at all stages of the project, the mechanisms and processes of legal protection of human rights should be neither pursued in isolation from the social, economic, and political context of African societies, nor assumed to be sufficient by themselves for the effective implementation of human rights standards. By focusing on the legal protection of human rights in specific countries, the project sought to take a realistic yet visionary view of the practical possibilities and limitations of these mechanisms and institutions as part of a broader range of strategies for the implementation of human rights in African societies. A planning meeting, held in Lusaka, Zambia, in July 1995, sought to clarify the conception and rationale of the project and identified a representative sample of countries in terms of geopolitical location, legal culture and system, regime of government, and role of the state and of customary or religious law. The countries selected at that meeting were Botswana, Egypt, Ethiopia, Ghana, Guinea, Kenya, Morocco, Mozambique, Nigeria, Rwanda, Senegal, South Africa, Sudan, Uganda, Zaire (as it was known then), and Zambia. Draft studies of the selected countries were presented and discussed at a conference in Dakar, Senegal, in December 1997, in collaboration with Rencontre Africaine pour la Défense des Droits de l'Homme (RADDHO).

Unfortunately, it has not been possible to include all those country studies in this volume.

The challenge is to utilize the conceptual and practical similarities of the struggles of African peoples for individual freedom and social justice in addressing specific country situations through national as well as continental and global efforts. It is true that the situation in each country should be understood on its own terms, as a basis for detailed strategies of legal protection of human rights in the context of the normative framework and institutional arrangements prevailing in the particular country. But the rationale of the present project is that such country-specific initiatives should benefit from insights gained from the experiences of other countries, as well as an understanding of historical and current developments affecting all African societies, though not necessarily in the same manner or to the same degree. In the final analysis, striving for the legal protection of human rights should be based on a clear understanding of the nature of the constitutional and legal orders under which such protection is supposed to materialize. But this endeavor also calls for reflection on the relevance and efficacy of human rights as setting the normative standards of protection.

The proposed approach balances the multifaceted diversity of Africa against the similarity of the experiences of its peoples with colonialism and its aftermath. On the one hand, one needs to be careful about generalizations in view of the diversity of cultural, ethnic, religious, and other features of African societies. On the other hand, the similarities of recent African experiences are too obvious and relevant to ignore in efforts to pool resources and develop responses to the drastic consequences of past colonialism and current differentials in global power relations. For the purposes of the legal protection of human rights in particular, those consequences include the establishment of European model nation-states premised on specific constitutional and legal assumptions, and ways in which that model was misconceived or misapplied in African settings. They also encompass patterns of political development, educational systems, and social trends as well as economic, technological, and other forms of postcolonial dependencies of African countries on developed industrialized countries.

These phenomena should also be understood in the context of increasing globalization. This term is commonly used today to emphasize notions of interdependence, the role of new technologies, the integration of markets, the shrinking of time and space, particularly, the intensification of worldwide social relations, whereby local events are shaped by apparently distant factors and actors. But one should also note that globalization raises possibilities of coercion, conflict, polarization, domination, inequality, exploitation and injustice, monopolies, disruptions and dislocations of the labor and other markets, the emergence of a global regulatory chaos that can be manipulated for economic or political gain. All these factors and actors should be taken into consideration in appreciating the contextual approach to the legal protection of human rights adopted in the following chapters.

Without claiming to do so definitively or exhaustively for any particular country, this project attempts to provide a coherent approach to understanding and documenting the relation between civil society and the state in Africa. Second, the project seeks to develop strategies for overcoming the sense of apathy and powerlessness among the population at large toward the state and its institutions, including its constitutional and legal order. The underlying rationale of this approach is that, despite its earlier noted limitations, the legal protection of human rights is both an end and part of the means for addressing the situation in African countries. But it is important to acknowledge first the reality and negative consequences of the present relation between civil society and the state, and its implications to the principle of constitutionalism and the repeated failure of African constitutions. Otherwise, it would be merely wishful thinking, if not harmful, to speak of the legal protection of human rights under African constitutions.

Following the Lusaka planning meeting of July 1995, I wrote to the selected authors with some suggested guidance for the country studies they were invited to prepare in light of discussions at that meeting. The guidelines emphasized structural and organizational consistency and comprehensive coverage in their country studies in order to develop valid general conclusions, make appropriate policy recommendations, and propose practical strategies for systematic action on the legal protection of human rights under African constitutions. To this end, all authors were asked to follow a similar format, as explained in Chapter 1, in addition to the following two points as a matter of general orientation:

1. The ultimate objective is to enhance and promote the legal protection of human rights under the constitution (or existing constitutional order, whatever it may be at the present time) of the country in question. As agreed at the Lusaka meeting, the concept of legal protection refers to the "total process of deploying the law for the purpose of vindicating human rights." Taking this focus as the agreed mandate does not mean that the legal process is the only, or even primary, way of protecting human rights, or that this subject can or should be studied in isolation from other approaches in broader local, regional and global context.

2. Each country study should be seen as the basis of a multifaceted strategy

which will include litigation, information exchange, training, and legislative advocacy. Accordingly, each study should include an assessment of the possibilities and problems of each aspect of this multifaceted strategy, while still focusing on the primary subject and organization of the study as explained below.

This book does not claim to cover every aspect of the legal protection of human rights under the African constitutions considered here, let alone other aspects of constitutionalism and politics or legal systems in general. To include specific subjects and themes that can be used by scholars, policy makers, and the public at large, there have been some necessary limitations. Nonetheless, this book is unique in its broad, systematic, and comparative approach to the constant imperative to remedy human rights violations through constitutional procedures and institutions.

Finally, I wish to acknowledge the unfailing support and assistance of colleagues at Interights and Afronet at all stages of this project. In particular, I am grateful for the additional work of Emma Playfair, Chidi Anselm Odinkalu, and Ibrahima Kane of Interights at all stages of the project. My special appreciation also goes to Rohit Chopra for helping me prepare this manuscript for publication.

Chapter 1
Introduction
Expanding Legal Protection of Human Rights in African Contexts

Abdullahi Ahmed An-Naʿim

The value added of international standards of human rights is that they are universally valid and legally binding on states that have ratified the relevant treaties or are bound by applicable customary international law principles, subject to clarification and qualification below. As such, human rights provide an external "common standard of achievement" for all nations and peoples, according to the Preamble of the Universal Declaration of Human Rights of 1948. Accordingly, states have the international legal obligation to provide for the protection of human rights under their own national constitutions, legal systems, and other official measures. In other words, international human rights law provides an independent frame of reference for ensuring the fundamental rights and freedoms of all persons subject to the jurisdiction of a state. It is from this perspective that each chapter in this book presents a detailed country study of the context and resources available for the legal protection of human rights under the constitution and legal system of a specific African state.

My objective in this chapter is to provide a theoretical framework for these country studies by clarifying the parameters of the role of the people themselves in protecting their own human rights because that is the only legitimate, principled, and sustainable way for realizing this essential objective. The premise of my analysis here is that an international human rights approach is both practically essential and conceptually problematic. This approach is practically essential because no state can be trusted to protect the rights of its own citizens, and it is conceptually problematic in that international human rights law maintains that the same state is bound to protect these rights. Making the protection of human rights a matter of state responsibility under international law means that an injury or harm is not a human rights violation unless the state is implicated in its happening by the acts or omissions of its officials or institutions. To simplify an example to make this point, the victim of bodily injury should always receive effective legal remedy against the perpetrator. But the act cannot be legally characterized as a human rights violation of torture, for instance, unless committed by or under color of the authority of state officials. In this sense, human rights violations can be committed only through the action of or omission by the state. Yet, the international law principle of national sovereignty and territorial integrity, as affirmed by the Charter of the United Nations, does not permit redress for human rights violations except through the agency of the state.

The question is therefore how to mediate this "paradox of self-regulation" by the state in order to induce, or coerce if necessary, the state to protect the rights of those subject to its jurisdiction against abuse and violation by its own officials and institutions? I believe, together with all the contributors to this volume, that this mediation must be undertaken by the people for themselves because that is the only way to reconcile the protection of human rights with the national sovereignty and territorial integrity of their own state. Direct so-called humanitarian intervention by other states or the international community at large in the territory of any state in the name of protecting the human rights of its people is problematic in principle and unsustainable in practice.[1] But to object to such external "enforcement" apparently raises another paradox. On the one hand, governments are unlikely to respect human rights without strong and effective accountability for their failure to do so. On the other hand, an oppressed people are by definition unable to achieve such accountability of their oppressive government. Here is an outline of an approach to mediating this second paradox, to be elaborated through the subsequent analysis.[2]

First, the choice for other states and the international community at large is not between rushing to "doing something" or passively watching flagrant and systematic violations of basic human rights. Rather, it is between the principled and institutionalized application of the same standards everywhere over time, on the one hand, and self-help and vigilante justice in crisis situations, on the other. The morally viable and practically sustainable approach is for other states to act individually and collectively in gradually investing in the capacity of the oppressed people to defend their own rights, while generally upholding the fundamental credibility of the rule of law in international relations. The possibility of direct intervention in the territory of states that engage in gross and systematic violation of human rights should remain as a last resort, provided it is exercised in a principled and consistent manner. But the primary response must be the promotion of local capacity for legal and political accountability of governments to their own people.

Second, this promotion of local capacity must be through the development of national institutions and mechanisms of accountability within the specific context of each country. In other words, such efforts must build on what actually exists on the ground because attempting to impose norms and models developed elsewhere is both objectionable as a colonial exercise in cultural imperialism, and unlikely to be workable in a sustainable manner in practice. Moreover, these efforts should always respect the independent agency and human dignity of its intended beneficiaries by gradually diminishing their dependency on external support.

But in the final analysis, the ultimate success of this approach is contingent on the willingness and ability of the people themselves to oppose oppression and violation of their rights to the maximum possible degree. The critical elements of this most fundamental requirement might be called the sociology and psychology of resistance and the context within which such resistance is supposed to take place. I will discuss these elements under the two sections following this introduction. In the last section of this chapter, I will draw on some of the findings of the country studies prepared under the project from which this book emerged, as explained in the Preface, to highlight differences in the level of achievement and challenges facing various African societies. But first, here are some further reflections on my earlier remarks about the nature and dynamics of the legal protection of human rights in general.

As a working definition, human rights are those claims which every human being is entitled to have and enjoy, as of right, by virtue of his or her humanity, without distinction on such grounds as sex, race, color, religion, language, national origin, or social group. This generally accepted definition does not provide an authoritative list of what these rights are or specify the precise content of any right in particular. It does not explain the criteria and methodology by which specific human rights can be identified and recognized, or settle controversies about economic, social, and cultural rights and whether there are, or ought to be, collective human rights other than the right to self-determination. In addition to addressing questions of more precise definition and content, one also needs to reflect on issues of how and by whom are human rights to be respected and protected, whatever they are and whatever content they may have. Theoretical definitions and enumeration of lists of human rights in the abstract is wishful thinking, unless supported by clarification of the process by which these rights are supposed to be implemented in practice.

To begin with, the assertion that human rights are claims to which all people are entitled, as of right, by virtue of their humanity firmly locates these rights and their implementation in the social and political realm of human affairs. Whatever these rights are, and whatever their precise content may be, their implementation necessarily requires allocation of resources over extended periods of time, and the establishment of institutional capacity to mediate between rights in case of conflict, and to adjudicate the competing demands in specific cases. The protection of human rights can only be realized through some form of wide-scale political organization that is capable and willing to undertake these functions. Whatever may be its failings and problems, as discussed in the next section, the postcolonial state in Africa is the most viable regime of political organization for these purposes for the foreseeable future. Though constantly contested by a variety of cultural (customary) institutions and networks, and recently increasingly undermined by globalizing forces, the state remains a fundamental framework for political interaction, social relations, economic development, administration of justice, as well as the provision of essential services at the national level. It is also the entity recognized and dealt with by all other states and external actors on such matters as international trade and economic activities, and diplomatic and foreign relations. The postcolonial state is the universally acknowledged medium of policy formulation, daily administration, and the embodiment of national sovereignty.

Thus, the very concept of legal protection of human rights assumes and presupposes the existence of a state that accepts responsibility for upholding the authority of human rights and has the institutional capacity and political will to effect such protection. That is clear enough regarding national constitutional and legal systems, as well as human rights norms and implementation mechanisms based on international treaties between states. Even principles of customary international law, to the limited extent they can establish human rights norms, are premised on state practice out of a sense of legal obligation.[3] It is true that formal legal obligations and implementation mechanisms are supported by such informal methods as pressure by nongovernmental organizations (NGOs) and the media or through diplomatic exchanges. But such efforts seek implementation of human rights obligations through legislation and enforcement by national jurisdictions, and not by direct action independent from the will of the state in question. Therefore, whether one is relying on a country's constitution and legal system, or invoking international legal obligations, the juridical sovereignty of the state means that its appropriate organs and institutions have exclusive jurisdiction over the interpretation and implementation of those rights.

Despite these legal and practical realities, the universality of human rights is intended to ensure the protection of certain minimum entitlements of all human beings, especially when they are not sufficiently protected under national legal and political systems. In practice, the present international standards of human rights are negotiated and adopted by delegates of state governments and become binding as treaties between states. Under international law, treaties create international obligations, but each state has the ultimate power to interpret and implement those obligations within its own exclusive national jurisdiction, though other actors may try to influence state action in this regard. It is true that intergovernmental organizations like the United Nations and its organs, NGOs, the media and public opinion, among others, seek to influence the human rights performance of various states. These activities are most welcome and indeed essential for the respect and protection of human rights. But the point to emphasize here is that such efforts can only work *through the agency of the state*, rather than through independent action within the territory of the state without its cooperation or at least consent.

Another point to note about the nature of the international source of the obligation to protect human rights is that, from an international law perspective, a state owes its legal obligations to other states parties to the treaty or customary practice. International obligations are normally supposed to be vindicated through interactions among states, whether unilaterally or through intergovernmental organizations like the United Nations and other mechanisms of multilateral relations. If other states parties to a treaty deem a state to be in breach of its obligations, it is up to those states to take necessary action under international law to ensure compliance or otherwise retaliate against the offending state. As a general rule, the whole system does not conceive of any legal role for nonstate actors, though they may well be able to exercise strong political or other influence on state actors.

This system is unlikely to work well for human rights treaties because their beneficiaries are individual persons and groups making claims against the state that is supposed to represent them in the international arena. For the system to work properly, states are supposed to have sufficient self-interest in monitoring and acting against breaches of international obligations by other states parties to a treaty or bound by a rule of customary international law. National self-interest is normally defined to include such matters as trade or economic relations, defense and national security, and natural resources. States may also deem the protection of their nationals against other states as part of their self-interest, though they may not be able to do it effectively in some situations. While many states claim commitment to international human rights standards, they are unlikely to risk their own self-interest in order to challenge another state's failure to honor its international human rights obligations toward its own nationals. This reality may explain why interstate complaint procedures under global and regional human rights treaties are rarely used, even against states that are universally condemned for their flagrant and massive human rights violations.

The same is true of claims to incorporate human rights concerns in the foreign policy of a state by making the protection of these rights a condition for giving aid to developing countries, through diplomatic pressure, or as part of the rhetoric of justifying so-called humanitarian intervention. But one should recall here that the rationale of international protection of human rights is that governments cannot be trusted to respect the rights of their own citizens, let alone those of citizens of other countries. Even if one is to assume a government's genuine commitment to the protection of human rights in other countries, its motives will probably be mixed because of the unavoidable complexity of the foreign policy interests of any state. Moreover, it is unlikely for declared intentions to translate into concrete and consistent action, regardless of changes in government and shifting priority in national politics. In any case, responses by other states are too slow and generalized to assist specific individual or group victims of human rights violations.

By the People for Themselves

It is therefore clear that the beneficiaries of human rights standards themselves must assume primary responsibility for protecting their own rights, whether against their own state, or by inducing it to support them against some external actors or conditions causing the human rights violation. This process can either relate to how to prevent the occurrence of violations in the first place, or effectively redress the wrong done to the victim in order to deter future violations. It should also be emphasized here that all persons and groups are "beneficiaries" of human rights standards, and not only the immediate victims of violations. Indeed, violators too can become victims when they fall out of favor with an oppressive government they used to serve in the past, or upon a revolutionary change of regime.

It may sound odd to speak of the victims protecting their own rights, but that is in fact true in all cases, whether at the national or international level, as it is always a matter of relative power relations between the violator and victim. That is, the question is how to move the violator to comply by finding an appropriate point of relative advantage or leverage point to that end. The availability to the victim of effective means of recourse that the violator will find difficult to resist is part of this process. But since this is unlikely to be readily available or self-evident, the issue is usually how to somehow shift the balance of power in favor of the victim, thereby prompting an actual or potential violator to comply with human rights norms in question.

Regarding the legal protection of human rights in national settings in particular, the first point to make is that being a victim does not necessarily mean that one is standing in an objectively and permanently weaker position in relation to the violator. In fact, the violator's power is usually dependent on the victim's perception of, and response to, the situation. If the victim is somehow able to refuse to submit to the apparent power of the violator, and able to resort to whatever means of resistance are available, the terms of the relationship between the victim and violator would already have begun to shift or change. Part of that transformation is an understanding of the nature of balance of power relations between the victim and violator, and calculation of how it might sufficiently shift or change in favor of the victim.

This psychological dimension of the relationship is closely linked to its political dynamics because violators cannot act without consideration of the consequences of their actions, especially the reaction of the actual or potential victims. The state itself is a political creature that does not have an independent existence from the people who control its apparatus and those who accept their commands. Despite all the material resources and coercive powers available to them, the ability of those officials who act in the name of the state is first and foremost political, including the willingness of the general population to accept or at least acquiesce to the state's actions. Since those in control of the state are a tiny fraction of those who accept its power, the ability of the former to enforce their will through direct force is untenable in the face of large scale and persistent resistance. Those who control the state would therefore need to persuade or induce the vast majority to submit to their power and authority, which is usually achieved by claiming to represent the will of the majority or acting in their best interest. In fact, not a single government in the world today openly claims that it is entitled to rule irrespective of its ability and willingness to serve the best interest of the population. The question is therefore how can violating the human rights of the population of a country be in the best interest of that very population?

From a practical perspective, there appear to be several possibilities for justifying the political authority of the state, such as safeguarding national security, the dictates of tradition or of moral or religious standing of the ruling elite. Political authority may even appear to be founded on the reality of effective control over the population through the sheer force of intimidation. Ultimately, however, none of these possibilities can materialize unless the population at large accepts or acquiesces to the authority of those in control of the state. Since human beings are always motivated by their self-interest in basic survival as well as material and moral well-being, such acceptance or submission is usually based on the people's belief that it is in their best interest. Whether it is based on the force of tradition or of moral or religious standing of the ruling elite, people will not submit to an authority that threatens or undermines their fundamental self-interest in human existence. It is better to speak of "human existence" in this context to indicate that it is more than purely physical survival and includes a sense of social justice and human dignity. Resistance may be delayed because of the psychological or material force of the bases of authority, but it can also mount in response to severity of oppression that weakens the legitimizing effect of an alleged rationale. For example, people may be culturally conditioned to submit to the authority of traditional or religious leaders, but this tendency will diminish in proportion to clarity of perceptions that those leaders are actually violating the interests of their constituencies. Even when people submit out of fear for their personal safety, there will probably come a point when the drive for human existence will overcome the force of intimidation.

For our purposes here, one can therefore conclude that the strength of a people's determination to insist on the protection of their human rights is proportionate to their belief that those rights are essential for their human existence. In other words, weakness in a people's determination to resist human rights violations reflects a lack or weakness of conviction that those rights are essential to their human existence. Conversely, the stronger that conviction, the more likely will people insist that the state respects and protects those rights against whoever violates them. The question that emerges from this analysis is whether a particular set of human rights has achieved, or is likely to achieve, the necessary level of acceptance among its purported beneficiaries as essential for their human existence.

The answer to this question is relative in the sense that the strength of a people's determination to accept the consequences of resistance is proportionate to their perception of the relationship between a given right and human existence. For example, people will more readily resist a threat to their physical survival than a denial of their right to participate in their own government or violation of their freedoms of expression or association that appears to be abstract and far removed from their daily concerns. But this, in turn, is a function of perception and understanding of the relationship between these freedoms and physical survival, which is also a relative matter. For instance, a denial of the right to participate in government is likely to be resisted to the extent that it is believed to be related to physical survival because bad governmental economic planning or poor response to natural disasters can threaten human life or essential health. The matter is also relative in the sense that people may also be moved to resisting non-life-threatening violations of their rights, but they are unlikely to do so at a serious risk to their lives. The question is therefore how do African peoples relate to human rights and perceive the relationship between those rights and their own human existence?

The type of norms that came to be known since the mid-twentieth century as "human rights" certainly had some philosophical, religious, and intellectual antecedents in the history of many societies. Moreover, the values and institutions that underlie these norms have come to be accepted by most societies today as a result of the internationalization of Western European and North American models of the nation-state, constitutional orders, and international relations through colonialism. In that sense, one can speak of the universality of human rights as a product of widely accepted moral insights and shared political experiences. But the idea of recognition and legal enforcement of these norms as overriding fundamental rights clearly emerged from Western political and intellectual experiences since the eighteenth century. Although not acknowledged for local populations during colonial rule of African and Asian societies, these rights came to be routinely included in constitutional bills of rights upon achieving independence in the mid-twentieth century.

The problem with the constitutional origins and international development of human rights from the point of view of African societies is that they did not participate in the early domestic development of these rights, or in their initial formulation at the international level. When these rights were developed in Western Europe and North America, African societies were not organized as nation-states with national constitutional orders and related institutions. Moreover, the colonial administration from which African societies emerged in their present nation-states was by definition a denial of any possibility of constitutional standing and participation for local African societies. At the time of the drafting and adoption of the Universal Declaration in 1946–48, as the constituent document of the modern human rights movement, there were only four African members of the United Nations (Egypt, Ethiopia, Liberia, and apartheid South Africa). The same European powers which upheld human rights for their citizens under national constitutions, and proclaimed the Universal Declaration for all of humanity, were at the time denying African societies their most basic human rights under colonial rule. Furthermore, as discussed in the next section, the concept of the nation-state, with its constitutional order and bill of rights, that African societies were supposed to implement after independence was a colonial impositions rather than the product of internal political, social, and economic developments. This is one aspect of the perception of lack of legitimacy of human rights in African societies.

Another aspect of this legitimacy issue is the apparent tension between certain African cultural and religious traditions, on the one hand, and some human rights norms, on the other. It is true that similar tensions exist in all societies, including liberal cultural relativism of Western societies against social, economic, and cultural human rights. But the issue seems to enjoy greater resonance in African societies because they did not yet have the level of political stability and economic development that would enable them to mediate such tensions for themselves in their own specific context. Moreover, issues of legitimacy and relevance in origins and current context are exacerbated in the African context through deliberate manipulation by those who wish to discredit or undermine human rights for their own political or ideological reasons. The ruling elite seek to legitimize their authoritarian regimes and oppressive practices, while religious fundamentalists and other cultural relativists perceive the human rights ethos as antithetical to their worldview and vision of the social good.

Given these realities, proponents of human rights in Africa should take challenges to the legitimacy of human rights in African societies very seriously. For example, they should not assume that the majority in their respective societies already understand and accept these norms, but are only unable to uphold them in practice because of oppressive regimes or authoritarian social structures and institutions. As indicated earlier, Africans may be failing to stand up for their human rights because they do not perceive international standards as essential for their human existence. Accordingly, the challenge facing the proponents of human rights is to demonstrate to their local communities the legitimacy and relevance of international standards in their own immediate context. This is by no means an easy task, but it can be done if taken as a sufficiently high priority by human rights advocates in Africa.[4]

Part of this process is to emphasize the importance of pursuing the legal protection of human rights in particular. First, the very concept of human rights in the modern sense of the term is that these are entitlements *as of right*, and not simply because of charity, social solidarity or other moral consideration, though those purposes may well be served in the process. In the present context of state societies in Africa, as opposed to what they may have been in precolonial times, no entitlement can be claimed as of right without legal mechanisms for its implementation or enforcement. That is, whatever other strategies one may adopt for the promotion and protection of human rights, there has to be ways and means for legal protection if human rights are rights at all.

Second, the availability of effective means of legal protection enables people to resist violations of their rights peacefully and in an orderly fashion, without having to risk their personal safety or suffer other serious consequences every time. As indicated earlier, this possibility is part of the process of shifting the balance of power in favor of victims or potential victims of human rights violations against the violator. The victim's apprehension that the cost of resistance might be too high is part of the violator's psychological advantage. Conversely, reducing and quantifying the consequences of resistance through the legal process will encourage victims to resist and support them in that process.

Another useful function of legal protection of human rights is that it provides society with opportunities for resolving conflicts within specific rights or between competing claims of rights. The deliberate nature and slow pace of the legal process is particularly appropriate for the sort of sociological and theoretical reflection necessary for resolving difficult issues like striking a balance between freedom of speech and protection of people's privacy and reputation. For example, should the incitement of racial or religious hatred, commonly known as "hate speech," be allowed as legitimate freedom of opinion and expression, or prohibited because of its negative social and political consequences.

An appreciation of these valuable functions of the legal protection of human rights will assist in building up political support for the success of this type of remedy or avenue of redress. Without strong political support, the legal protection of human rights is unlikely to receive sufficient human and material resources for its effective implementation. An understaffed and overcrowded legal process is hardly conducive to social and moral deliberation over the difficult policy issues that are likely to arise in human rights litigation. Even stronger political support is needed for making immediate accountability for any human rights violation so imperative and categorical that it becomes simply "unthinkable" for those who control of the apparatus of the state to act in that way.

Strategies for promoting political support include campaigns for raising public awareness about the importance and benefits of legal protection of human rights and exercising sufficient public pressure to ensure the success of such protection whenever it is sought by victims or potential victims to generate a momentum in its favor. But the main point that should be emphasized here is that the existence of sufficient political support for the legal protection of human rights cannot be taken for granted or assumed to exist without deliberate efforts for promoting and sustaining it over time.

As suggested earlier, the state is the essential context within which human rights are to be protected in practice. I now turn to a brief discussion of this subject in the African context, primarily in relation to the underlying issues of legal protection of human rights, before concluding with an overview of the current situation and future direction of developments in this regard.

The Postcolonial State in Africa

Notwithstanding the wide diversity of earlier forms of social and political organization and significant differences in their colonial experiences, all African societies today live under European model nation-states. Even those parts of Africa, like Egypt and Ethiopia, which were not colonized in the formal sense of the term,[5] have come to adopt the same European model in order to achieve national sovereignty and international recognition. Paradoxically, although in fact a poor copy of an alien model imposed by European colonialism, and while incapable for a variety of reasons of discharging its responsibilities at home and abroad, the postcolonial state in Africa is supposed to enjoy all the prerogatives and privileges of equal sovereignty. In this way African states are expected to protect their citizens and territories and to that end are deemed to be entitled to exclusive national jurisdiction over them, regardless of their ability and willingness to discharge the obligations of that claim.

Thus, although many African states are internally deficient and externally weak, their sovereignty is guaranteed by the world community of states in ways that stand in sharp contrast to the model of external recognition of their statehood on the basis of their empirical sovereignty on the ground. As explained by Robert Jackson and Carl Rosberg:

African states are direct successors of the European colonies that were alien entities to most of Africa. Their legitimacy derived not from internal African consent, but from international agreements—primarily among European states—beginning with the Berlin Conference of 1884–85. Their borders were usually defined not by African political facts or geography, but rather by international rules of continental partition and occupation established for that purpose. Their governments were organized according to European colonial theory and practice (tempered by expediency), and were staffed almost entirely by Europeans at decision-making levels. Their economies were managed with imperial and/or local colonial considerations primarily in mind. Their laws and policies reflected the interests and values of European imperial power, and these usually included strategic military uses, economic advantage, Christianization, European settlement, and so forth. Although the populations of the colonies were overwhelmingly African, the vast majority of the inhabitants had little or no constitutional standing in them.[6]

For our purposes here, it should be emphasized that African societies had little control even over the timing and dynamics of the process of decolonization that is supposed to have "restored" their sovereignty. Independence eventually came about as a result of shifts in the dynamics of European domestic politics and international relations after the end of World War II. The timing of independence was largely decided by the colonial power for its own considerations, rather than by internal developments within African societies. In order to immediately end colonial oppression and exploitation of African societies, the 1960 United Nations Declaration on the Granting of Independence to Colonial Countries and Peoples stipulated that the inadequacy of political, economic, social, or educational preparation should never serve as a pretext for delaying independence. In this way, increasing international moral and political pressures resulted in the separation of the juridical right of self-determination from the empirical capacity for self-government.[7] This blanket and unconditional preservation of juridical statehood and territorial integrity, regardless of ability and willingness to live up to consequent obligations, became the primary concern of the Organization of African Unity (OAU) since it was established in 1963.

This preoccupation with the preservation of juridical statehood does not mean that African countries are free from serious political conflict. The sovereignty and stability of African states are constantly contested in regional conflicts and internal civil wars,[8] as well as by the forces of diminishing sovereignty over vital national economic and social policy under current structural adjustment programs and unfavorable global trade relations. Such serious threats in turn led African states to be more concerned with their juridical sovereignty and political stability at almost any costs than with their ability to perform their essential functions of protecting and serving their citizens.

A particularly significant factor to note here is the nature of colonial administration and the political culture it cultivated in African societies. For decades, colonial powers exercised exclusive control over local populations by ruling through a few educated local elite and traditional rulers and the extensive use of divide and rule tactics. All that independence signified in most African states was the transfer of control over authoritarian power structures and processes of government from colonial masters to local elite. Notions of popular participation in governance and accountability of officials at the national and local level were never known to African societies during colonial rule or after independence. The political parties that were established during the struggle for independence often remained auxiliary institutions of personal power and rarely transformed into authentic organizations of public opinion or expressions of popular sovereignty.

Moreover, with external defense secured by agreement among colonial powers since the conference of Berlin, and largely preserved by the OAU since 1963, state security came to mean directing military forces inward at African populations as protection against rebellion or riot. National security has been transformed into the security of the regime in power, with no possibility whatsoever of transparency or political and legal accountability in the operation of security forces. Unable to govern effectively and humanely, postcolonial governments tended to compensate by using oppressive and authoritarian methods, usually employing the same colonial legal and institutional mechanisms maintained by several cycles of "native" governments since independence.

Since the state usually lacked effective presence in most of its territorial jurisdiction, ruling elite tended to focus on controlling the government apparatus and patronage system and to strive to retain the support of key ethnic leaders, instead of seeking genuine legitimacy and accountability to the population at large. Ironically, those shortsighted political strategies in fact facilitated the loss of power by most of the first generation of civilian African leaders to military usurpers who would succeed in controlling the government and the whole country by simply physically holding a few officials and key government installations in the capital. Within hours of a successful coup, military usurpers would be deemed to be in "effective control of the government" and thereby granted automatic recognition by "the international community" in almost every single case. In this way, both the domestic and international sources of recognition of independent statehood in postcolonial Africa tend to be exclusively concerned with sovereignty of the government, not of the people.

Whatever may have been the reasons or alleged justifications, the vast majority of first constitutions were actually either suspended or radically altered by military usurpers or single party states within a few years of independence. In other words, there appears to have been a fundamental weakness of the principle of constitutionalism itself in the vast majority of African countries. Subject to minor and partial exceptions, the idea that government must be in accordance with the rule of law in ways that uphold the fundamental individual and collective rights of all citizens has not been observed by postcolonial states. Constitutional instruments have also failed effectively to hold governments accountable to the principle of constitutionalism. Whatever the specific reasons may have been from country to country—and they are no doubt complex and often controversial—these are the sad realities in almost all African countries. Irrespective of the explanation one may wish to accept, local populations seem to be unwilling or unable to resist the erosion or manipulation of their national constitutions and governments by a variety of civilian and military leaders since independence.

In my view, the weakness of the principle of constitutionalism and actual failure of African constitutions are symptoms of the wider problem of the lack of dynamic relationship between civil society as it exists on the ground, on the one hand, and state institutions and processes, on the other. Part of the underlying causes of this problem, it seems to me, is the fact that the concept and nature of the present nation-state was an external imposition, rather than an indigenous growth that has evolved out of the lived experiences and cultural values of African societies. Far from having a sense of ownership and expectation of protection and service, as well as a general belief in their ability to influence its functioning, African societies apparently regard the postcolonial state with profound mistrust. They tend to tolerate its existence as an unavoidable evil but prefer to have little interaction with its institutions and processes.

These problems can be redressed through a variety of strategies to enhance the legitimacy and popular accessibility and utility of a constitution as a living institution. Analysis of drafting and adoption processes and of the content, interpretation, and application of the document are also necessary for assessing the ability of a people to hold officials and institutions of the state responsive to, and accountable for, the basic needs of the population. For the purposes of legal protection of human rights in particular, it is important to examine the cluster of norms, institutions, and processes pertaining to the rule of law, political participation, protection of fundamental rights, and so forth. However, as illustrated by the recent developments in Ethiopia briefly examined below, even with the most "promising" drafting and adoption process and despite the desperate need of the population for constitutionalism to take root and operate effectively, it is difficult to predict what will happen in practice. But since it is unthinkable, in my view, to abandon the possibility altogether, there is no alternative but to continue the struggle for moving the process forward whenever there is a setback for, or apparent failure of, constitutionalism in any country. From this perspective, it is critical to take a long-term view of the complexity and contingency of the process of ensuring the sustainability and practical utility of this principle in each country.

After decades of civil war and severe political and economic instability, Ethiopia finally appeared to have begun the process of securing the principle of constitutionalism, as explained in Chapter 2. However, developments in that country since the author finalized her draft for publication seem to seriously undermine that promising prospect. It is not possible to review these developments in detail or discuss various possible explanations and underlying causes in the political culture and recent history of the country. But the immediate trigger of the present crisis (as of August 2001) appears to have been the 1998–2000 war between Ethiopia and Eritrea, and the postwar relationship between the two countries in general. Major human rights problems during the war include the Ethiopian government's forceful expulsion of 70,000 Ethiopians of Eritrean parentage to Eritrea, after holding them in harsh detention conditions, without any possibility of challenging their expulsion. The government of Ethiopia also continued to hold under harsh conditions, and without charge or trial, thousands of people it suspected of sympathizing with insurgents within the country itself.

Moreover, disagreements over the causes and conduct of the war and postwar relations appeared to have been the cause of a serious division within the Tigray People's Liberation Front (TPLF), the main party in the ruling coalition, the Ethiopian People's Revolutionary Democratic Front (EPRDF). In the ensuing power struggle within the TPLF and EPRDF, the faction led by Prime Minister Meles Zenawi apparently won and succeeded in expelling the dissident group within the central committee of his own party.[9] To achieve its objectives, however, the winning faction has resorted to detaining the leading dissidents on allegations of corruption and manipulating the judicial process to keep them in detention. Such developments are to be expected in the politics of any country. Indeed, the fundamental purpose of the legal protection of human rights is precisely to prevent such abuse of the constitutional and legal system of the country for the political ends of the government of the day.

To summarize, this book presents studies on the legal protection of human rights under the constitutions of present African states that are the product of arbitrary colonial histories and decolonization processes. By their very nature, these states have tended to continue the same authoritarian policies and to enhance their ability to oppress and control, rather than to protect and serve, their citizens. The constitutional systems by which these states rule were hurriedly assembled at independence, only to collapse or be emptied of all meaningful content within a few years. The legal systems these states continue to implement are usually poor copies of the colonial legal systems, lacking legitimacy and relevance to the lives of the population at large. Many African states also suffer from cycles of civil wars and severe civil strife that undermine any prospects of the stability and continuity needed for building traditions and institutions of government under the rule of law. Their economies are weak and totally vulnerable to global processes beyond their control.

But the here goal is not simply to lament the deplorable status of the legal protection of human rights under African constitutions. Rather, the purpose is to provide a realistic basis for developing strategies to transform the situation in favor of greater and more effective protection. This objective is founded on the firm conviction that state practice must and can be changed in this way, provided appropriate strategies are implemented with the positive belief in the ability of African peoples to protect their own human rights.

Legal Protection of Human Rights

My purpose in this last section is not to summarize the various country studies but rather to highlight and draw upon some representative samplings of those findings for a general view of where different African countries are at present, and indicate what needs to be done to improve the quality and sustainability of the legal protection of human rights.

According to the guidelines that were agreed upon among all the authors, they were requested to organize and analyze their studies under six subheadings. They were all asked to begin with an overview of the historical background and demographic profile of the country and to highlight general political social, cultural, and economic conditions relevant to their subject. Against that general background, each author should proceed to examine the constitutional and legal framework for the protection of human rights, the status and performance of the judiciary and legal profession, the impact of political, social, and economic context, and the status and role of nongovernmental organizations, and offer some conclusions and recommendations.

Constitutional and Legal Framework

In this section, authors were asked to explain the origins, main developments, and current status of the constitutional and legal systems of their respective countries, followed by an overview of constitutional provisions relating to the protection of human rights. They were also requested to note ratifications of, and reservations on, the African Charter on Human and Peoples' Rights and the main United Nations human rights treaties. Special attention should be given to possibilities of using international human rights norms in domestic litigation and legal enforcement, regardless of how much this is happening in practice. In other words, this section is supposed to cover all aspects and possibilities of the formal legal view of the protection of rights, that is, what the law says should happen. The relationship between theory and practice should emerge from other parts of each country study.

Authors were also urged to discuss the status and role, if any, of customary (including religious) law and practice and its relation to the formal legal system of the state. Questions to be covered in this part of the chapter should include, for example, whether customary law and practice are subject to an overriding concern with the protection of constitutional and/or human rights. Is it possible, for instance, to challenge customary law as unconstitutional, or is there broader judicial review or other mechanisms to ensure respect for procedural or substantive constitutional and human rights standards in the application of customary law?

African countries may be characterized or classified in different ways, but for our purposes here, it might be useful to consider them in terms of whether the government is, on the whole, an aid or an obstacle to the legal protection of human rights. Whether a country's legal system is based on common or civil law is not the most important criterion in determining its attitude toward the legal protection of human rights. Similarly, whether a country has a federal system like Nigeria, or unitary system, as is the case in Mozambique and Uganda, is immaterial in principle, though the constitutional framework and institutional arrangements for legal protection under each type of system will probably be significantly different.

The influence of Western liberal theory can be seen in the fact that some African constitutions tend to recognize civil and political rights and generally disregard economic, social, and cultural or collective rights. None of the countries surveyed provide full-fledged constitutional protection for economic, social, and cultural rights. A few constitutions, like those of Ghana and Uganda, include economic and social rights as "Directive

Principles of State Policy." South Africa, which has apparently made the most advanced constitutional provision for economic, social, and cultural rights, still make them subject to progressive realization. It also remains to be seen how far South Africa can maintain its constitutional lead over the rest of the continent. But in all countries, additional protection of these rights can be drawn from international treaties providing for the rights when the treaties are ratified and their promises are fully incorporated into national domestic law.

In contrast, provisions for civil and political rights, like freedom of expression and association, can generally be found in every African constitution. Even repressive governments pay lip service to these notions, although they have developed some impressive ways of circumventing them, such as claw-back and ouster clauses and the use of military tribunals, as discussed below. Moreover, as already illustrated by the case of Ethiopia above, the existence of constitutional provision for specific civil and political rights is a necessary but insufficient condition for the legal protection of those rights. Regardless of the details of constitutional and statutory schemes, the question should always be whether the government is open and legally accountable to its citizens. Since many constitutions have been totally or partially suspended, drastically amended, or totally abrogated, the question may therefore be whether some form of constitutional framework for legal accountability remains despite the absence of, or the imposition of severe restriction on, a written constitution as a formal document.

Despite the existence of human rights protections in most African constitutions, however, repressive governments have found numerous ways to limit or eliminate these protections at the theoretical level, let alone as a matter of practice. The most important constitutional limitations and restrictions include the following. *States of emergency* appear to be the norm, rather than the exception, in several African countries, and the criteria and procedure for regulating them tend to grant considerable discretion to the executive branch of government. Once a state of emergency is declared, the executive can suspend the people's exercise of their civil and political rights in the interest of state security. For example, in a state of emergency it is common for the rules regarding preventive detention to be relaxed to "legalize" detention without charge or trial for exercising one's freedom of expression or association. Specific provisions of the constitution may be subject to *derogation* (partial repeal or suspension), based on the operation of other constitutional provisions, during an emergency or for other reasons. *Ouster clauses* are used to preclude or "oust" the jurisdiction of the courts over provisions of the constitution or other laws, thereby prohibiting them from hearing cases brought under the provisions in question. *Claw-back clauses* are also used to permit constitutional provisions and guarantees to be restricted by ordinary legislation.

Few of the studies actually discuss the rules of *standing to sue*, but the relevant provisions in most of the constitutions surveyed tend to limit standing to those who have suffered the actual violation of their rights. However, some countries, like South Africa and Uganda, have specifically broadened the rules of standing to permit public interest litigation. It is interesting to note that the bill of rights in the new South African constitution may apply to relations among private persons, as well as against the state and its organs and officials, as usual in Western constitutional schemes. The extent of the protection will vary, depending on the nature of the right in question, and it remains to be seen what the courts and other institutions will make of this provision.

Most of the countries studied have ratified the major *international human rights treaties*, without major reservations. Differences in legal systems are reflected in whether or not incorporating these international obligations into domestic jurisdiction requires specific legislation or procedure, while political factors determine whether or not those steps are taken for human rights treaties in particular. But the critical question here is whether national courts do apply such treaty obligations, or whether there are opportunities for realizing some degree of accountability for their governments before regional or international bodies, like the Commission of the African Charter on Human and Peoples' Rights and the UN Human Rights Commission. These types of issues were to be discussed in each chapter under the practical application aspects of the role of the judiciary, the legal profession, and NGOs.

The *legal systems* described in the country studies appear to be broadly based on Western models of either the English common law or continental civil law variety. As noted above, the choice of one system or another is a product of colonial experience and is not itself indicative of whether and to what extent human rights are legally protected in the country. But generally speaking, an imported legal system is likely to alienate the local people, as the law appears to them as both intimidating and inaccessible. Such perceptions are only exacerbated when courtroom proceedings are conducted in European languages that the parties do not understand. The result is particularly anomalous when all the major actors in the courtroom, judge, jury, attorneys, parties, speak the same local language just outside the courtroom, yet the proceedings inside are conducted in a foreign language.

Moreover, in former British colonies in particular, the "reception" of the legal system of the colonial power meant that English statutes existing as of a certain date were deemed to be the law of the colony. Statutes passed by the British Parliament after the date of reception were applied in the colony. That practice not only gave foreign law unusually high status in many African countries, but also meant that those imported statutes often remained in force in "independent" African countries in their original form, even when the original provisions in English law have long since been repealed or amended.

Given these anomalies, it is curious that almost all country studies took the colonial origin and nature of their legal systems for granted, without much comment. For most of the authors, the chief difficulty is not the statutes themselves or the foreign origin of much of the legal system, but rather problems of implementation and the constraints of resource limitations. Given their own training and the experiences of their own countries, it is not surprising that the authors of these studies find it difficult to imagine how a more authentically African legal system might be different from what prevails now throughout the continent.

One possible difference is the role of *customary law*, which is directly or indirectly recognized in almost all the legal systems discussed in these studies but plays different roles in each. In South Africa, for example, while customary law governs the domestic affairs (family law) of three-quarters of the population, its application must be consistent with the nondiscrimination provisions of the constitution. It will be interesting to see how the Constitutional Court of South Africa will attempt to mediate this tension between the individual right to equality and collective rights to cultural self-determination through the application of customary law. In Uganda, customary law is not codified and is deemed to be subordinate to statutory law. The party relying on a customary law rule must show the rule to be recognized by the native community whose conduct it is supposed to regulate. According to section 8(1) of the Ugandan Judicature Act of 1967, to be applied, customary law must satisfy two other tests: it must not be "repugnant to natural justice, equity and good conscience and not incompatible either directly or by necessary implication with any written law."

The Judiciary and the Legal Profession

Having covered the normative side of what the law says should happen, the contributors were to consider the institutional framework of the legal protection of human rights in their respective countries. To this end, authors were asked to first explain and discuss the general structure and organization of the judiciary, training of judges (or lack thereof), their institutional culture and professional tradition, and so forth. Second, they were to consider the theory and reality of independence of the judiciary in their countries, past and present, as well as its prospects in the near future. A similar discussion was requested for the structure and organization of the legal profession and its role (or lack thereof) in the legal protection of human rights. Issues to be addressed in this part include the composition, training, traditions, and organizations (bar associations, and so on) of the legal profession, and its role, if any, in the legal protection of rights, whether through the judicial process or by other means. For example, does the legal profession provide any legal aid or other services for human rights organizations? Is the legal profession engaged in training or education for the legal protection of human rights?

As can be expected, there are significant differences in the structure and organization of the judiciary in common law and civil law jurisdictions, as a result of colonial background as noted earlier. In common law countries, although the terminology may vary, the structures are fairly similar. Usually, there is a hierarchy of courts of generalized and specialized jurisdiction. Courts of general jurisdiction hear both civil and criminal cases and are usually divided geographically, with district courts feeding into regional courts. These lower courts of general jurisdiction are often referred to as magistrates' courts. There is usually a high court with unlimited original jurisdiction over both civil and criminal matters. It may also function as a constitutional court. Often there is no right of appeal for decisions rendered by the high court in its capacity as a constitutional court. The highest court in the system is the court of appeal, which will only rule on questions of law. Limitations may be placed on lower courts in terms of geographic area covered, subject matter jurisdiction, and size of claim.

Civil law or continental type of judicial structures can be found in countries colonized by France, like Guinea, and Portugal, like Mozambique. Some of its features are also found in North African countries. In this type of model, judges are trained lawyers whose judicial careers are essentially part of the civil service. Mozambique presents an interesting case of transition from a revolutionary socialist judicial system to a more common civil law system since the early 1990s. The "popular justice" system under the first organization of the judiciary after independence (Law 12 of 1978) encompassed all courts from the supreme court to local tribunals. Judges for local tribunals were all elected, while all other courts functioned with a combination of professional and elected judges. That popular justice system was an integral part of a wide process of social transformation after independence. Under the new system, popular local tribunals have become community courts, which operate outside the judiciary as organized under the 1990 constitution.

There are also differences in the recruitment and training of judges. In Senegal, magistrates are recruited in one of two ways. One way is from the ranks of lawyers, professors or other officials with varying levels of experience depending on the category (for example, ten years for lawyers and three years for university professors). Another way is for interested individuals who have a law degree but lack the requisite experience to pass an entrance examination that will admit them to a two-year training program at the National Center for Judicial Studies. In Uganda, judges receive no special training before or after their appointment. The lower ranks of the judiciary, the magistrates, need only a postgraduate diploma in legal practice from the Law Development Center. Judges are appointed from the ranks of the magistracy, the bar, or lawyers in the public service. It goes almost without saying that since there is no judicial training for judges, there is no specialized training in human rights either. In Morocco, judges are selected on a competitive basis and undergo a two-year training program consisting of five months at the National Institute of Judicial Studies, fifteen months of practical experience in the courts, and four months of practical experience in penitentiary institutions, companies, and prefectures. After the training program, candidates must pass another examination before appointment as judges.

Judicial independence can be undermined in two ways. First is the actual dependence of judges on the executive branch of government for job tenure and security. The second risk comes in the form of restrictions on judicial power to decide cases, as illustrated by the case of Nigeria under military rule. Separation of powers and independence of the judiciary in the liberal constitutional sense were unknown under the popular justice system that prevailed in Mozambique from 1978 until the adoption of the 1990 constitution.

As for dependence on the executive, judges are almost invariably appointed by various components of the executive branch. In a number of countries a nominally independent judicial service commission will nominate judges, but these commissions are often dependent on the executive branch of government. Lower-level judges may be appointed by designated agencies within the executive branch. In general, at the highest level (the high court and above) judges are nominated by the chief executive.

Security of tenure in office exists on paper, but it is likely to be rather easily circumvented in practice, as the judiciary is normally subordinate to the executive power. Thus, while the removal of judges is supposed to occur only for good cause, considerable discretion is vested in the executive branch of government in defining and applying that in individual cases. In Morocco, for instance, the executive can suspend a magistrate accused of serious error or transfer a magistrate to "any vacant post in the kingdom at any time." In theory, the judge can be transferred without his or her consent for a maximum of three months, but in practice it is difficult for magistrates to withhold consent or refuse a renewal of the period of "temporary" transfer. Originally relatively autonomous, the Sudanese judiciary has been subject to continual erosion of its independence since 1969. Judges serve at the pleasure of the president of the republic, who has complete power to appoint, discipline, and remove them. Judges may be removed from office unilaterally at any time in the name of protecting "the public interest."

In addition to dependence on the executive branch for their jobs, judges may also be incompetent or corrupt. The need for judges to curry favor with the executive power, whatever the original motivation, will, sooner or later, fatally compromise the quality of judicial decision making. Nigeria provides a clear illustration of these difficulties. Material and equipment, such as typewriters (much less computers) and stationery, are lacking. Most litigants must supply the stationery required for their case, including writing materials and file folders. As a result of the severe financial constraints and the low level of professionalism generally, court personnel, including magistrates, extort money from litigants. Nigeria may represent an extreme example of a much wider problem, however, as the judicial systems of all African countries studied under this project suffer from a lack of resources across the board. Court dockets are crowded, courtroom facilities are inadequate, delays are frequent, and there is a general lack of access to case reporters and other sources of legal precedent that are necessary for adequate judicial performance in common law jurisdictions. Dissemination of decisions that could be useful in human rights cases is often random or inadequate.

Legal education is generally available at law schools inside the country, which offer a standard curriculum. But access to the legal profession may be restricted by requiring lawyers to serve a training period as "articled clerks" before they can practice on their own, and the number of placements for articled clerks is limited. The system of articles of clerkship required for advocates is a problem in South Africa, where the finite number of places (about one thousand per year) is sufficient to meet only 60 percent of the demand, which means that available places are awarded to the most privileged law graduates.

As can be expected, the independence of local bar associations, and their willingness to take human rights cases and provide assistance to human rights organizations, closely corresponds to the overall climate for human rights in the country. In relatively open countries, like Uganda, bar associations and lawyers generally have more scope to litigate on behalf of human rights. In contrast, the Sudan Bar Association, established in 1935, had a distinguished record of advocacy of civil and political rights until the military coup of 1989 banned the preexisting bar association and instituted its own bar association.

Access to the legal system, particularly for poor, rural, and otherwise disenfranchised people, is also a problem. Lawyers are expensive, and their fees are beyond the reach of most potential litigants. The legal system is usually elitist, its practitioners concentrated in the cities, literally beyond the reach of the largely poor rural population. Public defenders, if found at all, are available only for criminal defendants in serious cases. The Legal Aid Project in Uganda is an example of privately sponsored and funded legal services for the poor. In South Africa, the Ministry of Justice, in response to legislation, has created a government-funded Legal Aid Board, whose goal is to render or make available legal aid to indigent persons involved in civil cases, work-related cases, divorces, appeals, and other constitutional matters. However, as with so many other aspects of the "new South Africa," the government's goals far exceed its capacity to fund them. South Africa is also exhibiting considerable creativity by experimenting with other, less expensive ways of delivering legal services to those who need them. The Legal Aid Board has established several community centers, housed at universities, to provide legal assistance for both civil and criminal matters.

Mozambique once more presents an interesting case. When only five out of about 350 Portuguese legal practitioners remained in the country upon independence, private law practice was banned, and Law 4 of 1975 allowed law students and paralegals to provide legal services under the supervision of the National Service for Legal Counsel and Assistance. However, as with other aspects of the administration of justice, the system for provision of legal services is in transition, with the establishment of the bar association in 1994, and the legalization of private legal practice. Since the vast majority of the two hundred legal practitioners are concentrated in the capital Maputo, the role of legal counsel in district courts is left to ad hoc "public defenders" who have no legal background at all.

Practice in Political, Social, and Economic Context

In light of the normative and institutional frameworks for the legal protection of human rights under the two preceding subsections, authors were requested to try to place the current practice and future prospects in general political, cultural, and economic context. In other words, authors were asked to assess the *actual practice and operation* of the formal normative and institutional frameworks they described. Questions to be addressed here should also include general reflections beyond a factual review of practice and obvious expectations. For instance, does the country's experience since independence support or repudiate the assumption that formally "democratic" governments are more likely to respect and protect human rights than nondemocratic governments? Which human rights, if any, do democratic governments tended to violate? What human rights, if any, do nondemocratic governments succeeded in protecting or promoting?

Authors considered the current role and operation of customary law, where applicable, especially as a possible source of human rights violations, and its future prospects in view of wider social, economic, and political developments. The main issue here is whether the role of customary law is likely to continue or diminish as a source of human rights violations. What are the dynamics of the relationship between the statutory regulation of the application of customary law and the political process, cultural and sociological factors, or economic constraints facing the state-law system? Another underlying issue suggested for the studies is whether customary law is so deeply entrenched that it would be difficult to displace it immediately or in the near future despite strong human rights objections to its continued application? If so, is it still possible to gradually influence the content and operation of customary and religious law?

Some authors under various sections of their studies gave part of the relevant information. But since most of the studies were more descriptive than analytic, I will offer here a couple of brief reflections on the role of customary law from a human rights perspective, as far as I can gather from the various country studies. One should first note the main features of the political, economic, and social context within which the role and status of customary law should be assessed. These features include general and drastic instability due to civil war or insurrection in the country. Another factor is the weakness and inaccessibility of institutional resources for the legal protection of rights, which forces people to find alternative mechanisms for the adjudication of disputes.

Regarding the application of customary law, the question is not whether it is possible or desirable to replace it by statutory or state law in the abstract. Rather, it is the relationship between the application of customary law and legal protection of human rights that is at issue here. At one level, since customary law will probably be perceived as more culturally authentic and practically accessible and useful by local populations than the much-maligned colonial legal systems, its forcible displacement may itself constitute a human rights violation. Statutory legal systems are incapable of properly serving urban populations, let alone rural populations who have even less access to them and are less able to afford their costs. Neither are they conceived and implemented in ways that are necessarily more protective of human rights than customary law. But the cultural authenticity or practical expediency of customary law should never be upheld at the expense of effective protection of human rights, especially those of women who suffer the most under various customary and religious law systems.

The challenge is therefore how to regulate the content and application of customary and religious law in order to better protect and promote human rights in local communities. Some of these studies clearly show that it is possible for the statutory state system to keep a tight grip on customary law, but that may not necessarily be for the right reasons or in appropriate ways from a human rights point of view.

Status and Role of Nongovernmental Organizations

Having discussed the theory and practice of the formal sector, as it were, authors were then invited to discuss and evaluate the *informal sector*, namely, the status and role of NGOs, whether openly identifying themselves as "human rights" organizations or not. Issues to be considered here include the mandate, constituency (popular support), operational capacity, funding, and accountability of local or national NGOs, their networks, and future prospects. For example, could they survive and be effective without external funding and technical assistance? What is the relationship between local or national NGOs, on the one hand, and international ones as well as foreign governments, especially of the North, on the other?

Reactions among the authors to NGOs are mixed. They are sometimes criticized for being elitist, out of touch with the population, or ineffective. But even the studies that criticized NGOs acknowledged some positive role for them. For example, the Nigeria study criticizes NGOs for being urban and elitist, but notes that the urban and elite bias of NGOs has begun to change since 1993 and the rise of the community-based environmental rights movement, focused on the oil-producing region and encompassing the rural communities there. According to this study, the public views NGOs in a positive light and relies on them for expression and protection of fundamental rights. NGOs are also criticized for lack of coordination among themselves and consequent duplication of effort, but there are also some attempts to address this problem. In Uganda, for instance, NGOs have begun to work together, coordinate their activities, share information, training, and other resources, and lobby the government and international donors. To facilitate these initiatives, Ugandan NGOs have formed an umbrella organization called the Development Network of Indigenous Voluntary Associations (DENIVA).

The human rights structure often reflects circumstances and political divisions in the country. In Morocco, for example, there are three national human rights NGOs: Ligue Marocaine pour la Défense des Droits de l'Homme (LMDDH); Association Marocaine des Droits de l'Homme (AMDH); and Organisation Marocaine des Droits de l'Homme (OMDH). The LMDDH, which is the oldest of the three, dating back to 1972, is associated with groups calling for more general and strict application of Islamic law. Various left-wing activist groups founded the AMDH in 1979. In response to the ineffectiveness of these organizations and increasing human rights abuses, a broad range of secular groups established the OMDH in 1988 under the aegis of the Bar Association. In 1990 all three organizations began working together and with the Bar Association to develop a national charter for human rights, which was signed in December 1990. They have continued to work together, although all have had difficulty institutionalizing their efforts, faced with the numerous challenges presented by the human rights situation in Morocco. These include government hostility and deficiencies of funds, material and human resources, and weakness of managerial and administrative capacity.

South African NGOs arose out of opposition to apartheid. Prior to 1993 NGOs mostly confined themselves to defending and providing other legal services to individual victims of apartheid. Many are now struggling to adjust to the drastic transformations of the last few years. The positive changes in the system carry with them a host of new and unfamiliar risks. Instead of opposing the government, NGOs now find themselves competing with it for funding, as foreign donors are increasingly channeling to the government funds that they used to provide to NGOs. In response, NGOs have to quickly develop unfamiliar fund-raising skills. Because of the dangerously steep drop in funding, NGOs cannot provide competitive salaries and are losing skilled leadership to the public and private sectors at a time when they are most in need of it. All this turmoil is having an impact on the quality of the services they provide.

There is broad agreement among those authors who addressed the question that NGOs are dependent on foreign sources of funding and technical assistance at the present time and will remain dependent for the foreseeable future. According to the Uganda study, for example, foreign funding can function to censor NGO activities because those NGOs that are dependent on these funds will not want to appear "subversive" in donors' eyes. The Nigeria study attributes poor in-country fund-raising to three factors: fear of government reprisal for becoming identified with human rights activities, the economic recession in Nigeria since the 1980s, and the failure of NGOs to reach out to the local resource base.

Conclusions and Recommendations

Finally, authors were asked to bring their whole discussion and analysis together to give an integrated and coherent evaluation of the reality and prospects of the legal protection of human rights in their respective countries. They were strongly urged to develop specific and concrete policy recommendations and propose practical steps for enhancing and promoting the legal protection of human rights in the country in question.

Notes

1. For a brief comment on this problematic concept and practice see Abdullahi Ahmed An-Na'im, "NATO on Kosovo Is Bad for Human Rights," *Netherlands Quarterly of Human Rights* 17, no. 3 (1999), pp. 229–31.

2. I have argued elsewhere for elements of this approach from a variety of perspectives. See, for example, Abdullahi A. An-Na'im, "The Legal Protection of Human Rights in Africa: Doing More with Less," in Austin Sarat and Thomas R. Kearns, eds., *Human Rights: Concepts, Contests, Contingencies* (Ann Arbor: University of Michigan Press, 2001), pp. 89–116; "The Cultural Mediation of Human Rights Implementation: Al-Arqam Case in Malaysia," in Joanne Bauer and Daniel Bell,

eds., *Human Rights in East Asia* (New York: Cambridge University Press, 1999), pp. 147–68; "Expanding the Limits of Imagination: Human Rights from a Participatory Approach to New Multilateralism," in Michael G. Schecter, ed., *Innovation in Multilateralism* (Tokyo: United Nations University Press, 1998), pp. 205–22; and "The Contingent Universality of Human Rights: The Case of Freedom of Expression in African and Islamic Contexts," *Emory International Law Review* 10, no. 3 (1997), pp. 29–66.

3. Besides the difficulty of proving the existence of principles of customary international law in general, the nature and dynamic of this source of international law is not conducive to precise specification of legal norms or to their effective implementation. See Ian Brownlie, *Principles of Public International Law*, 4th ed. (Oxford: Clarendon Press, 1990), pp. 4–11.

4. For a possible methodology for achieving this, and its application in different settings around the world see, generally, Abdullahi Ahmed An-Naʿim and Francis M. Deng, eds., *Human Rights in Africa: Cross-Cultural Perspectives* (Washington, D.C.: Brookings Institution, 1990); and Abdullahi Ahmed An-Naʿim, ed., *Human Rights in Cross-Cultural Perspectives: Quest for Consensus* (Philadelphia: University of Pennsylvania Press, 1992).

5. Egypt was greatly influenced by France following a brief invasion by Napoleon around 1802, and was subsequently occupied by Britain in 1882 as a "protectorate." Ethiopia was briefly occupied by Italy during the 1930s, and had to cope with much European interference in its internal affairs. But both countries retained their own native monarchies until they were overthrown by national revolutions, and were never colonized in the same way suffered by other African societies.

6. Robert H. Jackson and Carl G. Rosberg, "Sovereignty and Underdevelopment: Juridical Statehood in the African Crisis," *Journal of Modern African Studies* 24 (1986), pp. 5–6.

7. Ibid., p. 9.

8. Regional conflicts ranged from Tanzania's invasion of Uganda to overthrow Amin in 1978–79, Morocco's forcible occupation of large areas of Western Sahara since 1976, the Ethiopian-Somali wars of the 1970s and 1980s, invasions and destabilization tactics by apartheid South Africa against neighboring countries until the early 1990s, the Eritrea-Ethiopia war of 1998–2001, to the continuing conflict in the Great Lakes region of Central Africa. Many African countries have also suffered devastating civil wars, some continuing for many decades as in Sudan, or in several cycles as in Chad.

9. *Horn of Africa Bulletin* (Nairobi, Kenya: Life and Peace Institute), 13, no. 2 (March–April 2001), p. 13

Chapter 2
Ethiopia
Processes of Democratization and Development

Meaza Ashenafi

This chapter provides an overview of the legal and constitutional history of Ethiopia; an examination of the existing national and international regulatory frameworks for the protection of human rights; information on the structural, social, economic and political problems that limit the implementation of human rights laws; and, finally, measures that should be taken to move toward greater protection and promotion of human rights in Ethiopia.

Constitutional Legal Frameworks for the Protection of Rights

Early Constitutional Development

Before the drafting of its first constitution in 1931, Ethiopia was a feudal state with very few written laws or formal legal institutions.[1] Ethiopia was home to the powerful Christian kingdom of Axum during the early centuries of the Christian era and became a Christian empire in the fifteenth century. After 1600, it was divided up into a number of small kingdoms and was only unified again by Emperor Menilik II in the 1880s.

Around 1930, an interest in establishing a more modern legal system emerged, probably due to growing European influence, and Ethiopia's first constitution was drafted. Emperor Haile Sellassie I signed the constitution into law on July 16, 1931, stating that "laws bring the greatest benefits to mankind and . . . the honor and interest of everyone depend on the wisdom of the laws, while humiliation, shame, iniquity and loss of rights arise from their absence or insufficiency."[2]

Little, if any, of the emperor's speech was reflected in the first constitution, however. The constitution consisted of seven articles, only one of which addressed the rights of citizens, guaranteeing them equality before the law (Article 2[2]). The constitution created a parliament with two chambers appointed by the provinces with the approval of the emperor. All decisions of the chambers were subject to the approval of the emperor (Article 4). Despite the emperor's claim that he wanted to modernize Ethiopia, the constitution maintained the hereditary monarchy.[3]

Viewed from today's context, it is easy to dismiss the importance of the 1931 constitution. However, at the time, it was a significant break from the feudal tradition. It was the first Ethiopian law that dealt with citizens' rights in any way and it provided a point of departure for the drafters of later revisions to the constitution.[4]

In 1955, the constitution was revised and amended. The revised constitution made some important political and legal changes, though it carefully avoided any radical restructuring of the constitutional order. It had eighty-five articles, grouped into eleven chapters. The power of the emperor was reaffirmed, but his authority was to be exercised "in conformity with the provisions of the constitution" (Article 36). Chapter 3 provided for freedom of movement, due process of law, privacy and property rights, and freedom of religion, speech, assembly, and occupation. It also created an independent judiciary with the power of judicial review.

The civil rights recognized in the constitution were not self-executing, but required legislation to implement them. Over the ensuing years, civil, criminal, and other laws were passed to make these rights enforceable. Most of the laws were based on the civil law system and are still operational today. There was, however, an important limitation on the laws protecting citizens' rights. The emperor retained unlimited power to take any emergency measures "in the event of war or public misfortune" (Article 29).

Almost twenty years later, in 1974, the government attempted to make further constitutional reforms, as a result of growing pressure from opposition elements that demanded more legal protection and greater political freedom for the population. However, the reforms never came into effect, as the armed forces deposed the emperor in the same year.

The military dictator who took power in 1974 declared Ethiopia a socialist state, based on the Marxist-Leninist doctrine of rule of the proletariat. During the early years of the Derg (the common name for the military regime), the regime carried out killings, torture, imprisonment, and summary executions on a massive scale which was referred to as the Red Terror. To give the false impression of its desire for change and protection of the rights of the people, in 1987, the military regime adopted a constitution for the People's Democratic Republic of Ethiopia. Though the constitution was debated at the community level while it was being drafted, the process was basically a sham, intended to provide the illusion of popular legitimacy. In reality, the population was required to attend the debates and the entire process was carefully controlled and directed by the government.

Chapter 7 of the 1987 constitution was devoted to what it described as "Fundamental Freedoms, Rights and Duties of Citizens." It promised freedom of religion, speech, press, assembly, and association, equality for all, the rights of women, due process, and other economic and social rights. However, these rights were limited by the broad and vague provision that "the exercise of freedoms and rights and the discharge of duties by citizens shall be determined by law. The exercise of freedoms and rights by citizens may be limited by law only in order to protect the interest of the state and society as well as freedoms and rights of other individuals" (Article 58).

None of the provisions on rights ever became operational. The Derg passed laws and administrative orders repealing most of those rights. The Derg maintained its authoritarian grip on power for seventeen years, until it was eventually brought down in 1991.

The Federal Democratic Republic of Ethiopia Constitution

The Process

After the fall of the Derg in May 1991, the new government organized the Peace and Democracy Conference of Ethiopia during July 1–5, 1991. The delegates at the conference drafted the Transitional Period Charter, the document that was to be the fundamental law of the land until a new constitution could be adopted.

The charter outlined the basic directions to be followed in the drafting and ratification of a new constitution that would allow for the formation of an elected government. It also endorsed the Universal Declaration of Human Rights and specifically provided for freedom of conscience, expression, and ssociation and the rights of ethnic groups referred to as nations and nationalities to self-determination.

The transitional government consisted of the Council of Ministers and the House of Peoples' Representatives. Composed of delegates from national liberation movements and political parties, as well as other prominent individuals, the House of Representatives functioned as the legislature during the transitional period. It also established a Constitution Commission, responsible for drafting the new constitution.

The Constitution Commission was established by proclamation. Its members came from many different sectors of society. Of the commission's twenty-nine members, seven came from the House of Representatives, seven from political parties, three from trade unions, three from the Ethiopian

Chamber of Commerce, two from the Ethiopian Bar Association, two from the Ethiopian Teachers' Association, two from the Ethiopian Health Professionals' Association, and two were representatives of women.

The commission debated the new constitution in plenary sessions and meetings of specialized panels. It consulted legal researchers and experts, both foreign and local. It organized local and international meetings to discuss conceptual and practical constitutional law matters and it examined the constitutions of other countries. The commission disseminated a concept paper for public discussion, outlining alternatives on important constitutional matters, such as the structure and form of government. The public voted on some of the alternative proposals and the commission followed the outcomes of the vote. This, however, should not give the impression that the process was fully participatory. Those who were not sympathetic to the transitional government and were dismissive of the whole process did not take part in the consultation; they believed that participation would be "legitimizing" the process. Another group, which was not politically active, was not interested.

The commission's debates were lively. The chairperson of the commission encouraged decisions by consensus, though it was not always possible to reach a unanimous decision. The diversity of the commission members meant that a great number of interests were represented. Informal lobbying and negotiations were part of the process. Nonetheless, the Ethiopian People's Revolutionary Democratic Front (EPRDF), the ruling party, always dominated when an issue came to a vote, as it had the largest delegation.

The participation of independent lawyers in private practice, encouraged by the chairperson of the commission, ensured that minority views were heard. When the commission sent its proposals to the House of Peoples' Representatives, it included alternative versions for some key provisions, reflecting minority points of view. For example, the majority wanted a guarantee of the right of "nations and nationalities" to self-determination, including the right to secede. The position of the minority on the issue of self-determination was less radical. They supported decentralization of power less than secession. On the issue of land, the majority voted for the state ownership of land while the minority recommended a combined system of landholding, that is, state, private, and communal ownership. After two and a half years of deliberation, the commission submitted a draft constitution to the House of Representatives for further debate. The House of Representatives in turn forwarded the draft to the Constituent Assembly, a body composed of more than five hundred individuals directly elected by the population for the sole purpose of ratifying the constitution. The Constituent Assembly debated for several months before ratifying the Constitution of the Federal Democratic Republic of Ethiopia (FDRE) on December 8, 1994. The majority positions were adopted by the Constituent Assembly.

The draft constitution was, in the end, ratified with only minor changes. The majority at all stages knew that their position could not be seriously challenged. However, the fact that alternative views were presented and registered had its own merit in a country where the political culture does not allow alternative voices.

The challenge of implementation pending, the FDRE Constitution can be called the most democratic of all the constitutions Ethiopia has had; its substantive provisions limited the power of government and the chapter on human rights unequivocally guaranteed human rights protection by adopting international standards.

The Substance

The FDRE Constitution consists of 106 articles. It spells out human rights guarantees in detail, including the new generation rights such as the right to development and the right to a conducive environment. The constitution further provides procedural guarantees to ensure that rights are respected. The rights of those arrested, those accused, persons held in custody, and convicted prisoners to due process of law, speedy trial, and humane treatment are affirmed. For instance, on the right of persons arrested the constitution clearly delineates the authority of law enforcement by carefully defining the procedural guarantees to which an arrested person is entitled on issues of remand and habeas corpus. Article 19(4) reads: "All persons have the inalienable right to petition the court to order their physical release where the arresting police officer or the law enforcer fails to bring before a court within the prescribed time (48 hours) and to provide reasons for their arrest. Where the interest of justice requires, the court may order the arrested person to remain in custody or when requested, remand him for a time strictly required to carry out the necessary investigation. In determining the additional time necessary for investigation, the court shall ensure that the responsible law enforcement authorities carry out the investigation respecting the arrested person's right to a speedy trial."

The constitution also has provisions for the establishment of a human rights commission and the office of the ombudsperson. Under the leadership of the Parliament, national and international symposiums have been organized between 1998 and 2000, with the objective of discussing the different alternatives of creating institutions that best serve the country. Legislation to establish the human rights commission and the ombudsperson was adopted by the House of Peoples' Representatives on July 4, 2000 (proclamation no. 210/2000). Establishment of the institutions is eagerly awaited. The credibility and strength of the institutions will be essential if they are to contribute to the promotion and protection of human rights in Ethiopia.

On government structure, the constitution establishes a parliamentary federal government. The House of Peoples' Representatives, the supreme legislative body accountable to the people, is elected every five years by universal suffrage. Constituencies can exercise a recall procedure: "a member of the House, may in accordance with law lose his mandate of representation upon loss of confidence by the electorate" (Article 54[7]). The executive is formed and led by a political party, or a coalition of political parties, that wins the majority of seats. The highest executive power is vested in the prime minister and the Council of Ministers accountable to the House of Peoples' Representatives. Minorities have twenty seats reserved in the House of Peoples' Representatives. The president of the Federal Democratic Republic of Ethiopia is the head of state. The president is elected by a two-thirds vote of a joint session of the two chambers of Parliament, the House of Peoples' Representatives and the House of Federation. The president is elected for six years for a maximum of two terms. The office of the president has no substantive political function and power. The constitution delineates the powers of the central government, while endowing the regional states with all residual powers.

Human and Democratic Rights.   Chapter 3 of the constitution, entitled "Fundamental Rights and Freedoms," defines individual and collective rights. The commission debated whether to classify rights into different categories, rather than simply identifying them all as human rights. The majority position won and the rights were divided into two categories, human rights and democratic rights, the former enjoying greater protection. The rights to life, property, liberty, security, honor and reputation, equality, privacy, religion, and belief are grouped under human rights. The rights to freedom of opinion and expression, assembly and demonstration, movement, and personal and family rights of women and children, as well as rights to participate in the political process are considered democratic rights. It is unclear how the classifications were made and why certain rights, such as the right to privacy, were considered important enough to warrant the status of human rights, while others were only given the status of democratic rights.

Nonetheless, the classification of rights may be irrelevant, as the FDRE Constitution incorporates all the human rights conventions ratified by Ethiopia into domestic law (Article 9). Furthermore, the constitution provides that the fundamental rights and freedoms specified in the constitution shall be interpreted in a manner conforming to the principles of the Universal Declaration of Human Rights and the international human rights conventions to which Ethiopia is a party (Article 13).

International Human Rights Conventions.   Ethiopia is a party to many of the major international human rights conventions, including: International Covenant on Economic, Social, and Cultural Rights; International Covenant on Civil and Political Rights; Discrimination in Employment (Occupation) Convention; Equal Remuneration Convention; Convention on the Elimination of All Forms of Discrimination Against Women; Convention on the Rights of the Child; Convention on the Prevention and Punishment of the Crime of Genocide; Supplementary Convention on the Abolition of Slavery, the Slave Trade, and Institutions and Practices Similar to Slavery; and the African Charter on Human and Peoples' Rights.

Despite the ratification of these conventions, public awareness and the level of implementation of the treaties are minimal. One problem is that the treaties have not been translated into the languages of Ethiopia, although none of the official languages of the United Nations is widely used or recognized as an official language in Ethiopia. There is a concern expressed about whether the treaties actually become law before they are translated and published in the official legal journal. Hence, the dissemination and use of the conventions at the court level and elsewhere is limited by the failure to translate the treaties. Another problem is that new legislation implementing the principles enshrined in the international treaties has not yet been adopted. The rights and the remedies required to provide redress for the violations of rights need to be effectively guaranteed at the domestic level, as required by the human rights treaties. Subordinate laws falling short of the principles of the constitution should be reformed to meet the standard. For instance the provisions of the 1960 Civil Code regulating associations has proved to be insufficient to meet the various types of NGOs proliferating since 1991. To bridge this gap the Ministry of Justice (the authority that registers NGOs) has developed some directives to be followed in due course of registration. The requirements include a memorandum of association, a project plan, five pictures of five founding members, educational credentials of the founders, a letter from their area administration confirming that the founders are good citizens, and letters of promise from potential donors. These requirements may be excessive and have made the process a cumbersome task involving an average of one to two years (improvements have been observed lately) before registration. The NGO legislation, which has been under a drafting process for the past several years, should facilitate the exercise of freedom of association by shortening the list of requirements to essential information necessary for automatic registration. Similarly, laws have to be enacted or reformed to implement constitutions and conventions ratified by Ethiopia. In the same direction, the government has established the Law Reform Institute. So, the progress made in amending laws discriminating against women such as the family, pension, penal, civil service, and maternity laws is commendable. These reforms are initiated and lobbied for by the women's movement.

Customary and Religious Laws.   Unlike the legal systems of most African countries, the Ethiopian legal system does not recognize religious and customary law. The Civil Code, enacted in 1960, put an end to customary law as an official part of the legal system.[5] Customary law has not been part of the criminal justice system since the enactment of the Penal Code in 1947. Despite the ambition of legislators to standardize and modernize the legal system, the population has not abandoned the use of customary and religious law, especially in rural areas.

The FDRE Constitution softened the rigid stance of the former prohibitions against customary and religious law. It recognizes customary and religious law for "personal and family" matters, if both parties agree (Article 34[4]). This provision provoked a great deal of debate during the drafting of the constitution. In particular, many women opposed this change, arguing that it was a step backward in the protection of women's interests. Other people supported the change in recognition of the importance of various religious and cultural groups in Ethiopian society. In the end, the provision was a compromise, allowing certain matters to be governed by customary or religious law, unless one party preferred civil law. According to the constitution, legislation to regulate and harmonize the parallel operation of regular courts with customary and religious courts was to be adopted. There has not yet been any progress (that is known to the public) in this process.

The recognition of customary and religious laws for matters of family and personal relations, such as divorce, property division, child maintenance and custody, and inheritance raises the question of whether these norms conform to the provisions of the constitution. While the constitution guarantees the equality of all persons, most religious and customary laws do not treat women and men equally. It is difficult to understand, for example, how to reconcile the constitutional imperative of equality with a cultural norm that assumes there is no need for a girl's consent to be married. Some argue that any law or practice inconsistent with the constitution cannot be valid, but others claim that the fact that the constitution allows the application of customary and religious laws and practices indicates that these laws are exceptions to the general standards of the constitution. These latter groups further claim that once communities are permitted to use their religious and cultural norms, it is these same communities that must define these norms. Over time, judicial review of customary and religious laws should clarify the relationship between the different systems of laws. A recent development brought back the scenario of the Civil Code. The amended family law which was adopted by the Parliament on July 4, 2000, under its Article 74 affirms that despite the form of conclusion of marriage whether civil, religious, or customary, the effects including divorce are regulated by the provisions of the family law. This should provoke some questions on the status of the provision of the constitution permitting adjudication by religious and customary courts, particularly by those against regularization of matrimonial litigation under uniform civil law. So far this has not begun to happen.

Constitutional Interpretation.   The FDRE Constitution vests the power of constitutional interpretation in the House of Federation, a body composed of representatives of nations and nationalities elected by state legislators or by the people directly every five years (Article 61). The House of Federation has no legislative power; its major function is ensuring the harmonious coexistence of the different federal states under the political and economic umbrella of the federal state.

In its mandate of interpreting the constitution, the House of Federation is assisted by the Constitutional Inquiry Council (CIC), which is also a constitutional body. The CIC is composed of the president and vice president of the Federal Supreme Court, six legal experts appointed by the House of Peoples' Representatives, and three members designated from the House of Federation.

If a federal or state law is contested as being unconstitutional, any court or interested party may submit the matter to the CIC. If the CIC finds the case not warranting constitutional interpretation, it will remand the case to a court with jurisdiction or dismiss it. Where interpretation is needed, the CIC will issue a recommendation on how the constitution should be interpreted vis-à-vis the contested law. In accordance with the rules of procedure of the CIC adopted in 1996, issues raising point of constitutional interpretation could be submitted to the CIC by individuals or by federal or regional legislative or executive bodies. The issues should be submitted in written form and explain why they warrant constitutional interpretation. Twenty-three cases have been brought to the attention of the CIC so far. Twenty of the cases were dismissed as not warranting constitutional interpretation. Two cases have been decided and one case challenging the constitutionality of the electoral is pending. Cases range from issues of identity for nationalities to different issues of human rights violation. It is usually the prerogative of the CIC to dismiss a case on the ground of inadmissibility. For cases deemed admissible, the CIC's decision has to be approved by the House of Federation for that decision to be binding.[6]

The FDRE Constitution is unique in its arrangements for constitutional interpretation. In other countries, the power of judicial review of constitutional questions is vested either in general courts or in constitutional courts set up exclusively for constitutional interpretation. Some constitutional courts have the power to review the constitutionality of legislation before it is passed, as is the case in France. The procedure for determining the constitutionality of laws was an important subject of debate during the drafting and ratification of the constitution in Ethiopia. Many argued that vesting the power of constitutional interpretation in a legislative arm would disrupt the principle of separation of powers. However, the EPRDF was adamant about giving this power to the House of Federation, arguing that courts should not have the power to interpret a constitution made by the people.

The Judiciary and the Legal Profession

Parallel Court Structure.   From the unification of Ethiopia by Emperor Menilik in the1880s until the EPRDF took power in 1991, Ethiopia was a unitary state organized under a central government. The military regime made a show of decentralizing power by creating autonomous states, but, due to the authoritarian nature of the government, neither the public nor the decentralized provinces had a real role in decision making. Under the unitary state structure, the court system was also unitary. There was a clear hierarchy of courts, from the Supreme Court to the high courts to the Awradja (middle level) and Woreda (first instance) courts. The court structure is based on administrative divisions. The Woreda is the smallest, the Awradja, the second largest; the high court is based at the provincial level; and there is only one Supreme Court at the national level. To ensure reasonable access to the people at the Woreda and Awradja levels, high court judges hold periodic rotating sessions by going to Awradja level. The Supreme Court does the same for the provincial level cases. Moreover, to ensure that decisions are accessible with less procedural hurdles, small claims and misdemeanor offenses tribunals have existed under different names at much smaller constituencies. Specialized forums for such issues as tax and labor also exist.

The 1991 Transitional Period Charter established the basic structure for Ethiopian federalism. The charter provided for elected regional and local councils that would administer local communities. The charter further required that electoral boundaries be defined on the basis of nationality. The FDRE Constitution created a federal structure with nine states, the boundaries of which were decided on the basis of "settlement patterns, language, identity and consent of the people concerned" (Article 46[2]). The states have the unconditional right to self-determination, including the right to secede (Article 39[1]). Nations, nationalities and people in any state are also allowed to form their own states, if they have the approval of two-thirds of the state council and the population approves of the creation of the new state in a referendum (Article 47[3]). Article 39(5) defines "nation, nationality or people" as "a group of people who have or share a large measure of a common culture or similar customs, mutual intelligibility of language, belief in a common identity or related identities, a common psychological makeup, and who inhabit an identifiable, predominantly contiguous territory."

Under the federal system, the devolution of power to the regional states is radical and far-reaching. It is not a case of power at the center being delegated to the states. Rather, the states are assumed to be sovereigns that have delegated certain specific powers to the federal government for their common administration. Thus, the states retain for themselves all powers except those that they have expressly entrusted to the federal government. Whether they have the capacity to utilize this power in practice is another issue.

A principle of Ethiopian federalism appears in both the preamble and the body of the constitution. This principle is that Ethiopia is one political and economic community but in which different nations and nationalities exercise decentralized government authority. The provision of the constitution permitting secession, however, seems to dilute the principle of unity.

The court structure also changed with the new federal structure. A parallel system of federal and state courts was created by the constitution. Both federal and state courts have the three-level structure: courts of the first instances, high courts, and the supreme courts. The Federal Supreme Court is the court of final appeal for decisions originating in any of the federal or state courts. Regional courts undertake matters of federal jurisdiction by delegation. The delegation is based on jurisdiction, that is, a case having jurisdiction at the federal high court is delegated to the Federal Supreme Court and a case for the federal first instance is delegated to the state high court. This arrangement is made by the FDRE Constitution itself. By providing this mechanism of delegation on federal matters arising at states level, the constitution removed the immediate need of establishing a parallel federal court structure at the state level. This measure is useful, particularly in light of the material and human resource shortage the country is facing. The constitution provides for the establishment of federal high courts and federal first instance courts only when and where the House of Peoples' Representatives deems it necessary. So far no separate federal courts are established in any state. Other courts that have jurisdiction over small claims, misdemeanor, and various specialized issues can be established both at the state and federal levels by legislation and regulations. There are limits to what they can establish defined by different regulations.

Legislation has been enacted to define the jurisdiction of both federal and state courts, pursuant to the division of power between the federal government and the states. However, the issue of jurisdiction remains unclear on some matters of detail as expected for a new federal system. This needs to be clarified with time, test cases, and more legislation.

Judicial Independence.   The constitution requires the establishment of an independent judiciary. It also emphasizes that judges should not be influenced by government officials, but only by the law.

All federal judges are appointed by the House of Peoples' Representatives from a pool of nominees forwarded by the prime minister. The prime minister, in turn, receives the names of candidates from the Federal Judicial Administration.[7] State court judges are appointed through a similar process.

In addition to mandatory retirement at the age of fifty-five, the constitution provides three grounds for removing judges: violations of disciplinary rules, gross incompetence and inefficiency, and illness. The decision to remove a judge on one of these grounds is made by the Judicial Administration Council and is subject to the approval of the House of Peoples' Representatives.

Direct government interference with judicial functions is uncommon at the federal level. However, in some cases litigation in which a state is a party remains sensitive. Executive interference is more frequent at the state level. In some areas government officials harass judges and, in some instances, direct them on the outcomes of cases.[8] If the judges do not concede to the government officials, they are likely to face dismissal. Despite the procedures provided by federal and state laws for removing an appointed judge, there have been reports of judges being arbitrarily dismissed or even arrested for failing to do what government officials requested. For instance, a few years back in the regional state of Gamble it was reported that judges were arrested by administrative order. Thus far, it seems that the constitutional principle of judicial independence has not taken root. Increasingly, however, improvements are observed.

Another serious challenge is the shortage of trained judges in Ethiopia. Since 1963, Ethiopia has had only one law school that offers legal training. The school has been training an average of forty lawyers every year (the average does not include the early days of the law school when there were only a few students). Some Ethiopians received legal education abroad. In 1998, the government established the Civil Service College, which includes a legal education program that should begin to alleviate the shortage. The college is primarily intended to increase the capacity of state civil servants. The standard of training is under progressive review and improvement. On the average, one hundred students graduate yearly. Mekele University (a state university) has also upgraded its law diploma program to degree level. The degree program is expected to be launched in the academic year 2002. A private college called Unity College has also been offering a diploma course in law since 1998. Nonetheless, the problem remains, even with the improving number of trained lawyers. Many experienced judges have left the bench to go into private practice, a far more lucrative and independent career path. Furthermore, some former judges allege that they were dismissed from the bench because of their politics. In the last few years, the shortage of judges has created an enormous backlog of cases throughout the country. Recently, television reported that a divorce and property partition case has been pending in court for the past thirty-two years. The contention involves the partition of a matrimonial property from which the wife was evicted thirty-two years ago. This is not necessarily a typical example but it is all too common for a case to take more than six years before a decision is reached. Often appeals and execution orders take independent life cycles of their own which could mean several additional years.[9]

The quality of judicial decisions is another source of concern. Judges have neither the time nor the resources for legal research and investigation. Regular training opportunities for further professional development are sporadic. Having adequate experience is an important factor in judicial work; lack of experience is a serious problem of Ethiopian judges. Many of the judges are young with only a few years of working experience. Despite the rigorous effort on the part of judicial administrators to control corruption, misgivings still exist about some judges. Clerks and court secretaries also wield considerable power; there is a complaint that they have to be tipped for efficient service. The salaries of judges and other personnel in Ethiopia remain among the lowest in Africa, which does not help the fight against corruption. Little improvement has been made to the salary scale of judges.

These problems are exacerbated in state courts. Approximately 80 percent of qualified lawyers work in Addis Ababa. Most of the judges at the state level get only a few months of basic training.

Despite these daunting challenges, efforts are being made to improve the judicial system. More judges are being appointed at the federal level, regular training is offered for lower level state judges, a case database is being established by the Federal Supreme Court in a project supported by the Canadian International Development Agency (CIDA), and action is also being taken to introduce gender representation, particularly at the federal level.

The Legal Profession.   In spite of the obvious need for a strong legal profession, the Ethiopian Bar Association has not been very efficient. The bar was established over thirty years ago but has achieved very little so far. It has failed to persuade the government to grant it the authority to license and discipline lawyers and has generally been unable to command any respect from the government. The bar did not engage itself in public service until recently when it began free legal aid service to the poor in collaboration with other local NGOs.

Ethiopian Women Lawyers Association (EWLA), on the other hand, provides legal services to poor women, educates the public on women's rights, and lobbies for reform through legal research and publications. The objective of EWLA is to enhance the economic, social, and political status of Ethiopian women through the legal system. Because its mandate is so broad, many Ethiopians view it as a women's rights group, rather than a legal association. And the statute of the association affirms this view.

Political, Social, and Economic Context

As indicated above, the FDRE Constitution guarantees the rights of citizens, establishes the principle of separation of powers, decentralizes power, creates an independent judiciary, and introduces a system of periodic election. In short, the constitution espouses the basic values of democracy. The most difficult question is whether it is feasible to implement these democratic values. The demands of the constitution are considerable. It is not clear that Ethiopia has the infrastructure, institutional mechanisms, economic resources, political culture, informed and empowered citizenry, competent and independent civil service and judiciary, vibrant civil society, and free press that will be necessary to meet the demands of democracy. Since these resources are difficult to satisfy all at once, the question is whether they can be developed gradually over time, by building on what already exists. Addressing this challenge of implementation in the absence of most of the enabling conditions, the chairperson of the Constitution Commission said, "it is a classical chicken-or-egg question. But as with all such questions, we have to live with the dilemma it presents us. Indeed, the question is not with which we should begin—we should begin with both."[10]

According to the chief economic adviser to the prime minister of Ethiopia, since the change of government in 1991, Ethiopia's economic development has been encouraging. It maintained a gross domestic product (GDP) growth rate of 6 percent between 1993 and 1998, while inflation during the same period stood below 5 percent.[11] According to the United Nations Development Program (UNDP), Ethiopia's per capita GDP of $574 in 1998 was significantly lower than the $1,607 average for sub-Saharan Africa and the $1,064 average for least developed countries. Ethiopia is scored 171st out of 174 countries surveyed by the UNDP Human Development Index.[12] The persistent food shortage in Ethiopia has been exacerbated by unions and political parties, and freedom of movement. The permissible derogation of this provision includes laws passed by competent authority and restrictions imposed by courts in the interest of the welfare of the people of Ghana as are necessary in free and democratic society.

Right to Privacy of Home and Property

Article 18 of the constitution protects the right of individuals either alone or in association with others to own property. The only lawful grounds for the state to interfere with the privacy of home, property, correspondence, or communication is to guarantee the public safety and economic well being of the country, for the protection of public health or morals, or for the protection of the rights and freedoms of others.

Property Rights of Spouses

Article 22 is mindful of certain cultural practices which do not recognize the marital rights and contribution of wives to husbands' estates. In some cultural groups, such as the Akans, on the death of a husband, intestate, before the enactment of PNDCL 111, his property belongs to his extended family, thus depriving the wife. Article 22 of the constitution entitles spouses to reasonable provision from the estate of the deceased spouse.

Employment Rights

The rights to work under satisfactory, safe, and healthy conditions and to receive equal pay for equal work are provided for under Article 24 of the constitution. The provision enjoins employers to provide paid breaks and vacations, as well as remuneration for public holidays. Workers can join trade unions. The only justifiable restrictions are those imposed by law in the interest of national security, public order, and the protection of the rights of others (Article 24[4]).

Right to Education

The constitution provides for the right to equal educational opportunities and facilities with the view to achieving full realization of that right in the long term under Article 25. The constitution makes basic education available to all. Secondary and higher education is dependent upon the availability of resources. The right of individuals to establish private schools is also conferred by Article 25.

the last year's drought, however production for this year is expected to be the best in many years due to good rains. Social services such as health care are in bad condition. They lack both physical and human resources. The ratio of trained health personnel to the population is one physician for every 40,000 individuals, and one nurse for every 53,000 women. An assessment made in 1997 shows that trained health care personnel attend only 10 percent of births in Ethiopia, which means that out of the 2.9 million annual deliveries more than 2.6 million occur without professional assistance.[13]

So far, there are few opposition political groups, and many of those that do exist tend to be based outside Ethiopia. The political opposition groups claim that they are systematically excluded from the political process. They allege that they face harassment and do not have the same access to government resources, including public media, as the ruling EPRDF.[14]

In both the 1995 and 2000 parliamentary and local elections EPRDF won over 90 percent of the seats. In preparation for election 2000, the Inter Africa Group (IAG, a subregional NGO), organized serious televised debates. In the debates, the ruling party and different opposition groups introduced their programs and debated over their differences. The forum was organized both for parliamentary and local elections at the federal and state levels. The exercise was very useful in introducing opposition groups to the public. It has informed the public about their rights to alternative ideas and freedom of choice. The gain of this exercise in terms of sharing power was not huge. The incumbent party has better mobilization, more resources, and a larger network. Moreover, the opposition alleges that the ruling party has used state machinery to keep them away from power.

EWLA has also run a women's political participation campaign program stretching over one year before election 2000. The program was aimed at increasing the representation of women in the parliament. In the 1995 election women got only 14 of the 536 seats. This number has improved to 42 (all of them from the ruling party) in the 2000 election. In the twenty-five-member cabinet we only have one minister (minister of education). Women are still very much underrepresented and this will continue until measures of affirmative action are taken as in South Africa, Uganda, and other countries.

As described above, the efficiency of the judiciary is compromised by numerous problems. In addition, the judiciary faces other practical problems. When the EPRDF came to power in May 1991, the transitional government ordered the arrest of about 1,900 people suspected of gross human rights violations. They remained in detention for eighteen months without being charged while the transitional government set up a special criminal bench and a Special Prosecutor's Office (SPO). When the SPO was established, it released about 900 of the detainees, either on bail or after a preliminary investigation that did not produce enough evidence to charge the detainees with any crime. Between April 1993 and June 1993, the court released another 200 detainees. The SPO brought its first charges against 73 Derg members in 1994. In December 1997, the SPO filed charges against another 5,198 Derg officials, of whom 2,246 were already in detention. About 2,952 were charged in absentia, though a number of these defendants were apprehended later. Due to the serious nature of the charges against the Derg officials, they have been detained until their cases are decided. This is taking a very long time, given the number of defendants, the bulk of evidence presented, and the complexity of the cases.[15] Some defendants have been acquitted at the end of the trial, and there might be others in the future, but it will not be possible to compensate them, as the country does not have the legal mechanisms to address the problem of wrongful detention.

The police are not in a position to ensure respect for human rights, either. Inadequate training and insensitivity to human rights protection mean that the police do not or cannot protect the rights of the population. A recent incident affirms this problem: on April 11, 2001, forty students of Addis Ababa University were seriously attacked (a few deaths were reported) by the police force when they held a campus demonstration on issues of administration and academic independence. As of this writing, the problem is ongoing. Despite some progress, the gender insensitive attitude of the police is still strong. Police themselves have beenaccused of raping and abducting girls. They show no serious interest in investigating and reporting to the public prosecutor gender-based violence. They tend to take a long time to investigate cases. The inadequacy of equipment such as telephones, vehicles, and even stationery is apparent. Although there are a few allegations, systematic torture and brutality in prisons no longer exist. However, inadequate efforts are being made to improve police training. Training syllabi have been improved to enable more recent police trainees to understand their role in light of the civil rights protections made by the constitution to citizens. Similar problems apply in the case of public prosecutors. The police and public prosecutors work in collaboration; both their weaknesses and strengths reflect on one another. The office of the public prosecutor suffers from case backlogs. A case has to wait a year or two until the prosecutor presses a charge. Furthermore, the caseload minimizes the quality of litigation

The Civil Service is another problem area. It expanded continuously until the Structural Adjustment Program was implemented in the early 1990s, and the new government reduced the bureaucracy. The Civil Service, the largest employer in Ethiopia, suffers from inefficiency. In addition to structural problems, the sector lacks motivation and a sense of duty to public service. To rectify this problem the government has embarked on a large project to reform the Civil Service. The project is funded by UNDP. Measures will be needed to ensure the independence, credibility, and efficiency of these institutions in the protection and promotion of human rights. One such measure is the establishment of a strong and independent office of the ombudsperson that would keep an eye on and expose administrative injustice.

Status and Role of Nongovernmental Organizations

Nongovernmental organizations, particularly those dealing with human rights protection, are relatively new in Ethiopia and still very few in number. This is primarily due to the legacy of the Derg regime, which prohibited free association, assembly, and expression. During the Derg regime, a few international relief NGOs came to Ethiopia in response to the 1984 famine. Traditional credit associations have also existed for a long time as a community-based mechanism to deal with occasional expenses like funerals or weddings. These institutions are not political, but they may have the potential to become change agents.

After the 1991 transition, the new government established the constitutional legal framework to protect freedom of association. By incorporating the Universal Declaration of Human Rights, the Transitional Period Charter guaranteed these rights. The FDRE Constitution also guarantees freedom of association under its Article 30. It has also endorsed civil and political rights as part of the domestic law.

From 1994 to 2000, 436 local NGOs were registered with the Ministry of Justice. Almost all of them focus on welfare and development (food security, micro credit, health etc.). Some of these organizations have programs on civic education or gender equality. NGOs devoted exclusively to human rights work number very few. Some of the most active are highlighted below.[16]

The most controversial of these organizations is the Ethiopian Human Rights Council (EHRC) established in 1991. In the earlier years of its operation, EHRC often found itself in conflict with the government since some of its activities involved sensitive issues such as monitoring and reporting political prisoners. For example, a few years back the government froze the bank accounts of the EHRC until a court ruled that it had to release the funds.

Christian Relief and Development Association (CRDA) is the largest and probably oldest (twenty-five years old) umbrella NGO, consisting of a network of more than 180 mostly welfare NGOs. It provides capacity building assistance to its members in different forms. Traditionally it was more of a welfare organization but of late it has started to take up developmental issues as well. CRDA has played a critical role in the process that led to the adoption of NGO Code of Conduct in Ethiopia.

EWLA's activities focus on the protection and promotion of women's rights. Established in 1995, EWLA is one of the leading women's rights organizations. Its activities are centered around three major programs: research and legal reform advocacy, legal aid service, and public education. Over the last few years, the association has moved the debate on the issue of women's rights to the national agenda. It has initiated and mobilized support around reforming discriminatory laws and effectively lobbied for the amendments of family law, penal law, pension law, and others. It has provided free legal aid service to about 10,000 poor women on issues concerning divorce, property division, child custody, maintenance, and violence. EWLA has six branch offices at the level of states and thirty committees at different local levels.

Action Profession Association for People (APAP) is a civic and legal rights educational association formed and run by young lawyers since 1992. It is actively engaged in human rights education and legal aid provision. APAP has established offices in many regional centers.

HUNDEE is another local organization working on grassroots civic education, food security, and micro credit.

The Forum for Social Studies (FSS) is another association, established in 1998, to organize public debate, undertake policy analysis, and conduct research on development and related issues. Its priority areas of research and publication include poverty alleviation, population issues, land and agricultural production, gender studies, and economic and social policies. Over the past two years, FSS has held several public discussion forums and brainstorming workshops and published specialized studies and monographs.

The Ethiopian Economic Association (EEA) is a membership association of professional economists actively engaged in economic policy research and dialogue. There are also international and subregional organizations. One of the most active subregional organizations is the Inter Africa Group, established in the Sudan in 1998 by citizens of Ethiopia, Sudan, Eritrea, and Somalia for peace and humanitarian missions. Its office is based in Addis Ababa. Since 1991, IAG has been actively involved in election monitoring, organizing forums on issues of constitution making, economic policy evaluation, and political participation of opposition groups. PANOS Ethiopia, a country chapter of a British-based international NGO, is active on issues of environment and gender.

Civil society development is in a preliminary stage in Ethiopia. This still-young sector is making a significant contribution in different ways. The public recognizes this and understands civil society, particularly NGOs, as resourceful but on the other hand self-serving. The government tends to disregard the contributions of NGOs and to suspect that they abuse resources, as confirmed by the registration requirement. The government's approach has been not to regulate but to control. However, this is progressively changing as the government understands the role played by civil society, including NGOs. The long-awaited NGO legislation should set clear provisions that cut administrative requirements that would constrain freedom of association.

The relationship of local NGOs with foreign governments and international organizations has been good. Generally, foreign governments and international NGOs provide the funding, while local NGOs are free to define their own agendas. However, donors sometimes interfere and try to influence organizations' agendas, especially with smaller or newer NGOs. Dependency on donor funding is likely to continue for the foreseeable future. The government does not welcome the initiative of NGOs that wish to engage in profit-making activities with the view to financing their programs. The official explanation is that there is no provision in the Civil Code that allows NGOs to engage in profitable activites. The easy reply to this could be if it is not prohibited, that should mean it is permitted. An international NGO was initially denied registration because its statute provides that it may be engaged in paid service. It is hoped that the NGO legislation will deal with this also. Encouraging NGOs to build their capacity to generate income is useful in gradually reducing donor dependency or at least in complementing their support.

Conclusion and Recommendations

The crucial linkage between development, human rights protection, and democracy cannot be overemphasized. However, this does not mean that Ethiopia should wait until it attains economic independence to introduce democratic institutions and mechanisms. We have learned that democratization is a process, rather than an event, and that it is also a precondition to development. There are several steps Ethiopia must take to move this process along.

Detailed Legislation

It seems that Ethiopia needs legal reform for better protection of human rights. The principal legal framework for changes exists, but a detailed description is needed to guarantee rights and remedies in every branch of the law. This is important for several reasons. Ethiopia has a civil law system, but the courts need sufficient detailed laws for citation. Moreover, courts have not developed the necessary jurisprudence to enable them interpret the law consistently within the framework of broad legal principles.

Finally, there is little activism to interpret human rights laws more progressively, hence, laws that specifically articulate human rights principles are needed.

Clarification of Constitutional Issues

Several unsettled disputes about the interpretation and application of the constitution need to be resolved. Among them are the following:

1. Article 9 of the constitution provides for the direct incorporation of international human rights conventions into domestic law upon ratification by Ethiopia. Some sectors of the society including lawyers, however, argue that each convention must also be translated into the working language of the country and published in the official *Gazette* to become law. Since none of the United Nations' languages is used in Ethiopia, this disagreement has created confusion over the status of international human rights treaties. Whenever lawyers try to use international human rights law in court, they are asked to produce a translated official law. Some NGOs have translated some treaties into domestic languages. For instance, EWLA has translated seven international conventions into three local languages. However, these translations are not considered official and are useful only for public education. The government should focus on this issue of translating international instruments as a matter of priority and take official action to endorse already existing translations to ensure their applicability in courts.

2. The Constitutional Inquiry Council should be popularized. Challenging unconstitutional laws and administrative rules contributes to the culture of human rights protection. Procedures of application and types of admissible issues need clarification. The dismissal of twenty out of twenty-three applications by the CIC signals that there is a lack of clarity on types of admissible cases on the part of applicants.

3. The relative status of international law and the constitution is another area for further consideration. There are three general approaches to defining the relation between treaties and constitutions. In a few countries, treaties are considered superior to the constitution. In several others, the two are said to have equal status. In most countries, however, international conventions are deemed to have the same status as domestic legislation. The FDRE Constitution does not define the relation between international conventions and the constitution, but it does declare the supremacy of the constitution above all laws. Nonetheless, Article 13 provides that the human rights provisions of the constitution should be interpreted in conformity with international human rights conventions. This point again divides opinions among lawyers. Some argue that the supremacy clause is the final

word of the constitution on matters of hierarchy of laws, including international laws. Others argue that if the constitution is to be guided and interpreted in light of international laws, this must mean that international law prevails over the constitution and that the supremacy clause only relates to ordinary legislation. There are still others who think this argument is irrelevant because the provisions of the constitution and international conventions are compatible. However, some provisions of the constitution are, in fact, in conflict with international human rights law. For example, the provision on adjudicating power of religious and customary courts on matters of personal relations does not match the Convention on the Elimination of All Forms of Discrimination Against Women (CEDAW) provisions. The constitution also provides for the suspension of more rights during emergency situations than is provided for in the International Covenant on Civil and Political Rights (ICCPR). The relative status of the constitution and the international human rights treaties to which Ethiopia is a party needs to be explored and clarified in order for the treaties to be used effectively.

Human Rights Education

Violators of human rights as well as their victims are likely to be ignorant of human rights protections. To promote human rights effectively in Ethiopia, a country with massive illiteracy and poverty, there must be human rights education campaigns at both the formal and informal levels. The soon-to-be-established Human Rights Commission must take up this challenge of promoting human rights as a major program rather than focusing on remedial measures that it has no mandate to enforce. In this way, many human rights violations may be prevented altogether.

Enhancement of Professional Capacity

The legal profession is inadequate both in numerical terms and in the quality of training and experience. Moreover, there are no specialized training or graduate study programs in human rights. Unlike other African countries, Ethiopia does not have historical ties to a former colonial power to facilitate educational opportunities abroad, and many of those who do manage to go overseas to study remain abroad. Enhancing the capacity and quality of legal education is essential. Periodic refresher courses for judges and other key human rights workers would be an important step. The Bar Association should also take on more responsibility in this area.

Civil Society

The government should encourage the development of the civil society by providing an enabling environment that enables its growth and effectiveness. And the civil society itself should work to assure this space. Furthermore, all local organizations should be concerned about the protection of rights. They should be able to overcome the tendency of dissociating other development works with the promotion and protection of human rights. The society should be mobilized to ensure the rule of law.

Judiciary

It must be clear that in the absence of a well-functioning judiciary it is impossible to nurture public confidence in government or achieve the goal of development. Special attention should be paid to cultivate and strengthen human resource capacity through training and education. Effort should be made to attract people with experience to the bench. The Bar Association should strengthen its capacity to play its rightful role of contributing to legal development though publications, test cases, public forums, and so on.

Law Enforcement

The police have a special role in human rights protection. To discharge this critical duty they should be trained in human rights so that they will have the knowledge and skills necessary to protect human rights effectively.

Creating Greater Political Space for Less Powerful Groups

The government and the society need to understand and accept that alternative and competing political forces are needed to move forward. Most conflicts in Africa that lead to human rights violations are the result of winner-take-all politics. Also, engaging women and minorities in the country's governance would help make government policies and structures more responsive to their needs and concerns. This would help protect the rights of such marginalized sectors of the society, improve the quality of governance, facilitate the aspiration of development, and ensure harmony and peace.

Notes

1. Modern Ethiopia is bounded by Eritrea and Djibouti to the northeast, Somalia to the east and southeast, Kenya to the southwest, and the Sudan to the west and northwest. Ethiopia has a diverse population, made up of more than seventy dis-

tinct ethnic and linguistic groups. Its population is about 58 million and 85 percent of its people are subsistence farmers in rural areas.

2. James C. N. Paul and Christopher Clapham, *Ethiopian Constitutional Development: A Sourcebook*, vol. 1 (Addis Ababa: Faculty of Law, Haile Sellassie I University, 1967–1972).

3. Article 5 reads: "In order to prevent any uncertainty as to the succession to the Throne and avoid the gravest injury to Ethiopia, the right to the Imperial Throne, in the present Constitution, is reserved to the present dynasty."

4. Paul and Clapham, *Ethiopian Constitutional Development*, vol. 2, p. 912.

5. Article 3347 of the Civil Code reads: "Unless otherwise expressly provided, all rules whether written or customary previously in force concerning matters provided for in this Code shall be replaced by this Code and are hereby repealed."

6. Interview with Samuel Alemayehu, CIC head of secretariat and registrar. The CIC office is located in the Parliament.

7. The Federal Judicial Administration is presided over by the president of the Federal Supreme Court. The membership is composed of the vice president of the supreme court, judges of supreme, high, and first instance courts (two from each), and three representatives of the House of Peoples' Representatives. It was established by proclamation no. 24/96 to make decisions on important matters of judicial administration.

8. Interview with a former judge of Oromia Supreme Court (anonymous).

9. The estimation is not based on wide research but on the experience of the writer.

10. Speech made by Kifel Wodajo, chairman of the Constitution Commission, at the symposium on "The Making of the New Ethiopian Constitution," May 17–21, 1993, sponsored by the Inter Africa Group.

11. An interview with Neway Gebre-ab, senior economic adviser to the prime minister, *The Reporter* (Addis Ababa), vol. 2, no. 136.

12. *Women of the World, Laws and Policies Affecting Their Reproductive Lives, Anglophone Africa, Ethiopia, 2000 Update* (New York: Center for Reproductive Law and Policy, 2000).

13. Ibid.

14. EPRDF, the ruling party in power since the overthrow of the military, a coalition of four ethnic-based parties, the Tigray People's Liberation Front being the strongest.

15. *Trial Dateline Consolidated Summary of Red Terror Trials, No. 1*, March 1999, Trial Observation and Information Project (TOIP).

16. NGOs in this report are mentioned randomly, i.e., this is not an exhaustive list. And the order in which they appear does not reflect their importance. In view of the objective of the report, the focus is on NGOs working on different aspects of civil, political, economic, and social rights and those working at the national level.

Chapter 3
Ghana
Competing Visions of Liberal Democracy and Socialism

Nana K. A. Busia, Jr.

An inquiry into the legal protection of human rights in Ghana can be better appreciated if it is situated within the broad context of the political history of the country, paying particular attention to the types of regimes that have governed Ghana since it attained sovereign statehood in 1957. It is also necessary to examine the various sources of law available to the domestic legal institutions for the implementation of human rights. Ghana is currently under a constitutional democratic dispensation that may be conducive to possibilities for legal protection through the normal judicial process.

This chapter not only focuses on the role of the judiciary, but also considers the roles of other actors, such as quasi-judicial bodies and civil society groups, which contribute to the legal protection of human rights in Ghana. The chapter is divided into six parts to reflect and enable a more focused discussion of the above themes. The first part situates the discussion within the broad historical background beginning from independence, paying particular attention to how respective regimes—military and civilian—have responded to human rights issues. The second part examines in greater detail the Fourth Republican Constitution (1992), which provides the constitutional framework for the ongoing democratic dispensation, with a view to establishing the extent to which it provides for the protection of human rights, and the interpretation of such provisions by the courts. The third part looks at the nature of the legal profession and the training of lawyers in Ghana, as well as the means of recruitment into the judiciary in Ghana. The fourth part scrutinizes the judicial structures of the country and investigates as to whether or not they encourage the protection of human rights. The fifth part takes up the case of human rights NGOs and other civil society organizations and their roles in the pro-

motion and protection of human rights in Ghana. Finally, the sixth part critically evaluates the formal legal provisions for the protection of human rights
within the political, economic, and social context of Ghana. I conclude with
some specific recommendations for the promotion and protection of human rights in Ghana.

Historical Overview

With a total area of 238,537 square kilometers, bordering the North Atlantic Ocean between Côte d'Ivoire and Togo, Ghana has a population of
17,748,400 (1996 estimate), with a life expectancy of 55.9 years. The literacy rate in the country is 60 percent of the population aged fifteen and
over (1990). The main ethnic groups are: Akan, 44 percent; Mole Dagomba,
16 percent; Ewe, 13 percent; and Ga, 8 percent. Christians are about 42.8
percent of the population and Muslims 12 percent.

Since independence in 1957, Ghana has had four military regimes that
spanned a period of twenty-two years, while democratically elected civilian
governments have so far ruled for a total of about twenty years. Public
opinion holds that military/authoritarian regimes are more likely to violate human rights than elected civilian governments. Admittedly, this assertion might reflect certain tendencies of these two types of regimes. I will
show, however, that the nature of the problem of the legal protection of
human rights in Ghana is much more complex. Nana Akuffo-Addo, a foremost Ghanaian constitutional lawyer, for instance, insists that, in spite of
the frequent overthrow of democratically elected civilian governments by
the military, the Ghanaian political system and constitutional development
has always been liberal democratic in character.[1]

Though it began earlier, political agitation for independence against
British colonial rule received added impetus and increased organizational
strength when Kwame Nkrumah, who was the secretary of the United Gold
Coast Convention (UGCC), Ghana's first nationalist organization, broke
away in 1949 to form the Convention Peoples' Party (CPP). The CPP's support base came from lower-middle-class urban youth and the unemployed
in the cities and towns, referred to in Ghanaian political parlance as "ve-
randa boys" (*sans culottes*). The CPP's professed ideology, once in government, was African socialism, which gave higher priority to collective rights
over individual rights. The CPP also argued, at least on a rhetorical level,
that social and economic rights must take precedence over civil and political rights. The period of CPP rule (1957–1966) witnessed serious struggle
for political power in Ghana, struggle that sometimes turned violent.

By the mid-1950s, the struggle for power was mainly between the CPP
and the United Party (UP). The latter was an alliance of political parties, including the UGCC, made up mainly of traditional rulers, lawyers, doctors,

traders, and large-scale cocoa farmers.[2] The UP, therefore, was a constellation of elite, entrepreneurial, traditional, and professional interest groups of the upper middle classes. On the threshold of independence, the UP advocated for a federal constitutional system based on the belief that it offered better protection of local interests. The CPP favored a unitary system on the grounds that the country was a small contiguous nation with a population of approximately six million people, and constrained by a severe shortage of skilled civil servants. Sir Frederick Bourne, the constitutional adviser to the colonial government, with experience in India, accepted the arguments of the CPP. Nonetheless, the 1957 Constitution (also known as the Independence Constitution) sought to reach a compromise between the two proposed structures of government, and thus provided for regional assemblies in the then five regions of Ghana (Articles 63 and 64).

The Independence Constitution of 1957

The Independence Constitution was modeled on the British parliamentary system of government. However, three substantive limitations were imposed on the legislature under Article 31(2) of the constitution as follows: no law could be enacted to "make persons of any racial community liable to disabilities to which persons of other such communities are not made liable." Except for restrictions imposed for the preservation of public order, morality, or health, no law could be enacted to "deprive any person of his or her freedom of conscience or the right freely to profess, practice or propagate any religion." Article 34 provided that the taking of private property was subject to a right of adequate compensation, to be judicially determined.

There was also an important procedural limitation. Parliament could not, without the approval of the regional assemblies, make any enactment which, inter alia, sought to alter the boundaries of the regions and modify the provisions of the constitution (Article 32). The Supreme Court of Ghana was vested with the power of judicial review and original jurisdiction in all matters concerning the validity of any law in the country (Article 31[5]).

It is important, at this juncture, to draw attention to certain national political developments with implications for the courts and the protection of human rights. No bill of rights was provided for in the 1957 constitution. Also, the CPP, which formed the first independent government, argued that the tasks of nation-building and economic development are onerous in the postcolonial state. In order for Ghana to develop rapidly and catch up with the rest of the developed world, human rights should not impede the objective of rapid development.[3]

This period was also the height of the cold war, which made Africa part of the theater of superpower ideological rivalries and attendant proxy conflicts. Consequently, when the government of newly independent Ghana, which professed adherence to liberal democracy, proclaimed itself socialist, it became suspicious of opposition groups as potential agents of Western imperialism. According to the CPP's political logic it required virtually unlimited powers to contain such "subversive" opposition groups. This led to the enactment of the Deportation Act of 1957, which conferred authority on the executive to make deportation orders. This act, and others that followed, exposed the limitations of the Independence Constitution with respect to the protection of rights as well as the danger of leaving such rights to be determined by common law principles. The constitution's limitations came to the fore in the case of *Larden and Anor v. Attorney General* at the High Court of Ghana.[4] The applicants challenged the validity of their deportation from Ghana by an executive order on the grounds that they were Ghanaian citizens and as such could not be deported from their own country. While the case was pending, the CPP government passed a new law overruling the jurisdiction of the High Court. This new law was challenged by counsel for the applicants in *Larden and Anor v. Attorney General* on the ground that the 1957 constitution provided a limited exercise of the legislative powers of the state and as such the government could not pass the Deportation Act of 1957. The constitution, in their view, did not confer parliamentary sovereignty on the lawmakers of Ghana, as is the case under the English system of governance. The presiding judge rejected this argument and held that: "In England it is not open to the court to invalidate a law on the ground that it seeks to deprive a person of his life or liberty contrary to the court's notions of justice, and so far as the Independence Constitution, Section 31(1) is concerned, that is the position I find myself."[5]

The application was thus dismissed on the ground that the Ghanaian legislature, like the Parliament of the United Kingdom, was sovereign and as such no court could question the exercise of its legislative authority. Consequently, the CPP government, with a parliamentary majority of 78 seats (out of 104 members of Parliament), could literally do whatever it wanted except, as it was commonly asserted then, "turn a man into a woman." The CPP's stranglehold on political power meant that civil liberties suffered because of its alleged prioritization of economic development. The Preventive Detention Act (PDA) of 1958 was yet another piece of legislation that violated civil liberties. It allowed the minister of interior to detain without charge persons suspected of endangering national security. Habeas corpus applications were refused once a detention order had been properly made.[6]

The Republican Constitution of 1960

The 1957 constitution was replaced with a new constitution on July 1, 1960. It proclaimed Ghana a republican state within the Commonwealth, and, therefore, became known as the Republican Constitution. The effectiveness of the new constitution as a guarantor of civil liberties and individual freedoms and the power of the courts to test the constitutionality of acts of Parliament was put to a test very early in the case of *Re Akoto*.[7] This case challenged the Preventive Detention Act of 1958, under which the appellant (Akoto) was detained as in excess of powers conferred on parliament by the Constitution of the Republic of Ghana, with respect to Article 13(1) of the 1960 constitution which provided, inter alia, that:

Immediately after the assumption of office, the President shall make the following solemn declaration before the people:
"On accepting the call of the people to the high office of the President of Ghana I, _____, solemnly declare my adherence to the following fundamental principles: 'That no person shall suffer discrimination on the grounds of sex, race, tribe, religion or political belief. That subject to such restrictions as may be necessary for preserving public order, morality or health, no person should be deprived of freedom of religion or speech, of the right to move and assemble without hindrance, or of the right of access to courts of law.' "

The Supreme Court of Ghana held that under the Republican Constitution the power of Parliament to make law was unlimited. The solemn declaration by the president under Article 13(1) of the constitution was, in the view of the court, like the coronation oath of the United Kingdom, of no legal consequence. The 1960 constitution did not have any other provisions on human rights.

The CPP government was overthrown in a coup d'état by military and police officers who subsequently formed the National Liberation Council (NLC) government from 1966 to 1969. Up to this point, the Preventive Detention Act of 1958 had been widely used, and about two thousand persons were in detention at the time of the 1966 coup. The widespread arrests and detentions without trial under the PDA, as a result of its frequent application by party loyalists to exact respect and/or settle personal scores, created a climate of fear. These widespread detentions under the PDA stigmatized the CPP government as oppressive and without respect for civil liberties. The NLC was, therefore, popularly welcomed as a liberator. A proclamation was enacted to formally inaugurate the government of the NLC and to invest it with both the legislative and executive powers of the state. The NLC retained the PDA as the Protective Custody Decree of 1967 (NLCD 54) to curtail the activities of its ideological and political opponents. The powers of the judiciary remained as had been stipulated in the suspended

1960 Republican Constitution. The NLC initiated a transition back to a civilian constitutional order by putting into place the necessary logistics and institutional arrangements to conduct general elections in 1969. The bitter lessons of the first republic, arising mainly from the enshrined constitutional principle of parliamentary sovereignty, which enabled the CPP government, with its huge majority, to undermine human rights, informed the drafting of the 1969 Second Republican Constitution and all subsequent constitutions of Ghana. As a result, all Ghanaian constitutions following the first republic share these points:

1. The concept of parliamentary sovereignty was discarded in favor of constitutional supremacy. The constitutions were designated as the fundamental supreme law of the land from which Parliament drives its authority to make consequential laws. Any act or conduct inconsistent with the constitution was null and void to the degree of its inconsistency.
2. The constitutions should contain clear and explicit provisions on human rights with elaborate statements defining the content of the rights.
3. Since the entry into force of the 1969 constitution and subsequent ones, the courts have been vested with the power to act as the guardian of the constitution. The Supreme Court and the High Court have exercised this power since the 1969 constitution. The Supreme Court has always had original and exclusive jurisdiction to interpret the constitution, but shares concurrent jurisdiction with the High Court on the enforcement of the human rights provisions provided for in the various constitutions.[8]
4. The notion of "standing" (*locus standi*) in constitutionality litigation has been broadened to mean "any person" has access to the Supreme Court to seek interpretation of any particular provision deemed violated or under violation.[9] For human rights enforcement, standing may be subsumed under personal interest actions or public interest ones.[10]

The Second Republican Constitution of 1969

The 1969 elections ushered in the Progress Party (PP) with Kofi Abrefa Busia as prime minister under the Second Republican Constitution. This government was comprised of politicians and scholars with mainly liberal tendencies. There appeared, therefore, to be a desire to engender pluralistic politics with the assistance of the constitutional prohibition against a one-party government. The 1969 constitution laid a satisfactory foundation of the necessary formal rules for liberal democratic governance. It provided for pluralistic politics, regular elections, entrenched human rights provisions, separation of powers, and an independent judiciary. However, the ability of the PP government to rule in a liberal democratic fashion was tested in the celebrated case of *Salah v. Attorney General*.[11] The PP government had, pursuant to powers conferred upon it by section 9(1) of the transitional provisions to the 1969 constitution, dismissed 568 public officials who held positions in public statutory bodies from 1960. The applicant challenged his dismissal on the ground that he was appointed to his position before 1960, and, thus, was not covered by section 9(1). The Court of Appeal, at the time the highest court of the land, upheld his claim. The otherwise democratic prime minister, K. A. Busia, who was also the leader of the PP, went on national radio and television to make a broadcast severely criticizing the courts and stating that no court could compel his government to employ anyone. Furthermore, he issued a veiled threat to judges stating that if they wanted to play politics, he was prepared to take them on. The speech was generally construed to be contrary to the liberal democratic spirit of the 1969 constitution.

On balance, however, the PP government is generally perceived by the average Ghanaian as a regime with a very good record for the promotion and protection of civil and political rights in the country's history. At the time of the 1972 coup, there was not a single political detainee in the country's prisons. Nor were there reports of cases of torture or inhuman and degrading treatment or any other acts, of commission or omission, which by construction could have been deemed to have to amount to systematic violation of civil and political rights. Supporters of the regime argue further that because the regime embarked upon an aggressive program of rural development with the plan to make housing, education, electricity, and other facilities available to rural people, that in itself must be also viewed as a commitment to the rights stipulated in the International Convenant on Economic, Social, and Cultural Rights of 1966.

Military Rule

In 1972, the PP government was ousted in yet another coup d'état by middle-rank officers led by Colonel I. K. Acheampong. The coup leaders formed the National Redemption Council (NRC) government, which was subsequently transformed into the then Supreme Military Council (SMC) 1 and SMC 2 governments. In its official proclamation of power, the NRC, like the NLC government before it, arrogated to itself all legislative and executive powers of the state. The 1969 constitution, which had been carefully drafted to protect human rights, was suspended. On June 4, 1979, young army officers and noncommissioned officers staged a bloody, but successful coup against the SMC 2 military government and formed the government of the Armed Forces Revolutionary Council (AFRC) under the chairmanship of a young, charismatic army officer, J. J. Rawlings. This coup received support from the majority of Ghanaians. Like the NRC's proclamation, the AFRC government's proclamation also arrogated to itself all legislative and executive authority, as part of a supposedly temporary and limited mandate to "clean house" and conduct a moral revolution. Before it was overthrown, the SMC 2 government had, under intense public pressure, promised to return the country to multiparty politics, and elections were already scheduled to take place. After the SMC 2 was ousted, the AFRC government accepted this scheduled return to multiparty politics. The reign of the AFRC government, thus, became a short and violent interregnum of three months in which serious human rights violations took place for the first time in Ghanaian political history. The military head of state at the time, two of his predecessors, and three other senior service commanders were executed after a short and secret trial presided over by young army officers. In addition to the serious violation of right to life and unfair trial, soldiers on the streets indulged in other widespread human rights violations, targeting mainly women involved in petty trading but others perceived as having acquired ill-gotten wealth as well. Young enterprising women suspected of selling items above government regulated prices were stripped naked in public and subjected to all kinds of inhuman and degrading treatment. Others were tortured and, in many instances, if they were perceived as rich, had their property confiscated. It is a sad commentary on the rule of law and politics of Ghana that these acts received the approval of a great many Ghanaians at the time and were thus very popular acts of the AFRC government. The scheduled elections returned the People's National Party (PNP) to power under the Third Republican Constitution of 1979, but the PNP government was sacked by the military in 1981 after only two years in power. As Nana Akuffo-Addo has noted, "It can be seen that the periods of constitutional rule have been but brief interruptions of the seemingly inexorable determination of our military citizens to rule the nation."[12]

The long periods of military rule have negatively affected the healthy evolution of constitutional jurisprudence, including the interpretation of constitutional provisions on human rights. A dominant legal characteristic of all the military regimes has been the nearly unlimited nature of their powers of lawmaking and implementation. The courts could not test the "constitutionality" of decrees once passed because the rule of law was suspended. When the proclamations were thus taken as the law of the land to test decrees, this too proved futile, as further decrees were passed quickly in order to remedy any defect in the government's case.[13] The jurisdiction of the courts was further restrained through the insertion of ouster clauses; moreover, many decrees were passed with retroactive effect.[14] In some instances the courts were rendered incompetent to entertain, let alone examine, the merits for applications of habeas corpus.[15] Human rights were violated frequently under the military regimes; such violations included the frequent arrests of suspected political opponents and detentions without charge. Parallel judicial structures, which did not follow due process, were set up. The AFRC, in particular, created what could be rightly referred to as "kangaroo courts," which meted out rough and ready forms of justice that included torture, corporal and capital punishment, and the confiscation of private property.[16] The

AFRC then immunized itself against future prosecutions by means of indemnity clauses in the transitional provisions to the 1979 constitution.

Authoritarianism Under the PNDC: Challenge to Liberalism and Human Rights

The AFRC entered into wedlock with certain radical elements of Ghanaian society when it came to power in 1979. This political relationship formed the platform from which the chairman of the erstwhile AFRC, J. J. Rawlings, launched, in 1981, his second successful coup d'état, and formed the Provisional National Defence Council (PNDC) government. In his broadcast to the nation on December 31, 1981, Rawlings made it clear that he and the PNDC were launching a "revolution" in Ghana. This revolution was proclaimed against a background of economic crises in the country. Because of this economic crisis, the PNDC argued that liberal democracy could not address the social needs of the people with respect to education, health, transportation, and other basic needs. The PNP, therefore, was portrayed as elitist and insensitive to the plight of the ordinary people, and the judiciary was viewed with skepticism and suspicion. The PNDC portrayed the judicial system as fraught with difficult technical legal procedures, which enabled the rich to get away with "crime" and other civil wrongs to the disadvantage of the poor. The PNDC also maintained that individual civil and political freedoms were of interest only to the economic elite, who were depicted as "bourgeois" and "parasitic."[17]

The PNDC set itself the task of implementing an alternative revolutionary system of socioeconomic transformation of the state and social relations, in order to achieve equitable economic development. The makeup of the PNDC in 1982 thus reflected its revolutionary intent; it was comprised of militant trade unionists, former radical student leaders, young military officers, and noncommissioned officers. The PNDC's quest for the revolutionary transformation of state-society and intra-society relations led to the establishment of organs and institutions for the expression and exercise of popular power, which included Workers' Defence Committees (WDCs), People's Defence Committees (PDCs), PDCs in the armed forces and police services, the National Defence Committee (NDC), the Citizens' Vetting Committee, the National Investigations Committee (NIC), and public tribunals. These became the bedrock upon which the revolutionary ideals of the PNDC were erected. In spite of the initial excesses of these revolutionary organs and institutions, they represented, with regard to the realization of human rights, the first attempt in the history of Ghana to establish popular and inclusive institutions that enabled the peasants, the illiterate, the economically deprived, and marginalized youth and women to exercise power and take part in decision making.

In the first two years of the PNDC's revolutionary rule, the important yet difficult question of what type of economic development Ghana was to embark upon was initially not seriously addressed. However, in 1984, in a sudden reversal of its socialist economic principles, the PNDC wholeheartedly embraced the International Monetary Fund (IMF)/World Bank adjustment policies. This drastic turn necessitated a clamp down on all popular institutions and organs of the revolution, and this led to the implementation of an austere program of economic stabilization, known as the Economic Recovery Program (ERP). The PNDC had to demonstrate its autonomy from the various social organizations in order to be perceived as having the political will and effective control required to implement the ERP. In order to control various interest groups, the government set up a number of repressive organizations, notably the Civil Defense Organization (CDO), the Bureau of National Investigation (BNI), a people's militia, and commando organizations. By 1987, opposition to the IMF-sponsored austerity program had grown. Thus, the government created additional military and paramilitary/security organs in order to maintain control. Associations and individuals that sought to operate outside the PNDC sphere of control were perceived as "oppositional" and/or branded as constituting a threat to "state security," and severely punished with lengthy detentions, torture, and sometimes death. This vague and dubious legal concept of "state security" was overstretched to cover all activities within civil society of which the PNDC did not approve. Respect for human rights became dependent upon the good will of the PNDC government, which was never shown to its many perceived opponents. The government and its agents exercised arbitrary power in the hallowed name of "state security."

The PNDC conferred unfettered power upon itself, through its own decrees, such as PNDC Law 42, which brought the judiciary under executive control and ended the formal separation of powers that had been respected by previous military regimes, and PNDC Law 78, which provided omnibus definitions of offenses that left every Ghanaian vulnerable. PNDC Law 78 empowered the public tribunals to impose the death penalty for any crime specified as a capital offense by the PNDC or if the tribunal determines that capital punishment is warranted or merited in a particular case, even if such a crime is not normally punishable by death under existing operative statutes. The judiciary was further rendered impotent by PNDC Law 4, and as amended by PNDC Law 91, which made habeas corpus applications ineffective by providing the legal basis for the detention of real and perceived opponents of the regime. Moreover, the freedom of expression was stifled through the Newspaper Licensing Law of 1989 (PNDC Law 2), which prohibited the establishment of any newspaper without the consent and approval of the government. The PNDC regime, it is commonly agreed, had the worst human rights record in the political history of

Ghana. Arbitrary detention, torture, harsh prison conditions, and death sentences meted to political opponents were common occurrences in Ghana before the transition to democracy that began under the 1992 constitution. In a report issued by Amnesty International in 1991, an estimated 270 people had been sentenced to death (since 1982), including at least 23 who were prisoners of conscience.[18] Many others were forced into political exile.[19] However, it also must be said that the PNDC was an improvement over other regimes with regard to human rights promotion, by supporting some legislative measures which protected some economic and social rights. For example, the PNDC era saw legislation to promote the right to housing, access to justice, inheritance rights, and the establishment of the Ghana National Commission on Children to protect the rights of children.[20]

The Transition to Democracy

By 1989, when the cold war began to come to an end, and as national and international pressures mounted on most African governments, the question of a transition from PNDC authoritarianism to a democratic regime arose and was tied to the perennial problem of military disengagement from politics. The PNDC government had no other choice but to accommodate the clarion call for political pluralism, but did so by devising its own strategic response. The PNDC created a district assembly system in order to preempt any drastic constitutional changes, which might call for accountability for previous human rights violations. Pursuant to this, a local government law (PNDC law 207) was passed to give legal power to the district assembly system, which was presented to the Ghanaian populace as yet another alternative to the elitist liberal democratic system. The PNDC argued that the district assemblies would promote popular participation in decision making. A "Blue Book" was published by the PNDC, in which it promised the establishment of the district assembly as an important beginning and model for the evolving national democratic political process favored by the PNDC. Later, elections were organized on a nonparty basis, but with one-third of the members of the assembly appointed by the government. The public viewed this exercise as political gimmickry and boycotted the elections. The boycott created a political crisis which forced the PNDC to initiate real reforms, thereby leading to the eventual inauguration of constitutional rule in 1992.

In March 1991, the National Commission on Democracy (NCD), which had been appointed earlier in 1988, to advise the PNDC on how to transform the country to civilian rule, was called upon to survey Ghanaians on the new system of governance that they preferred. In order to do so, the

NCD toured the country and interviewed people. In its report to the then chairman of the PNDC, Flight Lieutenant J. J. Rawlings, the NCD affirmed that "all human rights derive from a very basic concern that all are entitled to social and economic rights that confer access to shelter, clothing, health, education, work, and a general state of well-being." The report stated, moreover, that "it is insistence upon this primary concern by a vast segment of the human race at various points in history that has led to revolutions and social upheavals." The report concluded that "our generation cannot close its eyes to this concern in the haste of fashioning a new constitution." The NCD report, therefore, affirmed human rights as a key concern of the people of Ghana, placing a premium on economic, social, and cultural rights. The Consultative Assembly, established in May 1992 to draft a new constitution, specifically addressed this concern.[21] From the start, the composition of the Consultative Assembly was an issue. It was acknowledged that whoever was appointed to the assembly was going to determine the framing of the constitution, and, thus, the composition of the assembly became a passionate issue in the transition period. Another contentious issue was whether or not to include indemnity clauses in the transitional provisions. The PNDC sought to indemnify itself and its appointees for any acts or omissions during its reign. This objective was realized through section 34 of the transitional provisions to the new constitution, which prevents the courts or any commission of inquiry from looking into the past conduct of the PNDC.[22]

According to the NCD report, the people also demanded that the assembly:

1. repeal repressive PNDC laws, most of which were still operative;
2. affirm freedom of the press by abolishing the newspaper licensing law and removing the ban on all the newspapers and magazines;
3. release all political detainees;
4. dissolve the paramilitary organizations created by the PNDC to intimidate political opponents; and
5. dissolve the election committees, which were created during and after 1988.

These demands were often punctuated with threats that, if they were not met, prodemocracy forces would adopt the *conférence nationale* model In this model, identifiable civil society organizations, social movements, political parties, and reputable citizens convened a national conference whereby they arrogate to themselves the sovereignty of the state; decisions and proclamations made by the constituted forum are deemed sovereign, which binds everybody including the incumbent government. A more militant and almost revolutionary version of this process was being practiced in neighboring Benin Republic. In the transition from authoritarianism to a democratic constitutional rule, the state and civil society engaged in a complex and dynamic relationship.

In April 1992, a draft constitution was presented to the people of Ghana to be voted on in a referendum, and 92 percent voted in favor. The following month, the Political Parties Law (PNDCL 250) was passed, and the ban on political activity was lifted. Presidential and parliamentary elections were organized in November and December 1992 respectively. The PNDC converted itself into a political party, the National Democratic Congress, with the chairman of the PNDC, Flight Lieutenant Rawlings, as its presidential candidate. He won 58.3 percent of the votes cast in the presidential elections. The opposition political parties boycotted the parliamentary elections, alleging that the presidential election was not free and fair. Nevertheless, on January 3, 1993, Rawlings was sworn in as president of Ghana under the 1992 constitution, inaugurating the Fourth Republic.[23]

The Fourth Republican Constitution of 1992

The Fourth Republican Constitution provides for traditional civil and political rights and economic and cultural rights. In addition it makes explicit provisions to protect the rights of vulnerable groups: women, children, disabled persons, and the sick. It is silent on group or solidarity rights, which in human rights parlance are called third generational rights, such as the right to good and satisfactory environment or to development. Nevertheless the 1992 constitution is, in terms of its substantive provisions on human rights, a qualitative improvement on the previous constitutions (1960, 1969, 1979) that Ghana has adopted since attaining republican status in 1960. This section presents the human rights provisions of the constitution.

Constitutional Provisions

The Fourth Republican Constitution was drafted and adopted in a drastically changed national and global political context. The discourse of the early 1990s advocated respect for human rights and democratic pluralism instead of authoritarianism. The triumph of liberal ideology in the wake of the collapse of the Soviet variant of socialism, plus the strengths of the previous constitutions as well as corrections of any mischief of the previous constitutions, influenced the drafting of the 1992 Constitution. Thus, the Fourth Republican Constitution of Ghana provides a generous list of freedoms and rights in accord with the International Bill of Rights. The International Bill of Rights is comprised of the Universal Declaration, the International Covenant on Economic, Social and Cultural Rights, and the

International Covenant on Civil and Political Rights. These rights are supplemented with a chapter on Directive Principles of State Policy (DPSP).

Chapter 5 of the constitution provides the fundamental legal framework for the protection of human rights in Ghana. The Constitutional Bill of Rights covers Articles 12 to 33, which are entrenched. A preambular statement calls on the executive, the legislature, the judiciary, all other organs of government and its agencies, and, where applicable, all legal persons in Ghana to uphold and respect the fundamental human rights and freedoms, which are enshrined in the constitution and are to be enforced by the courts (Article 12[1] and [2]). The constitution also affirms the principles of nondiscrimination as follows: "Every person in Ghana, whatever his race, place of origin, political opinion, color, religion, creed or gender shall be entitled to the fundamental human rights and freedoms of the individual contained in this chapter but subject to respect for the rights and freedoms of others and for the public interest" (Article 12[2]). The rights explicitly provided for are as follows.

The Right to Life

The constitution guarantees the right to life, with certain exemptions, such as in response to a criminal offense under the laws of Ghana under which a person has been convicted. Under the penal laws of Ghana, it is also unlawful to cause a woman to prematurely deliver a child with the intent of causing or hastening the death of the child.[24] Abortion is thus viewed as a contravention of the right to life in Ghana.

Right to Personal Liberty

Article 14 of the constitution guarantees personal liberty, except in certain instances such as: in order to execute a sentence or order of a court with regard to a conviction for a criminal offense; or for the education or welfare of a person who has not attained the age of eighteen. Article 14(2) confers rights on persons who are arrested or detained. These include the right to be informed of the reason for arrest and detention; the right to be arraigned for trial within forty-eight hours; and the right to be compensated for an unlawful detention.[25]

Respect for Human Dignity

Article 15 of the constitution provides for the inviolability of the individual, hence torture or other cruel, inhuman, or degrading treatment or punishment is illegal. The constitution also provides for detainees awaiting trial to be separated from convicted persons, and for juvenile offenders to be kept separately from adult offenders (Article 15[3] and [4]).

Freedom from Slavery and Forced Labor

Article 16 prohibits slavery and servitude, as well as forced labor (Article 16[2]). Exemptions include cases in which labor is required as a result of a sentence or order of a court, of a member of the armed services as part of his duties, and of a person who is a conscientious objector to the armed forces.

Equality and Freedom from Discrimination

Equality before the law is enshrined under Article 17 of the constitution. All forms of discrimination based on gender, race, color, ethnic origin, religion, creed, or social or economic status are prohibited, except in situations in which there is a need to redress social, economic, and educational imbalances (Article 17[4]).

Right to Fair Hearing

The right to a fair hearing within reasonable time before a court or tribunal for persons charged with a criminal offense is guaranteed under Article 19 of the constitution. The article guarantees the independence and impartiality of courts to try the case. The catalog of indices of fair trial in criminal and civil cases is indicated, including the rights to a public hearing, representation, and a presumption of innocence until guilt is proved.

Freedom from Deprivation of Private Property

Article 20 protects right to adequate compensation where property is compulsorily acquired or damaged and such acquisition is justified on grounds of public safety, public order, public morality, or public wealth. There are procedures for challenging the acquisition.

Freedom of Speech and Expression

In Article 21, the constitution provides for freedom of expression, which includes freedom of the press and other media, academic freedom, freedom of thought, conscience and belief, and the right to practice any religion. Other rights are consolidated with the right to freedom of speech, such as freedom of assembly, association, including the right to form trade

Right to Cultural Practices

According to Article 26, a person has the right to enjoy, practice, profess, maintain, and promote any culture, language, tradition, or religion. However, any customary practices, which dehumanize or are injurious to the physical and mental well-being of any person are prohibited (Article 26[2]).

Women's Rights

Article 27 of the constitution contains provisions specifically aimed at protecting the rights of women. It is the first of its kind in the constitutional history of Ghana. It states that special care shall be accorded to mothers during a reasonable period before and after childbirth; and during those periods, working mothers shall be given leaves. The provision also requires child care be provided by the state for children below school age, to allow mothers the opportunity to develop their careers. Women must also be given equal access to all training programs and receive equal treatment with respect to promotions (Article 27[3]).

Children's Rights

With respect to children's rights, Article 28 of the 1992 constitution adheres to the provisions of the UN Convention on the Rights of the Child of 1989, by affirming the nondiscriminatory principle which applies to the enjoyment of rights by all children, regardless of circumstances of birth or social status of parents. Guaranteed under the article are every child's right to family life and protection from threat to his health, education, or development. The article defines a child as a person below the age of eighteen years.

Rights of Disabled Persons

The constitution makes specific provisions for the protection of disabled persons against any unjustifiable differential treatment, exploitation, or discrimination. It also conferred on them the right of access to public places and provides incentives to employment.

Right to Health

The Bill of Rights does not specifically provide for the right to health, though it does provide for the rights of the sick. Under Article 30, a person acting on behalf of a sick person cannot deny that person the right to education or medical treatment on grounds of religious or other beliefs. The constitution does acknowledge the right to health as a goal the government should attain, under the Directive Principles of State Policy (Article 34[2]). It is also hoped that when the issue of the protection of the right to health arises, the courts will be guided by the Supreme Court ruling in *New Patriotic Party v. Attorney General* (CIBA [Council of Indigenous Business Associations] case, 1996). This judgment stated, *inter alia,* that the Directive Principles of State Policy are not in themselves legally enforceable by the courts; however, there are exceptions to the principle in that where the DPSP are read together with other enforceable parts of the constitution they then in that sense become enforceable.[26] In addition international human rights instruments would be considered in accordance with Article 33(5) of the constitution, which states: "The rights, duties, declarations and guarantees relating to fundamental human rights and freedoms specifically mentioned in this Chapter shall not be regarded as excluding others not specifically mentioned which are considered to be inherent in a democracy and intended to secure the freedom and dignity of man."

Application of the Constitution

In common law jurisdictions, such as Ghana, constitutional provisions and/or statutes may confer rights upon an individual; however, when a dispute arises as to the scope or enjoyment of these rights, it is up to the judiciary to make the final pronouncement on what the law, in fact, confers. Indeed, Articles 33 and 140(2) of the constitution confer authority on the High Court, and Article 130(1) confers authority on the Supreme Court of Ghana, to interpret and enforce the provisions of the constitution, including those provisions concerned with human rights. The Supreme Court is also vested with exclusive original jurisdiction in all matters relating to the constitutionality of legislation (Article 130[1][b]).

In the case of *New Patriotic Party v. Inspector General of Police,* the Supreme Court was called upon to determine the scope of the right to freedom of association and assembly as provided for under the 1992 constitution.[27] Since independence, police officers in Ghana have frequently denied permits to political opposition groups to hold political rallies or demonstrations on the "basis of maintaining public order." In two instances in 1993, the opposition New Patriotic Party (NPP) applied for permits to hold political rallies in compliance with the Public Order Decree of 1972.[28] In both of these instances, the permits were initially granted, but then withdrawn on the day of the planned rallies. The NPP, together with other opposition political parties, assembled anyway and demonstrated against the government's annual budget. A number of demonstrators were arrested and charged with demonstrating without permit, contrary to the aforementioned decree. The NPP, in response, declared that sections 7, 8, and 12(a) of the decree, which required the NPP to seek the permission of the police before embarking on a demonstration, were in contravention of Article 21(1)(d) of the 1992 constitution and were therefore inoperative because of this inconsistency. The Supreme Court unanimously decided that the cited sections of the Public Order Decree of 1972 were null and void to the extent of their inconsistency with Article 21(1)(d) of the 1992 constitution. Moreover, the Supreme Court ruled that under the 1992 constitution "no permit is required from the Police or any allied authority for holding a rally or demonstration or procession or the public celebration of any person or group within the intention of Article 21(d)."[29]

In addition, the Supreme Court required the inspector general of police, as defendant, to "duly obey and carry out the terms of these orders by circulating by way of formal notices of the orders of the court permanently and publicly displayed at all police stations and posts throughout the country setting out in extension three sections in the Public Order Decree, 1972 referred to in judgment and declaring them null and void and unenforceable and published once in the state owned electronic and print media and file a copy of these in the Registry of this court within fourteen (14) days of the date of this judgment." The police had for years prior to this decision used these powers to clamp down on political opponents of incumbent governments. There is a known pattern of consistent denial of permits to opposition political parties or groups that governments perceived as hostile.[30]

Another important case in which the Supreme Court clarified the provisions of the constitution is *New Patriotic Party v. Attorney General,* usually referred to as the December 31 case.[31] December 31, 1981, is the date of President J. J. Rawlings's second coup, in which he overthrew an elected government. As a result, December 31 became a national holiday. The NPP, however, contended: "The public celebration of the overthrow of a legally-elected Government of Ghana on December 31, 1981, and the financing of such a celebration from public funds was inconsistent with, or in contravention of the letter and spirit of the 1992 Constitution and more particularly Article 3(3)–(7), 35(1), and 41(b)."[32] In a 5–4 decision, the Supreme Court, in granting the NPP's claim, agreed that the celebration of the December 31 coup with public funds violated the spirit of the constitution.

In addition to the human rights provisions and freedoms stipulated in Chapter 5, the 1992 Constitution contains a set of rights under the Directive Principles of State Policy, which "guide all citizens, Parliament, the President, the Judiciary, the Council of State, Political parties, and other bodies and persons in applying or interpreting the Constitution or any other law and in taking and implementing any policy decisions, in the establishment of just and free society" (Article 34[1]). The Directive Principles reinforce many of the rights provided for in Chapter 5 and also supplement that list by including the right to work, the right to good health care, and the right to education (Article 34[2]). The established view of constitutional law is that the Directive Principles of State Policy are not intended by the drafters of the constitution to be justiciable, but rather are intended as an aid in constitutional or statutory interpretation and/or deemed to be aspirational. It appears, however, that some Supreme Court justices are of the opinion that the Directive Principles of State Policy can and do create legal obligations. Hence, in the December 31 case, the defense counsel contended that some of the articles invoked were merely Directive Principles of State Policy, and, as such, were not justiciable. Justice Adade held, however, that the constitution as a whole "is a justiciable document" because Articles 1(2) and 2(1) state that any law that is inconsistent with or in contravention of "any provision" is void to the extent of its inconsistency.[33]

In some instances, certain provisions of the DPSP may appear to form an integral part of the enforceable rights, either because they qualify them or are determined to be rights in themselves.[34] In sum, the DPSP provided for under the Ghanaian constitution are more than mere aids when it comes to the construction of human rights provisions contained in the constitution.

The constitutional provisions on human rights and fundamental freedoms include not only provisions for civil and political rights, but also provisions for economic, social, and cultural rights. In addition, the rights of vulnerable groups such as women, children, and the disabled have been adequately met under Chapter 5 of the constitution. There are also certain rights, which, though not provided for in the constitution, are, nonetheless, provided for under recognized international human rights instruments,[35] such as the right to satisfactory environment provided for by the African Charter on Human and Peoples' Rights, and in light of the CIBA case, are rights exercisable as human rights.

It could be argued that a limitation that affects the full enjoyment of the rights provided for in the 1992 constitution are the stipulations contained in sections of the transitional provisions, mainly sections 34, 35, and 37. These sections of the transitional provisions indemnify the PNDC and all its appointees from liability, individually or jointly, for any act or omission during the administration of the PNDC. Section 34(2) ousts the competence of courts, making it illegal for any court or tribunal to entertain any action or make any order or grant any remedy or relief on any claim pertaining to the said acts and/or omissions. It is not the first time in the constitutional history of Ghana that indemnity clauses have been inserted in the transitional provisions. All the military regimes after overthrowing constitutional governments ensure that constitutional constituent assemblies insert such immunity clauses before they finally disengage from politics by handing over power to elected incoming civilian governments.

However, differences exist between the PNDC indemnity clause and those of previous military regimes as contained in the transitional provisions of the constitutions. For example, section 13 of the transitional provisions of the 1969 constitution aimed at indemnifying the NLC members and its appointees from acts which led to and culminated in the coup d'état itself, the abrogation of the then operative 1960 constitution, and the establishment of the NLC. Further, the indemnity clause inserted in the 1969 constitution, unlike the PNDC's which appears to be permanent and absolute, had a maximum duration of five years after which the indemnity would lapse and not be applicable in law.[36]

The transitional provisions limit the protection of human rights for two reasons. First, they create a culture of impunity which is not consistent with the spirit of the constitution and possibly some of the evolving rules of public international law. Second, and perhaps more important, it appears that should there be a conflict between provisions of Chapter 5 (which provides for human rights) and the transitional provisions on any matter involving the protection of rights, the latter would prevail.[37] There is already an authority to sustain this contention. In the case of *Kwakye v. Attorney General* (1981), the plaintiff (who was a member of the SMC government which was overthrown by the AFRC) sought a declaration that he was never tried or convicted by any special court set by AFRC. Such a court set by the AFRC had purportedly sentenced him to twenty-five years' imprisonment. The plaintiff argued that the AFRC court was therefore in violation of his fundamental human rights as contained in the 1979 constitution, since the court was null and void and had no effect.[38] The state raised objections relying on the transitional provisions of the constitution, which were stipulated in section 15(2). The majority of the Supreme Court held that the court had no jurisdiction to hear the case.

Derogation by the State from Human Rights Obligations

Article 31 spells out clearly the circumstances under which the state could justifiably derogate from its human rights obligations or restrict the exercise of rights. The procedure for proclamation of a state of emergency is very comprehensive involving the Council of State, the president, and parliament. The article does not elaborate the kinds of rights which could be derogated from and the core nonderogable rights as provided for in international human rights treaties.

Additional Sources of Law

This section examines the international sources of human rights law which complement municipal law (in this case the constitutional law of Ghana) in the protection of human rights. Ghana is a party to several international human rights treaties. Ghana, as a common law country, operates a dualist system, which means that a piece of international law is not applicable in the domestic legal system unless it is incorporated by an act of Parliament. However, the domestic legal system of Ghana, as of other states, is being scrutinized by supranational bodies—the United Nations at the international level and the OAU at the regional level—with the view to ascertaining how such domestic laws are consistent with international human rights law. Better still, there is an emerging view that the International Bill of Rights constitutes part of customary international law which binds countries as of custom. This is also true of other international human rights instruments, such as the Convention on the Prevention and Punishment of the Crime of Genocide. It is submitted that the Ghanaian constitution recognizes the international sources of human rights law by providing in Article 33(5) thus: "The rights, duties, declarations and guarantees relating to the fundamental human rights and freedoms specifically mentioned in this Chapter [5, which is the chapter dealing with human rights] shall not be regarded as excluding others not specifically mentioned which are considered to be inherent in a democracy and intended to secure the freedom and dignity of man."

As a general rule, as stated above, an international treaty is not directly applicable in the domestic legal system except by a legislative incorporation (Article 75). However, when it comes to human rights law, it would appear that they would be applied even without the requisite legislative incorporation *New Patriotic Party v. Attorney General* (CIBA case, 1996–97).

Customary law is one of the sources of law in Ghana, but because its structure and formulations are informed by traditions and customs of the past, there is a tendency for it to be static in certain instances, lagging behind some of the changes in society. This in turn creates tensions between rights of individuals or peoples—which are by definition dynamic and very much in flux—and some of the customary rules. Women's rights in particular typify this tension, whereby authorities within society are very ready to invoke some dubious or outmoded customs to justify what would otherwise be a human rights violation. Yet there are some positive elements which the state needs to support and harness for the common the good of society. This act of balancing is what customary law in Ghana strives to achieve, albeit not without difficulty.

International Human Rights Obligations

Ghana is obligated under several international and regional human rights treaties which it has ratified. At the international level, Ghana is a party to, *inter alia*:

1. The Convention on the Elimination of All Forms of Racial Discrimination (CERD), although it does not recognize the competence of its committee to examine individual communications according to Article 14 of the Convention.
2. The Convention on the Prevention and Punishment of the Crime of Genocide.
3. The Convention on the Elimination of All Forms of Discrimination Against Women (CEDAW).
4. The Convention on the Rights of the Child (CRC).
5. The Geneva Conventions of 1926 and 1956 and the four Geneva Conventions on Laws of War and their two Additional Protocols.
6. International Labor Organization (ILO) conventions, including Conventions 29 (forced labor), 87 (freedom of association and protection of the right to organize), 98 (right to organize and collective bargaining), and 105 (abolition of forced labor).

At the regional level, Ghana is a party to the African Charter on Human Rights and Peoples' Rights and the Refugee Convention of the Organization of African Unity.

To date, Ghana has not ratified the International Convention on Economic, Social and Cultural Rights (ICESCR) and the International Covenant on Civil and Political Rights (ICCPR), which form the core of the International Bill of Human Rights. Ghana is also not a party to the Convention against Torture and Other Cruel, Inhumane or Degrading Treatment or Punishment (CAT). Thus, Ghana's willingness to accept international obligations with respect to human rights and to submit to international monitoring mechanisms is less than satisfactory. Moreover, Ghana has not abided by reporting obligations under the conventions it has ratified in time.[39] Ghana has not as yet domesticated, through legislative incorporation, any of the international human rights treaties that it has ratified.

Customary Law

Customary law is recognized as part of the laws of Ghana. Article 11(1) of the 1992 constitution makes common law part of the laws of Ghana, and Article 11(2) states that common law includes customary law. Customary law is defined in Article 11(3) of the constitution as "the rules of law, which by custom are applicable to particular communities in Ghana." According to case and statute law, customary laws are those that have acquired such status by legislative instrument or judicial pronouncement, or which are enforceable as rights under Article 26(1).[40]

The government has given the National House of Chiefs the task of studying, interpreting, and compiling customary law with a view to evolving a unified system of rules of customary laws. The Regional Houses of Chiefs are directly responsible for undertaking such study, verifying the existing customs in the different regions and making recommendations to the National House of Chiefs. Formal restatements of customary laws are also found in judicial decisions where customs are contested or applied by the courts.

However, customary practices can be pleaded as evidence before the courts in Ghana only if the party asserting it as evidence can prove that it exists in the particular locality. When a custom has been repeatedly established in court this way, the requirement of positive proof can be dispensed with through judicial notice of the particular rule of customary law.

In addition, under the law of evidence applicable before courts in Ghana, a norm of customary law must conform to the principles of natural justice, equity, and good conscience. Since the 1992 constitution, with its provision on cultural rights, it is doubtful whether statutory law should prevail over customary law. It would appear that the issue as to whether customary law can be challenged as unconstitutional has not as yet been tested thus far under the successive constitutions of Ghana. Since 1992, moreover, the National House of Chiefs has yet to formulate a uniform and systematized body of customary laws applicable in the different parts of the country.

At present, the application of customary law is contingent upon the extent to which a particular custom is consistent with provisions of Chapter 5 of the constitution. Article 26(2) states clearly that: "All customary practices which dehumanize or are injurious to the physical and mental well-being of a person are prohibited." It would appear, therefore, that in the case of conflicts between a customary practice and a right guaranteed in Chapter 5, the latter would prevail, where the former has been proved to be dehumanizing or injurious to the physical and mental well-being. Mindful of the tensions that can and do exist sometimes between the two legal regimes, the constitution enjoins the National House of Chiefs to work toward the elimination of outmoded and socially harmful customary practices. This is explicitly stated in Article 272(c) of the 1992 Constitution: "The National House of Chiefs shall undertake an evaluation of traditional customs and usages with a view to eliminating those customs and usages that are outmoded and socially harmful."

Sections 42 and 43 of the Chieftancy Act, 1971 (Act 370), stipulate a mechanism through which customary practices can be made legally enforceable. Section 42 states: "A Regional House of Chiefs may, either after receiving representations from a traditional council or on its own initiative, and shall if so requested in writing by the National House of Chiefs, draft a declaration of what in its opinion is the customary law rule relating to any subject in force in its region or any part thereof." Section 42(2) goes on to stipulate that the Regional House of Chiefs shall submit its draft declaration to the National House of Chiefs, which will study it and, if satisfied, submit it to the president. The president, in turn, in consultation with the chief justice of the Supreme Court, as stated in section 42(3), make a legislative instrument, which will put the rule into effect within the area in question. Section 43 also spells out the procedure by which a change in customary law might be made. In effect, what this suggests is that only certain rules of customary practice which can be shown to have gone through this procedure in accordance with sections 42 and 43 of the 1971 Act (370) can be deemed to be legally enforceable rules of customary practice.

The Legal Profession and Legal Education in Ghana

The General Legal Council is responsible for establishing a system of legal education, including arranging appropriate courses of instruction for those persons who wish to be admitted to the rolls of the legal profession. The council also regulates the admission of students to courses of instruction that are required for qualification as lawyers. The General Legal Council delegates the immediate and administrative supervision of legal education as it exists to the Board of Legal Education. The functions performed by the Board of Legal Education and the General Legal Council in relation to legal education are limited to preparing students and candidates for admission to the legal profession and do not extend to continuing education within the legal profession or the judiciary in Ghana.

Candidates for the legal profession must take a course leading to the award of the bachelor or laws (LL.B.) degree or its equivalent in a recognized institution. Students who qualify are then admitted to the School of Law in Accra for a two-year postgraduate professional course. The School of Law also admits graduates, with a first degree in any related field, such as political science or philosophy, from a recognized university who pass the entrance examinations at the school, to study to become professional lawyers. Such candidates, however, are required to undertake a four-year course, after which successful candidates are called to the Ghana bar and become solicitors and barristers. (There is no distinction, as in England, between solicitors and barristers once they become lawyers). A view gaining currency is that an LL.B. be made a second degree after candidates have completed undergraduate studies in another discipline. Individual lawyers may choose to pursue cases that have human rights implications; very often in Ghana most of such cases are couched as constitutional law claims. A number of reasons could be assigned. First, most of the judges and senior lawyers did not have the opportunity to study "purely" human rights jurisprudence during their university education, so they are not very familiar with the principles or conceptual framework, let alone the case law; the closest they have gotten to human rights law is constitutional law and administrative law. Second, most judges view human rights law generally as part of international law. Judges of common law jurisdiction, such as Ghana, are very uncomfortable handing down judgments based on human rights law unless unambiguous municipal law supports the reasoning. Also missing is a well-rooted culture of constitutionalism that could embolden a common law judge even in the absence of constitutional or statutory provisions on rights to venture to interpret the law purposely for human rights protection. Third, human rights litigation is not particularly lucrative, which makes it very unattractive to lawyers. Fourth, until recently human rights were viewed as a subversive concept inspired by foreign countries and internal opposition groups to undermine the security of the state, so lawyers who dared take up such cases risked reprisals or suffered the same fate as the clients they had to defend. This risk made it very unattractive to lawyers.

Since 1992 especially, there are about two or three law chambers (firms) that have argued "purely" human rights cases successfully in Ghanaian courts. Two such chambers which come readily to mind are Akuffo-Addo and Prempeh, and Minkah Premo and Co.

The Ghana Bar Association is a corporate body of all legal practitioners in Ghana. The association has branches in all ten regional capitals, in addition to the national office. It is impossible to cite reliable current figures of the number of practicing lawyers on the roll of the bar in Ghana since there is no periodic update of the roll, which takes into account deceased members of the profession. The Ghana Bar Association has a human rights committee constituted by some of the members of the bar to study important human rights issues and advise it to make national pronouncements, which it does as any other pressure group within the state; the bar has not as yet litigated on human rights cases as one corporate entity.

Legal practitioners in Ghana belong to other international and regional bar associations with interest and legal know-how for the protection of human rights. The most notable ones are Africa Bar Association (ABA), Commonwealth Lawyers Association (CLA), International Bar Association (IBA), International Federation of Women Lawyers (FIDA), and International Commission of Jurists (ICJ).

The Judiciary

Judicial Training and Qualifications for the Bench

The judiciary is the organ of the state vested with the power of interpretation of the laws of Ghana, including human rights law, under chapter 11 of the 1992 constitution. This section, which attempts an inquiry into the kind of training judges receive and the qualifications needed to become a judge, could furnish useful insights into their possible approach to human rights law.

Apart from a legal education, high moral character and proven integrity are the main qualifications for all judges of both the Superior Courts of Judicature and the lower courts. This is determined by the Judicial Council.[41] The different levels in the hierarchy of courts in Ghana is reflected in the length of legal experience required for appointment of judges to each court as follows: the Supreme Court, fifteen years as a lawyer; Court of Appeal, twelve years as a lawyer; High Court, ten years as a lawyer; regional tribunal chair, ten years as a lawyer; circuit and tribunal judges, five years as a lawyer; and chair community tribunal, three years as a lawyer or a person with other legal experience.

The judicial service supervises and coordinates the training of judicial officers under the broad supervision of the chief justice. It is the duty of the judicial secretary to ensure that facilities exist to train judicial officers. Seminars are organized occasionally in conjunction with other organizations outside the judiciary. There is no record of systematic human rights training for judges, but some are invited from time to time to attend conferences and colloquiums which address human rights issues. The colloquiums organized annually between the human rights unit of the commonwealth secretariat and Interrights is one such forum for judicial training on human rights jurisprudence. Other seminars include the annual conference of the African Society for International and Comparative Law, based in London and Accra, and the human rights procedures training program for magistrates and judges organized by the African Center for Democracy and Human Rights Studies, based in Banjul, Gambia.

The Institutional Framework for Human Rights Adjudication

In this section, I examine the formal structure of the institutions for human rights adjudication in Ghana, especially the judiciary and legal profession, and their respective capacities for human rights protection.

Judicial Enforcement of Human Rights

Enforcement of human rights can take several forms, including respect for, promotion of, and direct implementation of human rights. Legislative, judicial, executive, and administrative actions may be used for promotion or direct implementation. In this section, by judicial enforcement I mean a forum that has the competence to entertain and adjudicate over rights claims, that is, where the rights claims are justiciable.[42] Under the 1992 constitution, there are both judicial and quasi-judicial bodies vested with this competence. The Supreme Court and the High Court have concurrent but shared jurisdiction on human rights matters.[43] Quasi-judicial bodies with jurisdiction on human rights matters include the Commission on Human Rights and Administrative Justice (CHRAJ, Article 218) and the Media Commission (Article 167[b]).

The Structure of the Courts

The 1992 constitution vests judicial power in the judiciary and states clearly that no other organ of the state shall exercise judicial power (Article 125[3]). The judiciary has jurisdiction in all civil and criminal matters, and those relating to the constitution.

The Supreme Court's jurisdiction on human rights is derived from its general powers as the body with exclusive original jurisdiction in the interpretation and enforcement of the 1992 constitution. Accordingly, Article 130(1) states: "subject to the jurisdiction of the High Court in the enforcement of fundamental human rights and freedoms as provided for in Article 33 of this Constitution, the Supreme Court shall have exclusive original jurisdiction in (a) all matters relating to the enforcement or interpretation of this Constitution."

As a court of last resort in the land, it also has an appellate jurisdiction on human rights enforcement that may commence in the subordinate courts. Article 130(2) enjoins that all courts other than the Supreme Court must stay the proceedings and any matter of interpretation or enforcement of a constitutional provision and refers them to the Supreme Court for determination. Article 2(1) empowers the Supreme Court to entertain a claim from a person that an enactment or an act or omission is in contravention of the constitution and declare an action *ultra vires* in exercise of the authority conferred on it by Article 2(2). Whereas the High Court exercises original jurisdiction on all human rights issues, the Supreme Court has appellate jurisdiction over enforcement of human rights, based on personal interest actions as provided for in Article 33(1) and public interest ones commenced in the High Court under Articles 12(2) and 140(2). Both appeals, however, must go through the Court of Appeal before reaching the Supreme Court. Below the Supreme Court, the Court of Appeal has appellate jurisdiction over High Court and regional tribunals (Article 137).

The High Court, which is the Superior Court of the first instance, has jurisdiction in all civil and criminal matters, and appellate jurisdiction over subordinate courts (Article 140[1]). Article 140(2) provides that: "The High Court shall have jurisdiction to enforce the fundamental human rights and freedoms guaranteed by this Constitution." This article authorizes human rights actions through either personal interest or public interest litigation. This judicial competence is buttressed by the provision of Article 33(1), which concerns only personal interest human rights actions: "Where a person alleges that a provision of this Constitution on fundamental human rights and freedoms has been, or is being or is likely to be constructed in relation to him then, without prejudice to any other action that is lawfully available that person may apply to the High Court for redress."[44] Pursuant to the exercise of this jurisdiction, the High Court can, under Article 33(2), issue prerogative orders. A petitioner can also seek declaratory relief and injunctions from the court. Finally, the High Court also has supervisory jurisdiction over all lower courts and lower adjudicating authority (Article 141).

It would appear from the various provisions examined above that apart from the Supreme Court, the jurisdiction of both judicial and quasi-judicial institutions with respect to human rights matters stops at "interpretation" and *ultra vires* declarations. The issue of which forum an aggrieved person has to go to for enforcement of human rights has, since the 1992 constitution came into force, been a source of academic debate. In *Edusei v. Attorney General & Anor*, the Supreme Court by a majority of 3–2 held that the High Court is the proper forum for the enforcement of human rights claims and not the Supreme Court. In fact, this decision has generated even more passionate controversy.[45] In addition to the foregoing, the High Court may also enforce the recommendations of the Commission on Human Rights and Administrative Justice, which deals with human rights and administrative justice.[46]

Other claims have human rights implications or consequences but fall outside the provisions of Chapter 5 of the constitution. Such rights are actionable through the common law concepts of judicial review of administrative actions, tort, industrial law, and under the criminal law. It has been argued that the drafters of the 1992 constitution had an additional category of inferior courts and actionable causes in mind when they inserted in the constitution the "any other action" phrase in Article 33(1), so "as to make the jurisdiction of the High Court only cumulative not exclusive."[47]

In addition to the courts mentioned, the 1992 constitution provided for the establishment of regional tribunals with jurisdiction to try such offenses against the state and the public interest as may be prescribed by Parliament (Article 143).

Independence of the Judiciary

The independence of judges is guaranteed by the constitution by virtue of the mode of appointment and removal of judges. The chief justice, as the head of the judiciary, is appointed by the president in consultation with the Council of State and with the approval of Parliament (Article 144[1]). Other justices of the Supreme Court are appointed by the president on the advice of the Judicial Council, which has to consult with the Council of State, and is subject to the approval of Parliament (Article 144[2]). The president on the advice of the Judicial Council appoints justices of the Court of Appeal and the High Court and chairmen of regional tribunals (Article 144[3]). The removal of a justice of a superior court or a chairman of a tribunal is justified only on the grounds of established misbehavior, incompetence, or the inability to perform the functions arising from infirmity of body or mind (Article 146[1]). A very laborious procedure is spelled out by the constitution in order to remove justices of the superior courts (Article 146[2–11]).

Other Quasi-Judicial Forums

The Commission on Human Rights and Administrative Justice.   The main entity under the 1992 constitution that can be said to exercise quasi-judicial powers to entertain human rights and administrative justice claims is the Commission on Human Rights and Administrative Justice (Article 218[d] [iii]). According to Article 218, the functions of CHRAJ include the following: to investigate complaints of human rights violations, injustices, corruption, or abuse of power; to investigate certain public officials of state; and to investigate complaints concerning actions by persons, private enterprises, and other institutions where they allege human rights violations or corruption or misappropriation of public funds by an official. It also has the duty to educate the public on human rights. The role of the CHRAJ is largely arbitrative in non–human rights issues; it has the power to bring proceedings to a competent court to remedy any offending act or conduct (Article 33[2]).

In its capacity as a quasi-judicial body, the CHRAJ has handled cases concerning, for example, the right to education (including the *Parent-Teacher Association of Ghana International School v. Attorney General* and *Alpha Beta Educational Complex v. Ghana Education Service*), the right of the sick, and sexual harassment.[48]

Articles 217 and 221 list the qualifications for appointment to the post of CHRAJ commissioner. The candidate must be a lawyer of at least twelve years' standing (Articles 221, 136[3]). The commissioner is accorded the standing of a justice of the Court of Appeal, and his deputies are accorded the standing of a High Court judge.

Media Commission.   The Media Commission is invested with constitutional power under Article 167(b) to investigate, mediate, and settle complaints against or by the press or other mass media. Its function is to protect freedom of speech and expression as provided for in Article 21(1)(a). Proceedings are instituted by a written complaint by the victim or his or her representatives.

Procedures, Remedies, and Standing

To date, no human rights enforcement procedure rules have been enacted as envisaged by Article 33(4). This may be evidence of how unrooted the human rights culture is within the Ghanaian legal system. Or it could be that it is not one of Parliament's legislative priorities. Litigation on human rights enforcement can be commenced by the following procedure. An action may be commenced by a writ of summons order 2(1) of the High Court Civil Procedure rules, which state that declaratory relief can be sought by an aggrieved applicant. A declaration may also be sought. Human rights enforcement can also be instituted by the Originating Notice of Motion,[49] in consonance with Order 74 of the High Court Civil Procedure Rules. Prerogative writs may also be used. In the High Court, a prerogative writ is issued first with leave under Order 59 of the High Court Civil Procedures Rules, but when it is brought to the Supreme Court under CI 16 (that is, the Supreme Court Rules of Practice), no leave is required. Finally, with regard to the CHRAJ and the Media Commission, action can be commenced by way of petition.[50]

The facts of each case may give birth to different causes of action and therefore different remedies.[51] The courts can make a declaration that a right or rights have been violated and can award damages or compensation or make consequential orders of injunction, prohibition, and so on for such violations, in cases in which the plaint is couched as a specific human rights relief or remedy. On certain occasions, human rights remedies may not be available to a plaintiff, but other remedies may achieve the same result. For example, in military regimes when human rights are usually suspended or abolished alongside the suspension or abolition of the constitution, the right to administrative justice cannot be pursued as a human right remedy. The right, however, may be pursued by bringing industrial action of wrongful dismissal. The provision of a bill of rights in the 1992 constitution therefore envisages multiple remedies for facts that might be considered human rights violations (Article 33[1]).

The issue of *locus standi* (standing) is dependent upon the nature of the human rights claim that one wants to litigate. In cases that involve private human rights claims, whether made as an individual or as a group, the applicant(s) must demonstrate sufficient personal interest (Article 33[1]).

In respect to public rights, locus is accorded to any interested parties or citizens with a sense of civic duty (Article 12[2]) that can show their claim involves constitutional interpretation and an *ultra vires* declaration.[52]

A human rights petitioner to the CHRAJ must demonstrate the capacity in which the complaint is being brought in consonance with the CHRAJ's rules of procedure.

Human Rights NGOs

If we conceptualize human rights NGOs as civil society organizations, which specialize in the advocacy of human rights issues by using the International Bill of Rights as their normative framework, then human rights NGOs are a very recent phenomenon in Ghana. So defined, a number of human rights NGOs were created just before the inauguration of the 1992 constitution when the political climate was somewhat liberalized and, thus, enabled civil society to reemerge. The constitution also provided the normative framework for human rights NGOs thanks to its guarantee of the freedom of association.

The most notable human rights NGOs now operating in Ghana that became more active during this period include the Ghana chapter of the African Commission on Health and Human Rights Promoters (which was founded with the objective of rehabilitating political prisoners who were tortured while in police detention), and the Ghana Federation of Female Lawyers (FIDA), which advocates for women's rights issues and has gained the support of most women, including illiterate rural dwellers in Ghana. The Ghana Committee on Human Rights, which advocates for human rights with branches in some regional capitals, was an alliance of lawyers, trade unionists, journalists, academics, and political activists to campaign mainly against the violations taking place during the PNDC rule before the inauguration of the 1992 constitution. Another NGO, Human Rights Law Services (HURI-LAWS), has embarked upon litigation that relies on the 1992 constitution as well as on international human rights treaties. Of particular importance is the fact that it is the pioneer organization that litigates on economic, social, and cultural rights.[53] The Ghana Bar Association has also recently established a Human Rights Committee, and international human rights NGOs, such as Amnesty International, the African Society for International and Comparative Law, and Africa Legal Aid (ALA), have branches in Ghana.

Almost all the NGOs specializing in human rights depend upon outside funding or on international bodies operating in Ghana. In countries like Ghana where dramatic human rights violations have not been in the Western media for quite some time, it is harder for human rights NGOs to attract funding for their projects. When a regime is perceived, rightly or wrongly, as legitimate, donors tend to shy away from human rights issues, which are viewed as being particularly sensitive politically. Some of the emerging human rights NGOs also lack the capacity to indulge in high level professional advocacy. As is the case elsewhere in Africa, their activities are essentially urban based and focused. There are even a few cases of "letterhead" NGOs, in which questions of accountability and credibility have been raised.[54] In September 1996, the government sought to legislate on NGOs and to establish a coordinating body, which would provide a forum for cooperation between NGOs and the government. Section 11 of the draft NGO bill (1993) provided an NGO Advisory Council of twenty-one members, of which thirteen would be political appointees. This, however, was rejected as an example of creeping politicization of civil society formations, which are intended to be independent of the government and above the narrow partisan considerations of politics.

Other civil society groups which are not explicitly and exclusively human rights NGOs, but, nonetheless, contribute to the promotion and protection of human rights, include the Ghana Bar Association, the Trade Union Congress (TUC) of Ghana, the Ghana Journalists Association, the National Union of Ghana Students, the Christian Council of Ghana, the Bishops Conference, and the December 31 Women's Movement, which dates to the years of the revolution.

Political, Economic, and Social Context

The contemporary conceptualization of human rights makes the state the addressee of rights. This suggests that, in order for us to understand the human rights practices of a state like Ghana, such an understanding must be situated within the context of the structures of the state. The state of Ghana as it is known today is a colonial construct, and the colonial mode of governance was authoritarianism. The laws and security apparatuses of the state were designed to oppress those people it colonized. This system of dominance and exploitation was rationalized in the name of the alleged racial superiority of the colonizer over the colonized. The political legacy of colonialism has not had a positive effect upon juridical independence. And, unfortunately, human rights practices in Ghana have suffered from the strictures imposed by this baneful legacy.

There has been no substantial reorientation of the security services and governance. As stated in the beginning of this chapter, the CPP tradition tended to be more populist and radical, favoring economic, social, and cultural rights. The CPP government could be characterized as "developmentalist" for its alleged prioritization of economic development and nation-building and for group or collective rights over and above individual rights. The frontiers between rhetoric and reality were blurred and some the invocation of group rights or the general will was used to justify human rights violations, although there were objective challenges as a postcolonial underdeveloped state. This approach to human rights was jettisoned immediately after the coup of 1966, which in the main brought into power politicians of somewhat more liberal tendencies, and as such, ideologically opposed to the overthrown CPP government. The main members of the CPP government and its sympathizers were targeted by the NLC regime for detention and confiscation of property. They were debarred from politics and could not form a political party or contest and/or campaign in elections. Subsequently, the PP government dismissed CPP sympathizers from positions of public employment. Although the 1969 constitution was quite liberal, and in spite of its claimed tradition of belief in liberalism, the PP government, nonetheless, passed a law which effectively aimed at crippling the TUC and minimizing the trade union militancy that it had acquired under the previous radical CPP government. The TUC also, it must be stated, had ideological problems with the liberal PP government, and in the cold war political context of the time it saw the PP as reactionary and Western-oriented. A possible reason for the PP government's action was to prevent strikes and opposition to the austere IMF economic development program which the government had begun to implement. The workers who were members of the TUC were perceived to be left-leaning sympathizers of the erstwhile CPP government, who were going to resist the market and private sector orientation of the PP government.

The NRC government, which overthrew the PP government in 1972, aligned itself with the traditions of the overthrown CPP government. Thus, main actors of the PP government became political opponents, and were put in protective custody for reasons of "national security." The AFRC regime of June–September 1979 and the PNDC regime of 1981–92, both of which were under the chairmanship of President Rawlings, however, posed the main challenge to the enjoyment of human rights in the country. The revolutionary approach of these two regimes attempted to break with the liberal traditions of the country that had persisted in spite of frequent military takeovers and proscription of carefully drafted liberal constitutions. In the process of devising institutional mechanisms for addressing issues of structural human rights violations, such as poverty, lack of access to education and the justice system, and alienation of ordinary people from the decision-making processes of the country, the PNDC registered more serious human rights violations than any previous administration in the recorded annals of the history of Ghana. It would appear that most civil and political rights were traded off for the structural adjustment policies that the regime embarked upon.

The lesson learned from Ghanaian political history is that liberalism is a requisite minimum for the protection of civil and political rights, but it is inherently weak in addressing structural problems such as poverty, social inequality, marginalization of women and youth, alienation of rural peasants, which in human rights parlance is about collective rights and also economic, social, and cultural rights. On the other hand, as Ghanaians witnessed under the PNDC, a project that addresses such structural problems by addressing group rights without liberalizing the political system, results in serious human rights violations. This invariably derails the popular project of equitable development and social justice.

What is nonetheless commendable about the human rights scene in Ghana is that violations are not explained away with reference to ethnicity and religion. The two-party tradition has either consciously or unconsciously given Ghana a rational approach to politics focused on the promotion of the traditions stemming from the CPP and PP regimes. Human rights violations have occurred in the past for political reasons only because of the need of a particular tradition to retain power so as to progress its policies. Though this is not a practice to be commended, it has, nonetheless, enabled Ghana to avoid other scenarios of human rights violations in which ethnicity and religion are the main considerations.

This is not to apologize for the violation of any human right. Every individual has an inherent dignity as a person; his or her rights matter as do those of any other collective or group. This includes those experiencing the political violation of their individual rights. Any distinction of rights into categories at the emotional level is unacceptable and thus appears irrelevant. However, what I belabor to put across is predicated on the assumption—which is itself informed normatively by human rights law and practical experience in Africa and elsewhere in the world—that when the rights of a particular nationality or ethnic or religious group are systematically violated, that violation stands on the slippery slope of degenerating into genocide, the ultimate form of the violation of human rights. Ghana has witnessed sporadic human rights violations which have hardly been systematic or targeted at any particular identifiable social group, except during the PNDC era when that regime embarked on systematic human rights violations of the core rights of political opponents who were not of any particular social category. After a year or so of the "revolution," the regime started targeting those perceived as having become rich from ill-gotten wealth and the neo-Marxist intellectuals who had brought Rawlings to power, but later the violations became random and individual in character.

The 1992 constitution, it is submitted, is a synthesis of all these experiences and provides constitutional solutions to past political mischief. The human rights provisions of the 1992 constitution, as well as the judicial and quasi-judicial mechanisms to protect human rights, are adequate and satisfactory for the promotion and protection of human rights in contemporary Ghana. However, the way in which the Supreme Court will interpret human rights provisions has yet to be fully established. In recent years, a general perception has arisen that the chief justice's power of impaneling the court is being dictated by political considerations. As a result, certain judges are always brought to hear cases of political sensitivity. As human rights cases are by definition political, this approach is eroding the confidence that the Supreme Court enjoyed during the early years of the inauguration of the constitution when it handed down landmark decisions on human rights. Section 34 of the transitional provisions to the constitution, which indemnifies the PNDC and the previous military regimes from any judicial action for acts of omission and commission during their respective terms in office, is another concern. This section stipulates that should there be a conflict between individual rights and that of any provision in the transitional provisions, the latter will prevail.

On balance, however, the state and society in the Fourth Republic have made remarkable strides in human rights protection. There is still a long way to go, but a healthy human rights culture is evolving. In this respect the role of the Commission on Human Rights and Administrative Justice in human rights protection and promotion is commendable. As of 1995, it had established offices in ten regional capitals and twenty-eight districts. It had received 1,036 complaints at its national headquarters in Accra, and another 2,161 from its regional and district offices, for a grand total of 3,197 cases. Labor-related disputes represented about 62 percent of all complaints.[55] The privately owned media which has been proliferating in Ghana for the past ten or so years has made an invaluable contribution to the culture of constitutionalism and human rights. The FM radio stations in particular have also made an enormous contribution to the human rights culture, as they have allowed people to phone in and articulate in the vernacular their concerns, some of which can be construed as human rights issues.

The realization of economic, social, and cultural rights remains an important challenge. Since the introduction of the Structural Adjustment Program (SAP) as a strategy of economic stabilization in 1984, the economy has grown by 5 percent with inflation reduced by over 100 percent. This impressive macroeconomic performance notwithstanding, some economic rights have been adversely affected. By 1992, over 50,000 workers had been retrenched or made redundant. According to a report by the UNDP, 6.5 million Ghanaians, out of an estimated population of 17.7 million, live in absolute poverty, of which 38 percent are mostly in the rural areas of northern Ghana. Furthermore, government expenditure on education has been reduced from 3.8 percent of the gross national product in 1960 to 3.4 percent in 1991. Consequently, it is claimed that while enrollment in schools has dropped, the dropout rate has increased.[56]

Gender Dimensions

Despite the formal provisions of the constitution contained in Article 26(2), which outlaws all cultural practices which dehumanize or are deemed to be injurious to the physical and mental well-being of a person, there are still some social practices which amount to serious human rights violations, including female genital mutilation, child brides, child labor, and banishment of mostly old women from their communities because they are believed to be witches.

Nowhere does the tension between formal legal protection and the real social and cultural practices come out more clearly than in the area of women's rights. Curiously when it comes to the protection of women's rights all male societies are very quick to invoke cultural traditions to justify practices which are to all intents and purposes violations of women's rights. Constitutional and legal protection of rights are limited in practice by the conditions of poverty in which women live, lack of education, non-participation by women in political and public life, none of which augur well for the protection of women's rights.

Article 17 of the constitution enshrines equality before the law and eschews all forms of discrimination, including discrimination based on grounds of gender. An issue here, though, is that the constitution, by not placing a duty on the government to strive to eliminate the prevalent discrimination against women, has fallen short of regional standards of protection of women's rights, which specifically call upon state parties to eliminate discrimination against women.[57] In furtherance of protecting women's rights, statutes have been promulgated to protect women and in some instances criminalize practices deemed as a violation of their rights. Recent examples include PNDC Laws 111 and 112 which deal with the intestate succession law and the Registration of Marriages and Divorce Law of 1985, which sought to protect women against discriminatory forms of inheritance on the death (intestate) of the husband. In addition, PNDC Laws 263 and 264 impose criminal sanctions upon anyone who maltreats a surviving spouse and tries to take away from the spouse the self-acquired property of an estate. PNDC Law 263 also allows oral or documentary evidence to be used to establish proof of marriage in the absence of registration of customary marriage. Mothers are entitled in law to maternity leave under NLCD 157, which gives them time off during the nursing period of the baby.

These formal and legal protections are hampered by socioeconomic factors, which are mainly traditional cultural norms (or presented as such) and negate the enjoyment of the rights provided for by law. In this section I call attention to some of them and their impact on rights.

Outlawing harmful customary practices and rites which constitute violations of women's rights have not altogether helped in protecting the rights of women, as the practices linger on. For example, in spite of the stipulations of the Criminal Code (Amendment) Act, 1994 (Act 484), which insert a new section 69 into the criminal code, making it a criminal offense to excise, infibulate, or mutilate a girl, the practice is still carried out. Another disturbing cultural practice in the Volta Region, known as Trokosi, has recently come to the attention of human rights groups in Ghana. The Trokosi allows family elders to send young girls to particular shrines for the service of the fetish priests (sometimes as sex slaves) in order to counter past crimes of having offended ancestors by breaching certain customary injunctions. There is also a complex network of kinship relationships by which young girls from rural areas come to the city to live with the social elite as domestic servants. The conditions under which these young girls work are often very poor. They work from dawn to dusk without any remuneration or any holidays, and there are known cases of sexual abuse. This is slavery to all intents and purposes, but is not prosecuted as such because of the so-called familial relationship.[58] Women are further subjected to outmoded traditional practices of being tried by ordeal. They are often forced to perform a ritual and dangerous task at considerable risk to life to prove their innocence. Women accused of witchcraft are, in particular, subjected to trial by ordeal. They are forced to confess under duress to whatever they are accused of, including ridiculous stories such being party to the killing of Jesus Christ. Yet again, formal law criminalizes trial by ordeal in section 315 of the Criminal Code (Act 29). The women suspected of witchcraft are banished and ostracized from their communities and made to settle far away from their homes. This practice is comparatively more prevalent in Northern Ghana in places such as Yendi, Bimbila, and Gambaga. As yet another example of the issue under discussion, the PNDC passed a law (90) in 1984, making it a criminal offense and misdemeanor to make a bereaved spouse or relative undergo any custom or practice that is cruel in nature. This stipulation notwithstanding, in Ghana, women are subjected to widowhood rites which to all intents and purposes amount to inhuman and degrading treatment. The rites include obnoxious practices such as sprinkling pepper into the eyes of a widow and having her drink the water with which the corpse of the husband has been washed. In some communities, a widow is forced to walk naked through the streets of a given community at night, with a burning coal on her head.[59]

Available data, using the right to education as an example, demonstrate the limitations of formal/legal equality between men and women. Again social, traditional and economic factors conspire to undermine the exercise of the right. Though the constitution and Directive Principles of State Policy are geared toward realizing universal primary education, available data show how females are lagging behind males. In 1981, illiteracy was 65 percent for females and 44 percent for males. In 1990, the rate of female illiteracy stood at 49 percent and male at 30 percent. Enrollment of girls dropped from 50 percent at the preschool level to 20 percent at the high school level. The dropout rate for girls is higher than that of boys. A cursory survey of women's involvement in politics and public service reveals again the gulf between formal equality guaranteed by the constitution and realities. When the revolutionary PNDC regime was inaugurated in 1981, until it transformed itself into a democratic government in 1992, women made up only 6 percent of the Committee of Secretaries (which was the cabinet) and 3 percent of PNDC secretaries (the equivalent of ministers of state). When the constitution entered into force in 1993, there were four women on the twenty-five-member Council of State (a constitutionally created body to advise the president akin to a second chamber), two women out of a nineteen-member cabinet, and three women out of thirty-five ministerial appointments. Women then made up only 8 percent of a two-hundred-member parliament and less than 3 percent of the membership of the district assemblies. Women in the judiciary constituted 1 percent.[60]

Mindful of these limitations, the National Council on Women and Development (NCWD) established as a statutory body created by NRCD 322 in 1975, has been working with government departments such as agriculture, health, and finance. It also collaborates with NGOs. As of 1994, 119 NGOs had registered with the council. The government at the same time spent 0.006 percent on the activities of the council. The December 31 Women's Movement, formed as an NGO in 1982, after the PNDC revolution, works closely with the government in the advocacy of women's rights, especially economic empowerment and legal literacy. Thanks to its the chairperson, who is also the first lady, behind the scenes it has succeeded in getting passed a number of legislations which are protective of women's rights, for example PNDC Law 111, as cited above.

The International Federation of Female Lawyers established in 1985 a legal clinic that has helped with free legal representation of women, principally in the area of child maintenance. Since its inception, it has handled 2,347 cases.

A more fundamental issue regards the importance of the chieftaincy, which some argue reinforces traditional and ethnic prejudices because the institution is coterminous with the ethnic boundaries of the state. While the institution of chieftaincy undermines national unity, it is further argued that, because the chief derives his/her position from customary law and is largely hereditary, it is *prima facie*, a contravention of the constitution that makes Ghana a republican state.[61] Other commentators on the constitutional history of Ghana hold a different view. Kofi Kumado, for one, contends that the chieftaincy has adapted to social changes and in some instances has been very dynamic. Nana Akuffo Addo argues additionally that the diversity that the chieftaincy as an institution provides can be a source of national strength.[62]

The main challenge in the coming years, however, is how to keep the military out of politics, in order to enable the evolving culture of democratic governance and human rights practice to take root. The threat posed by the military is not to be taken lightly. If the current poor performance of the economy continues, it might be used as an excuse by the military to take over power in the hallowed name of "the poor masses." Such a violation of the democratic rights of the people will inevitably provoke resistance, which will most likely then provoke human rights violations.

In the end human rights protection in Ghana will continue to depend upon the struggle that civil society and social movements wage to demand their rights, as has been done in the past.[63]

Recommendations

A crucial goal that needs to be achieved is the ratification of international human rights treaties. The provisions of Article 33(5) of the constitution notwithstanding, it is essential for educational and promotional purposes and for protection within the international human rights implementation machinery that Ghana ratifies a substantial number of international human rights treaties. It is, therefore, recommended that human rights NGOs, activists, and intergovernmental bodies design a plan of action aimed at securing increased ratification of international human rights treaties by Ghana. Additionally, it is imperative that these ratified human rights treaties be published and publicized by the attorney general, who should also make copies of the treaties available to the public in simple language.

Human rights NGOs in the country should force the government to pay attention to its obligations under international human rights treaties through campaigns, concerted actions to increase public pressure, advocacy, and publicity. The advocacy and publicity could, for example, focus on calling attention to inconsistencies between Ghanaian laws and the specific human rights treaty to which Ghana is a party. Human rights NGOs should publicize the considerations of the Ghanaian government of reports by treaty bodies such as the Human Rights Committee and the African Commission on Human and Peoples' Rights. Human rights NGOs should monitor the Ghanaian government's compliance with its human rights obligations through the scrutiny and publicizing of state reports presented to treaty bodies and giving publicity to it, preparation of reports counter to Ghanaian national reports, constantly using the media to remind government of international human rights obligations. The media can also play an important role if journalists develop a particular interest in human rights projects and use simple, accessible language to communicate to the public.

Legal aid should be made readily available to victims of human rights violations by the government. Ghanaian human rights advocacy NGOs should do as some of their Nigerian counterparts did and take and litigate human rights cases of national importance on a pro bono basis. NGOs should provide material assistance to poor human rights litigants and undertake human rights "class action" cases whenever the opportunity arises, in order to further awareness of human rights issues.

With regard to education, human rights law should be taught at universities. There should be refresher courses for lawyers, judges, and law enforcement officers so as to keep them in touch with the rapidly evolving human rights scene and its developing jurisprudence. Human rights NGOs should continue to offer seminars and other educational projects to enable the public at large to understand their rights under the constitution and under human rights treaties. These NGOs should use local languages, dramatization, and street theater to educate the public on human rights issues.

Notes

I have benefited immensely from the writings of and interviews and discussion with some of the finest human rights advocates and scholars in Ghana. In this regard, I wish to especially thank Nana Akuffo-Addo, the foremost constitutional lawyer in contemporary Ghana; Emile Shot, the Commissioner for Human Rights and Administration of Justice in Ghana; Kofi Kumado and J. Quashigah, both of the Faculty of Law, University of Ghana, Legon; Ansah-Koi, Department of Political Science, University of Ghana, Yao Graham, editor of the newspaper *Public Agenda* and advocate for social justice; Kwesi Adu-Amankwa, secretary-general of Trade Union Congress of Ghana and a human rights activist. I am indebted to Mohammed Bawa, senior research fellow at the Africa Research and Information Bureau, London, for making helpful comments on a draft of this chapter; to my brother and intellectual friend Kojo Busia, USAID democracy and governance officer, Mali, for his profound insight on liberal discourse; and finally to my brother and friend Justice K. M. Premo, president of Human Rights Law Services (HURI-LAWS), for sparing the time to scrutinize the earlier draft of this chapter in great detail, providing very useful comments on the draft, and making research material available to me. I take sole responsibility and liability, however, for all the opinions and ideas expressed in the study.

1. See, for example, Nana Akuffo-Addo, "The Role of the Supreme Court in the Protection of Fundamental Human Rights—The Ghanaian and American Experience," paper presented at a joint conference of the Ghana Bar Association and the American Bar Association on the theme of "Development under the Rule of Law" in June 1996, Accra, Ghana.

2. Cocoa is a cash crop and Ghana's main source of foreign exchange.

3. See S. O. Gyandoh, Jr., *Liberty and the Courts: A Survey of Judicial Protection of Liberty of the Individual in Ghana During the Last Hundred Years: Essays in Ghanaian Law,* Supreme Court Century Publication (Legon: University of Ghana, 1976), pp. 57–91. See also Kofi Kumado and Nana K. A. Busia, Jr., "The Impact of Development in Eastern Europe on the Democratisation Process in Africa: An Exploratory Analysis," in Bard A. Andreassen and Theresa Swinehart, eds., *Human Rights in Developing Countries* (Strasburg: Engel Publishers, 1991).

4. (1958) 3 West African Law Report 114.

5. Ibid.

6. See *Re Okine* (1960) GLR 84 and *Re Dumoga and Twelve Others* (1961) 2 GRL 44.

7. (1961) 2 GLR 523.

8. Articles 106 and 28, 1969 constitution; Articles 118(1) and 35, 1979 constitution; Articles 130(33) and 140(2), 1992 constitution.

9. For a more detailed analysis of post-1969 constitutionalism in Ghana, see Akuffo-Addo, "Role of the Supreme Court," pp. 13–14.

10. On actions in personal interest, for further reading, see Justice K. M. Premo, "Beware of Article 33(1): Is It Delimiting or All-Embracing?" GQLJ 3 (1999), pp. 18–21. For actions in the public interest, Articles 12 (2) and 140(2).

11. (1970) CC 55.

12. Akuffo-Addo, "Role of the Supreme Court," p. 15.

13. *Rep. v. Director of Prisons*, Ex Parte Salifu (before J. Anterkyi) G&G 3 (1968), p. 374.

14. The classic example of legislation by military regime containing an ouster clause was the PNDC's 1982 public tribunals law (PNDC 24), section 9(1), repealed and reenacted as the 1984 public tribunals law (PNDC 78) section 24, which stipulated at section 24(1) thus: "No court or other tribunal shall have the jurisdiction to entertain any action or proceeding whatsoever for the purpose of questioning any decision, judgment, finding, ruling, order or proceedings of a Public Tribunal set up under the law; and for removal of doubt, it shall not be lawful for any court to entertain any application for an order or writ in the nature of *habeas corpus, certiorari, mandamus,* prohibition, *quo warranto,* injunction, or declaration in respect of any decision, order, finding ruling or proceeding of any such Public Tribunal." However, there have been some instances in which the courts have been very bold and asserted their authority by exercising the power of judicial review. See C. E. K. Kumado, "Judicial Review of Legislation in Ghana Since Independence," (1980) 12 *Review of Ghana Law* 67–103.

15. See PNDC Law 4 as amended by PNDC Law 90.

16. *Kwakye v. Attorney General* (1981) GLR 944.

17. See Proclamation which established the PNDC revolutionary government in 1981, and PNDC Law 42, passed as the quasi-basic law of the land, which provided in section 1(1) (b), the regime's conceptualization of human rights and social justice. For in-depth discussion of the PNDC approach to politics in Ghana generally, and particularly its perspective and practices regarding democracy and human rights, and the historical and political contex which informed it, see also Nana K. A. Busia, Jr., "Ghana (1982–1992): Une Si Longue Transition," in Momar Coumba Diop and Mamadu Diouf, *Les Figures du politique en Afrique: Des pouvoirs hérités aux pouvoirs élus* (Paris: Karthala, 1999).

18. Amnesty International Report, "Political Prisoners in Ghana and the Death Penalty," December 1991.

19. See Zaya Yeebo, *Ghana: The Struggle for Popular Power* (London: New Beacon, 1991).

20. On housing: PNDC Law 7 (Compulsory Letting of Unoccupied Rooms and Houses); PNDC Law 83 (State Houses [Allocation Policy and Implementation Commission]); PNDC Law 138 (Rent Control). On access to justice: PNDC Law 184 (Legal Aid Scheme). On inheritance rights: PNDC Law 111(Intestate Succession Law). On rights of children: AFRCD 66.

21. See "Evolving a True Democracy—Summary of National Commission on Democracy: Work Towards the Establishment of a New Democratic Order," presented by Justice Annan, Chairperson of the NCD, March 25, 1991, Accra, Ghana.

22. Section 34(1) stipulates that "no member of the PNDC and its appointees shall be held liable either jointly or severally for any act or omission during the administration of the PNDC." Section 34(2) makes it unlawful for any court or tribunal to entertain any action in any proceedings for past violations of human rights by the PNDC or any previous regimes. Section 34(3) further provided as follows: "For the avoidance of doubt, it is declared that no executive, legislative or judicial action taken or purported to have been taken by the Provisional National Defence Council or member of the Provisional National Defence Council . . . shall be questioned in any proceedings whatsoever and, accordingly, it shall not be lawful for any court or other tribunal to make any order or grant any remedy or relief in respect of any such act."

23. For a detailed and comprehensive discussion and analysis of the transition from PNDC authoritarianism to liberal democracy, see. Busia, "Ghana (1982–1992)."

24. See sections 58 and 59 of the Criminal Code of Ghana, 1960 (Act 29), as amended by Act 157 and as further amended by PNDC Law 102.

25. The article on personal liberty is one of the most elaborately expressed rights provided for in the constitution. This may be due to the fact that it is the right which has been most violated since independence by the military regimes especially but also in relation to the Preventive Detention Act of 1958.

26. *New Patriotic Party v. Attorney General* (CIBA case) (1996–97) SCGLR 729 at 788.

27. *New Patriotic Party v. Inspector General of Police* (1992–93) GBR 586 SC.

28. The Public Order Decree of 1972 (NRCD 68) obliges everyone to seek the permission of the police or any other authority to hold a rally, demonstration, procession, or any other traditional customary celebration.

29. Article 21(d) states: "(1) All persons shall have the right to . . . (d) freedom of assembly including freedom to take part in processions and demonstrations."

30. For example, *People's Popular Party v. Attorney General* (1971) 1 GLR 138.

31. *New Patriotic Party v. Attorney General* (December 31 case) (1994) 1 WASC 1.

32. Supreme Court suit 18/93, December 19, 1993, and March 8, 1994, unreported. Article 3(3) states that "any person who: (a) by himself or in concert with others by any violent or other unlawful means, suspends or overthrows or abrogates this Constitution or any part of it, or attempts to do any such act; or (b) aids and abets in any manner any person referred to in paragraph (a) of this clause; commits the offence of high treason and shall, upon conviction, be sentenced to suffer death." Article 3(4) states that it is the duty of all citizens of Ghana "at all times: (a) to defend this Constitution, and, in particular, to resist any person or group of persons seeking to commit any of the acts referred to in clause (3) of this Article; and (b) to do all in their power to restore this Constitution after it has been suspended, overthrown, or abrogated as referred to in clause (3) of this article." Article 3(7) states that the "Supreme Court shall, on application by or on behalf of a person who has suffered by any punishment or less to which clause (6) of this Article relates, award him adequate compensation, which shall be charged on the Consolidated Fund," for any suffering or loss incurred as a result of the punishment.

Article 35(1) states that: "Ghana shall be a democratic State dedicated to the realisation of freedom and justice." Article 41(b) requires that all persons: "uphold and defend this Constitution and the law."

33. *New Patriotic Party v. Attorney General* (December 31 case) (1994) 1 WASC 1.

34. Per Bamford-Addo, J.S.C., in *New Patriotic Party v. Attorney General* (CIBA case) (1996–97) SCGLR 729.

35. See *New Patriotic Party vs Attorney General* (CIBA case), (1996–97) SCGLR 729 at 788.

36. For a persuasive analysis of this issue, see C. E. K. Kumado, "Forgive Us Our Trespasses: An Examination of Indemnity Clause in the 1992 Constitution of Ghana" (1996) 19 *University of Ghana Law Journal* 83–101.

37. Article 299 states explicitly that: "the transitional provisions specified in the first schedule to this constitution shall have effect notwithstanding anything to the contrary in this constitution."

38. *Kwayke v. Attorney General* (1981) 9 GLR 644.

39. See Walter Suntinger, "Ghana," in *Human Rights in Developing Countries Yearbook 1994*, ed. Peter Baehr et al. (Boston: Kluwer Law and Taxation Nordic Human Rights Publications, 1994), pp. 209–10.

40. Daana Seidu, "Chieftaincy and Adjudication in Ghana—Some Problems" (1998) 3 GQLJ 9.

41. The Judicial Council and its composition are provided for in Article 153. Its members are the chief justice, who is the chair; the attorney general; a justice of the Supreme Court nominated by the court itself; a justice of the court of appeal nominated by the court itself; a justice of the High Court nominated by the court itself; two representatives of the Ghana Bar Association; two representatives of the regional tribunals; a representative of the lower courts or tribunals; the judge advocate general of the Ghana armed forces; the head legal directorate of the police; the editor of the *Ghana Law Reports*; a representative of the Judicial Services Staff Association nominated by the association; a chief nominated by the National House of Chiefs; and four persons who are not lawyers appointed by the president.

42. For persuasive and insightful analysis see Justice K. M. Premo, "The Role of the Judicial Enforcement of Economic and Social Rights in National Development: The Case of Ghana," paper presented at eleventh annual conference of the African Society of International and Comparative law, Harare, Zimbabwe, August 1999. Premo calls attention to a very significant distinction in the use of a concept of human rights enforcement in Ghana. He points out that there are forums which can and do handle claims which may not be couched as human rights claims, but, nevertheless, may, to all intents and purposes, result in the enforcement or application of human rights. Yet such forums may not have the constitutional competence to entertain any claim couched as constitutional human rights remedy as provided under the constitution. See Premo, "Role," 2.

43. Article 130 (1). See also minority opinion in *Edusei v. Attorney General and Anor* (1996–97) SCGLR 1 and *Mensima v. Attorney General* (1996–97) SCGLR 678.

44. Premo, "Beware of Article 33(1)," pp. 18–21.

45. See, for example, Kofi Kumado, "Courts as Protectors of Rights Under the 1992 Constitution of Ghana," paper presented at a seminar on Human Rights Issues in Ghana, organized and published by Konrad A. Stifling (Accra, 1997), and Premo, "Beware of Article 33(1)," Dominic Ayine, "Public Interest Litigation as an Aspect of Human Rights Enforcement" (1999) 3 GQLJ 14–17.

46. Such a competence can be derived from Articles 218(d)(iii), 229, 140(1) and (2).

47. Justice K. M. Premo, "Selected Topics on Judicial Enforcement of Human Rights in Ghana," paper presented at the eleventh annual conference of the African Society for International and Comparative Law, Harare, Zimbabwe, 1999.

48. For report of cases handled by the CHRAJ, see the CHRAJ Annual Report since 1995 and *Ghana Quarterly Law Journal,* published by the African Society of International and Comparative Law.

49. *PPP v. Inspector General of Police* (1971) 1 GLR 138.

50. CHRAJ Complaints Procedure Regulation 1, 1994 Constitutional Instrument No. 7.

51. Article 33(1) of the 1992 constitution; and *Mensima v. Attorney General* (1996–97) SCGLR 623.

52. Article 2(1) *Tuffuor v. Attorney General* (1980) GLR 637, *New Patriotic Party v. Attorney General* (December 31 case) (1994) 1 WASC 1, *New Patriotic Party v. Attorney General* (CIBA case) (1996–97) SCGLR 729.

53. *Concerned Parents and Teachers Association (CPTA) and Two Others v. Morning Star Preparatory School and Eight Others, the Minister for Education and the Attorney-General,* unreported case, suit no. Misc 339/98 High Court. In this case the plaintiffs were parents with wards in some schools in Ghana that were in the opinion of the CPTA charging exorbitant school fees which impeded the right to education. The CPTA is a registered incorporated body with the Registrar-General's department. An objective of the CPTA is to ensure conformity and adherence to relevant provisions of the constitution (particularly Articles 25 and 38) and rights of the child in general, other regulations established by the Ghana Education Service (GES) and other UN documents relating to rights of the child. See also Justice K. M. Premo, "Litigating Educational Rights in Ghana," Proceedings of the Tenth Annual Conference of the African Society for International and Comparative Law (1998), p. 89.

54. "Letterhead NGOs" is a pejorative term that refers to nonoperative NGOs who nonetheless seek funds from donors for individual gains.

55. See CHRAJ, *First Annual Report (1993–94)* (Accra: Safeway Printing, 1995).

56. Suntinger, "Ghana."

57. See Article 18(3) of the African Charter on Human and Peoples' Rights.

58. See Nana K. A. Busia, Jr., "Slaves of a Culture: The Case of Domestic Servants in Ghana," Occasional Paper, Centre for Development and the Environment, University of Oslo, 1991. See also Sheila Minkah-Premo, "Comparative Analysis of the Right of Women Under the African Charter and the 1992 Ghanaian Constitution's Bill of Rights," paper presented at the Eleventh Annual Conference of the African Society for International and Comparative Law (1999?).

59. See generally Johanna O. Svaniker, *Women's Rights and the Law in Ghana* (Accra: Friedrich Ebert Foundation, 1997).

60. *The Status of Women in Ghana (1985–1994): Executive Summary of National Report for the Fourth World Conference on Women,* prepared by National Council on Women and Development, Accra, Ghana.

61. Interview with Yao Graham, executive director, Integrated Social Development Centre/Third World Network, Ghana, October 1996.

62. From interviews with Kofi Kumado and Nana Akuffo-Addo in October 1996.

63. See Gyimah E. Boadi, "Civil Society Associations in PNDC State and Democratization in the 1990s," paper presented at the workshop "Civil Society in Africa" at the Harry Truman Research Institute for the Advancement of Peace, Hebrew University of Jerusalem, Israel, 1992.ß

Chapter 4
Guinea
Building the Rule of Law for Social Development

Ibrahima Kane

Guinea is a small West African country (245,875 square kilometers) in the shape of an arc, hemmed in by the Atlantic Ocean, Guinea-Bissau, Senegal, Mali, Côte d'Ivoire, Sierra Leone, and Liberia. The country gained independence from France in 1958 and its first president was Ahmed Sékou Touré. Relatively sparsely populated, the country has a very young population with more women than men, and the majority of the population lives in rural areas.[1] The main religion is Islam, followed by Christianity and traditional religions.[2]

Guinea is a geological plum.[3] With 18 billion metric tons of high-grade bauxite, it holds two-thirds of the world's known reserves. The deposits are not only easy to mine but are also profitable. Its iron ore is high grade and reserves are estimated at 15 billion metric tons; its diamond reserves are reckoned to be 300 million carats of which two-thirds are gem quality; gold reserves in the northeast of the country have deposits whose grade varies between 300 and 600 grams per gravel ton. Uranium and oil deposits have also been discovered. Guinea also has the largest reserves of hydroelectric resources in West Africa (6,600 megawatts). A project to build a dam on the Konkouré, which the French developed before independence, was abandoned after they left. On the agricultural front, the country has extraordinary potential.[4] Guinea's four geographic-ecological regions—coastal Guinea, the valleys of Middle Guinea, highland Guinea, and forest Guinea—are complementary and could easily provide food self-sufficiency while also allowing produce to be exported. Guinea also has significant sea and river resources thanks to high fish populations off its coasts and in its many rivers.

Guinea was governed from 1958 to 1984 under a "revolutionary" political system, led by a single party which regulated economic, political, and social life, and under whose leadership massive human rights violations were perpetrated. From 1984 onward, led first by the military and then by a civilian regime, a liberal political regime has sought to build a state governed by the rule of law, one in which human rights and individual freedoms are respected. In 1990, a new constitution was introduced which established an independent judiciary and allowed multiparty presidential, legislative, and local elections to be held. But after several years of democratic pluralism, it must be recognized that this system has created more problems than it has solved: ethnic and regional rivalries, nepotism, and corruption are the most obvious evils in Guinea and are endangering the country's very existence.

Despite Guinea's great potential, the replacement of the centrally planned collectivist management of the "socialist" period by a liberal economic system has not been enough to lay the foundation for real economic and social development. At the dawn of the third millennium, Guinea is ranked 162 out of 178 in the annual rankings of the United Nations Development Program (UNDP)[5] and 167 out of 190 in the rankings of the World Health Organization.[6]

How has a country so well endowed by nature produced such disastrous results, both in human rights and in economic and social development? Is there a link between the massive human rights violations which the country has experienced and the lack of economic and social development? To answer these questions, we will examine in turn the regulatory and institutional framework for the protection of human rights in Guinea, the economic, social and political context in which the country has developed since its independence and the role played by different actors, particularly civil society.

Legal and Constitutional Framework for the Protection of Human Rights in Guinea

Of all the Francophone countries of West Africa, Guinea has been without a doubt the least influenced by the French constitutional system, in terms of both administration and human rights protection. This is due to its political history under colonialism, the unusual conditions under which it gained independence, and the personality, philosophy, and politics of its first president, Ahmed Sékou Touré. On September 28, 1958, the population of Guinea, under the leadership of the main political party of the colony, the Democratic Party of Guinea (PDG), voted overwhelmingly for the country's independence.[7] Its citizens had resolved to take their fate into their own hands because, quite simply, they preferred "to be poor and free rather than rich and slaves."[8]

Paris's reaction to this "insult" was immediate: the severing of all links with the new republic, immediate repatriation of all archives, and all French officials in the country, suspension of all investments, cessation of financial aid, and so on.[9] Undaunted by France's negative attitude and wishing to extract the maximum benefit from this situation, the new authorities were quick to set up the institutions of an independent republic: a fifteen-member constitutional commission was immediately formed to write a constitution whose main lines had already been sketched out by the Political Bureau of the PDG. After ten days in seclusion, this committee produced a draft constitution which was presented to the former colonial assembly which had been transformed into a national constitutional assembly. The constitution was adopted unanimously on 10 November 1958 after only two hours' debate.[10]

The political and social context was characterized on the international front by the cold war, and on the national front, by ethnic and regional divisions and, as a backdrop, by a population with a very low level of education. Guinea's new authorities hardened their position and chose confrontation with the former colonial power. The new president of independent Guinea, Sékou Touré, explained: "since the legal presence of the colonial regime has been utterly abolished in Guinea, it is time to take positive action to exercise our option to *destroy*, in the behaviour of every man, in the attitude of every man, woman and child, everything which still smacks of the presence of the colonial regime to which we have been subjected for half a century."[11]

During the entire period of the First Republic (1958–84), President Sékou Touré and his party would methodically make use of the country's constitution as "a law at the service of the Guinean revolution, . . . an evolutionary tool, . . . a simple and effective tool" and, at the cost of serious and massive human rights violations, use it to establish what one author has called "a constitutional dictatorship,"[12] in which the republican state gradually faded away in favor of the single party and its head, now decked out in the titles of "President of the Republic, Secretary General of the Party-State, supreme leader of the Revolution" (Article 44 of the first Republic Constitution). This period was one of the blackest in the political history of Guinea, and of the region, with numerous coup attempts, either real or invented, which led to arrests and arbitrary detentions, "people's" trials organized against the "enemies of the Guinean Revolution," forced millions of Guineans into exile in neighboring countries (mainly Senegal and Côte d'Ivoire) and Europe.

In 1982, the Guinean authorities, under pressure from the international community and a significant sector of the population, notably women, liberalized the regime somewhat, adopting a new constitution in which human rights were better protected. In April 1984, President Sékou Touré died suddenly. Faced with the politicians' inability to decide on a successor but also wanting to put an end to "a bloody and pitiless dictatorship that crushed the shining hopes" of the Guinean people,[13] the army took power and set up a Military Committee for National Recovery (CMRN). This committee organized a transition period of six years during which all the "wicked" laws were repealed and replaced by laws which took greater account of civil liberties. For the first time in Guinea, a new Basic Law was debated and passed by referendum. Adopted on 23 December 1990 in the aftermath of the fall of the Berlin Wall and at a time when protest movements were emerging all over Africa to demand accountable government, plural democracy, and respect for rule of law and human rights, Guinea's Basic Law integrated certain principles and rules of the liberal democratic model with the rule of law, without really breaking with the country's constitutional heritage.

In December 1993, presidential elections were held, followed two years later by legislative and local elections. The Second Republic was thus well on its way and, since then, the new authorities have undertaken the difficult task of modernizing Guinean society. We will now examine one by one the guarantees provided for citizens in terms of basic rights and freedoms and the effects which the imbalance of the constitutional powers in favor of the executive has had on the effectiveness of their protection.

Guarantees of Citizens' Rights and Freedoms

We shall go through each of Guinea's three constitutions in order to identify those rights and freedoms which are recognized as citizens' entitlement and to examine the mechanisms of their protection. Emphasis will be placed on the current constitution.

Recognition of Basic Rights and Freedoms

Under the First Republic, the ideological and political orientation of the PDG resulted in a political system founded on the supremacy of the party over the constitutional institutions, closely resembling the Soviet model of power. Like the constitutions of the Eastern European countries, the constitutions of 1958 and 1982 offered few rights to individual citizens, while imposing duties which were often difficult to respect. The 1958 constitution gives the least detail on civil and political rights and freedoms. This is certainly partly due to the speed with which it was written,[14] but also to the desire of the PDG's leaders to control tightly Guineans' political and social space.[15] Thus, they only allowed citizens the following rights: the right to participate in the management of public affairs (Article 39), freedoms of expression and association, freedom to hold demonstrations (Article 40), the right to the sanctity of the home and to private communication (Article 43), freedom of conscience, the right to legal defense (Article 36), and protection against arbitrary detention (Article 42), racial discrimination, and racist and regionalist propaganda (Article 45). And as a country which extolled solidarity between peoples, the right to asylum was accorded to all those persecuted "for their struggle to defend a just cause or for their scientific and cultural activities" (Article 46). The rights protecting life and physical integrity are conspicuous by their absence from the text, which is also silent on the right to a fair trial and to free movement within Guinea.

The 1982 constitution introduced some significant changes in the formulation of civil and political rights by replacing the state with the single party, the PDG, in the management of public affairs. The right of association was struck out because the PDG was "the meeting place and debating hall for all currents of national life and the supreme means of the people to exercise power and the principal guiding force of its actions" (preamble, 1982 constitution). Moreover, the constitution left it to subsequent legislation to give substance to nearly all the recognized civil and political rights.[16] Only freedom of conscience (Article 8) and the ban on arbitrary arrests (Article 9) escaped the heavy hand of the legislator. The text allows for the protection of the integrity of the person (Article 23[1]) and the right to develop freely (Article 23[2]) although this must occur while respecting the "democratic and social order" determined by the PDG. It also permits each citizen to institute legal proceedings with the Party-State authorities against any authority or person who has caused him prejudice (Article 25). The socialist tone of the political regime explains the importance given to economic, social, and cultural rights in the constitutions of the First Republic, even if in terms of content it is the constitution of 1982 which goes furthest in their formulation.

Whereas the 1958 constitution only contained one article which made direct mention of economic and social rights (the rights to work, to rest, to social assistance, to training [Article 44(1)], to join a trade union, and to strike (Articles 44(2)]),[17] the 1982 constitution, the aim of which, it must be remembered, was to "construct a strong, prosperous and just nation, a socialist society, and to pursue indefinitely the goal of greater and greater progress in all areas" (preamble), widened the scope to education, which became mandatory and free (Article 24), to health and social security (Article 20[1]), to assistance for the elderly, handicapped and disabled (Article 20[2]), to the relationship between men and women in economic, social, and cultural life (Article 21[2]), to the family (Articles 21[2–4] and 22), and to the natural resources of the country which became the property of the people (Article 26). That constitution even set moral integrity criteria for those wishing to hold official position (Article 29) and prohibited corruption and the misappropriation of public funds (Article 30).

As for the duties, these dealt essentially with the economic, social, and cultural aspects of the life of a society and were presented as duties of the citizen and of the state. But they were so vaguely formulated that putting them into practice became highly problematic. The definition of these duties in the 1958 constitution was very simple: in return for the rights granted to them, citizens had to respect the constitution and the laws of the land, pay their taxes and fulfill their social obligations (Article 47), and if the nation was imperiled, defend it (Article 48). But within the context of the Party-State the citizen's task became more complicated. To the "duties" of the first constitution were added the following: to carry out their civic duties (Article 15), to show solidarity with all other citizens (Article 17), to work according to their abilities (Article 18) but with the strictest respect for discipline and working hours (Article 19), to care for collective property, to fight against the misuse and squandering of public property, and to be "constantly striving to safeguard and develop the best interests of the people" (Article 27). Even more difficult to abide by, because of their vaguely worded nature but also because of the frequent denunciations of ongoing "coup plots" in the revolutionary Republic of Guinea, were the requirements to not betray the people or the country (Articles 16[2])[18] and to maintain "revolutionary vigilance toward all elements hostile" to the regime (Article 31). Opponents and critics of the regime paid the price for the "weakness" of these constitutional norms.

The current constitution, drawing on painful lessons learned from the single party regime, proclaims the adherence of Guineans "to the ideals and principles, rights and duties" established in the United Nations Charter, the Universal Declaration of Human Rights, the Charter of the Organization of African Unity (OAU), and the African Charter on Human and Peoples' Rights. At the same time it fundamentally rejects "any regime founded on dictatorship, injustice, corruption, nepotism and regionalism" and commits to "creating, in a united country, a state founded on the rule of law and on respect for democratically established law" (preamble, 1990 constitution). With regard to civil and political rights, the 1990 constitution begins by setting down two essential principles, the sacrosanct nature of the person and the inviolability, inalienability, and irreversibility of the rights and freedoms described in the constitution which "are the foundation of all societies and guarantee peace and justice the world over" (Article 5).

The liberal nature of this constitution is not open to doubt: to the rights recognized in the previous constitutions, it adds others deemed essential in the fight against repressive government, such as the right to free personal development (Article 6[1]), the right to life and to physical integrity (Article 6[2]), the right to profess one's faith and political and philosophical opinions, to express, demonstrate and spread ideas and opinions via the spoken and printed word and images (Article 7), the right to a fair trial

(Article 9), the freedom to live anywhere in Guinea and to travel freely within the country, as well as to enter and leave it freely (Article 10[3]), the protection of privacy (Article 12[2]), the right to property (Article 13), and the right to resist oppression (Article 19[4]). The constitution reestablishes the right of association (Article 10[2]), but imposes two conditions on political parties before they can be recognized: they must have representation throughout the country and they must not be identified with a particular race, ethnic group, religion, or territory. According to certain authors, the fear of a resurgence of the tribalism, regionalism, and ethnic divisions, which poisoned political and social life during the First Republic and during part of the military transition, is the reason for the introduction of these legal constraints.[19] In applying the provisions of the new constitution, several laws of relevance to the protection of civil and political rights were passed covering political parties, freedom of the press and of the national communications council, the state of emergency, and martial law.

In the field of economic, social, and cultural rights, the 1990 constitution maintained most of the rights proclaimed by the constitutions of the First Republic, while sometimes reinforcing them with new ones: the right to health was supplemented by the right to physical well-being (Article 15), workers, the elderly, and the handicapped were given the right to state assistance and protection (Articles 17[2]) and 18[5]), the rights to the country's resources were made not just irreversible but also had to equally benefit all Guineans (Article 19[2]), and public officials were made solely responsible for their own actions and must make sure that these were performed for the good of all (Article 23). Guineans were also given a right to the preservation of their heritage, culture, and environment (Article 19[3]), and young people were given the right to be protected against exploitation and moral neglect (Article 17[1]).

In the chapter on duties, the 1990 constitution elaborated on the substance of some of these duties. Henceforth, the Guinean citizen was required to abide by the constitution, laws, and rulings (Article 20[1]), to be loyal to the nation, to promote tolerance and the values of democracy (Article 20[2]), to respect the dignity and opinions of others (Article 20[3]), to pay taxes "according to his means" and to fulfill his social duties (Article 20[4]). Parents had to provide education for their children and protect their physical and moral health while children, in return, had to provide care and support for their parents (Article 16[2]). Better still, they placed the burden of some of these duties on the state. These relate to promoting the population's well-being and health (Articles 15 and 21[1]), strengthening national unity (Article 21[6]), providing public institutions and services (Article 21[4]), guaranteeing the safety of the population and of property and keeping the peace (Article 21[3]), guaranteeing equal access for all citizens to the civil service (Article 21[5]), promoting national cultures and languages (Article 1[2]), protecting marriage and the family (Article 16[1]), creating an environment enabling citizens to exercise their right to work (Article 18[1]), and guaranteeing the diversity of opinions and information sources (Article 21[2]). Nowhere to be found in this constitution or its implementing laws are the substance and terms of the penalties to be applied if these duties are not performed. It is as though these duties were formulated simply to provide the public authorities with the right to freely dispose of the rights of others.

It should be noted that the constitutional recognition of many rights did not necessarily imply the existence of a legal or political regime conducive to their being respected. For instance, the right to life did not prevent the inclusion of the death penalty in Article 14 of the new Criminal Code.[20] Similarly, the formal ban in the constitution on torture and cruel, inhuman or degrading treatment (Article 6[2]) and Guinea's ratification of the Convention Against Torture on 10 October 1989 was not followed (in the wake of the penal reform of December 1998) by the harmonization of the clauses of this treaty with the Criminal Code and the Criminal Procedure Code, especially the definition of torture,[21] nor by the introduction of the principle that it is within the jurisdiction of all Guinean courts to judge all perpetrators of acts of torture and the responsibility of the state prosecutor "to undertake an immediate and impartial enquiry each time there are reasonable grounds to believe that an act of torture has taken place on any part of the territory under his jurisdiction."[22] However, the Criminal Code has an entire chapter dealing with crimes and offenses against the constitution (Articles 123–139) which covers the gamut from breaches of civil rights to acts of racism, ethnocentrism, and regionalism, and includes violations of civil liberties, collusion between public officials, and the encroachment on administrative and judicial authorities.

Moreover, the constitution contains a significant innovation restricting the powers of the legislature, which in future can only pass laws in the area of rights and freedoms which are "indispensable to keep the peace and maintain democracy" (Article 22[2]). If the notion of keeping the peace is generally seen as a catch-all which can be used to justify abuses, the notion of democracy, on the other hand, can contribute a great deal, as can be seen by the interpretations which certain African court judgments have made of the notion of an open and democratic society in order to give a more protective slant to certain human rights.[23]

The Protection of Basic Rights and Freedoms

Citizens are guaranteed the protection of their basic rights and freedoms through the constitutional right to legal remedy should their rights be violated either by the state and its agents or by private individuals. In

Guinea, this protection is based essentially on the legal bodies which monitor state activity and which rely on a constitutional principle, the independence of the judiciary. Setting these mechanisms in place has been, for various political reasons, an arduous process.[24]

Under the First Republic, the legal authorities, "the guardian of individual freedom", did not really have the means at their disposal to ensure that citizens' rights were respected, as was guaranteed by the constitution (Article 37), for the simple reason that the country did not possess courts whose jurisdiction covered administrative and constitutional disputes. Only a High Court of Appeal had been established to replace the French Court of Appeal to review the verdicts of the lower Guinean courts as a last resort and only in criminal, commercial, and civil cases.[25] According to the 1982 constitution, all disputes, whether legal or not, had to be submitted to the authorities of the Party-State which were responsible for supervising the activities of the organs of the state (Article 32). It was only with the advent of the military regime that a court could be established to hear appeals against verdicts handed down in any court in the land.[26]

The system improved in 1990 with the creation of a genuine Supreme Court with real powers to supervise the activities of the administration and thus respect for human rights by all public authorities. This court, whose status is set by a State Authority Act, can be used to enforce basic rights and freedoms in certain situations. For example, when the president of the republic, or one-tenth of the members of Parliament, ask for a review of constitutionality within eight days following the passing of a law by the National Assembly (Article 64). Under the constitution, "no provision of a law which is found not to comply with the Basic Law can be enacted or enforced" (Article 64[5]). A State Authority Act, such as the one on the status of magistrates, is still not formally enacted into law until declared by the court to be in compliance with the constitution (Article 67). When the president or a member of Parliament applies to the court to declare that a treaty contains unconstitutional clauses, the treaty can only be ratified or approved if the constitution is amended (Article 78[1]). And the law authorizing ratification or approval cannot come into effect or be enacted until the court has ruled that it is in compliance (Article 78[2]).[27] When the president or the National Assembly submits a bill to a referendum, they must submit the text to the court so that it can judge its constitutionality. A text judged unconstitutional cannot be submitted to a referendum (Article 45).

The constitution settled definitively the position of treaties, especially human rights treaties, in the juridical order. In effect, the hierarchy of norms is as follows: the highest law is the constitution (Articles 45 and 91). Following that are international treaties, once approved and ratified (Article 79), organic laws (Article 67), ordinary laws (Article 59), and regulations (Article 60). As a result, all the human rights treaties approved or ratified by Guinea, with the notable exception of the African Charter on Human and Peoples' Rights (which forms an integral part of the constitution), have supralegislative status and can be directly invoked before Guinean jurisdictions. The application of any law which is contrary to them can be set aside by a judge at the request of a citizen. It is notable that the Guinean authorities have not, to this day, entered any reservation to any of the various treaties to which Guinea is a party. However, Guinea has made declarations in relation to certain articles in the International Covenant on Civil and Political Rights (Article 48[1]), and the International Covenant on Economic, Social and Cultural Rights (Article 1[3], Article 14, and Article 26[1]).

Efforts have also been made by the authorities in recent years to comply with some of their convention obligations such as the presentation of periodic reports before the supervisory mechanisms of certain treaties. Thus Guinea presented reports before the Committee on the Rights of the Child (1997), the Committee for the Elimination of all Forms of Discrimination Against Women (1998), and the African Commission on Human and Peoples' Rights (1998). However, the process of harmonizing national laws with the human rights treaties is not yet under way in the country.

Guineans thus have at their disposal, at least formally, a whole range of rules guaranteeing their rights and freedoms. But implementation of these rights and freedoms does not only depend on a judge's ruling on an issue. It is also a consequence of the relationship between the different institutions which share state power, principally the president of the republic and the National Assembly. And in this regard, in Guinea, as in most African states, the lion's share of this power has always resided with the president of the republic who has often used it to abuse human rights, particularly during the reign of the Party-State.

How the Power Imbalance Favors the Executive Branch

Guinea, both now and in the past, provides an interesting example of the way the executive branch uses the constitutional framework to strengthen its dominance over the other state bodies. To prove this, we will examine the powers of the president of the republic and the rules which govern the relationship between the executive and legislative branches in their dealings with a number of interesting human rights issues.

The Presidential "Dictatorship"

This can be best appreciated at the level of normal presidential prerogatives, emergency powers, and those powers the president shares with his deputies. One can observe a continuity in the way in which the different constitutions have organized the absolute control maintained by the president over all constitutional institutions. The concentration of powers in the hands of the head of the executive, already present under the First Republic and expanded still further under the 1982 constitution, continued under the Second Republic, although it would be true to say in a less excessive manner. No less than twenty-two articles of the 1990 constitution are on the powers of the head of the executive branch. Regarding his emergency powers, the president can decree a state of emergency or martial law after consulting the Speaker of the National Assembly and the president of the Supreme Court (Article 74). In such cases, he may take "all necessary measures to defend territorial integrity and to restore or keep the peace" (Articles 74[2]). However, if he wants to extend the edict, he must get the National Assembly's permission (Articles 74[3]), but, as in the First Republic, the implementation of emergency powers "ends up concentrating all legislative and statutory powers in the hands of the president from the moment he decrees (these measures)."[28] And if one adds to all these prerogatives the fact that the president of the republic can, after receiving parliamentary authorization and via edict, temporarily intervene in areas normally within the sphere of the law (Article 66) and that he can, in the event of a "persistent failure to agree" and at his own risk,[29] dissolve the National Assembly, it can be concluded that the president is really the "monarch" of the republic.

Parliament Under Supervision

In a political system in which real power is in the hands of the head of the executive branch, Parliament can only play a secondary role even if, at times, the powers conferred upon it by the constitution can give the illusory impression that it constitutes a genuine counterweight. The first constitution of the First Republic illustrates this perfectly. Contrary to the other Francophone states which adopted the French method of limiting the scope of the law, Article 9 of the 1958 constitution stipulates that "the scope of the law is limitless." Members of Parliament could therefore, theoretically, limit the excessive powers of the president of the republic and above all enforce the rule of law through the powers devolved upon them, in particular in the area of human rights.

However, the establishment of the single party and the constitutional reform that took place in 1963 and set up a permanent committee which sat during parliamentary recesses dealt a harsh blow to Parliament's independence. The combination of the president's constitutional powers and the PDG's social and political hegemony resulted in Parliament's role being reduced to rubber-stamping the president's wishes. This concept was ratified by the second constitution of the First Republic. Indeed, from 1982 onward, laws were no longer initiated by members of Parliament but by the National Congress, the National Revolutionary Council, the Central Committee and the PDG's politburo (Article 64). Bills were then examined by the National People's Assembly, which was only a branch of Parliament.[30] The date and the agenda of sessions were also set by the party politburo.

Under the 1982 constitution, the scope of the law was carefully delineated and gave the PDG, in practice, all legal means to define human rights according to its whims: these means consisted of defining a development plan, civil rights and the basic guarantees given to citizens in the exercise of public freedoms, nationality, civil status and capacity, matrimonial property systems, inheritance and gift laws, the definition of indictable offenses, the criminal procedure, amnesty, labor and civil law, property systems, real rights, civic duties, and the organization and administration of public authorities (Article 66).

It should be pointed out that the guarantees of immunity for members of Parliament in the performance of their duties were struck from this constitution, which made their legal position even more vulnerable. While the Second Republic "restored" the legal guarantees traditionally enjoyed by members of Parliament (Article 52), it still kept Parliament in a state of "vassalage." In broad terms, the National Assembly could only pass laws whose scope was restricted (Article 59). What was new was that its duties in terms of human rights were clearly defined: The assembly sets the rules governing the guarantees of basic freedoms and rights, the conditions in which they can be exercised, and the restrictions which can be placed on them, civil rights, nationality, and so on. The assembly also defines the basic principles governing the general organization of national defense and the keeping of the peace, education, the property system, real rights, civic and commercial duties, the right to work, to belong to a trade union, to social protection, to cultural development and to protect the country's heritage and environment. In addition, the assembly passes budget and planning acts containing the multiannual guidelines for state development and program acts which set out, sector by sector, the targets of the state's economic and social activities.

One final aspect of the weakness of Parliament concerns the overall intellectual level of the members of Parliament and their understanding of the country's problems. In general, they owe their position more to how militant they are and how successful they have been at mobilizing the electorate than to their mastery of the issues debated in Parliament. This situation gives a certain advantage to the executive branch, which can thus control the entire process of lawmaking.

The Institutional Framework for the
Protection of Human Rights

In this section we will concentrate on the legal institutions which generally work together to administer justice and protect human rights in modern legal systems, that is, the courts, the magistrates, and the legal officials, which include lawyers and state solicitors. These institutions were introduced to Guinea by the French colonial system which established two systems of justice in the country: one for the French and one for the indigenous population. The latter dealt with Africans and applied Muslim customary law, while the former dealt with Europeans (or assimilated non-Europeans) and applied French law.

Customary or local law courts were created in 1903 in French West Africa to rule on disputes among the indigenous population.[31] They grouped together a number of courts (reconciliation courts, courts of first degree, customary courts, courts of second degree, local law high courts, Muslim courts, and a chamber that could overturn or confirm decisions) whose role was essentially, in cases involving customary disputes, personal status, the family, divorce, inheritance, and lineage, to reconcile the parties, that is, to allocate blame rather than to punish crimes. In other words, it was a system in which "the parties seek to expatiate on their wrongs in a public forum rather than to obtain legal recognition of their rights."[32] With the exception of the customary courts and the Muslim courts, which were presided over respectively by local worthies and by cadis, the other courts were all run by colonial officials assisted by indigenous nonpresiding judges.

As for the "French" courts, they were to judge French citizens or nonnatives according to the rules governing the courts in France. They were ordinary courts, made up of two regional courts in Conakry and Kankan and a dozen district courts spread out among the cities of the interior. Appeals were heard at the Court of Appeal in Dakar, the headquarters of the federal colonial institutions of West Africa and final appeals at the French Court of Cassation in Paris, while administrative proceedings were judged by the Combined Court in Dakar with the right to appeal to the State Council in France. This legal system was run by both French and African staff (magistrates, registrars, lawyers, and so on).

Immediately following independence, above all to compensate for the departure of huge numbers of French civil servants who formed the backbone of legal officialdom, and for the transfer of all the colonial archives, the Guinean authorities began to consolidate the legal system. On the one hand, they officially abolished customary law by deciding that throughout the territory of the new republic, "the same law will apply to the same disputes regardless of tradition, religion or region."[33] On the other hand, they merged the criminal and administrative courts. Gradually a new legal system took shape: a court of appeal made up of three sections (civil, correctional, and commercial) was established in October 1958 and a final court of appeal was set up at the beginning of 1959 to oversee it.[34] A High Court of Justice was also created to judge offenses against internal and external national security. Its composition was mainly political; it is presided over by the president of the National Assembly assisted by three ministers (justice, interior, and security and defense).[35]

A district court with wide powers was set up in each administrative region, apparently "to bring justice closer to the people"; the Kindia, Labé, and Nzérékoré district courts would later form a regional court.[36] Special courts were also set up: a labor court, an administrative court, a special court to deal with economic fraud, a military court, and people's courts at the level of PDG branches whose aim was to solve minor disputes at the local level.[37] These courts applied the new Guinean code of law and all French laws which had not been declared contrary to the peace and the independence of the nation.[38]

To get the legal system working, aid was requested from supporters in the international community and the rest of Africa and graduates were recruited from the University of Guinea.[39] Only the people's courts were presided over by nonprofessional magistrates. At the same time, restrictions were imposed on the legal professions: initially, only Guinean nationals[40] were permitted to be lawyers, notaries, and bailiffs. Private practice of these professions was later abolished and they became civil service jobs, performed by agents of the Guinean state.[41]

As the single party got stronger and political, economic, and social problems multiplied, courts which seemed to be aimed at the "marginalization" of the ordinary courts proliferated.[42] One by one, the following were set up: a special court to deal with forest fires, brush fires, and illegal medical practices, a special court to deal with traffic accidents, a special court for cases involving the theft of cattle, telephone and telegraph wires, possession and use of drugs, and a special court for fraud and economic offenses.[43] In addition, the High Court of Justice was transformed into a revolutionary court and the National Assembly into a supreme revolutionary court "by a public decision of the President of the Republic."[44] This process was completed in 1973 with a major legal reform which officially transformed the peoples' courts into ordinary courts.[45] From this date on, the courts echoed the structure of the party and became its legal arm on all civil, commercial, and criminal matters.

At the village level, there were people's village courts headed by a president, the mayor of the local revolutionary authority (prl), assisted by two people's judges elected by the party and by an official in the role of registrar. At the district level, there was a people's district court, the head of which was the district commander assisted by two people's judges elected by the party for two years and an officer of the republican guard (police). At the regional level, a people's regional court was presided over by a magistrate or by a professional registrar with two people's judges and a registrar. At the level of each province, a criminal court and a court of appeal were set up, each presided over by a judge, two advisory magistrates, and four people's judges chosen from a list of political and administrative staff drawn up by the authorities. Special courts were also set up: a children's court, a property court, a mining court, and an economic and financial court.[46] At the pinnacle of this pyramid was the Court of Cassation, whose structure and role remained unchanged.

The establishment of this collegiate legal system was not unproblematic. Not only did nearly all the people's judges have no professional qualifications, but even those who were supposed to be professional magistrates had not received adequate legal training.[47] In reality, and in the absence of a training college, the latter had one year of practical training after graduation, at the end of which they were officially appointed to the courts. Admittedly, work experience, seminars, and study days were organized for them within the country, but the lack of contact with the outside world did not allow them to fill the many gaps left by their university education and to acquire new legal knowledge. And in addition these judges were not protected from the wrath of the party or the administrative authorities by any special status.

On the other hand, the "people's lawyers" were given professional status by a 1980 edict, which organized them into colleges and produced a list of disciplinary regulations.[48] A national college for the whole country and colleges at the level of each of the courts of appeal were run respectively by the republic's public prosecutor and by the public prosecutors of the courts of appeal. In any case the only qualification required of these "people's lawyers" was that they be good party militants.[49]

Given that the party leaders now had the legal power to control the workings of the legal system, the speedy trials organized by the people's courts and their staff, most often at the direct request of the Party-State authorities, against the real or presumed enemies of the Guinean regime, who obviously would not enjoy even the most basic of fair trials, contributed to the discrediting of the PDG's regime which used these numerous "coup plots" to distract the population's attention from their own failings. In his study on Guinea, Maurice Lovens has described the functioning of this legal system with its "investigations behind closed doors and absolute judgments" and the key role played by the president.[50] Sékou Touré explained to his compatriots that when they saw action being taken against someone, they should not question it.

Know only that this man or this woman has betrayed the trust of the people, betrayed Guinea. . . . *With the full powers given to the government,* we have the means to reduce the number of counterrevolutionaries in this country. However severe the means, we will use them without hesitation, without regret, whenever the higher interest of the Nation requires it. . . . If the people's best interests demanded the deaths of a thousand or two thousand people, we would do it without hesitation in order to allow the masses to live happily in honor and dignity.[51]

There were indeed thousands of victims of this system and without the "masses" living "happily in honor and dignity." Sékou Touré's death in April 1984 put an end to this system, which was abhorred by the Guinean people. When they took power, the military made legal reform a priority. The first national conference and the regional conferences which grouped together all those working in the legal system organized by the military during June 1984, three months after taking power, made recommendations to reform the Guinean legal system. The recommendations included the abolition of the post of people's judge, the abolition of the special courts (the economic and financial court, the property court, the mining court, and the supreme revolutionary court), the resumption of the children's courts, the setting up of a Higher Magistrate's Court; and the setting up of a Center for Legal Studies for the practical training of staff.

Among the first measures taken by the military as a result of these recommendations were the abolition of the people's courts and their replacement by traditional style courts (district courts in the largest subprefectures, regional courts in the thirty-three prefecture capitals, and three in the capital, a Court of Appeal in each provincial capital, and a Supreme Court made up of four chambers—legal, administrative, economic and financial, and constitutional).[52] The military also set up special courts: a military court, a labor court, a children's court, and a High Court of Justice.

But due to the lack of human and financial resources to get such a substantial system working,[53] the authorities had to reconsider their ambition to reform Guinean justice: the High Court of Justice was transformed into National Security Court, the ordinary courts to two Courts of Appeal (Conakry and Kankan), six regional courts, thirty district courts, and the Supreme Court was replaced by a National Chamber of Annulment whose role was to examine appeals against the rulings of the courts.[54]

At the same time efforts were made to provide this legal system with competent staff. From 1986 onward, grants were regularly offered to magistrates for initial or ongoing training in France, Senegal, and Côte d'Ivoire. Legal officials' posts were no longer closed to the general public, and their previous occupants were rehabilitated and allowed to return to their jobs. Lawyers, for example, were given a new status,[55] which allowed them to fully perform their role in the administration of justice. After the 1990 Constitution was passed, new rules for the organization and workings of the judiciary were introduced. Some were contained in the constitution itself and others in a series of laws decreed by the transitional authorities.[56] A new law, which corrected some of the weaknesses of the Edict of July 5, 1986, concerning the legal system, was also passed.[57] The number of regional courts was revised upward (nine instead of six) while the number of district courts was reduced to twenty-five, commercial courts were merged with the civil courts (courts of appeal and regional courts), and new criminal courts were set up (assize court, criminal court, police court). Staffing problems (lack of magistrates), practical problems (lack of suitable premises), and financial problems (the tight budget allocated to the Justice Department) resulted in a new law being passed three years later, which simplified the legal system, clarified the roles and responsibilities of the different actors, and tried, once again, to bring justice closer to the people.[58]

With French aid, the Center for Judicial Training and Documentation (CFDJ) was set up in Conakry. As well as being responsible for the initial training of magistrates, the CFDJ aimed to provide ongoing training for registrars and criminal investigation department officers. A cooperation agreement with the Center for Judicial Training and Documentation in Senegal meant that Guinean judges and registrars could be sent to Senegalese courts for supplementary and ongoing training.

Organization and Workings of the Judicial System in Guinea

According to Article 80 of the constitution, the judicial system is entirely independent of the other powers which together exercise sovereignty in Guinea. As in all countries claiming to exercise the rule of law, judicial power rests upon a number of principles whose goal is the fair administration of justice and, thus, a scrupulous respect for human rights in the country. These principles, essentially, are founded in the constitutional provisions relating to the independence and impartiality of the judiciary[59] and reiterated in the laws which govern the organization and functioning of the main courts responsible for dispensing justice in the country, that is, the ordinary courts, the special courts, and the Supreme Court.[60] They consist, in sum, of all the principles which combine to realize the right to fair trial. They set down the essential rules relating to access to justice, the organization of the courts, and the proper conduct of proceedings which can be found in the constitution, the international human rights treaties to which Guinea is party,[61] and under international customary law. With this background, we will distinguish here between the rules governing the organization and functioning of the ordinary courts and those of the courts of exception.

The Rules Governing the Organization and Running of the Ordinary Courts

There are four ordinary courts: the district courts, the regional courts, the courts of appeal, and the Supreme Court.

District Courts.   These are the lowest level of Guinean courts. They are located in all the prefecture capitals except, for practical and financial reasons, in those which have a regional court. As a first resort and whatever the value of the litigation, the district court deals with all cases to do with people's status and capacity, claims for payment, revision or withdrawal of maintenance, and civil and economic claims not exceeding 50 million Guinean francs (about U.S. $36,000). As a first resort, and under the conditions defined by the Civil, Economic, and Administrative Codes, the district court also delivers judgments on payment orders and other court orders and, when within its geographical jurisdiction and according to the conditions set out in the Criminal Procedure Code, on criminal offenses defined in the Criminal Code. The district court consists of a single judge who performs the duties of a public prosecutor, examining judge, and trial judge. According to the law, one or several supplementary judges or examining judges can be appointed at this level when needed.

Regional Courts.   There are eight regional courts which are located in the capitals of the administrative regions, Boké, Faranah, Kankan, Kindia, Labé, Mamou, Nzérékoré, and in the capital Conakry. According to the law, the regional court has a wide and general jurisdiction, that is, it deals with all cases which are not expressly or exclusively the responsibility of another court. It is also the ordinary judge of administrative litigation, except for *ultra vires* cases, which go directly to the Supreme Court. It has exclusive and mandatory jurisdiction in matters defined by the Civil Procedure Code (marriage, divorce, inheritance, and so on) and may fulfill any other function assigned to it by a specific law.

The regional court is made up of a single judge except when it is sitting in judgment on a social or economic issue in which case it is presided over by a college of judges. Then it is made up of a president and two nonpresiding judges. When adjudicating on a social issue, the makeup of the court of judgment is determined by the Labor Code.

The regional courts, with the notable exception of the one in Conakry, are divided into two chambers: a civil and administrative chamber which also deals with social and economic matters, and a criminal chamber. The one in Conakry has five chambers (one civil, social, and administrative, two economic, and two criminal) and seven examination chambers, including one headed by the dean of examining judges. The examination chambers are headed by judges who report to the president of the regional court, who are supervised by the indictments chamber of the court of appeal and who receive submissions from the republic's public prosecutor. The first chamber is headed by the dean of judges, who coordinates the activities of the other chambers and who hears civil litigation complaints and enforces rogatory letters on criminal matters. According to the law, the first chamber specializes in offenses resulting from the violation of provisions of the Economic Activities Code, the second, third, fourth, and fifth sections with offenses against property, persons, and the state, and the sixth and seventh chambers in offenses relating to drugs or customs, maritime or forest offenses, and offenses committed by minors.[62]

The public prosecutor's office of the regional court, also known as the attorney general's department, is directed by the public prosecutor, assisted by his deputy and "substitute" public prosecutors. The one in Conakry, taking into account the capital's specific needs, is divided into four chambers which deal respectively with crimes and offenses against the state, goods, or persons (first chamber), offenses and misdemeanours relating to drugs, violation of the press laws, customs, maritime and forest crimes, as well as other specific offenses (second chamber), the followup and wording of conclusions and comments on the cases pending at the Public Prosecutor's Office, and representing the state before civil courts and before those trying cases concerning offenses committed by minors (third chamber), and trials involving *flagrante delicto* (fourth chamber).[63]

A major innovation in the new Criminal Procedure Code is a provision for the appointment (to a number of regional courts chosen by the Ministry of Justice) of judges responsible for the execution of sentences whose task is to monitor prisoners' sentences and to resolve problems which they encounter in the prison system (Articles 774–779). He has the power to give permission for work releases, semi-detention, and day passes, and order, where reasonably justified, special prison measures (Article 774).

The Courts of Appeal.   These are the courts of second degree which rule on the facts and the law on appeals against verdicts given by the regional and district courts, the professional disciplinary bodies such as the Bar Council, the decisions of all other courts whether professional or arbitral in the cases defined by the law or by the wish of the parties. They also have jurisdiction over cases which are sent back to them after final appeal to the Supreme Court. There are two courts of appeal: one in Conakry and one in Kankan. Each court of appeal has, at its head, a president, chamber presidents, and advisers. Each chamber is made up of at least three judges who deliver judgment in college.

The court of appeal in Conakry has five chambers; the one in Kankan only has three. The courts of appeal sit in ordinary hearings, formal hearings, or general assembly. An ordinary hearing deals with judgments on verdicts from regional courts or cases sent back after appeal. These hearings are held in the presence of three magistrates, one of whom is a chamber president, who deliver judgment in college, and of the public prosecutor. Solemn hearings are held for the appointment of members of the court and for new judges' oath-taking ceremonies. They are presided over by five judges including the president of the court of appeal. General assemblies are held to establish or amend the rules of procedure of the courts of appeal and to deliver judgment on decisions made by professional bodies (in particular the bar). They are convened at the request of the president and include all the court of appeal judges.

The public prosecutor's office of the court of appeal is directed by a public prosecutor and is made up of attorney generals and their deputies. The public prosecutor is also legally responsible for the practical and financial management of the court of appeal. Under the terms of the law, he must consult with the president. The registrar's office at each court of appeal consists of a chief registrar and of secretaries to the registrar and public prosecutor.

The Supreme Court.   This is the highest legal body of the whole legal and government system. As explained above, its jurisdiction covers *ultra vires* and appeals against court verdicts. It also supervises the expenditure of the executive branch, is responsible for guaranteeing the constitutionality of State Authority Acts and international treaties, makes sure that the constitution is respected, and arbitrates in legal disputes between the executive branch and the National Assembly. The executive branch also seeks its opinion on specific questions on the constitution. The Supreme Court is administered by a president, assisted by an executive staff and a general secretariat. It is divided into three chambers, each with a president and four advisers (except for the auditor general's department, which only has two advisers): one administrative and constitutional chamber whose president is the president, one civil, criminal, commercial and social chamber, and one auditor general's department.

The public prosecutor's office is represented by one public prosecutor assisted by a state attorney general and two deputies. In addition, there are public auditors at the auditor general's department and registrars who report to the chief registrar.

The members of the Supreme Court are appointed by the president of the republic who, in the case of the president, must consult the president of the National Assembly. In legal and administrative matters, the Supreme Court can be approached in the two months following the handing down of the verdict to be questioned. And to be acceptable, the request must be in written form, detailing the names and addresses of the parties, a summary of the facts, legal arguments and conclusions of the party who is challenging the verdict and a copy of the verdict. It is then lodged with the registrar of the Supreme Court by the appellant who, unless a recipient of legal aid, will have first deposited the sum of US$25 in the court's account at the Central Bank of Guinea. Once this process has been completed, the opposing party is informed of the appeal within a period of two months, and he also has two months to prepare his defense. The procedure for social cases is almost the same except that the opposing party is notified by a letter, sent recorded delivery whose receipt must be acknowledged.

In criminal cases the notification of appeal is lodged with the registrar of the court which is nearest to the home of parties who are not in prison, and nearest the prison in the case of detained persons. It is signed by the registrar and by the appellant and he and his lawyer then have ten days to present the arguments to support their appeal. Within the next three days the registrar informs the opposing party of the appeal made against him. In this case as well the appeal can be lodged only when a deposit of US$25 has been made in the court's account at the Central Bank of Guinea. The opposing party must produce his defense within two months and he is not obliged to use a lawyer. The statements by each party are lodged with the registrar who shares their contents with each party.

Supreme Court verdicts are delivered at a meeting of one or more chambers of the Supreme Court or an Advisory General Assembly. The hearings are public and the lawyers retained by the parties are allowed to make verbal statements, although they can include only the concluding and general arguments which have already been submitted in written form. The Supreme Court can annul or reverse the rulings, judgments, or edicts of judges within its remit. It can also, when requested to do so by the parties, suspend judgments and rulings until it has delivered a verdict on the appeals lodged with it. Its decisions are binding on citizens and on the public authorities. The court's judgments are published in the *Supreme Court Bulletin* and, in exceptional cases, in the *Official Gazette*.[64]

Rules Governing the Organization and Running of the Special Courts

There are three special courts: the military court, the National Security Court, and the High Court of Justice.

The Military Court.   As its name suggests, the military court judges all violations of a military nature as set out in the Criminal Code.[65] As such, it can pass judgment on perpetrators of or accessories to military offenses or any other offenses committed within the military forces, in military establishments, or during military service whether military or not. In a case dealing with an infringement or petty offense, the military court is made up of a president, who will be a judge from the legal system, assisted by three military personnel who will be either of the same grade or higher than the defendant. When dealing with a criminal case, the president, a judge, is assisted by six nonpresiding judges (two magistrates from the judiciary assisted by four military judges of the same or higher grade than the accused). The state is represented in military matters by a military public prosecutor assisted by military deputies appointed by edict and nominated by the national defense minister. The rules of procedure of the court in peacetime and in wartime are set out in Book 6 of the Criminal Procedure Code.

The National Security Court.   This is a special court responsible in peacetime and wartime for judging crimes and offenses against the internal and external security of the state.[66] One of its salient characteristics is that it is a mixed civil and military court and that its procedures differ according to the case to be judged and its particular requirements. Thus its makeup and procedures differ according to whether the offense or crime was committed in peacetime or in wartime, by civilians or military personnel, and whether through the media or not. This type of court has been abolished in several countries in the region (notably Mali and Senegal) due to the political nature of the crimes and offenses which come before it, and also because these courts have been severely criticized by the Human Rights Committee of the United Nations, which considers them to be political courts.

When dealing with a civilian case, the National Security Court is made up of a president, who is a Supreme Court judge, and two professional magistrates. The registrar of the court's duties are performed by a chief registrar and assistant registrars. The state is represented by a public prosecutor, assisted by two attorney generals, of whom one is a senior army officer, and two deputy attorney generals, both magistrates from the legal system. When military personnel are among the accused, the bench also includes two senior serving army officers and two substitutes of the same rank. In every case, members of the court are appointed by the president of the republic. In peacetime, when offenses against national security have been committed through the media, they are judged before criminal courts. The law states that cases which come before this court are "prepared by the minister of justice, who forwards them to the public prosecutor for indictment."[67]

The National Security Court can, after having passed judgment on the state, examine requests for damages. According to the law, the judges of the National Security Court, in delivering their verdict, do not need to "enumerate the arguments which led them to reach a verdict."[68] They can simply express their innermost conviction. The decisions of the National Security Court are final, except that an appeal can be made to the Supreme Court to challenge whether a verdict is correct in legal or regulatory terms.

The High Court of Justice.   The jurisdiction of the High Court of Justice covers the highest authorities in Guinea, the president of the republic when accused of high treason and ministers accused of crimes and offenses committed during the performance of their duties. The High Court is made up of a president, a judge elected by the General Assembly of the High Court by secret ballot and by absolute majority of its members, and six magistrates elected from the members of the National Assembly. A deputy president and three deputy judges are elected in the same manner.

For a case to be put before this court, a resolution must be passed by the National Assembly by secret ballot and by a majority of three-fifths of its members. Once passed, the president of the National Assembly hands this resolution to the public prosecutor at the High Court. The pretrial examination of a case is the responsibility of an examination board made up of three incumbents and one deputy chosen at the end of each year from among the magistrates sitting at the court of appeal by the General Assembly of this court without the participation of members of the public prosecutor's office. The state is represented by the public prosecutor at the Supreme Court, assisted by the first attorney general, and the office of registrar of the court is assigned ex officio to the chief registrar of the Supreme Court.

Judicial Administration

This description of the Guinean court system would be incomplete if we did not add that, apart from the Supreme Court, which manages the budget allocated to it by the National Assembly itself, the courts in the country are under the administrative and financial supervision of the Justice Ministry. On the financial side, legal staff's salaries and allowances, like those of all Guinean civil servants, are paid from the operating budget of the Ministry of Justice. In 1997, these staff expenses represented 35 percent of the Ministry of Justice's budget, about US$2,262,758 or 0.31 percent of the Guinean national budget.[69] On the administrative side, their work is entirely managed by the ministry, either indirectly via the Judicial Service

Commission (CSM) in the case of judges, or directly, in particular for the public prosecutors, court registrars, and staff lower down the hierarchy. In the case of the latter, they are supervised by the General Inspectorate of Legal Services within the Justice Ministry, a task that includes: ensuring that the procedural rules are followed in the preparation and follow-up of case files; supervising the registrar's offices (keeping the registers, enforcement of fines, serving summonses, and so on); inspecting judges, the public prosecutor's offices and the examination chambers; and carrying out inquiries following complaints made by litigants.[70]

This inspectorate, made up of a general inspector, his deputy, and nine inspectors, all magistrates, conducts at least two inspections of the courts each year and publishes a report on the state of the courts, which is a very useful source of information on the real status of Guinea's judiciary. For example, its first report (1996–98) contained the following highlights:[71]

- Guinean justice is extremely slow: of the 677 cases sent to the examination chambers in 1996, only 208 or about 30 percent were finished and sent before the court for judgment. One year later, this had increased to only 35 percent. This is hardly surprising considering that 205 of the country's 219 magistrates were recruited and trained under the First Republic and that training at that time was very slapdash and the position itself highly politicized. Cases now require more and more technical knowledge, which many magistrates lack. This slowness can also be attributed to the very poor financial situation of the courts, particularly the registrar's offices, which have practically nothing at all, and to the severe shortage of detention centers.[72]
- Despite the slowness of the justice system, the number of civil and criminal cases is increasing. In 1996, 2,317 cases were dealt with by the public prosecutor's office; this number had almost quadrupled by 1997, to 8,723 cases.[73]
- It must also be noted that justice is more an urban than rural phenomenon. Nearly 53 percent of cases before the public prosecutor's office (4,573 out of 8,723) came before the court of appeal in Conakry which, with the capital's regional court, dealt with nearly 90 percent of all civil cases.
- The high number of cases dismissed (470 out of 1,524 cases) gives a good indication of the lack of legal knowledge of law enforcement officers (police, gendarmes, and others) and of the reign of arbitrariness in the country. This goes to show, once more, that legal reforms which are not accompanied by attempts to change people's mentality almost never produce the structural changes desired.

Guinean law requires the president of the republic to preside at the annual opening of the new session of the courts,[74] during which an exchange of opinions is organized on current issues regarding the running of the justice system in Guinea.

This overview of the rules governing the organization and running of the Guinean courts enables us to highlight a number of structural problems currently afflicting them. Since the judge and prosecutor in the district courts are one and the same person, in other words, both the state's representative and the judge, Article 41 of the Criminal Procedure Code not only violates a basic principle of the law, that of the right to a fair trial, which states that the duties of cross-examination must be separated from those of judgment, but also allows the attorney general to give orders to the judge who is supposed to be subject only to the law. The interference of the executive branch in the judiciary is even more blatant in Article 86 of the Criminal Procedure Code, according to which, when a court has a number of examining judges, the republic's public prosecutor can designate the judge to be used for each case. It is easy to imagine situations in which the public prosecutor would avoid giving a sensitive case to an examining judge known for his independence simply because he would like to control its outcome.

Equally worrying is Article 634(7), according to which the attorney general "prepares cases" that come before the National Security Court, the very archetype of a political court. This seems to be a way of giving a task to the executive branch which, in the French legal tradition which is the basis for Guinean law, belongs within the judiciary itself.[75] The military courts are also a cause for concern in the sense that the Criminal Procedure Code authorizes them to try civilians. This practice is condemned by several of the organizations monitoring the application of human rights treaties which Guinea has signed, including the African Commission on Human and Peoples' Rights and the United Nations Human Rights Committee.[76]

Judges

Guinean justice is handed down by a body of officials with special status known as judges. Traditionally, under civil law systems, and Guinea is no exception to this, a distinction is made between those who sit during trials (judges) and those who stand (prosecutors). But all are regulated by the same statute that sets the rules governing the organization and running of the body.[77]

According to the law, judges must hold Guinean nationality, be entitled to its civil and political rights, have high moral standards, hold a master's degree in law or an equivalent qualification, and have graduated from a magistrates' college. In addition, lawyers at the bar who have been practicing for more than five years as well as professors, assistant professors, and senior lecturers at law faculties who have been teaching for at least two years can also be appointed as judges. They are appointed by the president of the republic after nomination by the attorney general, who is advised by the Judicial Service Commission (CSM) and take office after taking their oath before the court of appeal.

Judges examine cases, preside over arguments at hearings, and deliver verdicts. The importance of their role in the administration of justice means that they enjoy a certain number of professional guarantees: they cannot be removed from office, are guaranteed their independence and have a special body which is responsible for managing their careers. The principle of security of office means that judges cannot "without their prior consent, be moved to a new job even if it constitutes a promotion"[78] nor be dismissed, suspended or forced into early retirement by the authority of the executive branch. This is a constitutional principle (Article 81[1]) considered in civil law countries as one of the main pillars of an independent and impartial justice system. As an exception to this principle, however, judges can be transferred by the president of the republic "when the demands of service require it" provided he first obtains the "argued approval of the Judicial Service Commission (CSM)" (Article 9[2]). If the CSM is weak, the vagueness of the term "demands of service" means the principle can be robbed of all substance.[79]

The principle of independence means that the judge can, after examining the information and evidence provided by the parties and on the basis of Guinean law, freely give a verdict on the case before him. This principle is also guaranteed in the constitution (Article 81[3]) and reinforced by the law, which protects judges "against threats and attacks, of whatever nature, directed against them in the course of or as a result of the performance of their duties."[80]

According to the constitution, the Judicial Service Commission (CSM) is the body which plays a key role in managing judges' careers. Not only does it give an opinion on each appointment, transfer and promotion of judges but it also has disciplinary power over them. The law states, in fact, that the president of the republic must obtain the opinion of the CSM before appointing a judge and must consult it on any question concerning judges' independence. The CSM is also legally responsible for updating the judges' promotion register each year, which it submits for the consideration of the attorney general.

As the disciplinary body, the CSM rules on "any failure by a judge to observe his duties as a judge, or the honor, sensitivity or dignity" of his role.[81] The penalties which it can apply range from a reprimand on the record to removal from the promotion register, demotion, early retirement, or removal from office, with or without loss of pension rights. The law has given nine "elders," including four ex officio members and five members appointed by edict every four years, the responsibility of performing this delicate task. In all cases, the CSM is under the jurisdiction of the attorney general. When sitting on a disciplinary matter, the CSM is presided over by the president of the Supreme Court and gives its judgment without the participation of the president of the republic or the minister of justice. The accused judge is guaranteed a fair hearing before the CSM. The CSM deliberates in camera and its verdicts cannot be appealed even before the Supreme Court.[82] When a judge is accused of an offense or crime, he can only be prosecuted with the consent of the CSM. If this consent is given, in the case of a petty offense, he stands trial at the appeal court, and in the case of a crime, he stands trial at the criminal chamber of the Supreme Court. The verdicts of the court of appeal and Supreme Court are final.[83]

State prosecutors are responsible in the courts for defending and upholding the best interests of society and the law by making sure that it is fully and completely enforced. With this aim in mind, they manage the activities of the criminal investigation department, prosecute the presumed perpetrators of a crime, direct inquiries, prepare case files, make submissions calling for punishment, and make sure that sentences are enforced.[84] These different tasks explain why state prosecutors "are directed and supervised by their superiors and are under the authority of the minister of justice."[85] The main consequence of this is that they are totally dependent on the minister of justice, who not only manages their career but can also transfer them from one court to another.

On disciplinary matters, state prosecutors do not enjoy the same protections provided to judges since the task of disciplining them is the direct responsibility of the minister of justice. Like all civil servants, state prosecutors have the duty of discretion and are under legal obligation not to undertake any other public or private activity or stand in an election without a dispensation from the minister of justice.[86] Unlike in other countries of the region (Côte d'Ivoire, Mauritania, and Senegal), state prosecutors are not formally prohibited from forming a trade union or exercising the right to strike.

Training is the responsibility of the Center for Judicial Training and Documentation (CFDJ) attached to the Justice Ministry.[87] Apart from professional training of judicial staff, this center is responsible for contributing to the training of legal officials, maintaining legal documentation, and making the documentation available to the personnel. It is directed by a team of a director, a deputy director, and three division chiefs (teaching, equipment and documentation). Apart from magistrates' initial training, the center organizes training for working magistrates, such as sessions on familiarization with new legislation (business law, new codes), composition of judgments, and using computers. As far as documentation is concerned, the center's mission is to provide magistrates with as many documents as possible to help them perform their task of protecting citizens' rights. In this regard, it receives aid from several of Guinea's partners such as the French Development Agency and the International Francophone Agency.[88] The center's web site (http://www.mirinet.net.gn/cfdji) is already up and running, and the creation of a data bank of information on the justice system is planned to increase the dissemination of information on Guinean law.

Despite all these modernization efforts, the Guinean magistracy still faces serious obstacles in its attempts to convert the independence with which it is constitutionally endowed into a reality. This can be seen at the level of the institutional, financial, psychological, and technical conditions in which judges work in Guinea. Institutionally, the law continues to place nearly all the country's judges under the administrative and financial supervision of the executive branch of government. The power to appoint judges is the exclusive responsibility of the president of the republic, while the management of their careers falls to the minister of justice. In other words, it is the executive authorities which, as under the PDG, continue to direct and to directly manage judicial affairs while casually flouting the structures set up for these tasks by the law. So for example, in October 1997, the president appointed a number of judges without consulting or convening the CSM. Similarly, on November 20, 1996, without consulting the CSM the minister of justice suspended a judge for eight months for having delivered a guilty verdict against a bank.

With a monthly salary of US$175–250 and without any housing allowance or danger money,[89] the 219 Guinean judges live in a precarious financial situation which leaves them vulnerable to reprehensible professional behavior (corruption, misappropriation of public funds, nepotism, patronage, ethical offenses), consequently damaging the credibility of the judiciary.[90] Their working conditions exacerbate this phenomenon. Courts lack even the most basic equipment; their buildings are almost all dilapidated, particularly in the regions, the equipment which is essential to the proper running of legal matters (filing cabinets, typewriters, photocopiers, codes and legal documents) are generally lacking. At times, some verdicts are not implemented simply because the public enforcers needed are unavailable. And this is to say nothing about the chronic lack of detention centers, which means that a good number of sentences, especially in criminal cases, are never served.[91]

Judges' professional failings are still enormous despite the best efforts of the CFDJ: the filing of cases is not thoroughly mastered, hearings are very often held irregularly and often with scant regard for the rights of the defense, the knowledge of applicable law is very weak,[92] many judgments and verdicts are delivered but not written up, which means that parties are unable to lodge an appeal through the means available to them.

Legal Officials

Lawyers

Lawyers are the legal officials with the power to assist, represent, and plead for an individual or legal entity before the courts and disciplinary bodies in their defense. The profession is open to any Guinean national with a certain level of legal qualification, high moral standards, and having two years' practical training in a law office.[93] Articled lawyers are required to take legal and judicial training courses organized by the Justice Ministry in conjunction with the Association of Barristers.[94] This program consists of a course in theory, one in ethics, and one in computers. Lawyers who have qualified in Guinea are enrolled on a register and become members of a bar which is administered by a council elected by the Association of Barristers headed by the president of the bar. The Bar Council has eight members, five full members and three alternate members elected for a two-year term. The president of the bar is elected by the lawyers who have been registered with the association for at least five years.[95]

According to the law, the Bar Council can deal with all issues relating to the profession, including making sure that lawyers perform their duties correctly and protecting their rights. In so doing, the Bar Council fulfills at least five functions:

- *the administrative function* of enrolling or deleting lawyers from the Association Register, admitting or refusing admittance to articled lawyers, registering contracts established by lawyers, and organizing the general research and documentation services necessary for the profession;
- *the regulatory function,* by which the Bar Council determines and amends the articles of the Association of Barristers;
- *the financial function,* whereby it manages the association's money, prepares the budget, sets fees and manages lawyers' accounts;
- *protecting the profession's ethical standards,* whereby it monitors whether lawyers are abiding by the principles and rules of probity, impartiality, and moderation, which are the basis of the profession and the best defense of its honor and interests; and
- *the disciplinary function,* which authorizes it to investigate misconduct by lawyers, to examine case files and to impose penalties on lawyers guilty of misconduct.[96]

When it sits on a disciplinary matter, the Bar Council is presided over by the president of the bar and the accused lawyer is guaranteed the right to a fair trial. Disciplinary proceedings do not, however, preclude the public prosecutor or civil parties from taking other legal action against criminal offenses by lawyers. Appeals against the verdict of the disciplinary council go to the court of appeal, from where a final appeal can go before the Supreme Court.[97]

As in the case of magistrates, the profession of lawyer is not compatible with any commercial activity, partnership in any commercial business, holding public or ministerial office, being an auditor, any job in the civil service, or any appointment by the Justice Ministry, except for that of public custodian. On the other hand, they are allowed to hold a professor's or lecturer's post in national law faculties.[98]

Legal offices are normally inviolable in all countries under civil law. Neither the police nor the security services are allowed access, not even to conduct a search of the premises, unless they are accompanied by the president of the bar or his representative. Guinean law is silent on this subject. However, it requires that the president of the bar be informed of a decision to tap a lawyer's telephone line.[99] Guinean law also allows lawyers "in regular practice in any state with reciprocal arrangements, and after informing the president of the bar, to act in a case before the Courts of the Republic of Guinea."[100] This rule was at the root of a dispute between the Guinean authorities and the bar in the "Alpha Condé case."[101] What in fact happened was that, despite the examining judge having given permission for three Senegalese lawyers to act in the defense of a Guinean opposition politician, the authorities refused outright to allow into Guinea the African (from Benin, Côte d'Ivoire, Mali, and Senegal) and European lawyers (from France and Belgium), chosen by Alpha Condé to defend him. According to the authorities, Guinean law allowed foreign lawyers to be used only when a reciprocal agreement was in place, and an agreement of this kind existed only with Côte d'Ivoire.[102] It took pressure from the international community and legal arguments, based on the provisions of the African Charter on Human and Peoples' Rights, for the National Security Court to overcome the resistance of Guinean authorities.[103]

Finally, it should be noted that Guinea currently has eighty practicing lawyers and seventy-six articled lawyers who are almost all based in the capital, Conakry, the main economic and business center of the country. Obviously this causes serious obstacles to the adequate protection of human rights, in particular the right to a fair trial, in the regions and rural areas in which by far the greatest part of the population lives. This was made especially clear during the March 1999 trial, before Kankan's regional court, of around fifty people arrested after the Kankan-Siguiri riots, whose defense lawyer was the only one to be found in Kankan, the country's second largest city.[104]

The State Solicitor

The state solicitor is to the state what lawyers are to the average citizen, that is, the part of the legal system which defends the best interests of the public authorities every time the state is a party to a trial. According to the law, the state solicitor must be a judge appointed by the president of the republic on the joint recommendation of the justice and finance ministers. His task is to direct, coordinate, lead, and supervise the activities of the public agency known as the Office of the State Solicitor, which is responsible for monitoring all cases brought before the courts which are likely to result in the state being declared either a creditor or a debtor, to safeguard its rights in areas in which the relevant laws have not entrusted this prerogative to another agency, and to pay the fees of legal officials.[105] In this regard, it handles all issues relating to the examination and settlement of litigation (enforcement of legal and/or administrative decisions as a result of which the state comes out either owing or being owed money) within its jurisdiction, receives summonses, writs, and statements of claim served against or notified to the state, monitors ongoing cases, directs the defense and decides whether appeals may be made, and administers, among other things, the payment and settlement of lawyers', attorneys', and legal officials' fees.

The agency itself comprises a litigation office, a collection office, and a documentation and archives department. Since its creation in 1993, the Office of the State Solicitor has dealt with some 3,500 litigation and claims cases involving the public authorities. It collected nearly 14 billion Guinean francs (about US$9 million) and paid out more than 2 billion Guinean francs (about US$1.5 million) to third parties as a result of legal proceedings against the state.[106]

Political, Social, and Economic Context

Several authors who have studied Guinea's postcolonial political life agree that the political history of the country is one of missed opportunities for building an economically strong country and a truly democratic society. In 1958, when he became supreme leader, President Sékou Touré benefited from significant advantages which could have helped him build a real nation and lay the foundations for Guinea's economic and social development. At his death he left behind him a country which had been completely ruined and devastated by the totalitarian Party-State.

When the military took power in 1984 after a coup, they made a commitment to lay "the foundations of a genuine democracy and guarantee that there would never again be a dictatorship." Six years later they swapped their uniforms for civilian clothes, and wrote themselves a new constitution which allowed them to stay in power. By 2000, the new republic that they founded "in a spirit of unity and national reconciliation to create a state based on the primacy of law and on the respect for democratically established laws" (preamble to the constitution), was yet to fulfill this promise. In reality, all the successive governments, and especially their leaders, have used the law to establish and maintain their control over the population instead of using it to protect rights and freedoms, thus causing the deterioration of the people's legal awareness and rights.

The Party-State Revolution

When, immediately following the 1958 referendum, the French broke off relations with Guinea, and Sékou Touré and the PDG took power, many development experts considered Guinea to be the most promising West African country due to its mineral and agricultural potential. As in many Third World countries at this time, the Guinea of President Sékou Touré chose to pursue so-called noncapitalist social and economic policies, which put all the means of production of the country's wealth in the hands of the state and introduced central management. The course of action was obvious—the thorough decolonization of all the country's institutions. The first measures taken by the government were aimed at putting this new economic policy into action: the import-export business was nationalized in January 1959, the banks in 1960, then the bauxite mines in 1961, and so on throughout the remaining industries.[107] The Guinean franc, a nonconvertible currency, was created on March 1, 1960 to ensure the country's monetary independence but mainly to combat capital flight.[108] Economic plans were developed with the aim of setting up noncapitalist development institutions. Between 1960 and 1984, four national development plans were drawn up, leading to the creation of about 170 state-owned enterprises, of which the largest were in the mining industry. Collective arrangements were put in place for the peasants (state farms, production brigades, and agropastoral farms) and the agricultural sector was mechanized.[109]

After making the smaller parties dissolve themselves, the PDG organized the state into a strict hierarchy which gave it control over the whole population. In 1978, the single party institutions merged with those of the state to give birth to what was an atypical system in Africa, the Party-State.[110] From then on state institutions were controlled by the party through its militia, its women's, youth, and workers' associations, and its neighborhood, village, and district committees.[111] The PDG set up a whole series of mechanisms with which to control the population. For instance, it set up a supply system to give the population access to essential goods; education and health care were free, rents were low, leisure activities were organized for the people, and all university graduates had the right to a job in the civil service or in a state-owned enterprise.[112] Priority was given to young people whose level of schooling soon improved. Two universities (Conakry and Kankan) and forty secondary schools were established, although the infrastructure in other parts of the educational system (primary, secondary, and technical) was not developed much. Following a number of reforms, the teaching of national languages in schools, adult literacy campaigns, and links between schools and industry were introduced. National languages even ended up replacing French in primary schools during the regime's most radical phase in 1978.

The situation of women also improved. Since the vast majority of PDG militants were women, and thus constituted a significant political force, their status was entirely transformed: the minimum age for marriage was set at 17, women's consent was required before a marriage could be contracted, polygamy was prohibited,[113] as was repudiation. Later, a law was passed giving rights to childless widows.[114] Female genital mutilation was forbidden.[115] Progress was also made in the employment arena as several careers were opened up to women, including the army, police, and customs. The authorities even led by example by appointing a woman to what was at the time a highly strategically important post, that of United Nations ambassador. As in other so-called socialist countries at the time, in return for these state measures, citizens had to perform a number of duties which were defined by the PDG. And whoever failed to do so could "legitimately" be exposed to the full wrath of the authorities.

The situation worsened when it became clear that most of these measures were not having the desired result. For example, economic results were disastrous. Not only did the economy not take off but it remained totally turned toward foreign markets because it relied solely on the mining industry.[116] In the agricultural sector, mechanization and the collectivization of land did not increase production. Yields and the level of farmers' technical knowledge remained low.

Those in power saw these setbacks as clearly not due to their economic choices nor to their management mistakes, but as the result of deliberate acts of sabotage perpetrated by the enemies of the Guinean revolution. They therefore used very severe repression against entire sections of the population, particularly those ethnic groups that were accused of being "Trojan horses of imperialism."[117] And this repression was even more pitiless since the authorities had developed a unique concept of the purpose of the law in Guinea. "We are not," said the president of the Guinean National Assembly at that time, "and never will be the kind of people who get tangled up in their own legality, the kind of people who are smothered by their own laws."[118]

Between 1960 and 1977, at least ten coup plots were denounced and followed by bloody purges. Events took a dramatic turn after the defeat of a landing attempt in Conakry by Portuguese troops supported by Guinean opposition politicians on November 22, 1970, which resulted in the death of more than 350 civilians. This Portuguese "aggression" was also at the root of the deteriorating relations between Guinea and some of its neighbors (Côte d'Ivoire and Senegal), which it accused of aiding and abetting the invaders. Boiro Camp, a detention center and "death camp" for the victims of the PDG's purges, became a potent symbol of these dictatorial excesses.

In nearly all cases, mock trials, organized at first by the special courts and subsequently by the notorious people's courts, were used to throw hundreds of law-abiding and honest citizens into prison and to subject their families to terrible humiliations. As Salifou Sylla explains, the country had reached a point where anybody with a morsel of authority made casual use of it, often to their own private ends: "Verdicts were handed down in the offices of the party militia, in police stations, by both political and administrative officials. In a word, if you had a certain level of authority, you could render a verdict and sometimes even throw someone in prison without trial. It is useless to speak here of the legality of sentences, since despotism and force took the place of the law."[119] This "blind" repression left the majority of the population totally disenchanted with the official legal system and, especially in rural areas, they turned once more to the customary and traditional methods of settling disputes. This all led to a progressive "crumbling" of the Guineans' legal awareness to such an extent that "the law and justice system [were] seen as unbearable constraints to be avoided at all costs, and to be got around and violated by any means available."[120]

Repression also created a deep divide between the state bureaucracy and its acolytes, who were generally rather incompetent and living off trickery and corruption,[121] and the rest of the population, which was forced, in the rural areas, to fall back on subsistence agriculture and, in the urban areas, to rely on petty trade and family support for its survival. Those who could no longer tolerate the system had no other choice than to go into exile in the neighboring countries (mainly Côte d'Ivoire and Senegal) or in the West, where the boldest among them would try to get organized to fight against the dictatorship of Sékou Touré and his PDG party. In its workings, the dictatorship of Sékou Touré and the PDG was reminiscent of the system of "dark despotism" described by Edem Kodjo in the mid-1980s in his work *Et demain l'Afrique*. Kodjo attributed Africa's gross underdevelopment to "dark despotism," which he characterized as "the exact opposite of development."[122]

The Military Transition

From the moment they took over power in 1984, Guinea's military sought to wipe the slate clean of the painful past and to build a really democratic society based on the rule of law and economic liberalism.[123] To do this, they decided on a four-phase program: enforcement of human rights, rebuilding of the country's economy, rehabilitation of the education and health sectors, and preparation of an institutional reform.

Having made a solemn vow to respect human rights and to "build the foundations of a true democracy, making sure that no personal dictatorship could be established ever again,"[124] and having freed more than three hundred political prisoners, the military attacked the Guinean legal system which had been totally discredited during the First Republic. All "wicked" laws and edicts were annulled and a national conference on the legal system was convened only three months after the takeover. Some of the recommendations of this meeting, such as the abolition of the people's courts, the setting up of new legal institutions, and the rehabilitation of legal officials (lawyers, bailiffs, and notaries) as professions open to all, were acted upon immediately.

Furthermore, a Board of National Inquiry was set up to investigate those responsible for the massive human rights violations and misappropriations of public funds under the former regime. The trial of sixty senior officials of the former regime was even planned to take place sometime in 1985, but was abandoned after the attempted coup d'état which was seemingly initiated by the former prime minister of the junta, Colonel Diarra Traoré. The violent reaction of the president to this attempted coup d'état, and the consequences for its protagonists and their supposed allies, reminded people of a dark page of the country's history which they believed had been turned forever.[125] The former regime's practices were once more put into use: torture, inhuman prison conditions, self-accusations by those put under arrest, in camera trials in the National Security Court, and a military court especially created for the occasion. There were even extrajudicial executions.[126]

Economic reforms were undertaken with the support of the World Bank and International Monetary Fund (IMF) within the framework of the financial and economic recovery programs, and later a structural adjustment program (SAP), whose stated goals were to correct the greatest macroeconomic imbalances and to increase the mobilization of internal resources and the liberalization of the economy. The initial reform measures allowed the economy to stabilize financially and some foreign investors to return to the country, either by buying or making significant capital investments in those few state enterprises which were solvent. But they also resulted in real social upheaval: nearly forty thousand public employees lost their jobs between 1985 and 1991, inflation escalated alarmingly,[127] and essential social sectors like health and education had their budgets drastically reduced.

The situation was hardly any better in the rural areas with the crumbling of what little social infrastructure there was. In fact, the disappearance of the single party, economic liberalization, and the inexperience of the military accelerated the breakdown of society and encouraged patronage and corruption at all levels. Social movements (such as public employees' strikes, and people's demonstrations) arose pretty much all over the country but were severely repressed, sometimes even bloodily.[128] Journalists and human rights activists also became the victims of these widescale acts of violence.

In addition, ethnic tensions reappeared following the attempted coup d'état during which accusations were made against putschist military men, the majority of whom were of the Malinké ethnic group and who were accused of wanting to reinstall a "Malinké" government. Following the attempted coup, a timid rebalancing was carried out within the government, as Bernard Charles pointed out, in favor of the Soussous, the ethnic group to which the leader of the military junta belonged, and the Peuhls. According to him, the military changed the proportion of public posts held from 50 percent by Malinkés, 29 percent by Peuhls, and 11 percent by Soussous at the end of the PDG's regime, to 42 percent Malinké, 31 percent Peuhls, and 13 percent Soussous after 1985.[129]

All these difficulties showed that Guinea's integration into the liberal economy was an extremely slow and difficult process due to social, economic, and political problems. Even the military appeared impotent in the face of the evils eating away at Guinean society, which, between 1984 and 1991, assumed worrying proportions. This could be seen by the repetition in official speeches of references to the problems undermining Guinean society: corruption, incompetence and civil servants' lack of dedication, the massive increase in crime, particularly juvenile delinquency, trafficking of all kinds throughout the country, the lack of public spirit, the serious human rights violations by both the population and the police, the degeneration of the latter which "instead of arresting thieves, steal for themselves."[130] It was against this backdrop, in 1990, that a new constitution began to be discussed, a discussion which would lead to the setting up of the country's first democratic institutions. These discussions, however, represented more of a token gesture to donors and international opinion than the laying of the foundations of a real democracy in Guinea.

A Trompe l'Oeil Democracy

It is important to note that these discussions took place in an international and African context which left governments of the day little choice regarding the form of government to be established. In fact, the implementation in Guinea of economic adjustment policies at the instigation of the Bretton Woods institutions had a "constitutional side" in the sense that the liberalizing of the economy inevitably had to be accompanied by an "adjustment" of the legal rules which regulated the organization and running of the Guinean state itself by putting in place a liberal democracy intended to establish an environment in which economic actors could compete freely.[131] This was also reflected in Western incentives for establishing democratic regimes in Africa's political systems through multilateral cooperation agreements like Lomé IV, which linked the European Union with African, Caribbean, and Pacific countries, as well as bilateral arrangements.[132]

From 1985 onward, new decentralized administrative institutions and bodies had been set up, with the aim, it was said, of making a clean break with the former method of centralizing the political and administrative system, and of promoting local development by giving the population a greater hand in the management of its own affairs. This process resulted in the establishment of 303 rural development communities and 38 urban communities, 5 of which were in the city of Conakry, 270 areas, and 1,700 districts.

The draft constitution submitted to the Guinean people, while supporting the Western concept of democracy, did not utterly break with the country's constitutional heritage since it sanctioned the hegemony of the president of the republic. Passed by referendum on December 23, 1990, the new constitution was enacted, and a whole series of measures were enacted a year later, to implement it. On December 23, 1991, State Authority Acts on political parties, the Social and Economic Council, the freedom of the press and its regulatory body, the judicial system, and the state of emergency and martial law were passed by the Transitional Council for National Recovery (CTRN), the body responsible for setting up the institutions of the Second Republic. These measures resulted, for the first time in Guinea, in a real opening up of the political space with the emergence of a whole range of political movements, trade unions, and media.

Political pluralism was evidenced by the creation and legalization of several political parties which, at least for the most important among them and despite the safeguards set out in the constitution,[133] were identified with the ethnic group and/or region from which their leaders came. So, the Party of Unity and Progress (PUP), whose members came mainly from lowland Guinea, became the "party" of the Soussous, the ethnic group of its president, the Guinean People's Assembly (RPG), whose main activists come from highland Guinea, was the "party" of the Malinké, where its secretary general comes from, while the Union for the New Republic (UNR) and the Renewal and Progress Party (PRP), whose members mainly came from Middle Guinea, presented themselves as the "parties" of the Peuhls. To date, nearly forty political parties have been recognized, and a dozen of them have formed a coalition of opposition parties which is called the Coalition of Democratic Opposition (CODEM).

As for the trade unions, the only trade union from the era of the single party, the National Confederation of Guinean Workers (CNTG), which was the only institution to survive the military coup, now shares its territory with new trade union workers' organizations, like the General Union of Guinean Workers (UGTG), the Trade Union of Guinean Workers (USTG), the Free Union of Guinean Teachers and Researchers (SLECG), the Transport and General Workers' Union (STMG) and employers' unions like the Union of Road Hauliers (UTR).

As for associations, the first laws on the subject allowed associations, nongovernmental organizations, and cooperatives of all sorts to be set up with the aim of defending citizens' rights in different areas of society. A real revolution took place in the media with the publication, for the first time in the country, of about ten newspapers, which are varied and provide an alternative to the official media.

The institutions of the Second Republic began to be set up in 1993 with the Supreme Court, followed by the first multiparty elections in the country which were held at the end of the year, with the main event being the election of the first president of the Second Republic. Of the eight candidates who sought election by the Guinean people, the electorate finally chose the incumbent president General Lansana Conté after an exceptionally violent campaign during which ethnic tensions increased to such an extent that the results from nearly all the electoral constituencies of highland Guinea were quite simply canceled by the Supreme Court.[134] These first elections confirmed the administration's lack of impartiality (at the central, territorial, and judicial levels) and showed it to be totally subservient to the elected president's party.[135]

In the legislative elections which followed two years later in 1995, the electoral campaign and the voting itself took place in a much-improved environment. About twenty political parties took part in the elections which resulted in the president's party winning 71 parliamentary seats out of a total of 114. These results were not seriously challenged and the parties which won parliamentary seats took them up as normal in the National Assembly and took part in its activities. The local elections which were held in late 1995 confirmed this move toward institutionalization with the victory of opposition and independent candidates in several constituencies in the country (particularly in highland Guinea and the capital, respectively). Nevertheless, the increasing focus of political life on ethnic and regional issues was getting more and more worrying with, as a backdrop, an increase in the number of acts of violence and vandalism.[136]

As far as constitutionally guaranteed rights and freedoms were con-

cerned, it must be admitted that the unfavorable social and political climate and the persistence of government habits inherited from the PDG
made it almost impossible for these rights and guarantees to be exercised:
marches, demonstrations, and political meetings were systematically forbidden, local journalists and the correspondents of some international radio stations were regularly harassed in their work, arbitrary arrests and
detentions were rife, and torture was common practice in police stations,
gendarmeries, and military camps. However, it is also true that there was
increased recourse to legal institutions with the aim of putting an end to
these practices and that this was showing significant results. For instance,
the Supreme Court has been trying, through the use of precedents which
are increasingly available, to reinforce its role as guardian of the constitution and public freedoms.

But it was really the "gang" trial, from February to October 1995, of the
groups of youths who went on a rampage through the country's cities,
which gave the legal system the opportunity to start a real public relations
operation.[137] Indeed, the high level of publicity given to the sessions of
Conakry's assize court allowed the court to start a broad campaign to educate the population on judicial procedures, and the place and role of the
legal system in a state of law. For once, the accused were well defended by
lawyers of their own choosing, the hearings were open and the court was
able to deliver its verdict without any pressure from the public authorities.
But, above all, the debates allowed a very dark picture to be drawn of the
state of society, its true condition, its state of moral decrepitude, its weaknesses at every level (family, school, state structures) and the real risks of
collapse that it faced.

Since the late 1980s, the regional context has been characterized by political and social instability in two neighboring countries, Liberia and Sierra
Leone, where civil wars are raging which have not only obliged the Guinean
authorities to intervene militarily in these two countries, within the framework of the Economic Community of West African States (ECOWAS), but
which have also witnessed, since 1991, the regular influx of more than
500,000 refugees into Guinean territory.

But once again, it was the deterioration of the economic, financial, and
social situation in 1995 which caused upheavals in the country and encouraged part of the army to break its habitual silence. What happened was
that a group of officers and troops, in support of demands for better wages
and living standards, organized a mutiny on February 2 and 3, 1996, which
led to another coup attempt and which resulted in killings, pillaging, acts
of vandalism, and the destruction of public property, including the Palace
of the Republic. As was the case following the first attempted coup d'état,
the instigators of the mutiny and their accomplices were arrested, and

some were allegedly tortured and put on trial before the National Security Court. This time, the trial was public and the due process rights of the accused appeared to have been respected.

The immediate consequence of this affair was the decision by the president of the republic to devolve some of his powers and to appoint a prime minister, Sidya Touré, whose mandate was, among others, to work toward the stabilization of the economy, which was stumbling, and to seek solutions to the social demands which were growing every day. In reality, when the prime minister took office, the economic situation was disastrous, and its consequences were more and more unbearable for the population.

Women have seen a steady backslide in their status. Despite a law prohibiting it, polygamy was reintroduced into social practice and the public authorities tried, via sectoral policies, to give renewed vigor to the image of women as wives, mothers, and housewives.[138] Thus in 1994, women represented only 21.8 percent of state employees and 4 percent of higher government officials.[139]

All these factors explain why, as the 1998 presidential elections approached, protest against the government, particularly in those regions most affected by the social crisis, took a more serious turn. The authorities responded to strikes, street demonstrations, meetings, and one-day stoppages organized by the trade unions, political parties, and the unemployed, with the traditional methods of intimidation inherited from the era of the single party: arbitrary arrests and detentions, torture, murders. The election took place in a particularly tense atmosphere and even before the results were declared, the main challenger to the outgoing president, Alpha Condé, was arrested and accused of wanting to overthrow the regime by force.

What can be concluded from all the ins and outs of the Alpha Condé affair is that the existence of a whole arsenal of modern legal weapons is not necessarily enough to eliminate the influence of the public authorities on the legal system. The protection of human rights in general and the independence of the legal system depend on the real willingness of the public authorities to respect the rules that govern a state of law, as well as on the level of commitment of other actors in society to defend their rights and prerogatives. In Guinea, both of these facets of human rights protection are missing. Therefore, ten years after the new constitution came into force, an event which gave a lot of hope to a population which had been traumatized by nearly thirty years of authoritarian practices, a long road remains to be traveled before the citizens of Guinea truly enjoy proper protection of the constitutional rights and freedoms to which they are entitled. Certainly, efforts have been made to create a legal, political, social, and cultural environment which should ensure better protection of human rights and lead to an improvement of Guineans' living standards. But the imbalances within the administration which favor a very strong executive branch, the continuing presence within the administration, still permeated by a kind of "nomenklatura" dating from the First Republic, of authoritarian practices and reflexes, the more and more frequent resort to ethnicity and/or regionalist attitudes by political actors, and the progressive development at the highest levels of the state of a single party mentality all discourage calm discussion of a wide-ranging plan which will allow the country, so rich in natural resources, to get out of the vicious circle of impoverishment in which it has been sunk for more than forty years.

Status and Role of Nongovernmental and Other Human Rights Organizations

As described above, citizens' groups which take on the task of resolving the problems surrounding the respect for their rights and freedoms is a very recent phenomenon in Guinea. Previously this was the responsibility of the PDG, "the only and exclusive leading political force which integrate[d] all the different sectors of society by applying the principle of democratic centralism,"[140] and its satellite organizations dealing with women's, trade union, and youth issues. There were only a few opposition organizations, mostly based in France, which integrated this dimension into their platform of opposition to Sékou Touré's regime.

It was only after Sékou Touré departed the scene and his political system with him that the first organizations appeared in the form of associations for the defense of human rights: defense of human rights in general, and defense of the victims of repression of the former regime. But as the new political, economic, and social situation developed to include greater participation by the population, this phenomenon took off until it had spread more or less throughout the country. The process was consolidated by the arrival in the country, at the end of the 1980s, of large numbers of foreign NGOs which allowed NGOs to have a presence in most areas of the life of the society, from health, human rights, and local development, to women, young people, the disabled.

In response to this situation, the military authorities quickly put a very simple legal framework in place in 1986 which allowed many Guineans to set up initiatives in the area of human rights promotion and protection.[141] This law established a very simple procedure for recognizing NGOs: the founding document of the NGO is deposited with the Ministry of the Interior and Security which must then issue a deposit receipt which allows the organization to function while waiting for its official recognition by ministerial order. This is given when the ministry has checked that the statutes, aims, and methods of the new body comply with the laws and regulations in effect in the country. But, as the experience of the Guinean Organization for the Defense of Human and Citizens' Rights (OGDH) shows, the sensitivity of human rights issues has made life difficult for those citizens who have got involved in this sector in Guinea.

In June 1990, a group of Guinean citizens founded an association to defend human rights and deposited its file with the Ministry of the Interior and Decentralization, which gave the leaders of the new organization a deposit receipt. But these leaders were then refused permission to organize any activities since the organization had not been formally recognized. After several fruitless attempts to arrange a meeting with the minister, they decided to make direct contact with the president of the republic to inform him of the situation and ask him to intervene with the minister of the interior in order to sort out the organization's status.

A letter dated January 25, 1991, from legal counsel Mamadou Lamine Touré, annotated in the hand of the president himself, informed the leaders of the organization that "in common with other associations whose statutes, social goals and methods comply with the laws and regulations in force in the country, the OGDH should receive legal recognition from the appropriate authority." He then asks them to "communicate [their] request to the Minister of the Interior and Decentralization for it to be granted." And at the same time, a letter from the secretary general of the Office of the President of the Republic, Rene Gomez, was sent to the Minister of the Interior with the comment "to be granted."

Despite the intervention of the president, the ministry continued to categorically refuse recognition of the OGDH. On August 27, 1992, the leaders of the organization, following their participation in a protest demonstration with the leaders of the opposition parties, received a copy of an order of the Minister of the Interior and Security suspending the activities of the OGDH because "since it is supported by the government, it should not take part in a demonstration of this nature."[142]

For the leaders of the NGO, more than a little at sea, this order represented a recognition of the OGDH by the authorities; this seemed to be even more the case when, seven months later, another ministerial order was received by the OGDH terminating the suspension.[143] The OGDH was even able to organize activities with the Friedrich Ebert Foundation and the International Federation of Human Rights which were presided over by government representatives. But this illusion was short-lived since, a few days before a seminar which they were planning to hold in Conakry, they received a letter from the secretary general of the Ministry of the Interior which informed them that it would be impossible to hold this meeting since "research in [the] department's archives has revealed that [the] organization has never been approved. Since [it] does not have legal status,

[it] cannot legally engage in any type of activity whatsoever."[144] Finally, it was only in April 1995, under pressure from certain Western embassies and international NGOs, that the authorities agreed to issue a recognition order for the OGDH.[145]

Today the legal situation of NGOs is a bit more stable and relations with the authorities somewhat calmer. A sign of this is the participation of several ministerial departments in NGO activities and the efforts made by the government to improve the working environment for NGOs, in particular with the merging of the Service de Coordination des Interventions des ONG (SCIO) and the Service National d'Assistance Technique aux Coopératives (SENAPEC) into one national department of assistance to cooperatives and of coordination of NGO activity (SACCO), attached to the Ministry of the Interior and Security to closely monitor all issues relating to NGOs.

The defense and promotion of human rights are guaranteed in Guinea by a plethora of associations, NGOs, and trade unions which deal at the same time with specific issues of civil and political rights, or of economic and social rights or, sometimes, more generally with civic education.[146] For the purposes of analysis, the main organizations working in this sector can be classified in two broad categories: NGOs *promoting* human rights and NGOs *protecting* human rights. The first category includes the traditional human rights NGOs, such as the OGDH, the Guinean Association for the Defense of Human Rights (AGDH), and the Committee for Civic Rights (CDC). To these can be added the NGOs or bodies dealing with specific social categories, such as the Guinean Coalition for Children's Rights (COGUIDE), the Guinean Association of Women Lawyers (AFJG), the Association for the Defense of Women's Rights (ADDEF), the Coordinating Council for Women's NGOs in Guinea (COFEG), the Guinean branch of the Network of African Women Ministers and MPs (REFAMP-Guinée), the Unit for the Struggle Against Harmful Traditional Practices Affecting Women and Children (CEPETAF), the Guinean Women's Association for the Integration of the Disabled (AGFRIS), the workers' unions, the Guinean Women's Association for the fight against sexually transmitted diseases (AFGMASSI), and the Guinean Journalists' Association (AJG); organizations for the popularization of the law, such as the Foundations for the Study and Promotion of the Law in Guinea (FEPGUI), the Justice, Aid and Development Association (AJAD), and Africa-Law; and the development organizations such as the Association for the Development of Community Action (ADIC).

As far as the protection of human rights is concerned, the list would include the OGDH, AGDH, ADDEF, AFJG, and the unions, to which the legal clinics of the COFEG, COGUIDE, AJG, and AJAD could be added. Nearly all these organizations are based in Conakry and only a few of them have branches in towns in the interior. Organizationally, they all share the same failings: very weak institutionalization, strong slant of the membership toward one ethnic group, very vague objectives, no headquarters, no permanent and qualified staff, very limited financial resources, lack of co-ordination of activities, and so on. This explains why the main activity of these organizations is organizing seminars, study days, and sensitivity training sessions. The only NGOs to have strayed from this beaten path are:

· the OGDH, which regularly organizes training activities for its members and for government officers (police, gendarmes), produces teaching aids, and publishes reports on the human rights situation in the country;
· the Free Union of Guinean Teachers and Researchers (SLECG), which is undertaking an education program on human rights in primary schools in Guinea that also involves certain state bodies. Within this framework, it has produced a working document for teachers and a car-toon book for pupils;
· the Foundation for the Study and Promotion of the Law in Guinea (FEPGUI), which publishes a bulletin on Guinean justice in which in-formation on the current legal situation in the country can be found (texts of laws, jurisprudence, and legal theory); and
· the Association for the Development of Community Action (ADIC), which, in highland Guinea, is trying to popularize a number of laws con-cerning human rights by translating them into the national languages and by using rural radio.

Many of these activities have been undertaken in collaboration with inter-national NGOs based in Guinea. But it must be said that these relationships are generally unequal, and it is not unusual to see some international NGOs forcing the hand of their Guinean "partners" by providing them with ready-made projects, and thereby determining what the bulk of their activities would be. During the last two years, some NGOs like the OGDH have be-gun to open up to the outside world, and are beginning to strengthen their international relations by forging links with regional or international hu-man rights organizations like the Inter-African Union for Human Rights and the International Federation of Human Rights. In the end this will greatly help Guinean NGOs to escape the "localism" in which the country has been imprisoned since the days of the First Republic.

The financing for these activities of promotion and defense of human rights is, for the most part, provided by private organizations like the Friedrich Ebert Foundation, Plan International and bilateral and interna-tional cooperation agencies such as the Canadian International Develop-ment Agency (CIDA), the French Development Agency (AFD), the United States Agency for International Development (USAID), the German Agency for International Cooperation (GTZ), the United Nations Development Program (UNDP), the World Bank, and UNICEF.

Guinea is certainly one of the few West African countries in which donors deal directly with NGOs to implement programs which have been agreed upon with the country's government. This situation, which puts international NGOs based in Guinea in direct competition with the local NGOs, is not the most appropriate for the good management and coordination of the human rights programs developed by the Guinean public authorities.

The Guinean authorities have still not quite realized the important role that human rights NGOs play in Guinean society or the benefits they could derive by using them to carry out a good number of the activities of human rights protection and promotion which Guinea must undertake in order to meet its international commitments. Here as elsewhere, the lack of vision and of a national project and the inheritance of the First Republic explain this inactivity.

Conclusion and Recommendations

Nearly half a century after gaining international sovereignty, and ten years after the implementation of a constitution whose main goal was to create a genuine state of law, that is, "a system or regime in which the state is subject to the law, and where everyone enjoys guarantees which protect him from the omnipotence of the public authorities,"[147] the Republic of Guinea has not yet been able to establish the mechanisms and procedures to guarantee its citizens effective protection of their rights and freedoms. This situation, as we have seen throughout this analysis, is mainly due to the dictatorial regime under which the country spent more than twenty-five years and which totally devastated the country politically, economically, socially, and culturally. It is also due to the policies of the military who, after they took power, were not able to find adequate responses or solutions to the evils inherited from the dictatorial regime. Even today, ethnicity, regionalism, lack of public spirit, corruption, nepotism, impunity, and casual violations of human rights are the main failings in Guinean society. The fact that this situation persists is linked to three factors.

Citizens' Lack of Knowledge of Their Rights and Duties

The Republic of Guinea is, with Guinea-Bissau, definitely the country in the region where the civic feeling is the weakest. In other countries the rapid spread of the media, especially private radio stations, has given citizens much greater access to the most basic information (parliamentary debates, the contents of the constitution and of laws which have been passed, the position of different parties on issues of national interest), while the Guinean citizen is confined within a kind of localism. The information he receives comes from the publicly owned media: national radio, the rural radio stations of the four geographic regions, the television and the daily newspaper, *Horoya*. Even today, a few private newspapers (the *Lynx*, the *Lance*, the *Indépendant*, to name only those which appear most regularly), most of which are weekly papers with very limited print runs (5,000–8,000 copies a week), try to provide more diversified information in the face of enormous obstacles (legal, practical, and financial). In the absence of private radio stations, which elsewhere have become the best channel for spreading information in general and legal information in particular, Guineans must either be satisfied with filtered official information or resort to foreign radio stations (Africa No. 1, Radio France International, and the BBC) to get reasonably reliable information on the social, economic, and political life of their country.

Since the new constitution came into force, the opportunities for informing the population about its rights and duties and the administrative, political, and legal institutions established by this constitution have been very rare. To our knowledge, apart from meetings organized around the consultation of the population in 1990 and the media campaign on the legal system in 1996, Guineans know little of their laws. And everyone knows that the effectiveness of a system to protect human rights depends largely on the trust which citizens place in the law and the institutions whose responsibility it is to uphold the law. Efforts must thus be made to encourage a full civic involvement which would be an excellent rampart against the dictatorship or authoritarianism.

The Weaknesses of the Judiciary

The weakness of the judiciary is directly linked to the political history of the country. Since independence, the legal system has acted as the obedient arm of the executive authorities in its legal interventions which resulted in the massive and repeated violations which we have described. Even today, the legal authorities find it difficult to act as an independent institution with the power of imposing punishment: judges still depend on the president of the republic and the attorney general for their appointment, promotion, and financial well-being, the legal system's budget is insufficient, and judges still do not have legal status guaranteeing their independence and impartiality as set out in the constitution. The image of a justice system at the mercy of the authorities is so deeply embedded in the mind of Guineans that they balk at seeking its aid when their rights are violated. No progress can be made until the legal institutions are given the independence that will allow them to freely punish the excesses or failings of the other authorities and until justice is brought closer to the people.

The Authorities' Lack of Political Will to Promote and Protect Citizens' Rights

This is the central issue for the legal protection of human rights in Guinea. Indeed, despite all the lip service which the Guinean authorities have paid in recent years to the promotion and protection of human rights, they have not undertaken any major initiatives to give substance to the commitment they have made to turn their backs on the practices which have so tarnished the country's image. The massive and repeated human rights violations under the First Republic and the killing of former PDG officials and military arrested following the 1985 coup attempt have not been properly investigated, and executive authorities still violate the law daily, attacking Guineans' property and persons.

Clearly, it cannot be envisaged that any progress will be made in the human rights arena unless the executive authorities are involved in the conception, planning, and carrying out of programs to promote and protect human rights. Establishing a constructive dialogue between the state and other sectors of society would be a step toward a bigger commitment by the Guinean government to greater respect for the law and to a more effective protection of human rights.

* * *

From this, it is possible to make the following recommendations:

Educate the Population on Human Rights

The essential method of educating the population on the subject of human rights in a country where two-thirds of the population cannot read or write is by using the media (mainly radio and television). It is imperative to establish private radio stations, supported by grants from the government, to undertake awareness activities. The main drivers of these activities should be the state and civil society organizations (development associations, organizations for the defense of human rights, teachers' unions, women's organizations, etc.).

The success of such an undertaking will depend on strengthening the institutional and operational capabilities of these civil society organizations by using public and private money. Such tasks and activities could include: training of teachers and journalists in human rights; media campaigns for civic education (radio and television); teaching the subject of human rights in schools and colleges; organizing public debates on burning human rights issues; broadcasting, via radio and television, summaries of the work of the National Assembly and of trials which have important implications for the country; and amending the constitution to make primary education obligatory for all Guineans.

Improving the Running of the Legal System

Recommendations for improving the legal system's operation include: legislative reform to eliminate all links which subordinate magistrates to the executive authorities (appointment and promotion) and to establish a genuine status for magistrates; improvement of judges' living and working conditions; allocating a fixed percentage of the state's annual budget to the legal system which should be at least double the current percentage; developing exchange programs for magistrates with other countries in the region; systematic publication of the decisions of the courts of appeal and the Supreme Court and ensuring that magistrates are properly informed of these decisions; training of magistrates and lawyers in human rights and in using the international mechanisms for protecting these rights; setting up a legal aid fund mainly for rural areas; and reform of the legal system to make it easier for the population to have access to the administrative courts.

Strengthen Collaboration Between the State and Civil Society Organizations

The state and civil society organizations should work together to the benefit of human rights by the following: establishing an independent commission of inquiry into human rights violations in Guinea since independence; legislative reform to allow associations for the defense of human rights to be party to civil and criminal trials; extensive reform to harmonize Guinean legislation with the country's international commitments on human rights; establishing a liaison committee between the public authorities and civil society to deal with all human rights issues at the local, regional, and national level. This could take the form of a national human rights commission designed along the lines of the Paris Principles; publication of an annual report on the human rights situation in Guinea which will name those responsible for human rights violations (this report would be examined by Parliament in public session as a result of which recommendations would be made to the executive authorities on how to end these violations and punish those responsible for them); and training members of Parliament and civil servants in human rights law enforcement.

Notes

1. According to the results of the general census of December 1996, the population was 7,200,000, 45 percent of the population is under 15, there are 93 men for every 100 women, and about 70 percent of the population lives in rural areas. See UNDP, *Guinée: Rapport national sur le développement humain 1997*.

2. Muslims make up 87 percent of the population; 4.3 percent is Christian.

3. Bernard Charles, "La Guinée," in *Encyclopédie universelle*, p. 60, *Le Monde*, April 5, 1984, p. 5.

4. Charles, "La Guinée," pp. 54–55.

5. See *PNUD: Rapport mondial sur le développement humain 2000*, p. 193.

6. See *OMS: Rapport sur la santé dans le monde 2000*, p. 204.

7. Of the 1,405,986 registered and 1,200,151 who actually voted, 1,130,292 voted for independence and 56,959 for maintaining links with France. See Ibrahima Baba Kaké, *Sékou Touré, le héros et le tyran* (Paris: Editions Jeune-Afrique Livres, 1987), p. 84.

8. Speech by Sékou Touré delivered on August 26, 1958, quoted by Bernard Charles, *La République de Guinée* (Paris: Editions Berger-Levrault, 1972), p. 20.

9. See Kaké, *Sékou Touré, le héros et le tyran*, p. 86.

10. See Charles, *La République de Guinée*, p. 21.

11. See Maurice Lovens, "Etude comparative des constitutions du Ghana et de la Guinée (III)," *Cahiers économiques et sociaux*, 2, no. 1 (June 1964), p. 95 (emphasis added).

12. See Salifou Sylla, "Guinée," in *Constitutiones Africae* (Brussels: Editions Bruylant, 1988), p. 29.

13. Communiqué no. 1 of the CMRN, dated April 3, 1984, quoted by Salifou Sylla in "Le régime militaire guinéen, un anti-modèle?" in *Revues des Institutions Politiques et Administratives du Sénégal* (January–June 1985), p. 380.

14. See Lovens, "Etude comparative des constitutions," p. 91.

15. Maurice Lovens points out that the constitution was cut to the PDG's measure, i.e., it is "a tool for its use, and amenable to a wide variety of interpretations" (ibid., our translation).

16. The right to equality (Article 6), freedom of speech, press, association, freedom to demonstrate and hold public meetings (Article 7), the sanctity of the home, and the right to private communication (Article 10), incitement to racial hatred and regionalism (Article 13).

17. The right to asylum could also be given to a foreigner "persecuted for scientific *and* cultural activity" (Article 46, emphasis added). It is only necessary to point out that the cumulative requirement of this article made it very difficult to put into practice.

18. This article in fact condemns this form of treason as "the greatest crime" a citizen could commit.

19. Arnaud de Raulin and Eloi Diarra, "La transition démocratique en Guinée," in Gerard Conac et al., *L'Afrique en transition vers le pluralisme politique* (Paris: Editions Economica Collection "La vie du droit en Afrique," 1993), p. 314, and Arnaud de Raulin, "La constitution guinéenne du 23 décembre 1990," *Revue juridique et politique Indépendance et coopération* 2 (April–June 1992), p. 189.

20. Law 98/036 of December 31, 1998.

21. Torture is not defined as a separate crime in Article 287 of the Criminal Code. Its use is merely considered as aggravating a crime: "All offenders who, in

carrying out their crimes, use torture or other barbaric acts, will also be put to death."

22. Article 12 of the Convention Against Torture and Other Cruel, Inhuman, or Degrading Treatment or Punishment.

23. For example, in South Africa in the case of *State v. Makwanyane and Mchunu* (1995) 1 LRC 269; see *Human Rights Law Journal*, 16, nos. 4–6, p. 170ff.

24. In this section, I have used some of the points made by Pierre Roy in his article "La Guinée à l'aube de l'Etat de droit (la loi fondamentale du 31 décembre 1990)," *Penant (revue de droit des pays d'Afrique)* 102, no. 809 (1992), pp. 133–151.

25. Edicts 18/PRG of February 29, 1958, and 38/PRG of July 9, 1959.

26. Edict 15/PRG of July 14, 1984, on the creation of a Supreme Court amended by Edict 110/PRG of July 5, 1986.

27. According to Roy, this latter clause was directly transposed from the jurisprudence of the French Constitutional Court into Guinean law. See "La Guinée à l'aube," p. 154.

28. Ibid., p. 143.

29. Since, as laid down by Article 76(4), if the next elections "result in a majority of MPs in the National Assembly in favor of the position taken by the previous majority on the point which resulted in the dissolution of Parliament," then he must resign.

30. According to Article 34, Parliament consists of: the National Congress, the Supreme Constitutional Assembly, the National Revolutionary Council and the National People's Assembly.

31. Edict of November 10, 1903, amended by the edict of March 22, 1924.

32. See Kéba Mbaye, "Contentieux judiciaire," in *L'organisation judiciaire, la procédure civile et les voies d'exécution, Encyclopédie juridique de l'Afrique*, vol. 4, p. 27.

33. Edict 47/PRG of December 29, 1960.

34. Edicts 18/PRG of February 21, 1959, and 38/PRG of July 9, 1959.

35. Edict 29/PRG of April 20, 1959.

36. Edict 46/PRG of December 29, 1960. See Salifou Sylla, "Destruction et reconstruction d'un appareil judiciaire: Le cas de la Guinée," *Afrique contemporaine*, 50 (La justice en Afrique) (1990), p. 39.

37. Edict 498/PRG of November 19, 1964 amended by Edict 64/PRG of March 2, 1965; Law 50/AN/66 of February 28, 1966; Edict 069/PRG of February 19, 1966; and Law 58/AN/62.

38. Edict 001/PRG/58 of October 3, 1958.

39. See Kaké, *Sékou Touré, le héros et le tyran*, pp. 88, 89.

40. Edict 25/PRG of March 28, 1959.

41. Edicts 253/PRG of June 23, 1964, and 271/PRG/64 of July 9, 1964. According to Judge Kassory Bangoura, this prohibition "obeyed the theory of free justice" introduced by the then regime. See "Le rôle de l'avocat dans l'administration de la justice et la promotion du développement," in *Table ronde sur le rôle et la place de la justice dans le développement de la Guinée (19–24 octobre 1992): Compte-rendu intégral des travaux* (Conakry: Government of the Republic of Guinea, 1992), p. 65.

42. See Sylla, "Destruction et reconstruction," p. 40.

43. Law 053/ANP/81 of November 9, 1981.

44. Law 019/AN/68 of September 30, 1968.On all these new courts, see Sylla, "Destruction et reconstruction," p. 40.

45. Law 018/AN/73 of June 6, 1973.

46. Law 022/AN/77 of October 20, 1977; Law 044/APN/80 of November 7, 1980; Law 053/APN/81 of November 9, 1981. All the information on the people's courts has been taken from Sylla, "Destruction et reconstruction."

47. Ibid.

48. Edict 002/PRG/80 of January 7, 1980.

49. Salifou Sylla points out in addition that the majority of these "people's lawyers" were "nurses, teachers or other state employees who were appointed to the job or who improvised as lawyers." "Destruction et reconstruction," p. 42.

50. Lovens, "Etude comparative des constitutions," p. 101.

51. Sékou Touré, *La Guinée et l'émancipation africaine*, p. 188 quoted by Lovens, ibid. (our emphasis).

52. Edict 115/PRG/84 of July 14, 1984.

53. Salifou Sylla suggests another reason, i.e., that the new authorities also wanted to break with the practice of making the legal institutions correspond to state institutions with the aim of "breaking the political and administrative authorities' habit of interfering in the work of the courts" in "Destruction et reconstruction," p. 43 (our translation).

54. Edicts PRG/85 of August 10, 1985, and 109/PRG/86 of July 5, 1986.

55. Edict 111/PRG/86 of July 5, 1986.

56. In Articles 60, 64, 67, 70, 74, 82, 83, and 84 of the constitution and State Authority Acts 008/CTRN and 009/CTRN of December 23, 1991.

57. Law L/95/021/CTRN of June 6, 1995.

58. Law L/98/014/AN of January 16, 1998.

59. Notably Article 81(1), which assures the judge of security of office and that he is subject only to the authority of the law and the provisions relating to the nomination and administration of the career of a judge (Articles 81[2] and 82).

60. First Article Law L/98/014/AN of January 16, 1998.

61. Notably the International Covenant on Civil and Political Rights, the Convention Against Torture and Other Cruel, Inhuman, and Degrading Treatment or Punishment, and the African Charter on Human and Peoples' Rights.

62. See Yaya Boiro and Cheikh Yérim Seck, *La justice en Guinée: Une publication de l'ONG Afrique droit*, preface by Isaac Yankhoba Ndiaye (Paris: Harmattan, 2000), p. 70.

63. Ibid., p. 71.

64. Judgments are currently not published in the Court Bulletin, apparently for financial reasons.

65. Criminal Code, Sections 1–6: Treason, espionage and other breaches of national security, assassination attempts, coup plots and other crimes against state authority and the integrity of the national territory, crimes of a nature to disturb the state such as massacres, rape and pillage, and belonging to a rebel group.

66. Criminal Procedure Code, Article 634(4). These crimes are defined in the Criminal Code, Articles 70–105.

67. Criminal Procedure Code, Article 634(7).

68. Criminal Procedure Code, Article 348.

69. *Official Gazette* of Guinea, no. 6/97 of March 25, 1997, quoted in Boiro and Seck, *La justice en Guinée*, p. 31.

70. See Attorney General Maurice Zogbelemou Togba's speech to the National Assembly, "Pour un renouveau de la justice guinéenne," *Bulletin de la justice guinéenne*, 1, March 1997, p. 122.

71. *Bilan des activités du ministère de la Justice: Juillet 1996–juillet 1998* (Conakry: Fondation pour l'étude et la promotion du droit en Guinée).

72. Up to 1996 the Justice Ministry ran only nine prisons. See Togba, "Pour un renouveau de la justice guinéenne," p. 120.

73. This surge in the number of cases presented is undoubtedly linked to the information campaign on the judiciary broadcast throughout Guinea by the country's

main media (national radio, rural radio, television) for nearly ten weeks from April 22 to June 22, 1996, to explain the organization and running of the new courts and the new laws for the protection of the population. At the same time, the publicity surrounding the trial of the "gang" (of youths who, between 1995 and 1996, plundered nearly all the large shops in Conakry; see *L'Indépendant,* no. 134, August 10, 1995, p. 11) on the radio and on television certainly also encouraged people to go to the courts and to rely less on private justice, which seemed to be people's preferred method in the early 1990s.

74. State Authority Act L/91/011/CTRN of December 23, 1991, Article 39, on the status of the magistracy.

75. See on this subject *Comité des droits de l'homme des parlementaires: Rapport de la mission d'observation au procès de M. Alpha Condé et ses coaccusés (7 août–11 septembre 2000),* Union interparlementaire, October 2000, p. 9.

76. See, for example, Twelfth Annual Report of the African Commission on Human and Peoples' Rights, OAU/AHG/222(XXXVI), p. 42, and general comment no. 13 of the Committee on Human Rights, para. 4, HRI/GEN/1/Rev.5 26 April 2001 p. 126.

77. See State Authority Act L/91/011/CRTN of December 23, 1991.

78. Ibid., Article 9.

79. As a demonstration of the weakness of Guinea's CSM, for example, in October 1997, the president of the republic appointed a number of judges without consulting or convening the CSM. Similarly, on November 20, 1996, the Minister of Justice suspended a judge for eight months for having delivered a guilty verdict against a bank without consulting the CSM. For a description of these two events see Boiro and Seck, *La justice en Guinée,* p. 131.

80. State Authority Act L91/011/91/CTRN of December 23, 1991, Article 17(1).

81. Ibid., Article 21.

82. Ibid., Article 34.

83. Criminal Procedure Code, Articles 618 and 620.

84. See Boiro and Seck, *La justice guinéenne,* p. 131.

85 Article 10(1) Edict L91/011/CTRN, December 23, 1991.

86. This dispensation only means that he can teach or perform duties "which will not harm the dignity of the magistrate or his independence" (Article 11[2] of the Magistracy Statute).

87. Edict D/98/026 of February 10, 1998.

88. Program for the "modernization of the collection, management and diffusion of legal information" (COGEDI).

89. For purposes of comparison, Senegalese magistrates, in addition to a salary of about US$400, receive at least two allowances (US$330 housing and US$250 judicial office allowance), which gives them a monthly take-home pay of about US$1,000.

90. See Boiro and Seck, *La justice en Guinée,* p. 129.

91. On these issues, see Lamine Sidimé, "L'administration d'une bonne justice et son impact sur le développement," in *Table ronde sur le rôle et la place de la justice dans le développement de la Guinée (19–24 October 1992): Compte-rendu intégral des travaux* (Conakry: Government of the Republic of Guinea, 1992), pp. 25–35.

92. It is interesting to note that several Supreme Court judgments mention court judges' lack of knowledge of Guinean law. For more information on these judgments, see *Le Bulletin de la Justice guinéenne,* 1, March 1997, Jurisprudence section, p. 104ff.

93. Edict 11/PRG/86 of July 6,1986, Articles 3 and 18. On legal qualifications

(being a former magistrate or the holder of a master's degree in law or an equivalent or higher qualification or holder of the CFDJ diploma) see Article 3(3); on moral standards (not having been convicted of any criminal offense against honor, probity or good morals) see Article 3(4); on practical training see Article 3(7).

94. Order 2235/MJ/SGG/97 by the Minister of Justice,

95. Edict 11/PRG/86 of July 6, 1986, Articles 4, 5, and 8.

96. Ibid., Article 11. See Boiro and Seck, *La justice en Guinée*, pp. 137, 138.

97. Edict 11/PRG/86 of July 6, 1986, Articles 84 and 79 and following.

98. Ibid., Articles 20–21. They can nevertheless be given temporary posts by the state, but, if so, the lawyer in question must inform the president of the bar, who informs the Association Council, which then decides if the lawyer can remain on the register. Ibid., Article 21.

99. Article 652(1) of the Criminal Procedure Code.

100. Edict 11/PRG/86 of July 6, 1986, Article 86.

101. Alpha Condé, the president of the main opposition party, the Guinean People's Assembly (RPG), was prosecuted for breaching national security.

102. For more on this affair, see *Comité des droits de l'homme des parlementaires: Rapport de la délégation du Comité sur sa mission en République de Guinée (10–14 janvier 2000)*, CL/166/19(c)-R.3, April–May 2000, p. 15ff.

103. Article 7(c): "Every person shall have the right to have his cause heard. This comprises . . . the right to defense, including the right to be defended by counsel of his choice." In fact, this article is a Guinean constitutional provision, according to the terms of the preamble,.

104. See *Comité des droits de l'homme des parlementaires: Rapport de la délégation du Comité sur sa mission en République de Guinée (10–14 janvier 2000)*, CL/166/19(c)-R.3 April–May 2000, p. 15.

105. Edict D/93/176 of September 13, 1993, Article 2(2).

106. See *Programme d'assistance à la justice (propositions du Gouvernement à la Banque mondiale)*, Conakry, January 2000, p. 11, quoted in Boiro and Seck, *La justice en Guinée*, p. 144.

107. See Annie Chéneau-Loquay, "La Guinée en reconstruction: six ans après, redressement ou dérapages?" in *Neue Herausforderungen Im Nord-Sud-Verhaltnis (Socioökonomische und okologische Krisenfaktoren in Guinea*, Loccumer Protokolle 54/91 (Evangelische Akademie Loccum, 1991), p. 71.

108. See Kaké, *Sékou Touré, le héros et le tyran*, p. 95.

109. See Chéneau-Loquay, "La Guinée en reconstruction," p. 74.

110. The 1982 Constitution made the Party-State system constitutional.

111. In 1982 the PDG had 2,441 local revolutionary branches (PRL), 314 sections, and 35 federations under the aegis of a central committee topped by a politburo.

112. See Chéneau-Loquay, "La Guinée en reconstruction," p. 79.

113. Guinean Civil Code, Article 315. And any man who breaks this law is subject to a prison sentence of five to ten years (Civil Code, Article 318).

114. Law 025/APN/80/CP of April 5, 1980.

115. Criminal Code, Article 216.

116. See Yves Topol, "Réajuster l'économie: Premier bilan des réformes," *Politique africaine*, 36, p. 57, who notes that during the First Republic, "bauxite provide[d] 97 percent of the state's income in foreign currency" (our translation).

117. See Kaké, *Sékou Touré, le héros et le tyran*, p. 96.

118 P. F. Gonidec, *Constitutions des états de la communauté* (Paris: Sirey, 1959), p. 51 (translated by the author).

119. See Sylla, "Destruction et reconstruction," p. 41.

120. See Sidimé, "L'administration d'une bonne justice," p. 32.

121. It has even been said of them that they were "very formidable mafia organizations." See Chéneau-Loquay, "La Guinée en reconstruction," p. 82.

122. Edem Kodjo, *Et demain l'Afrique* (Paris: Editions Stock, 1985), pp. 159, 164.

123. See Salifou Sylla, in "Le régime militaire guinéen," pp. 375ff.

124. Ibid., p. 375.

125. "They had said that blood would never flow again in Guinea. The defeated leaders would be imprisoned to stand trial. *In the name of men's rights, women's rights, children's rights, this right, that right, it will never happen again in Guinea.*" Radio broadcast in July 1985 quoted by Amnesty International in *Existe-t-il une volonté politique d'améliorer la situation des droits de l'homme?* AFR 29/05/95/F, p. 2 (our translation and emphasis).

126. On this issue, see *République de Guinée: Préoccupations d'Amnesty International et évolution de la situation depuis avril 1984*, EFAI 91/RN/235 AFR 29/03/91.

127. It fell from 72 percent in 1986 to 37 percent in 1987 before stabilising at 30 percent in 1988. On this issue see Jacques Schwartz, "L'Ajustement au quotidian," *Politique africaine*, 36 (1990), p. 94.

128. See Amnesty International, *République de Guinée*, pp. 8ff.

129. See Bernard Charles, "Quadrillage politique et administratif des militaires?" *Politique africaine* 36 (1990), p. 20.

130. President Lansana Conté, speech, December 22, 1985.

131. See Jean du Bois de Gaudusson, "Les Nouvelles tendances du constitutionnalisme en Afrique," quoted by Roy, "La Guinée à l'aube," p. 136.

132. France, for example, did not hesitate to make clear to the leaders of its former African colonies during the sixteenth France–Africa summit (Sommet France–Afrique de la Baule, June 18–19, 1990) that from then on its bilateral cooperation would be "more lukewarm towards authoritarian regimes and more enthusiastic toward those who took the path of democracy," and it even gave its definition of a democratic regime, i.e., a "representative system, free elections, competing parties, a free press, an independent legal system, freedom from censorship." See interview with President François Mitterand in *Le Monde*, June 20, 1990.

133. See Article 3(2) of the constitution: "[Political parties] must have representation throughout the country. They must not be identified with a particular race, ethnic group, religion or territory."

134. See Supreme Court, Constitutional and Administrative Chamber Order 94–001. President Lansana Conté was reelected with 50.93 percent of admitted votes, and of his opponents, Alpha Condé received 20.85 percent, Bah Mamadou 13.11 percent, Siradou Diallo 11.64 percent, and Facinet Touré 1.37 percent. See also *L'Etat de droit: sources d'information sur vingt pays d'Afrique et de Haiti* (Paris: Editions Ibiscus, April 1997), pp. 133–141.

135. The cancellation of the results of the vote in highland Guinea seems to have been linked to the authorities' wish to avoid a second round of voting for the president which would have resulted in the PUP candidate's defeat.

136. Acts which caused the cancellation of the election results in Conakry (Kaloum commune) and in Kissdougou in the center of the country.

137. For more than ten months, a daily summary of the trial was broadcast on national radio and television.

138. See Lucie Belle-Isle and Kefing Condé, *Monographie de la femme en Guinée*, African Development Bank, Central Project Department, Women and Development Unit, May 1994.

139. See *Les Nations Unies en Guinée*, October 1999–January 2000, p. 7.

140. Preamble to the 1982 constitution.

141. Edict 72/PRG/SGG/86 of 7 March 1986 on the status of NGOs.

142. No. 92/3435/MIS (our translation).

143. No. 93/1778/MIS/DAP.

144. Letter No. 01278/MIS/CAB (our translation).

145. No. 95/2231/MIS/CAB/DAP.

146. For example, between 1986 and 1997, fifty NGOs dealing with women's issues were set up. See *Rapport initial, deuxième et troisième rapports combinés relatif à la mise en oeuvre de la Convention sur l'élimination de toutes les formes de discrimination à l'égard des femmes en République de Guinée,* November 1998, p. 36.

147. Conclusions of the international symposium "L'Etat de droit au quotidien: Bilan et perspectives dans l'espace francophone" (Cotonou September 11–14, 1991), quoted by Maurice Glélé Ahanhanzo, "L'Etat de droit, les droits de la personne et les libertés publiques dans la Constitution du 11 décembre 1990," in *L'évaluation critique de la mise en oeuvre des droits de la personne humaine et de la pratique de la démocratie au Bénin* (Actes du Colloque), (Cotonou, Benin, 1999), p. 50.

Chapter 5
Morocco
The Imperative of Democratic Transition

Abdelaziz Nouaydi

Each society has its own experience, but these unique experiences can be used to benefit other societies. Such is the case with Morocco in North Africa and its struggle to incorporate human rights protections into its constitutional, legal, and political systems. Morocco's history as a nation-state stretches back over twelve centuries. Idriss II founded the first Moroccan dynasty in 788, and established Fès as its capital in 808.[1] Nearly all 30 million members of this Arab-Berber society are Muslims, and the influence of Islam is visible in the political system. The king is the Commander of the Faithful and owes his political status largely to his religious status.[2] Family law and personal status law are tied to a conservative reading of the *shari'a*, the prescriptive code based on the Koran and the oral tradition of the prophet Muhammed. Its official interpretation determines religious, legal, and political practices in Islamic societies. The influence of the closely watched Islamic movement has been evident since the 1980s, especially in the universities. Moroccan society is, however, an open one, permeated by Western values.

French colonization (1912–1956) has had a profound impact on Moroccan economic, bureaucratic, cultural, and legal structures, as well as on the educational system. These influences have been reinforced by television, women's access to education and employment, and the state's promotion of a tolerant form of Islam, allowing for a variety of religious practices and styles of dress, as well as coeducational schools. However, the openness of Moroccan society is dependent on the evolution of the economic and social context. A sharp deterioration of the economic situation could reinforce elements of the society that reject supposedly Western values. Fundamentalism, in particular, could benefit from a downturn in the economy.

The evolution of the political situation in Morocco will have an impact on that of its neighbors, especially Mauritania, but also Algeria and Tunisia. The region is in transition and interactive. The Moroccan political system, which has already adapted itself to difficult internal and external pressures, is going through a decisive period. The possibility of a democratic transition coexists with the threat of chaos. The years to come may see great improvements in the respect for human rights, but, nonetheless, considerable risks remain.

This chapter will begin by examining the political and social contexts, before turning to an analysis of the legal and institutional contexts, the status of the magistracy and the legal profession, and the role of NGOs. I conclude with an analysis of the status of and prospects for the evolution of human rights and make several recommendations for further development.

Political and Social Context

The relationship between democracy, improvements in the legal framework, and the respect for human rights is clear if one looks at the evolution of the Moroccan political system. It should be recalled at the outset of this discussion that nondemocratic government in itself violates several human rights: rights dealing with political participation, such as the right to free, fair, and regular elections; the right to freedom of association; the right to equal opportunity in political competition; and the right to freedom of expression and information. In Morocco, we can talk of four phases in the evolution of the political situation and the respect for human rights.

Balance and Cooperation (1956–1960)

In the period just after independence in 1956, the monarchy and the parties born out of the nationalist movement balanced each other politically. Morocco had been ruled by a hereditary monarchy for three centuries, which was maintained, after French colonization in 1912. In 1934, the nationalist movement began its struggle for independence on the political front, and, in 1954, the nationalist movement became an armed struggle as well. The monarchy has gained more legitimacy by the exile of King Mohamed V and his family between 1953 and 1955, and his support from exile of the demands of the nationalist movement. France, concerned with protecting its interest in North Africa by maintaining Algeria as a colony and avoiding a total war of liberation in the Maghreb, agreed to negotiate for the independence of Morocco and Tunisia in 1956.

As a result of the balance and cooperation between the monarchy and the nationalist movement parties (Istiqlal and the Union Nationale des forces populaires, or UNFP), leaders from the nationalist movement were able to participate in, and sometimes even dominate, the government between 1956 and 1960. During this period, the government passed laws that provided significant human rights protections. Among them were

1. the law of July 16, 1957, on trade unions which governs the creation and activities of trade unions;
2. the Code of Public Freedoms of November 15, 1958, which consisted of three laws (*dahirs*): the law on the right of association, the law on public assembly, and the legal code governing the press in Morocco; and
3. the Code of Criminal Procedure of February 10, 1959.

These laws were of a liberal nature. They allowed that in order to exercise public freedoms, it was only necessary to declare one's intent to do so, rather than apply for an official permit. The spirit of the Code of Criminal Procedure was apparent in its introduction, which reads: "Only a penal procedure that presumes innocence of the accused, sets absolute limitations on arrest and detention, guarantees the inviolability of the home, respects the exercise of property rights, ensures the rights of the defense, in a word, protects citizens against errors and abuses committed in the name of society, is worthy of a free society."

The liberality of these modern laws protecting public and private freedoms was the result of two main factors: first, the French protectorate system had deprived Moroccans of public and private freedoms (interdiction of the rights to assembly and to demonstration), and, second, the nationalist elite and the monarchy were steeped in modern (especially French) legal culture. Moreover, the monarchy was willing to prevent the unique party because the Istiqlal was dominant. The nationalist movement, on the other side, wanted to modernize the monarchy. The new Moroccan government wanted to lay the foundations of a liberal political system even before the adoption of the first constitution. The task was especially delicate for a monarchy that had always ruled according to the traditional methods based on the *Makhzen* and the *baiah*,[3] which contrast to modern constitutionalism founded on the ideas of natural rights, the social contract, and the separation of powers between branches of government.

Conflict and Repression (1960–1975)

This period was defined by the confrontation between two conceptions of power and society as exemplified by the monarchy and the Union Nationale des Forces Populaires (UNFP). UNFP represented the left wing of the nationalist movement and drew its strength from its role in that movement, its close ties with the liberation army, and its alliance with the Union

Marocaine du Travail (UMT), which was the only trade union at the time, and the Union Nationale des Etudiants du Maroc (UNEM).

UNFP called for a constitution adopted by an elected assembly that would establish a parliamentary constitutional monarchy. Economically and socially, UNFP stood for socialism based on the mobilization and development of natural and human resources, the recuperation of land from French colonists, the nationalization of the country's main utilities, and the closure of French and American military bases in Morocco.

On the opposite side of this power struggle was the monarchy. From the time Hassan II took the throne after his father's death in 1961, he sought to consolidate royal power. According to his conception of the monarchy, the king should both reign and govern; that is, he should determine general policy, appoint and depose the government at will, control the legislative process, appoint top civil service and military officials, and handle foreign policy. This conception of power was enshrined in the first constitution established by Hassan II in 1962. Finally, with regard to the economy, the king supported a market economy and close ties with the West.

Between 1960 and 1975 waves of repression unfurled on the country, targeting UNFP militants. Thousands were arrested, tortured, and sentenced to heavy sentences. In 1965, Mehdi Ben Barka, leader of UNFP, was abducted in Paris and disappeared. The powerful Moroccan minister of interior, General Oufkir was directly implicated in this political crime. He remained close to Hassan II until the 1972 coup d'état in which he was implicated. Mass political trials were conducted during the sixties and seventies. Hundreds were forced to exile and hundreds of others were victims of enforced disappearances.

This political conflict led to a deterioration in the legal protection of civil liberties, as well as, more generally, a deterioration of the status of human rights in Morocco. The legal protections were whittled away, throughout the 1960s and 1970s, through a series of constitutional amendments aimed at neutralizing the opposition through legal processes. For example, in 1962, the articles of the penal code pertaining to police custody and detention pending trial were changed to give police more latitude in detaining people (dahir of September 18, 1962). Following a failed military coup on July 10, 1971, the dahir of July 26, 1971 changed the code of military justice to make it possible to renew police custody every time it appears necessary, thus allowing police to detain suspects indefinitely.

After an armed uprising of revolutionary groups in March 1973, the legislature amended the law on public freedoms on April 10, 1973, to make it more restrictive. So the executive power was given competence to suspend and put an end to the existence of newspapers and associations without prior decision of justice. The prison penalties were reinforced. Also, in

1973, UNEM was accused of being a subversive organization operating under the influence of the extreme left and banned. In 1974, judicial reforms were carried out. As discussed below, these reforms increased the dependency of the magistrates and restricted the rights of defendants.

Openness and Repression (1975–1990)

After two attempted coups in July 1971 and August 1972, an armed uprising in March 1973, and a series of political trials in 1973 and 1974, the monarchy found itself dangerously isolated at the national level. Within this climate of opposition, Hassan II decided to take back the Western Sahara, until then under Spanish occupation. This nationalist issue quickly brought unanimity among the political class and also gave rise to another consensus on the need to undertake the gradual democratization process. The Union Socialiste des Forces Populaires (USFP), an offshoot of the UNFP and today Morocco's largest leftist party, opted in 1975 for a strategy to fight for democracy. This means: first, that the party no longer professes to overthrow the monarchy by violent means as some of its components do; and second, that the party will fight for democracy by democratic means. Local and state legislative elections were held between 1976 and 1977. Though these elections were manifestly fraudulent, the opposition did not choose to boycott the institutions. Though this period of limited liberalization was seriously flawed, nonetheless, some important changes were made. The government lifted the ban on UNEM in 1978. The Confédération Démocratique du Travail (CDT), a trade union association with close ties to the USFP, was organized in 1978 as well. And, in 1979, the Association Marocaine des Droits de l'Homme (AMDH) was founded, as well as a legal Marxist-Leninist political party, the Organisation de l'Action Démocratique et Populaire (OADP).

However, this period of political liberalization quickly came to an end, stymied by the negative impact of economic liberalization within a context of extreme social inequality. The government brutally repressed CDT strikes in 1978 and 1979, dismissing hundreds of striking teachers and nurses. In June 1981, the CDT launched a general strike to protest price increases. The strike turned violent in Casablanca, and the army intervened. Dozens of deaths were recorded. The hundreds of people who were arrested were tried rapidly and received heavy sentences.

After the violence in Casablanca, the government imprisoned the CDT leadership and banned the USFP newspapers *Libération* and *Al Moharrir*. Militants members, mainly the leadership of AMDH, were arrested. The USFP crisis worsened in September 1981 with the arrest and conviction of the party leader Aberrahim Bouabid and two other party political bureau members as the result of a party communiqué that declared its opposition to a referendum on self-determination in the western Sahara, a plan the king had accepted at the OAU summit in Nairobi. The king later pardoned the CDT and USFP leaders.

In 1988, the Organisation Marocaine des Droits de l'Homme (OMDH) was established, its founding rejuvenating the human rights field in Morocco. In the midst of the end of the cold war, Moroccan civil society underwent something of a transformation: human rights organizations, associations for women's rights, trade union alliances, and demands for political, social, economic and legal reforms increased the pressure on the political system to democratize. Moreover, more rioting occurred in December 1990, principally in Fès on the occasion of a general strike called by CDT.

Political Openness and Social Crisis (1990–1996)

By the beginning of the 1990s, it had become obvious that the political, economic, and social system in Morocco could no longer maintain itself and continue operating without substantial changes, including greater political participation, improved social justice, and a more rational economy. Major internal and external pressures challenged the Moroccan political system. It became apparent that neither the economy nor the political system was run according to the rules of healthy competition. Ties with those in power determined economic success. In the period since independence, a parallel economy of rents based for the most part on privileges, corruption, tax fraud, contraband, and drug trafficking had been established. Neither the industrial infrastructure, manufacturing, agriculture, or tourism, nor the educational, legal, and judicial systems was managed in a way that prepared Morocco for the era of globalization.

Rural areas remained on the fringes of modernization, with the exception of the privileged estates owned by a Moroccan elite, inherited from French colonists, which were used to produce export crops mainly to Europe: oranges, tomatoes, fruits, flowers, and so on. The impoverishment of the rural areas spread to the cities, where problems of housing, employment, and living conditions grew worse from day to day.

As a result of the economic and social crisis, the opposition pushed for constitutional and political reforms. In their memoranda to the king in 1991 and 1992, the opposition parties demanded greater powers for the Parliament and government, respect for human rights, the appointment of a human rights mediator, freedom for political prisoners and amnesty for exiles, guarantees of the independence of the magistracy, and free and honest elections.

In light of the proposed constitutional revision of 1992, OMDH proposed that the constitutional guarantees for human rights be strengthened. In particular, it called for the constitution to confirm the importance of international human rights laws, increase the monitoring of the constitutionality of laws, clarify the powers of the Parliament and the government, establish an ombudsman or defender of the people, and reinforce the guarantee of judicial independence. Moreover, women's rights organizations forcefully demanded the revision of family law.

External demands were no less pressing. Reports by Amnesty International, particularly the January 1990 report on torture and mistreatment during police custody, and discreet diplomatic efforts, particularly by the United States and France, contributed to the positive changes that took place between 1990 and 1994.

In May 1990, the king created the Conseil Consultatif des Droits de l'Homme (CCDH), a human rights advisory board. In 1991 many people who had disappeared or been held as political prisoners since the early 1970s were freed. In 1992, the government amended the Code of Criminal Procedure to reestablish the guarantees of the 1959 laws regarding police custody and detention pending trial. The constitutional revision of September 4, 1992, was a response to the growing demands of the population (see below).

In June 1993, Morocco ratified four major human rights conventions: the Convention Against Torture, the Convention on the Elimination of All Forms of Discrimination Against Women, the Convention on the Rights of the Child, and the Convention on the Protection of Migrant Workers and Their Families. That same year, the Ministry of Human Rights was created. In July 1994, in response to demands by democratic forces and the human rights community in Morocco and abroad, 424 political prisoners were freed under a royal amnesty.

However, these important measures did not significantly affect the fundamental structures of the political system. There is potential for greater transformation, but the respect for human rights in Morocco hinges on structural reforms to and wider participation in the political system. In fact, no significant progress toward these goals has been made since 1994. Thus, the constitutional, legal, and institutional framework is incomplete and inadequate as it stands to ensure effective protection of human rights, as I will show below.

The Constitutional and Legal Framework of Human Rights Protection

The constitution and the international conventions that Morocco has ratified offer considerable tools for the protection and promotion of human rights. However, the poor enforcement of these constitutional and conventional guarantees means that they represent potential, not substantial, change.

Constitutional and Conventional Provisions

The Constitution

Since the constitutional revision of 1992, the preamble of the constitution reaffirms Morocco's attachment to human rights as they are universally recognized. This appears to mean a commitment to international human rights standards and conventions. In addition, the Moroccan Constitution enumerates a set of principles and rights. In the order in which they appear in the constitution, these include:

1. recognition of the multiple party system and banning of the single party system (Article 3);
2. nonretroactivity of the law (Article 4);
3. equality of all Moroccans before the law (Article 5);
4. the right of free worship for all (Article 6);
5. equality of men and women *in their political rights* (Article 8) (emphasis added);
6. the right of all citizens to circulate and settle throughout the kingdom (Article 9);
7. freedom of opinion, expression, and assembly (Article 9);
8. freedom of association and the right to belong to any labor or political organization (Article 9);
9. any limitation of freedoms guaranteed in Article 9 must be in accordance with the law (Article 9);
10. the right not to be arrested, detained, or punished except in accordance with the law (Article 10);
11. the inviolability of the home (Article 10);
12. the requirement that all searches be carried out in conformity with the law (Article 10);
13. inviolability of correspondences (Article 11);
14. equal access of citizens, under the same conditions, to civil service and government employment (Article 12);
15. equal rights to education and employment for all citizens (Article 13);
16. the right to strike (Article 14);
17. the right to property and the right to free enterprise, although these rights may be restricted temporarily if the nation's economic and social development require it; expropriation must be carried out according to the forms provided under the law (Article 15);

18. proportional taxation (Article 17);
19. independence of judicial authorities from legislative and executive powers (Article 82); and
20. irremovability of magistrates (Article 85).

This list does not include all that is provided for in the constitution, as Morocco's commitment to universally recognized human rights makes it possible to extend the list to include those international conventions to which Morocco is a party. Nonetheless, these constitutional and treaty-based rights are only effective to the extent that they are protected by internal legislation and enforced by local judges.

International Conventions

Morocco has ratified some of the most important international human rights conventions, including:

1. International Covenant on Civil and Political Rights of 1966 (ratified 1979);
2. International Covenant on Economic, Social, and Cultural Rights of 1966 (ratified 1979);
3. Convention Against Torture and Other Cruel, Inhumane, or Degrading Treatment and Punishment of 1984 (ratified 1993);
4. Convention for the Elimination of All Forms of Discrimination Against Women of 1980 (ratified 1993);
5. Convention on the Rights of the Child (ratified 1993);
6. Convention on the Protection of Migrant Workers and Their Families (ratified 1993);
7. Several International Labor Organization (ILO) Conventions (including convention nos. 29 and 105 on forced labor, convention 98 on the right to organize and collective bargain, convention 100 on equality in remuneration, convention III against discrimination in work, convention 138 on minimum age for work, and convention 182 against worse forms of employing children).

However, along with its ratification of these conventions, Morocco has also lodged several reservations that go against the objectives of the conventions, and, thus, limit their effectiveness under Moroccan law. This is particularly true for the reservations added to the Convention on the Elimination of All Forms of Discrimination Against Women. During the ratification of this convention, Morocco registered comments and reservations on Articles 2, 9, 15, 16, and 29 of the convention. Morocco declared that in the case of Article 2 (which condemns discrimination against women in all its forms and imposes a set of obligations on states parties to reach that goal) it would apply the Convention to the extent that it does not contradict Islamic *shari'a* and, in particular, the Moroccan Family Code. The government also declared that it could not accept the provisions of Article 15, paragraph 4, regarding the right of a woman to choose her place of residence, except where these provisions did not contradict Articles 34 and 36 of the Family Law Code, which provides that a woman obey her husband and cohabit with him.

Morocco also lodged official reservations to Article 9, paragraph 2, which guarantees the equality in nationality matters between men and women. The government explained that the right to Moroccan nationality does not allow children born in Morocco to take on their mother's nationality unless the father is unknown or not a Moroccan citizen. Children born in Morocco to a Moroccan mother and a foreign father may acquire their mother's nationality on the condition that they make a declaration stating that they wish to obtain that nationality two years before they reach adulthood (which is age twenty-one in Morocco) and that they reside in Morocco at the time of this declaration.

The government also made reservations regarding Article 16, which forbids any discrimination in matters related to marriage. According to the Moroccan reservations, the provisions of the article are contrary to Islamic *shari'a*, which guarantees the rights and responsibilities of both spouses in a balanced and complementary framework in order to safeguard the sacred bond of marriage. As for its reservations regarding Article 29, which provides for dispute settlements between states concerning interpretation or application of the convention, Morocco explained that disputes may only be submitted to arbitration upon the consent of all parties concerned.

The statements and reservations on Articles 2 and 16 are particularly serious. They defend the Family Code of 1957, which was based on an archaic interpretation of Islamic *shari'a*. The code enshrines discrimination against women, especially in the context of marriage. According to Moroccan family law, therefore, a woman is the ward of her husband and is required to obey him and obtain his permission to leave the home. The only formality required for a husband to divorce his wife is to summon her beforehand. It is not even necessary for her to appear when summoned, nor can a judge prevent her divorce. A woman, on the other hand, may only obtain a divorce through a court and must prove serious harm. When a marriage is dissolved, the children usually depend on the alimony their father pays to their mother. A judge often decides the amount of the alimony, and it is usually insufficient and sometimes remains unpaid.

Ratification of international conventions further suffers from the government's refusal to allow the treaty bodies to hear complaints from individuals or other states. For example, Morocco has not ratified the optional protocol of the International Covenant on Civil and Political Rights, which gives the Human Rights Committee (HRC) jurisdiction to hear complaints from individuals about violations of the convention. Nor does Morocco accept the competence of the Committee Against Torture to receive and examine communications from individuals or party states in accordance with Article 21 and 22 of the Convention Against Torture.

Moreover, ratification is rarely followed by legislation to update or harmonize domestic laws with the provisions of the conventions. As a result, local judges, who are not trained in international human rights law, do not consider enforcement of international standards to be a priority. Therefore, judges, who are trained to enforce domestic laws and influenced by the conformist culture from which these laws arise, are not pressed by political authorities or the constitution to enforce international law.

Finally, conventions are published in official bulletins years after they have been ratified. For example, two of the conventions that were ratified in 1993, the Convention Against Torture and the Convention on the Rights of the Child, were not published until early 1997. The convention against discrimination against women was published in 2000. Thus, judges may not even be aware that an international human rights convention has become law or what the provisions of a particular treaty might be.

Human Rights in Moroccan Legislation

Legislation in support of constitutional provisions is crucial for the legal human rights system. This section examines Morocco's statutory protections for a few large categories of rights: rights connected with political participation, rights involving the physical freedom, safety, and integrity of the individual, and rights considered social or economic.

It should be noted that since human rights are indivisible, each right has political dimensions as well as economic and social requirements, and it is difficult to classify them in distinct categories.

Rights of Political Participation

Rights of political participation principally include freedom of association, freedom of assembly, freedom of opinion, expression, and information, and the right to free, fair, and regular elections. The right to a fair trial extends beyond the sphere of political participation, and it will be discussed in the section below on institutional guarantees of human rights.

Freedom of Association, Assembly, and Expression.   These rights are enshrined in the Moroccan Constitution and the International Covenant on

Civil and Political Rights and are governed by the dahirs of November 15, 1958, that instituted a liberal declaration system, in which people who want to exercise these freedoms need only declare their intent to do so to the judicial authorities (Press Code) and to Ministry of the Interior local authorities (association and assembly laws). Trade unions are allowed under the dahir of July 16, 1957; specifically, it guarantees the freedom of all salaried employees to establish a union by common agreement among co-workers. This provision even applies to state officials, with the exception of those responsible for public order and state security.[4]

However, changes introduced in 1973 restricted these rights. As for freedom of association, the 1973 amendments established the possibility of suspending associations by government decree. In addition, associations may be dissolved by the courts *if* it appears that their activities are of a nature to disturb the "public order" or aim to harm territorial unity or the monarchic system (Articles 3 and 7 of the Associations Law). It is not necessary for the courts to cite examples to support its decision, nor is it necessary that the "public order" actually be disturbed.

The 1973 amendments to the law on the press increased the amount of penalties for journalistic offenses (like defamation or incitement to crime or disturbing public order) and reduced the time during which a journalist under prosecution can ask that a witness be called or cite documents in his or her defense. The Minister of the Interior retained the power to seize any edition of a newspaper or periodical whose publication would be of a nature to "disturb the public order" (Article 77 of the Press Code). He also acquired the power to suspend a newspaper or publication that allegedly undermines the institutional, political, or religious foundations of the kingdom. In such cases, the prime minister may also ban the newspaper or periodical by decree, without going through the judicial system (Article 77 of the Press Code).

The 1973 amendments restricted freedom of assembly by allowing that a civil servant mandated by the public authorities to attend the meeting could proclaim the dissolution of the meeting if he or she deems that the meeting disturbs or is likely to disturb the peace or public order (Article 7 of Public Assembly Law).

Finally, it should be added that, in practice, the supposedly liberal declaration system established by the Code of Public Freedoms for matters such as founding an association or a newspaper or holding a public meeting has been transformed into an authorization system. Thus, in order to hold a meeting or found a newspaper or an association, a person must have in hand the receipt given by the authorities after the declaration. This proof of one's declaration is often not granted if the authorities are hostile toward those making the declaration.

Right to the Physical Freedom, Safety, and Integrity of the Individual

The right to freedom and safety, affirmed in Article 10 of the constitution and Articles 7 and 9 of the International Covenant on Civil and Political Rights, is governed by the Code of Criminal Procedure, and, in particular, by the articles on police custody and detention pending trial. These articles were modified in 1962 to make them stricter, but in 1992, they were returned to their original form. Thus, in 1962, the length of police custody for suspects was doubled from forty-eight hours to ninety-six hours, with the possibility of a further extension of another forty-eight hours with the written authorization of the public prosecutor or the examining judge.

In matters concerning betrayal of national security, police custody could last 192 hours and could be extended as often as the authorities felt necessary. The dahir of September 18, 1962, also doubled the allowable length of detention pending trial and permitted the public prosecutor's office to detain suspects pending trial whenever the accused cannot provide sufficient guarantees that he will appear in court, whereas this had previously only been allowed in cases in which the accused had been caught in the midst of committing a crime. The prosecutor's office had the power to determine whether an accused should be detained or not, and no court could review the prosecutor's decision.

In 1992, following pressure from the human rights community, six articles of the Code of Criminal Procedure were modified by law 67–90, which the Moroccan Parliament unanimously approved on April 25, 1991. This law was promulgated by dahir 1–91–110 of January 1, 1992. According to this law, the following articles were modified as follows:

- Article 68: "In cases of betrayal of the internal or external security of the state, the duration of police custody is set at ninety-six hours renewable once upon written authorization by the King's Attorney or the King's Attorney General, each in his own right."
- Article 69: "The officer (of the criminal investigation department) must inform the family of any person in police custody as soon as he decides to place this person in custody. He must also send a list of persons taken into police custody in the previous twenty-four hours to the King's Attorney and the King's Attorney General every day."
- Article 76: "In cases of *flagrante delicto* or when the accused cannot provide sufficient guarantees of his appearance in court, when the offense is punishable by a prison sentence, the King's Attorney or his representative may place the accused under a committal order after informing him that he has the right to seek counsel immediately and after questioning him about his identity and the charges against him. He may also

cite that the accused appear in court without holding him in custody, if the accused can put up bail in the amount determined by the prosecuting attorney or a personal guarantee. The counsel of the accused has the right to attend the preliminary questioning. The King's Attorney must submit the accused for a medical examination, to be carried out by a specialized doctor, whenever so requested by the accused, or on his own initiative if he has observed evidence to justify such an examination."

- Article 127: "The investigation judge shall inform the accused of his right to choose his counsel immediately, and if he does not do so, counsel may be appointed to him if he so requests. This shall be entered in the record. . . . The counsel has the right to be present when the accused is questioned as to his identity. The examining judge shall expressly inform the accused of the charges against him and advise him of his right to remain silent. This shall be entered in the record. The examining judge must submit the accused for a medical examination, to be carried out by a specialized medical doctor, whenever so requested by the accused, or on his own initiative if he has observed evidence to justify such an examination."

- Article 154: "Detention pending trial cannot exceed a duration of two months. After this deadline, if it appears necessary to continue detention pending trial, the examining judge may extend it by an order stating the reasons for the extension upon an address by the King's Attorney General also stating the reasons for the extension." No more than five extensions may take place during the same period. "If the examining judge does not decide to refer the accused to the criminal chamber during that period, then he is rightfully liberated, and the preliminary inquiry is pursued."

Law 67–90 also modified Article 2 of the dahir 1–74–448, dated September 28, 1974, on transitional measures as follows:

- Article 2: "In criminal cases of *flagrante delicto,* as described in Article 58 of the dahir cited in Article 1, unless the penalty decreed is death or imprisonment for life, the King's Attorneys General or a deputy public prosecutor especially appointed by them, shall question the accused as to his identity and proceed with the interrogation, after having advised him that he has the right to seek counsel immediately. If he does not call in counsel, the judge presiding over the criminal chamber will appoint one to him."

The chosen or appointed counsel has the right to be present during questioning. He also has the right to communicate freely with the accused and to consult the file on the proceedings in the court. If the case appears to be suitable for judging, the above-mentioned prosecutors or deputy prosecutors place the accused under a committal order and refer him to the criminal chamber of the court of appeal within fifteen days. If the case does not appear to be suitable for judging, the investigation continues.[5]

However, neither the changes in these articles nor the ratification of the Convention Against Torture brought about profound changes in the behavior of the officers of the criminal investigation department, the public prosecutor's office, or the judges. In its comments on the government report to the Convention Against Torture, OMDH noted that "there is as yet little monitoring of police custody, and that several defendants and their counsels have protested in court that custody dates were falsified."[6]

Moreover, in general, the obligation to inform the family of the person arrested is not respected by the police. Judges do not always order medical examinations for the accused, even when they are requested to do so and there is evidence to justify examination. OMDH has also found no evidence that the criminal investigation department has ever prosecuted officers for mistreatment of prisoners in police custody. In practice, the presence of counsel during questioning before the prosecutor is merely a formality. The counsel cannot ask questions or have his or her comments entered in the record.[7] (The counsel is not present during police custody where mistreatment often occurs.)

Worse still, OMDH and AMDH recorded an increase in torture and deaths of defendants while in custody in police stations and gendarme headquarters in 1996. Unfortunately, complaints of torture have not led to more transparent administrative investigations or judicial investigations.[8] Except in some recent cases, law enforcement officers who brutalize or even kill people in their custody went unpunished. Deaths are generally blamed on the victims themselves (as a result of, for example, suicide, death during an escape attempt, or serious disease). This is true even when it is established at the autopsy that the person was subject to violence while in police custody.[9]

Economic, Social, and Cultural Rights

The internal judicial framework is haphazard where economic, social, and cultural rights are concerned. The fact that Morocco ratified the Convention on Economic, Social, and Cultural Rights in 1979 has had no real impact in itself on these rights in Morocco. Social inequality and disparities between urban and rural areas, aggravated by structural adjustment policies imposed, with the supervision of international financial institutions on an undemocratic manner, have caused serious prejudice to the economic, social, and cultural rights of the majority. Particularly hard hit are the poor, especially poor children, the disabled, poor women and the elderly; in short, the vulnerable, and those who have been made vulnerable by official policies.

Regarding the rights of children, Morocco's ratification of the Convention on the Rights of the Child has not changed the status of the majority of children. In the first place, the convention remains largely unrecognized by the courts as it has not been published in the *Official Bulletin* (until 1997).[10] In addition, in violation of the standards set in the Convention on the Rights of the Child, which protect children from economic exploitation, Moroccan law authorizes that children may work starting at the age of twelve, and even this restriction is regularly disregarded. Moreover, girls can be legally married at the age of fifteen (with their consent). In terms of education, girls (especially girls in rural areas) are discriminated against.

During the discussion of Morocco's report to the Committee on the Rights of the Child in October 1996, the committee noted in its observations that Morocco does not make children's rights a priority. This is clear from the fact that the convention itself had not yet been published in the Morocco's *Official Bulletin* at that time. The committee expressed concern that the deteriorating economic and social situation in Morocco has had negative consequences on the status of children, particularly due to structural adjustment policies.

The committee asked the government to adapt its legislation to the convention and to ratify ILO Convention 138 on the minimum age of employment. It also expressed its concern for the status of girls, particularly with regard to employment, violence, and their very low level of education especially in rural areas.[11] (Since then the government has addressed some of these issues; in 1999 it ratified ILO Convention 138 and has taken measures to extend girls' education, especially in rural areas.)

The state has not enacted the measures dictated by the convention to promote and protect the right to employment. Unemployment is spreading, and unfair dismissals, particularly of union activists, are common. Labor law is often disregarded in the private sector, as well as in the informal sector of the economy.

The right to health has essentially become a question of one's economic status and purchasing power. There is no safety net for most of the population. Health services must be paid for, even in public hospitals. In these hospitals, corruption, trafficking in medicine, small budgets, and deteriorating equipment are some of the barriers between poor people and the right to health. The shortage of drinking water in the countryside, unsanitary housing, the high cost of food, and various forms of pollution are further factors influencing the right to health for the majority.

Institutional Guarantees: The Status of the Magistracy and the Human Rights Bureaucracy

This section describes the status of the magistracy and the role of the new human rights institutions in Morocco, the Conseil Consultatif des Droits de l'Homme and the Ministry of Human Rights. The role of lawyers will be analyzed in the section on NGOs, as the Moroccan equivalent of the American Bar Association is not an official institution.

The Status of the Magistracy

The Courts

Morocco has ordinary courts, administrative tribunals, commercial tribunals, penal courts, and a constitutional council. The penal courts include regular courts and special courts. Ordinary penal courts are courts of first instance which also have some competence in civil cases. There are also courts of appeal, which are the first level of review of decisions of courts of first instance but also have original jurisdiction over the most serious criminal cases. The Supreme Court is not a final court of appeal; it examines only the procedural validity of lower court decisions. Special courts are exclusively penal courts. Their competence depends on the status of the defendant or on the type of crime. After the abolition of the juvenile courts in 1974, the remaining special courts include: the Permanent Court of the Armed Forces, the Special Court of Justice, and the High Court.

The Permanent Court of the Armed Forces is presided over by one civilian judge and is composed of military judges. The prosecutor is in the armed forces, as is the clerk. This court is competent to try cases where the defendant is a soldier or gendarme. It also tries crimes against the national security of the state (regardless of the accused perpetrator), crimes against military personnel, and crimes concerning illegal possession of firearms. Rulings by the Permanent Court are final and can only be overturned by the Supreme Court.

The Special Court of Justice is competent to try state officials accused of corruption, theft or embezzlement of public or private funds, and abuse of power. Officials may only be indicted by this court upon written orders from the minister of justice and upon condition that the amount allegedly stolen or embezzled exceeds 25,000 DH (dirhams; approximately US$2,770). The Special Court of Justice is distinguished by the speed of its procedures and the severity of its sentences.

The High Court is competent to try members of the government accused of crimes committed during their office exercise. Members of the government may be accused in Parliament by means of secret ballot. The members of the court are elected by Parliament from its members and are also nominated among Supreme Court judges (for the investigation committee). The prosecutor of this court is the Supreme Court prosecutor.

Administrative tribunals were created by law in 1991. They are competent to rule on actions involving the civil liability of the administration and complaints of abuse of power regarding decisions by the administrative authorities (for example, decisions to not give passports or to not give receipt after a newspaper declaration). These tribunals are also competent in electoral disputes, cases of expropriation, and fiscal matters. There are currently seven administrative tribunals across the principal regions of the kingdom.

The Magistracy

Judges are recruited based on a competitive examination (open to graduate students in law with a bachelor's degree). Candidates must go through two years of training (including five months at the National Institute of Judicial Studies, fifteen months of training in the tribunals, and four months of training in penitentiary institutions, businesses, and prefectures). After this training, they take another examination, and if they pass, they are appointed as judges by royal decree after nomination by the High Council of the Magistracy.

The independence of the judiciary is proclaimed by the constitution, as is the principle of irremovability of judges. However, three laws passed in 1974 reduced the independence of the judiciary from the executive branch.[12]

The principle of irremovability was threatened by the law of November 11, 1974. This law allows the minister of justice to immediately suspend any magistrate accused of a serious misdemeanor, before the case is submitted to the High Council of the Magistracy for adjudication. The minister may also appoint any magistrate to any vacant position in any region in the kingdom at any time. In principle, this appointment may not exceed a period of three months without the consent of the judge concerned. In practice, however, it is difficult for a judge to refuse the renewal of the appointment. The law of November 11, 1974, also prohibits judges from forming unions.

In addition, the High Council of the Magistracy (governed by November 11, 1974, law) which is competent in matters of promotion and discipline, has only advisory status before the king. It is presided over by the king, followed by the minister of justice. It also includes the presiding judge of the Supreme Court, the attorney general, and the presiding judge of the Civil Chamber of the Court, all of whom are appointed by the king. There are only four elected judges: two representatives of the courts of appeal and two representatives of the courts of first instance. Finally, the secretary of the council is a judge appointed by the minister of justice.

The law of July 15, 1974, on judicial organization grants presiding judges, who are appointed by the minister of justice, the power to comment on the competence and behavior of judges in their courts and, thus, to influence the other judges' chances for promotion.

The law of September 28, 1974, enhanced the role of the public prosecutor's office at the expense of the bench, the defense, and the rights of the accused.[13]

Material conditions have also had a negative impact on the administration of justice in Morocco. Courtrooms are inadequate, both in number and in size. There are not enough judges or court personnel, nor is there proper equipment for the courts. As a result, each judge has a very high caseload.

In addition, there are problems of corruption, the trading of favors, and the incompetence of certain judges. In trials observed by OMDH in 1996, in cases involving the government's campaign against drug trafficking, OMDH noted that the public prosecutor's office refused to allow counsel to be present at the preliminary inquiry and that lawyers were denied the right to communicate with their clients. In those trials, counsel was prevented from providing legal assistance to the accused. Contrary to the guarantees of the Code of Criminal Procedure, requests for medical examinations to prove torture, which was widespread in these cases, were rejected by the court despite visible evidence of violence on some of those accused. Moreover, throughout the hearings, all petitions by the public prosecutor's office were granted, while those of the defense counsel were almost systematically rejected.[14]

The Human Rights Bureaucracy

The human rights bureaucracy is essentially made up of the Conseil Consultatif des Droits de l'Homme and the Ministry of Human Rights.

Conseil Consultatif des Droits de l'Homme

The Conseil Consultatif des Droits de l'Homme (CCDH) was created in 1990 following mounting criticism of Morocco by national and international NGOs concerning human rights. Unsurprisingly, the first case submitted to the CCDH stemmed from Amnesty International's report on torture during police custody (issued in 1990). Unfortunately, the CCDH has some serious weaknesses in its makeup, its mandate, and its procedures, and these limitations are apparent in its actions.

First, the CCDH is dominated by representatives of the government, parties close to power and individuals chosen by the king. Representatives of opposition parties and human rights NGOs are in the minority. Significantly, not until 1998 was a single woman on this council for the promotion of human rights.

Second, the CCDH only has an advisory role. It can only make suggestions to the king for the promotion and protection of human rights. The CCDH has formed five working groups concerned with the following: penal legislation; the state of prisons; information and contacts with organizations (NGOs and intergovernmental organizations); human rights in the Tindouf camps;[15] and economic, social, and cultural rights. However, the king and the majority of the council decide which individual cases may be submitted to the CCDH, and decisions are made by the majority.

Since its foundation, the CCDH has only been able to improve the human rights situation in Morocco when its recommendations coincided with the king's wishes. For example, the CCDH was responsible for preparing the reform of the above-mentioned articles of the Code of Criminal Procedure before they were submitted to the king and then to the Parliament. In 1994, the CCDH prepared lists of political prisoners who were later freed by the king after the king asked them to draw up the list. At present, the CCDH seems to be wallowing in complacency. It has done little of significance since 1995.[16]

The only area in which the CCDH appears to be active is in exchanging information and making contacts with international organizations and institutions. Its members have made several trips to improve Morocco's image abroad. It should also be noted that council members are paid an annual salary of 15,000 DH (approximately US$1,500) in addition to their revenue from other public and/or private sources.

The Ministry of Human Rights

The Ministry of Human Rights was set up under the government appointed on November 11, 1993, and the ministry's mission was established in a decree from the prime minister dated May 24, 1994. According to this decree, the ministry is responsible for coordinating with other ministries to ensure that government policies promote, defend, and respect human rights and further the establishment of the rule of law. In order to meet this objective, the ministry studies legislative and statutory texts and recommends reforms aimed at harmonizing Moroccan legislation and statutes with international standards. It investigates instances in which human rights are not respected in Morocco and pressures public authorities to respect them more closely. According to the decree, the ministry can recommend the establishment of institutions to promote human rights. It can use all pedagogical means in which to spread the culture of human rights.

The ministry maintains a dialogue with national and international NGOs, as well as intergovernmental human rights organizations, and assists the government at international conferences on human rights. It is also mandated to monitor the implementation of human rights conventions. Finally, the ministry is supposed to respond to requests for advice from ministers on draft laws or programs to ensure that their proposals will further the protection of human rights.

The ministry is divided into four departments: dialogue and protection of human rights; international relations; legal studies and promotion of human rights; and administrative and financial affairs.

At the time it was set up, the ministry was placed in the hands of a former chairman of OMDH, Omar Azziman. He met with Moroccan NGOs, labor unions, women's rights associations, and organizations to protect children and the family, organized meetings to publicize and prepare for the Beijing Conference on Women, and signed an agreement with the Minister of National Education on the establishment of human rights education in Moroccan schools.

Unfortunately, during a cabinet shuffle in 1995, Azziman was replaced by a politician from a right wing party close to the interior ministry—Mohamed Ziane. The change of ministers marked the beginning of a much less active period for the Ministry of Human Rights. Unlike Azziman, Mohamed Ziane was by no means an activist for human rights; indeed, he was a declared enemy of the opposition in particular and of change in general. During his time as minister, he put a brake on activities to promote and protect human rights. He was dismissed in 1996, leaving the Ministry of Human Rights to the Minister of Justice (from the same party and a worse enemy to human rights cause). In 1998, under the government of Prime Ministrt Abderrahmane Youssoufi, a new human rights minister, Mohamed Aujjar, was appointed.

NGOs for Human Rights Protection and Promotion

In Morocco, various types of nongovernmental actors are calling for improved respect for human rights, including opposition political parties, trade unions, and youth organizations that are often linked with the opposition parties. This section analyzes the organizations focused in particular on the struggle to defend and promote human rights, including human rights NGOs, women's rights organizations, and the lawyer's association. These three types of organizations do not work in isolation from each other. Indeed, their actions converge, with many individuals working through all three structures.

Human Rights NGOs

History

Morocco has three national human rights NGOs: the Ligue Marocaine pour la Defense des Droits de l'Homme (LMDDH), the Association Marocaine des Droits de l'Homme (AMDH), and the Organisation Marocaine des Droits de l'Homme (OMDH).

Ligue Marocaine pour la Defense des Droits de l'Homme (LMDDH).   This organization was founded in 1972 by the Istiqlal party in reaction to the left wing's attempts to establish a national committee for the fight against repression. In the end, because of the fierce repression, the left wing never created a national committee, but LMDDH was established in its place. Along with its relationship with Istiqlal, the organization is distinguished by direct reference to Islam in its statutes. For its first 16 years, LMDDH was not very active, primarily because it is linked with Istiqlal, a moderate party, close to the monarchy, and because, between 1972 and 1988, repression mainly targeted the party's political enemies (especially UNFP and USFP). But, in 1988, it became active when the OMDH was created.

Association Marocaine des Droits de l'Homme (AMDH).   This association was formed in 1979 by members of the USFP, Parti du Progress et du Socialisme (PPS), and other left-wing parties. Between 1979 and 1982, the AMDH was very active, setting up several local branches and asserting a strong position against human rights violations. It condemned the repression of strikes in 1979 and 1980, called for the release of political prisoners and the disappeared, and called for legislative reforms. Between 1983 and 1988, the association underwent a serious crisis, when a split within USFP between those who opposed and those who favored participation in the electoral process spilled over into the AMDH. Those who were opposed to participating in the electoral process, many of whom had been victims of government repression, were the principal national leaders of the AMDH.

The AMDH finally recovered from this schism in 1988, to some extent thanks to the formation of the OMDH that same year. Although initially a politically active, left-wing organization, AMDH has progressively become more professional and open to civil society. Its language and methods have improved with reference to human rights standards. Its composition is more pluralist.

Organisation Marocaine des Droits de l'Homme (OMDH).   Faced with the vacuum left by human rights NGOs from 1983 to 1987, and with serious human rights violations (including political prisoners, disappearances, torture, and the deterioration of economic and social rights), Morocco's Bar Association relaunched a debate on the subject of human rights protection in a seminar in Oujda in December 1987. A group of members from the leftist parties USFP, PPS, and OADP and unaffiliated human rights activists worked for several months to set up OMDH. The organization is distinguished by its independence, professionalism, and energy.

It should be noted that these NGOs have moved from viewing each other with distrust to establishing a relationship based on respect and cooperation. In 1988, LMDDH and AMDH, recognizing that the presence of OMDH would put more pressure on them to perform, established a coordinating committee that ascertained several positions common to all three organizations. All three NGOs worked with the Bar Association of Morocco to formulate a national charter of human rights that was signed by them in December 1990. In February 1994, the three NGOs addressed a joint memorandum to the minister of human rights raising their main concerns relating to legislation reforms and human rights.

Resources, Methods, and Problems

The main resources available to NGOs in Morocco are human resources, that is, the people who work for them. The relationships that these NGOs have developed with Moroccan civil society and international human rights NGOs also help to support their effort. For example, OMDH is affiliated with the International Federation for Human Rights, the Arab Organization for Human Rights, the International Commission of Jurists, and the World Organization Against Torture.

The Moroccan NGOs have their own information channels and also take advantage of the relative openness of opposition newspapers to publicize their activities and explain their positions. OMDH, AMDH, and LMDDH make use of opposition newspapers according to their political affiliations; for example, OMDH and AMDH mostly use the left-wing newspapers (*Al Ittihad Al Ichtiraki, Al Bayan, Anoual*). AMDH also has its own monthly journal called *Attadamoun* (Solidarity). The NGOs have some financial resources from private contributions, but these are limited.

The NGOs' principal demands are for legislative reforms and other signs of real respect for human rights. In order to push the political authorities in this direction, the NGOs document human rights violations, hear complaints, and carry out investigations and studies on alleged human rights abuses. They take the information they gather and then contact the authorities. For the most part, they address their concerns to the Ministry of the Interior, the Ministry of Justice, and the Ministry of Human Rights. Because these basic steps are rarely effective, the NGOs have also adopted various forms of public pressure, including the publication of press releases, reports, comments on trials, counterreports in response to the government reports to human rights treaty bodies, and through cooperation with international NGOs and the media. The NGOs try to raise awareness of human rights and offer training in documentation of violations, observing elections, and so on. Sometimes they also offer services to victims of human rights violations. For example, OMDH has a medical commission that provides counseling services to former disappeared people of Tazmamart (a center for secret detention from which twenty-eight survivors came out of the sixty detainees between 1973 and 1991).

The NGOs are faced with several challenges in their work: official hostility, widespread poverty, an environment that is sociologically and culturally unfavorable to human rights. The NGOs have also found the task of institutionalizing their work difficult. This is connected to the lack of training for their members, as well as a lack of financial and administrative support for their activities.

The OMDH has a number of qualified officials, but it has not yet learned how best to use its members and mobilize its supporters. The AMDH has become more professional, even acquiring a few full-time salaried officers. Nonetheless, it too has difficulties using its human resources to the fullest. The LMDDH is much less active and institutionalized than the OMDH and AMDH, and its identity tends to get merged with that of its chairman Abdelhadi Kabbab, a parliamentary lawyer and Istiqlal official who led the organization since its creation.

Women's Rights Organizations

History and Objectives

Organizations promoting women's rights have multiplied since 1985, the year of the United Nations Conference on Women in Nairobi. The main general objective of most of these organizations is to improve the legal status and material conditions of women in Morocco. Five specific objectives can also be identified. The first is the revision of the Code of Personal Status, which allows forms of discrimination against women. The second is the fight against violence toward women. Violence takes many forms: within the family, in the street, at the workplace, and includes the structural violence affecting poor, marginalized, and exploited women.

The third objective is to increase women's participation in the political process, which is a necessary condition for the improvement of their legal and social status. The fourth objective is to improve the condition of women in the workplace, focusing on issues such as equal treatment and the fight against economic and sexual exploitation. Finally, the fifth objective is the elimination of discrimination against women and girls in conformity with the standards of the United Nations Convention on the Elimination of All Forms of Discrimination Against Women (CEDAW).

Women's rights organizations are generally linked with the opposition parties. The Association Démocratique des Femmes du Maroc was formed in 1985. Although is has ties with PPS, it has acquired a measure of independence from that party. In 1996–1997, it prepared a shadow report to the government's report presented to the Committee on the Elimination of All Forms of Discrimination Against Women in January 1997.

In 1987, the Union de l'Action Féminine (UAF), which has ties with OADP, was created. This vibrant organization initially reached the public through its newspaper *8 Mars* (March 8, International Women's Day). In 1992, it gathered one million signatures demanding the revision of the Code of Personal Status to make the code conform with the spirit of CEDAW.

The Organisation Marocaine des Droits des Femmes was formed in 1992. Like the Union de l'Action Féminine, it also works toward the implementation of the CEDAW.

There are numerous other women's rights organizations, including the Ligue Démocratique des Droits des Femmes, Solidarité Féminine, Convergence des Femmes Marocaines, and Association Marocaine des Femmes Progressistes.

On March 8, 1997, all the above organizations, along with AMDH, OMDH, the Comité de Défense des Droits de l'Homme (an offshoot of the Marrakech branch of AMDH, led by lawyer Ahmed Abadarine), and the Association of Amnesty International Groups in Morocco, published an open letter to important figures in the government and civil society. The communiqué asked the government to take back the reservations it had expressed on the CEDAW, to publish the convention in the government's *Official Bulletin,* to establish equality between men and women in all areas, and to harmonize all Moroccan legislation with the United Nations Convention on the Elimination of All Forms of Discrimination Against Women. It also asked important figures in civil society to contribute to raising consciousness of women's rights as indivisible from, and essential to, human rights, to fight against preconceived ideas that enshrine discrimination against women in Moroccan society, and to support greater women's participation in the public and political sphere.

The strongest and most bureaucratic political parties, USFP and Istiqlal, have women's organizations that are officially bound to them and that function only as arms of their parties. The Istiqlal women's organization and the National Secretariat of the Women of USFP are partisan organizations whose priority is to increase women's participation in politics.

Forms of Actions, Status, and Prospects

One of the primary forms of action of the women's rights NGOs is to conduct and publish studies on the status of women in education, employment, and the family.[17] Many such studies have been carried out since the early 1990s, generally funded by foreign foundations with projects in Morocco, particularly the Friedrich Ebert Foundation of Germany. They also prepare more action-oriented reports on the status of women; for example, they participated in the preparation of Morocco's report for the Beijing Conference in 1995.

The women's rights organizations also undertake campaigns to raise public awareness and create political pressure around different issues affecting women. A prime example of this is the 1992 signature drive to petition changes to the Code on Personal Status. Women's rights organizations also provide some direct services to women and girls. In 1995 and 1996, members of OMDH set up a legal and psychological assistance center in Casablanca for female victims of violence. A vocational training center for girls has been operating in Fès since 1995 under the auspices of the Union de l'Action Féminine.

The women's rights organizations' actions are publicized and reported on by opposition newspapers. The UAF newspaper, *8 Mars,* has been an important tool for getting information to the public about the work the NGOs are doing. Unfortunately, its publication has been irregular since the early 1990s.

In the face of such pressure by women's rights activists, the state has tried to limit their effect. In 1993, at the height of the campaign for the revision of the Code on Personal Status, the king, in his position as Commander of the Faithful, invited the leaders of the women's movement to address their demands to him. He admitted to certain weaknesses in the government's record on women's rights and requested that he be allowed to remedy them. For the most part, this appears to have been a public relations ploy by the king to stifle the campaign to revise the Code on Personal Status. The reforms carried out after the women's rights activists' audience with the king involved a few positive changes regarding marriage and the legal representation of children by their mother upon their father's death. However, polygamy continued to be legal. Moreover, the only formality required for repudiation of wives by husbands remained that the husband has only to summon his wife beforehand (it is not necessary for her to be present, and judges cannot prevent repudiation if the husband desires it).

Although the campaign did, to some extent, sensitize and mobilize a large number of actors around the fundamental issue of the status of women, nonetheless, the most urgent reforms necessary to harmonize Moroccan law with international human rights standards have yet to be carried out. The principle achievement with regard to family law is that it is no longer taboo to attempt to change family law so that it is reflective of a more humane and nondiscriminating interpretation of Islamic *shari'a*. Nonetheless, it should be noted that, while the campaign to revise family law was supported by democratic forces, Islamists opposed it.[18]

Like other NGOs, the women's associations are hampered in their efforts by the widespread problems of poverty and illiteracy in Morocco. Another difficulty is the hostility of the authorities toward their work to improve the status and condition of women and to push for democratic change. The NGOs activities are largely confined to urban areas, led by an elite group of educated and politically aware women, and are rarely developed into national and long-term strategies. They lack the resources to carry out coordinated actions that include both urban and rural areas.

If they are truly in favor of democratization of society and the state, democratic forces, essentially composed of the most influential opposition parties, have a fundamental responsibility to make the promotion of women's rights a top priority.

Lawyers' Associations.   Lawyers act locally through their associations. These organizations are democratically chaired by a chief barrister, who deals with professional matters (related to the profession). At the national level, lawyers are represented by the Moroccan Bar Association.

Lawyers, academics, and other members of liberal professions (such as doctors and architects) have always formed the majority of membership in human rights NGOs. In Morocco, lawyers have a tradition of independence (from the government) and have often spoken out to improve the human rights situation in general, and the conditions of the administration of justice and the independence of the magistracy in particular.

Their associations do not tend to suffer from the financial difficulties that beset many human rights NGOs. However, their influence is constrained by the conditions within the courts. Moreover, the lawyers' associations have not been free of corruption. The democrats and activists who uphold the honorable standards of the profession, must diligently work to maintain these standards, particularly through the better training of young lawyers and by promoting ethics by means of the self-regulation imposed by the lawyers' associations. Some courageous lawyers continue to lead the way, including Abdelaziz Bennani, former chairman of OMDH, and Abderrahmane Benameur, chairman of AMDH. We can say that lawyers' work in human rights is done principally through human rights NGOs.

Conclusion

The constitutional framework for protection of human rights in Morocco, including the incorporation of international human rights treaties into domestic law, holds great potential for the improvement of the country's human rights situation. However, internal legislation remains inadequate. Furthermore, the law is applied in a selective and distorted manner due to serious structural imbalances, lack of democratic foundations, and weaknesses in the independence of the judicial system.

Democratic forces in Morocco have a number of difficult tasks ahead of them, including:

1. Peacefully moving the political system toward greater participation and social justice. Thus far, the opposition parties, NGOs, and unions have played a positive role in this effort. Their actions will become more effective if they are based on increased, enlightened participation at the grassroots level and improved dialogue and cooperation with each other.
2. Changing behaviors, mentalities, and structures in order to increase equality, social justice, and constructive citizenship through example and education. A special investment should be made in young people and women. Universal and top-quality education is essential for meeting the challenges for human and sustainable development. Democratic forces and NGOs shall push in this direction.
3. The role of Morocco's relationship to its external environment, in particular, the developed countries of the North, is important. The European Union (EU), whose interest is in maintaining a stable zone on the southern shore of the Mediterranean, seems mostly concerned with preventing the development of fundamentalism, illegal immigration, drug trafficking, and the destruction of the environment by means of a gendarme approach that deals with symptoms, but not the root causes of problems in Morocco. Instead of adopting a policy of constructive involvement in the development of the region's wealth and the status of its people, the EU persists in basing its relations on unequal trade. Moreover, the EU continues to raise increasingly insurmountable barriers against Moroccan agricultural exports, exports that at one time were encouraged by the EU (because they met its needs). In 1995–1996, for example, during negotiations to renew the fisheries agreement for Moroccan waters, the EU pressured Morocco to drop its demands, based on scientific studies, to reduce the European fishing fleets and allow for longer biological resting periods with no fishing so that the fish population can be rejuvenated. (These pressures continue in 2000–2001.)

4. The reform of the legislative framework of rights remains an immediate priority, especially with regard to women's rights, public freedoms, and the physical integrity of the individual. These improvements can only be effective in the context of an integrated policy of participatory, democratic development.

5. Far-reaching reform of the status of the magistracy and the conditions of the administration of justice is a fundamental element in the overall reform process. The rule of law requires an independent, competent justice system with appropriate legal and material means to ensure the capacity to carry out fair trials.

6. This is a decisive time for Morocco. Much depends on the will and ability of the main political actors to bring about peaceful change toward greater democracy and social justice.

Notes

1. Yves Lacoste, "Histoire (du Maghreb), de l'Antiquité à la colonisation, une Histoire mouvementée," in *L'Etat du Maghreb* (Paris: La Découverte, 1991), p. 43.

2. See Mohamed Tozy, "Monopolisation de la production symbolique et hierarchisation du champs politique religieux au Maroc," in *Le Maghreb musulman en 1979* (Paris: CNRS, 1983), pp. 219–234.

3. The *Makhzen* is the sultan (king), the army, the administration (particularly the tax administration and the notables (families close to the king). The *baiah* is the procedure whereby the representatives of the population present their allegiance to the sultan, while the sultan commits himself to protecting Muslim lands and attending to the welfare of the population.

4. Najib Ba Mohamed, *Les Libertés publiques* (Casablanca: Gaetan Morin, 1996), p. 118. See also, the Royal Decree 010–66 of October 12, 1996 (*Official Bulletin* of October 19, 1966, p. 1163)

5. Dahir 1–91–110 of January 1, 1992.

6. In June 1993 at the occasion of International Conference on Human Rights.

7. OMDH, *Observations on the Preliminary Report Presented by Morocco to the Committee Against Torture* (Arabic Edition), December 1966, p. 50.

8. OMDH, *Rapport annuel sur la violation des droits de l'homme au Maroc* (Rabat: Edition Attadamoun [Solidarité], 1996), p. 22.

9. *Attadamoun* (AMDH journal), 44 (1996).

10. OMDH, *Rapport annuel* (1996), p. 34.

11. *Al Ittihad Al Ichtiraki* (Casablanca daily newspaper) dated October 1, 4, and 23, 1996 (no author but reporting the committee observations).

12. See the laws (dahirs) of July 15, 1974, on the judicial organization of Morocco; September 28, 1974, entitled "Transitional Measures"; and November 11, 1974, on the status of the magistracy.

13. Abdelaziz Nouaydi, "The Right to a Fair Trial in the Moroccan Criminal Procedure," paper presented at the Heidelberg Symposium, Max-Planck Institut (January 31–February 3, 1996), pp. 18–20, 31–32, published in *The Right to a Fair Trial*, ed. David Weisbrodt and Rüdiger Wolfrum (Berlin, 1997).

14. OMDH, *Rapport annuel* (1996), pp. 21–22, 30: OMDH, *Rapport sur la torture*

au Maroc, annexe aux observations de l'OMDH sur le rapport gouvernemental au comité contre la torture (December 1996).

15. Tindouf, in Algerian territory, is the location of the camps of the Polisario Front, a (guerrilla) organization with claims to the Western Sahara with Algerian support. In these camps, many Moroccans (mainly Sahraouis), who would like to return to Morocco, are held prisoner by the Polisario Front.

16. Since 1998, the CCDH, with the impulsion of Youssoufi government and King Hasson II, request issued recommendations to settle the cases of disappearances in Morocco. In these recommendations it produced a list of disappeared persons, recommended amnesty for victims (!) and for state agents responsible for disappearances, and recommended indemnification to victims and their families. These recommendations have been approved by the king. A commission in charge of indemnification has allowed substantial amounts of money to some victims. But the recommendations and treatment have been much criticized by human rights NGOs and some of the victims' families. For more details see Abdelaziz Nouyadi, "Elite and Transition to Democracy in Morocco: The Example of the Advisory Council of Human Rights," presented at Middle East Studies Association symposium in Orlando, Florida, November 17, 2000.

17. See the following publications (collective authors) *Droits des Femmes au Maghreb: L'universel et le spécifique* (Casablanca: Friedrich Ebert Stiftung and the Association Démocratique des Femmes du Maroc, 1992); Aicha Belarbi, ed., *Couples en question* (Casablanca: Le Fennec, 1990); Abderrazak Moulay R'chid, *La femme et la loi au Maroc* (Casablanca: Le Fennec, 1991); PUMAG, *Femmes et violence* (Casablanca: Friedrich Ebert Stiftung, 1993); Fetouma Benabdenbi Jirrari, *Marocaines et sécurité sociale* (Casablanca: Le Fennec, 1992); Latifa Akherbach and Narjis Rerhaye *Femmes et médias* (Casablanca: Le Fennec, 1992); *Femmes et éducation: Etat des lieux* (Casablanca: Le Fennec, 1994), Rachid Fiali Meknassi, *Femmes et travail* (Casablanca: Le Fennec, 1994).

18. See the interview with Latifa Jbabdi, UAF chairperson, in the weekly newspaper *Annachra*, no. 72, July 17, 1996. *Annachra* is published by the Jeunesse de l'USFP (youth organization of USFP), which is a strong defender of human rights causes.

Chapter 6
Mozambique
Nurturing Justice from Liberation Zones
to a Stable Democratic State

Luis Mondlane

> The Mozambican people have fought for a long time for the triumph
> of human rights. The victory represented by national independence is,
> itself, an expression of the fundamental rights of people and citizens.
> It has provided the ground for the enjoyment of human rights at the
> national level. Economic and social rights were extended throughout
> the country after independence.
>
> —President Joaquim Chissano, address to Parliament,
> December 8, 2000

The current legal framework for the protection of human rights in Mozambique represents an important achievement by the people of Mozambique. This chapter examines the present status of the protection of
human rights within that framework. I contend that national independence is the foundation for the protection of these rights. National independence is, per se, the enjoyment of the right to self-determination, a
right of the people that is enshrined in the African Charter, and a precondition for the provision and expansion of other rights for the people of
Mozambique. This chapter will assess the protection of human rights in
the context of the implementation of the socialist project in the first
decade after independence. It will also assess the status of human rights
in the present period—a time when Mozambique is in transition from a
planned economy to a capitalist market economy. I will argue that development is an important precondition for the extension of human rights to
every citizen, and across the nation as a collective. Extreme poverty affects
the enjoyment of rights in Mozambique; development, as a means of eradi-

cating poverty, can create the conditions of possibility for genuinely empowering citizens in terms of their rights. Additionally, the first and the second Mozambican constitutions are of critical significance in any consideration of the legal framework for the protection of human rights in Mozambique. The 1975 constitution chronicles the legal foundations of the new state. The 1990 constitution articulates extensive reforms in the political and economic spheres and, as such, is a new constitution rather than an amendment of the existing one. Hence, both of these constitutions signify crucial moments in the country's constitutional history.

Mozambique gained independence from Portugal on June 25, 1975, after a ten-year liberation struggle led by the Front for the Liberation of Mozambique (FRELIMO).[1] As the sole Mozambican movement effective in carrying out the Mozambican liberation struggle, FRELIMO was the only movement recognized by the Portuguese government as a legitimate representative of the people of Mozambique. Hence, the Central Committee of FRELIMO was the body that adopted the first constitution on June 20, 1975.

The first constitution established a one-party system ruled by FRELIMO, where the president of FRELIMO was inherently the chief of state and the commander-in-chief of the armed forces. The constitution, thus, established the unitary power of the state, in which the People's Assembly (the Assembleia Popular or Parliament) was the highest sovereign power holding legislative functions. In this system, the head of state was also the president (speaker) of the People's Assembly. The main feature of this system was that power was concentrated in the same hands, that is, in the same party (which was also the only party with a legal existence). The president of the republic, therefore, was also the president of the People's Assembly, the head of the executive.

The new state was defined as the fruit of a long resistance against Portuguese colonialism, the reward of the heroic and victorious struggle of the Mozambican people. It was a sovereign state: an independent and popular democracy. Some of the fundamental objectives of the new state included: the elimination of colonial, oppressive, and traditional structures; the creation of an independent economy and the promotion of cultural and social progress; the building of defense capabilities; the creation of an accessible and widespread justice system; and the consolidation of independence and national unity. A specific goal of the state was the eradication of illiteracy and ignorance, as a means of promoting the development of a national culture and character.

The 1975 constitution reflected all of these objectives and is a statement of a new beginning. Article 71 of the constitution stated that all previous legislation contrary to the constitution stood automatically repealed, and did not remain in force. Articles 1 and 2 proclaimed its sovereignty and democratic character. Additionally, the document was significantly different from the constitutions of other African countries that gained independence in the decades of the 1950s and 1960s. Most of these constitutions only contained provisions about general principles and power sharing with a limited consideration of human rights. The first constitution of Mozambique, in contrast, provided for a bill of rights. The bill of rights of the 1975 constitution entails principles of equality before the law, the principle of nondiscrimination, the principle of equality between men and women, and a set of economic, social, and cultural rights. The bill also specified that it was a state obligation to provide basic services and needs, especially to the less privileged sectors of society. It should be noted, however, that in this bill of rights, greater importance was accorded to collective rights than to individual rights. The same position was reflected in Article 8 of the constitution, which declared the land and natural resources of the country as state property and granted the state the right to determine how these resources should be used. Though the 1975 constitution had no section that specifically addressed the right to life, it can be argued that the Criminal Code in force, as per the constitution, did not sanction capital punishment.[2]

The actual implementation of the constitutional project resulted in considerable achievements in the political, economic, and social spheres. This amounted to applying—on a national scale—a political, administrative, and social organizational project that had already been piloted in the liberation zones during the liberation struggle. In 1965, in the northern provinces of Cabo Delgado and Niassa, the Portuguese authority began to be expelled from extensive zones—the liberated areas. In such places, colonial rule had no longer any administrative or economic power. Its presence was only signaled through bombardment and military operations. It was soon perceived by FRELIMO that the absence of colonial power did not eradicate other forms of antidemocratic authority exercised by Régulos (traditional chiefs), or for that matter, did not counter the oppression of women and youth in the context of traditional society. Simultaneously, new exploitative agents appeared to replace the colonists. I argue that the main impact of the liberated zones was the elimination of oppressive structures and the establishment of the people's power. The main social form of organization was collective. From farming to trade, cooperatives were set up in the liberated areas.

Additionally, people delivered justice in community settings. The central role of the people's court was to identify the root causes of crime and find out adequate mechanisms for rehabilitating or reeducating the offender. Reeducation was achieved not through isolation but through deepening contacts of the offender with people and their work. The idea was to liberate such offenders from influences leading to crime.[3] Experiences of communal justice nurtured in the liberated zones were applied throughout the country after independence.

Through the enjoyment of rights of political participation, hitherto voiceless sectors of society were able to express their social interests and, more importantly, act on them. Their contribution was particularly sought on issues that were relevant to their own lives and to their communities. Toward this end, women, young people, the elderly, peasants, and workers, in particular, were organized under "dynamiting groups" (*Grupos Dinamizadores*), forums where they could openly discuss their problems. Women's emancipation, in particular, was a key focus is of the new state policy. As President Samora Machel stated in his opening speech at the First Conference of Mozambican Women, March 4, 1973, "the emancipation of women is not an act of charity, the result of humanitarian or compassionate attitude. The liberation of women is a fundamental necessity for the revolution, the guarantee of its continuity and the precondition for its victory. The main objective of the revolution is to destroy the system of exploitation and build a new society, which realizes the potentialities of human beings."[4] The emancipation of the hitherto disenfranchised sectors of society was related to the state's goal of countering obscurantism. FRELIMO'S policies abolished traditional systems of authority on the grounds that these systems would cause problems, related to tribalism and regionalism, for the new state. Traditional authorities provided "nothing on which to base the foundations for a modern state."[5] For instance, the government took a strong position against traditional practices, such as polygamy, that women were subject to under traditional society. In sum, the process was one of building a participatory democracy, and thus dramatically transforming the status of the sectors of the population that had been marginalized in colonial and traditional societies. For the first time in the history of Mozambique, people participated in parliamentary elections. As a result, peasants and people from rural communities were elected as members of Parliament, the highest representative posts in the country.

Also in consonance with the goals of the program, the cabinet decided to nationalize private clinics and create the National Health Service, although, it was only much later, on July 24, 1975, that President Machel actually announced the nationalization of private clinics and schools and the creation of the national education system. Along the same lines, private legal assistance was also abolished. Nationalization enabled the new state to provide for basic services for the majority of the population, in accordance with the spirit of the struggle for liberation.

During this period, access to justice also improved through the implementation of the popular justice system. The first constitution set out the basic foundations of the people's courts and stipulated the independence of the judiciary, which were later regulated by the People's Court Act (Law 12/78, of December 2, 1978). (I will refer to this law in more detail later in the chapter, while considering the judiciary and the legal system.) While the fundamental law placed the courts under the authority of representative bodies such as people's assemblies at all levels (Article 69 of the constitution as amended by Act 11/78, of August 15, 1987, and Article 1 of Act 12/78), for the purpose of administration they were under the direction of the minister of justice. He had the power to appoint, transfer, or remove judges.

During colonial rule, the formal justice system had been limited to urban areas, serving mainly colonial settlers and a tiny minority of black Africans—*assimilados*. The majority of Mozambicans, mostly living in rural settlements, were governed by African customary law that was enforced by Portuguese officials (*administradores, chefes de posto administrativo*) who were sought by traditional chiefs and headmen to implement the law. The new system—the popular justice system—in contrast, drastically expanded access to justice across the country, by extending justice beyond the district level, and reaching small administrative divisions, communal villages, and headquarters in urban areas. This new system was shaped by the experiences of the liberated areas during the war for independence where people had taken a part in administering justice. Lay judges delivered justice, and communities elected their judges from among the respected men and women in the local community.

The new system was popular because, by setting up collective courts, it allowed people to exercise a direct control of the administration of justice. A professional judge (president) and a minimum of three lay judges comprised the court at all judiciary levels (district, province, and supreme). Below district courts and following the administrative divisions, there were courts at the level of localities, administrative posts, communal villages in rural settlements, and boroughs in urban centers. Lay judges, elected by the communities in which they served, made up these courts. Lay judges took part in both finding matters of fact and in determining concrete punishment. They reinforced popular control over the judiciary, thus ensuring the effectiveness, transparency, and impartiality of the courts. Additionally, they brought to the court system an understanding of communal rules and day-to-day experiences, which often differed from those embodied in formal or positive law. Popular courts also introduced an important innovation—assigning power to the attorney general to request judicial review regardless of the time elapsed, when court decisions amounted to a gross violation of the law or were manifestly unjust.

The socialist project briefly outlined above soon brought about tangible results in the economic and social spheres. However, the destabilization war, which began in 1976 (less than six months after independence) and lasted until 1992, destroyed Mozambique's economic and social infrastructure. Initially, the aggressor was the Rhodesian regime of Ian Smith. With the independence of Zimbabwe, the apartheid South African regime took on the role of directing the war against Mozambique. It is during this period that the MNR (Movement for the National Resistance, or RENAMO) was formed with the objective of continuing the war against Mozambique. As Joseph Hanlon puts it, the objective of foreign intervention was to destroy the dream of socialism, to convince the people that socialism was not an alternative to development.[6]

The war destroyed vital economic facilities such as industrial plants, hospitals, schools, population centers, bridges, roads, and the power line transportation system. Millions of people were internally displaced from their original homes, and equal numbers were forced to move to neighboring countries. This mass displacement led to the destruction of the social fabric. As families were torn apart, massive killings destabilized the basic foundations of the African family, affecting the culture and the structural organization of society. Such an environment, in which life itself is under threat, is inimical to the enjoyment of human rights. The result was a spectrum of violations of human rights. The nature of the political situation in Mozambique led to the adoption of legal measures that ran counter to human rights principles.

The New Security Act (Act 2/79 of March 1, 1979) is a case in point. It introduced capital punishment and severe imprisonment for crimes against state security and the national economy. The act also contains provisions for sanctioning acts that would be crimes under international humanitarian law. Article 49 of the Security Act stated that crimes listed in the act fell under the jurisdiction of provincial courts, barring when and where constitutional guarantees had been suspended according to the constitution. In other words, the article awarded competencies to common courts, for the trial of crimes against the security of people and the state. However, Act 3/79, which created the Revolutionary Military Court, stipulated something quite different. The Revolutionary Military Court was an exceptional tribunal with powers to try serious crimes without the provision of appeal for the accused. Article 23 of Act 3/79 accounted for the transitory character of the court. It stated that as soon as the Ministry of Justice assured conditions for the exercise of the competence currently assigned to the Military Revolutionary Court by common jurisdiction competence would be transferred to such judicial bodies.

The creation of an exceptional court—the Revolutionary Military Court—consisting of five judges appointed by the minister of national defense was highly controversial, since it called into question the objective of administering justice in an unbiased manner. In fact, the creation of the court represented a derogation of the principle set forth by Article 52 of the Security Act, which allowed for the judicial review of every case where capital punishment had been applied, *even in cases where the defendant had not appealed.* This competence was assigned to the People's Supreme Court. It can be argued that at the time there was no Supreme Court, but a Superior Court of Appeal. Was the military court, then, administering martial law in a nondeclared state of war? I have already argued that Mozambique was in a state of de facto war, whether this war was declared or not.[7]

It was also during this period that physical punishment was introduced (Act 5/83 of March 31, 1983). Apart from imprisonment, the court had the right to determine the application of lashing as a complementary sanction in cases where defendants were convicted of crimes contained in the Security Act, such as economic crimes, robbery, hijacking, and rape. This statute was phased out long before it was formally abolished in September 1989 (Law 4/89).

Legal Framework for the Protection of Human Rights

The Constitutional Protection of Human Rights

One of the most significant legislative measures taken by the People's Assembly was the adoption of a new constitution in November 1990. Stipulating extensive reforms in the political and economic spheres, the text is a new constitution rather than an amendment of the existing one. I will, hereinafter, refer to it as the 1990 constitution. The establishment of a pluralistic democracy and an affirmation of a commitment to a market economy are the significant changes introduced by this paramount law. In addition, the independence of the judiciary and its total separation from the executive branch is a central aspect of the constitution. The extensive bill of human rights enshrined in the fundamental text is also a core feature of the new constitution.

Equality and Equal Protection

Article 66 proclaims the equality of all citizens before the law and guarantees the equality of men and women. According to this provision, citizens shall enjoy the same rights and be subject to the same duties regardless of color, race, sex, ethnic origin, place of birth, religion, educational level, social position, legal status of their parents, or their profession. Article 67 stresses the right of equality of men and women in all spheres of the political, economic, social, and cultural domains. It may appear redundant, but given the discriminatory practices based on sex that still prevail in Mozambican society, which derive, on the one hand, from formal law and Western culture, and from customary law on the other, one can understand the need for such guarantees. In step with international norms of human rights, these constitutional guarantees bear testimony to the struggle for the liberation of women in Mozambique.

The Right to Life

Article 70 guarantees the right to life and physical integrity and forbids torture and cruel or inhuman treatment. As a logical consequence, it prohibits the death penalty. Additionally, the article asserts that human life should be lived with dignity and freedom, hence the relevance of so-called personal rights, such as security of person, privacy, and freedom of movement.

Freedom of Expression and Information

Article 71 deals with the right to honor, good name, and reputation, and the right to privacy. For example, this section prevents the media from declaring those suspected of criminal activity guilty before they are deemed so by a court of law. The right to defend one's public image is related to the right to freedom of expression and information enshrined in Article 74. Indeed, the freedom of expression and information is a concrete reality in Mozambique. After the adoption of the new constitution, the Ministry of Information does not control the media. Today, state-owned media organizations and privately owned ones operate with the same goal: to impart and disseminate information to people, for their benefit.

Freedoms of Participation, Assembly, and Association

Article 73 provides for the rights and duties of participation in public life and, thus, toward the consolidation of democracy. Such rights are further elaborated in Articles 75, 76, and 77, which provide for freedom of assembly and association and the freedom to form political parties.

Economic and Social Rights and Duties

The constitution dedicates one chapter to the treatment of economic and social rights and duties. The chapter encompasses the right to ownership, the right to work, to just employment, the freedom to form professional associations or trade unions, the right to strike, to education, to physical education and sport, medical and health care in case of disability or old age. According to Article 56 of the constitution, the right to ownership can only be subject to limitation (expropriation) on grounds of public need, use, or interest, as defined by law. It further states that in case of expropriation, a fair compensation will be awarded. Regulations on private investment deal with the matter (Law 3/93, of June 24, 1993). It is worth highlighting the peculiar characteristic of this chapter—it stresses not only rights but also duties. For instance, Article 88 states that work right and duty of all citizens regardless of sex. The importance of such statements does not need any justification. Through this clear position adopted by the constitution, rights are accompanied by correlative duties.

Procedural Rights and Guarantees

The provisions of Articles 82 and 100 guarantee access to justice. According to the former, a citizen has the right of recourse to the courts against any act violating his/her ordinary status or any of his/her rights recognized by the constitution. Article 100 provides the right of access to courts and legal assistance. Every citizen must have complete access to the justice system, irrespective of his/her social or economic condition. However, economic factors constrain the full exercise of this right. Mozambique is one of the most impoverished countries in the world, with 70 percent of its population living below the poverty line, earning less than US$1 a day. As such, when the majority of the population does not have decent living conditions, food, shelter, and clean water, there is no way they can afford counsel fees. In addition to economic factors, legal, social, and cultural obstacles hamper access to justice as well.[8] Furthermore, the state law that still prevails in Mozambique was forcibly imposed during colonial rule and, as such, is alien to sociocultural realities. Thus, since positive law is not in tune with the cultural context it applies to, it is not understood by the people. This has led to a crisis within the legal system and the judiciary—a crisis that revolves around the issue of the legitimacy of the law applied in conflict settlement or even in criminal cases. This is discussed in greater detail later when I elaborate on legal pluralism.

In addition, habeas corpus is one of the most important guarantees related to procedural rights. It is a constitutional remedy for unlawful detention. The constitution refers to ordinary legislation to deal with procedures. The guarantee is currently regulated by the Penal Procedural Code adopted in 1929 in Portugal. The provisions of habeas corpus were first introduced in the Portuguese Constitution of 1911, but it was only in 1945 that a regulation was approved to deal with the matter (Decree 35,043 of October 20). The preamble of the regulation states: "freedom without order is crime; authority dissociated to order is discretion." The constitution also provides for important guarantees of human rights such as the right to legal representation, the presumption of innocence until proved guilty by a competent court, and the independence of the judiciary. The right to liberty of movement and legal mechanisms for tackling unlawful detention or remand custody are the cornerstone of the adversarial model in criminal procedure yet integrate substantial elements of the inquisitorial system.

The Constitutional Bill of Rights and Public International Law

Although the Universal Declaration of Human Rights is not an international treaty with any judicial binding force for the international community, it nonetheless constitutes one of the main sources for the interpretation of the phrase "human rights" contained in the United Nations Charter. It also serves as a source for national court decisions when its principles are incorporated into state constitutions. This also holds for various international conventions such as the International Covenant on Civil and Political Rights, the Convention Against Torture, and the African Charter on Human Peoples and Rights. On examining the constitutional bill of rights in the 1990 constitution, one can make the case that the phrasing of some provisions is that of the Universal Declaration or relevant international treaties. The incorporation of international norms into domestic law (especially in the constitution) and accession to international treaties are concrete mechanisms for adopting international law. This incorporation entails important consequences for the protection of human rights. When international norms are integrated in the constitutional bill of rights, they are elevated to the category of constitutional norms at the domestic level. They become norms of paramount hierarchy in the country. As a consequence, they become justiciable at the domestic level.

Incorporation also translates as the obligation of the Mozambican state to respect existing international norms and to create the necessary conditions that will enable citizens to enjoy the rights provided for in the constitution. The Mozambican case is an exemplar of the current trend of the constitutional incorporation of international norms as a better means to the realization of human rights. This phenomenon is not new, nor is Mozambique a pioneer in this regard. However, it is a praiseworthy feature of modern constitutionalism in Mozambique. Thus, for example, Article 62(2) of the constitution establishes that the Republic of Mozambique accepts, observes, and applies the principles of the African Charter. Furthermore, in the definition of the main objectives of the state, Article 6(d) of the fundamental statutes provides for "the defense and promotion of human rights and equality among citizens before the law." By so doing, the state obliges itself to abide by these norms, and, at the same time, the citizen sees in them a powerful instrument for the defense of his or her rights.

Apart from the constitutional charter of human rights, the legal framework for the protection of human rights includes international treaties to which Mozambique has acceded and a wide range of ordinary legislation, with special attention to the prevailing system of penal procedures. According to UNDP sources, Mozambique has acceded to the following treaties: the Convention on the Elimination of All Forms of Racial Discrimination, the International Covenant on Civil and Political Rights, the Convention on the Elimination of All Forms of Discrimination Against Women, the Convention Against Torture and Other Cruel, Inhuman, or Degrading Treatment or Punishment, and the Convention on the Rights of the Child.[9] Surprisingly the International Covenant on Economic, Social, and Cultural Rights is not included in this list. The simple fact that substantial norms of the covenant are integrated in the fundamental text of both the 1975 and 1990 constitutions *does not represent accession to the treaty*. It can also be argued, contrary to this position, that the covenant has inspired the formulation of economic, social, and cultural polices in Mozambique. Indeed, a close examination of governmental programs carried out after independence demonstrates that positive steps in the implementation of rights enshrined in the covenant were, indeed, taken.

In my view, there are historical reasons for the lack of accession to the treaty. The covenant provides for the state's obligation to undertake appropriate steps toward the implementation of the treaty and for reporting to the UN system. Such measures require considerable resources that poor states cannot afford. Besides, new states that were former territorial colonies did not want to undertake obligations that had been decided by earlier colonial administrations. With the end of the cold war, however, and the dissolution of blocs based on political affiliations, such arguments do not hold. Today there is no sound argument for not acceding to the covenant.

An essential feature of democratic rule of law, which Mozambique has been striving to consolidate, is that along with the establishment of fundamental rights and freedoms, there is also an effective protection of these rights. In a just society the equality of freedoms and rights among citizens is a given; the rights guaranteed by the justice system are not dependent on the political negotiation, nor are they tied to social interests.[10] The protection of rights by courts is the most important form of redressing denied rights. Article 161 of the 1990 constitution, therefore, explains that: "It is the function of the courts to guarantee and strengthen the rule of law as an instrument of legal stability, to guarantee respect for the laws, to safeguard the rights and freedoms of citizens, as well as the judicial interests of other legal entities." Article 82 is even more explicit, asserting that, "all citizens have the right of recourse to the courts against any act which violates their rights recognized by the Constitution and the law."

The constitution is the fundamental law of the country. Every state agent and the state itself must respect the rule of law that is the constitution. In addition, ordinary legislation must respect the constitution. This is the reason why the constitution allows for declarations by a court that a given law is or is not in accordance with the fundamental text of the constitution. Constitutional control can be preventive or incidental if raised in a particular case that seeks scrutiny of the constitutionality of a legal provision. Article 183 of the constitution stipulates preventive control by specifying the entities that can request the declaration of unconstitutionality or illegality of any normative act to the Constitutional Council, namely the president of the republic, the president or speaker of Parliament, the prime minister, and the attorney general.[11] However, insofar as the incidental control of the constitutionality of norms is concerned, the common courts have the competency to decide on any issue that is prior to a pending case. In any civil, labor, social, or criminal matter, if a question of a constitutional nature arises that is different from the main issue, the court must deal with it before it can address the main issue of the case.

Legal Pluralism

The State Law and Unofficial Law

Mozambique is a cultural mosaic, including within its territory different ethnic groups, cultures languages, and religions. In Mozambique, there is a coexistence of the state law inherited from the colonizer with a complex set of normative systems of law ranging from African customary law to religious law.[12] Positive law in Mozambique, therefore, is based on Portuguese law, which was operative in Mozambique at the time of independence, but with some important changes that have been effected over time.

Portuguese law was imposed on the peoples and cultures of Mozambique. This alien legal system was sustained by domination and the force of arms. For the majority of the population, this law was, and still is, viewed as an imposition. The perception has always been that it falls short of the requirements that will grant it cultural legitimacy. A legal system in any society does not exist as an end in itself: its ultimate purpose is to bridge the gap between the values at the conceptual level and applied justice. Through the cultural dimension of law, the foundation of the law should be in line with the will and aspirations of the people. Moreover, its manifestation and realization must take place in such a way that can be understood and identified in terms of fundamental societal values.

The Legitimacy of the State Law

In Mozambique, there is a long overdue need for the law to conform to what is socially just today. The law being applied is founded in archaic legislation, some of which dates to the nineteenth century. For instance, the

Penal Code, approved in 1886, was conceived for a context that was starkly different from the sociocultural reality of Mozambique, whether in the past or today. After independence, the legislative authority did amend sections, parts of sections, and articles within laws. However, such partial amendments can cause severe distortions in the whole system, in the bargain neglecting the more critical aspects of the laws. For instance, the crime of arson is punishable with a minimum sentence of sixteen to twenty years of imprisonment. That is to say, someone who burns a hut worth US$200 is likely to face such heavy punishment. In rural communities, setting fire to a hut is a common means for retaliation in cases of provocation or even jealousy. In such a case, the disproportion between the action and the sanction against the action is apparent. It follows that people cannot understand the rationale for such a law. This particular sanction was perhaps adequate for nineteenth-century Portugal, in the wake of the fire that devastated Lisbon, but certainly does not hold the same relevance for life in contemporary Mozambique.

The inadequacy of the law is also exemplified by a custodial case in the northern province of Niassa, where matrilineal and patrilineal values are in conflict. In the case in question, a father had been transferred to Maputo and requested custodial rights over his son. The court ruled that custodial power should be granted to the father on the grounds of the best interests of the child, since the father was in a position to provide adequate health care, shelter, and education for his son. However, the mother's community did not comply with the court decision, since according to the matrilineal system the community followed, the child belonged to the mother's family. The decision was not enforced. The case highlights the urgent need for reforming legislation in Mozambique. The legal system needs to be replaced with another system that is based on values that are founded on an evolutionary African society, a system that fruitfully combines positive law with customary law.

It has been a long time since the law ceased to openly address the question of customary law systems and religious law systems. There is some acknowledgment of these systems, but the matter has not been given the status of a central issue. For instance, Decree 43,897 of September 6, 1961, was aimed at safeguarding the statute of private law for Africans. Article 1 of the act stated that "local uses and customs, regulating private juridical relations, both already compiled, not yet compiled and those currently ruling in *regedorias* (chieftancies) are recognized." In contrast, while the constitution affirms "the Mozambican personality, its traditions and all its sociocultural values" (Article 6), there is no recognition, in any part of the constitution, of customary law and local languages. Similarly, while the Civil Code of 1869 awarded a special place for local uses and customs, the 1967 code, still in force, is quiet about this matter. In regard to the municipal courts and judges of peace and their competencies in civil matters, Decree 43,898, of September 6, 1961, in Article 23 (1)(a), contains the following phrase: "To prepare and decide civil proceedings, whichever the value, as long as the applicable law is not codified uses and customs."

It suffices to assert that only a small percentage of the population has access to the formal justice system, leaving the majority to govern their lives and resolve conflicts according to the norms of customary law. Customary law must be situated in a dialectic perspective with formal law and within a context of constant social change. Such law systems often contain values that run against principles that are universally accepted, especially those principles shed in the constitutional charter of human rights. The equality of men and women before the law is a case in point. There is, thus, a need to eradicate norms of customary or religious laws that are contrary to these principles.

The Judiciary and the Legal Profession

During the era of the colonial administration, the judicial system only covered the geographical space corresponding to the provinces that had courts. The rest of the administrative subdivisions had only municipal courts and judges of peace. It was only after colonialism, that one could find professional judges in the provincial courts. In other cases, public servants like district administrators and heads of posts and localities were also empowered with judicial functions. At the top of the hierarchy, there was a court of appeal in the capital city, which established the relationship with the Supreme Court of Justice, based in Lisbon. At the level of the rural administration of justice, the function was exercised by a traditional authority, which applied customary law. This was the structure of the judicial system until the time Mozambique became independent. The framework was that of a hybrid judicial system, where the agents for the administration of justice were either magistrates sitting in the Ministry of Justice (and who were, therefore, dependent on the executive powers) or agents of public administration. It was a system dominated by the executive.

With independence, this framework underwent a series of radical changes with the implementation of a people's justice system that was extended throughout the national territory, based on the experience of the administration of justice in liberated zones during the freedom struggle. The 1975 constitution created, at the top of the system, the People's Supreme Court. This court, however, did not immediately start functioning due to a paucity of human and material resources. Law 12/78, of December 2, 1978, established the following hierarchy of the courts: the People's

Supreme Court, and provincial and district people's courts in localities and boroughs in towns. The people's courts in provinces and districts consisted of a judge appointed by the minister of justice and three elected judges, whereas the courts at the grassroots level were only manned by elected judges. The judges participate in tandem with professional judges in discussion of the matter of fact, incorporating a sense of popular justice based on their own experience. It then rested with the professional judge to apply the relevant laws for the case under judgment. The courts at the base, composed of elected judges who were entrusted with cases of small infringements or civil cases of regrettable consequences, often sought to reconcile the parties in the case and applied alternative penalties to imprisonment. They judged according to common sense, principles of equity, and the sociocultural values prevailing in the region.

Given the limited number of lawyers (judges and advocates) that stayed on in the country after independence, one can understand the difficulty of setting up such a system. The situation was made worse by the fact that there was no faculty of law in the only Mozambican university. A faculty of law was only established in January 1975, during the period of transition government. It was only with the efforts of the early graduates of this faculty that the system of popular justice could be implemented in the country.

The Independence of the Judiciary

The 1990 constitution has introduced major changes in the state system and, in particular, in the judiciary. It has launched the foundations for the emergence of a new judicial power that is independent from the legislative and the executive. The independence of the judiciary is the cornerstone of the separation of powers in a democratic rule of law. The constitution (Article 172) provides for a self-governing body of the judiciary—the Superior Council of the judiciary. The creation of this body, the separation of community courts from the formal judicial system, and the creation of the Constitutional Council are the most significant changes in the judiciary. Accordingly, Parliament has adopted two important statutory regulations: Act 10 of 1991, which pertains to a judge's functions, and Law 12 of 1992, which deals with the organization and functioning of the court system.

Apart from constitutional guarantees, the independence of the judiciary is secured through self-government and self-discipline of the judiciary and through material, financial, and administrative autonomy. Judges are independent and only observe obedience to the constitution and other statutes (Articles 162 and 164 of the constitution). Autonomy entails that judges are free from interference in the execution of their duties, whatever the nature (political or administrative) of that interference or the source of pressure (public opinion or pressure group). Judicial power is of a specific nature in the sense that, though exercised by distinctive individuals, it maintains, in every jurisdictional act, its identity, indivisibility, and plenitude. Judicial power cannot be delegated; on the contrary, every judge is representative of this power. Therefore, with the exception of operational or administrative instructions, superiors cannot direct judges of lower courts on how to deliver justice in a case.

The Superior Council of the judiciary is comprised of the chief justice and his deputy, one associate justice elected by his peers, four members designated by Parliament, two members appointed by the head of state, four provincial judges elected by their peers, and four officials also elected by their peers. This multisectarian composition allows the necessary checks and balances among the three state powers and also brings a diversity of perspectives into the organ. Additionally, the system opens doors and windows to both state powers and to civil society. Members designated by Parliament do not have to be lawyers or from the judiciary. In fact, just one of the presidential appointees has to be a lawyer. The system of appointing judges also enhances the independence of the judiciary. The Superior Council appoints judges at provincial and district levels. The president of the republic appoints judges of the Supreme Court after consultations with the council. The same holds for the chief justice and his deputy, but their appointment is subject to ratification by Parliament.

One could argue that the current legal framework appears to be very comprehensive and, one may even say, near ideal. However, what is imperative is the establishment of conditions for the full realization of the already established law. Both the state and society must collaborate toward realizing these conditions. As a means to ensure the independence of judges, statutory regulations provide for adequate housing, salary, medical assistance, and protection for judges (Article 53 of Act 10 of 1991). Yet, given the present economic constraints that Mozambique faces, it is simplistic to expect that all these conditions can be fully met. It is a rather tricky situation when a judge has to take a lift from a defendant or party in a case that is going to trial. If the state does not comply with the law in allocating the adequate entitlements for judges, that may jeopardize the independence of the judiciary. When the impartiality of the court is threatened, the legitimacy of the court system is also at risk. In a nutshell, the crisis affecting the judiciary and the legal system stems from problems of legal legitimacy that are compounded by the scarcity of material and human resources. It is reassuring, however, that the political will to tackle the situation is clearly present.

The Court System

The hierarchy of the court system in Mozambique includes the Supreme Court, eleven provincial courts, and more than eighty district courts. The provincial and district courts are still manned by one professional judge and a minimum of three lay judges. The Supreme Court is presently composed of seven professional judges and eighteen lay judges, who only take part in first instance trials. At the bottom level, there are a number of community courts functioning outside the formal justice system. This is a natural legacy of the former people's courts at the grassroots level, created by Law 12/78.

Courts are the bastions of human rights in the land. Courts are reactive rather than proactive; however, they provide remedies in case of human rights violation. Now, given that human rights are recognized and accepted by positive law, through their declaration in the "constitutional charter" of fundamental rights and freedoms, and through internationally accepted principles, they should logically be justiciable in a court of law. Hence, they should be used as legal arguments in courts, and, as a matter of fact, they are. What is absent, however, is a culture of legal practice where lawyers use such norms in their arguments.

The legal protection of rights is fulfilled, in principle, through every field of the legal domain. However, this protection needs to be both effective and timely. Given that it was only recently—about two years ago—that the court administration finally managed to provide a professional judge for every provincial court, one can imagine the long road ahead. What makes the task even more difficult is the fact that the country has 130 districts. It is a legal requirement to establish a district court in every one of these divisions to be presided over by a professional judge; currently, however, lay judges who have attended courses lasting six months to one year preside over district courts. Because of the shortage of trained personnel, a Supreme Court judge was appointed director of the recently created Law and Judicial Training Center. The center will administer inducting courses for lawyers joining the judiciary, courses for district judges and justice officials, and will also carry out social and legal research programs. It is expected that such initiatives will decrease the load of the Supreme Court.

As mentioned above, at the bottom level of the legal system, there are a number of community courts functioning outside the formal justice system. The creation of these community courts, through Act 4/92 of May 6, 1992, is already a positive, albeit tentative, step toward the recognition of customary law.

Like the former people's courts at the bottom level, the community courts handle minor civil cases and matters relating to marriages according to customary law. With regard to criminal cases they can handle only petty crimes that do not warrant imprisonment as a penalty. Community courts are the natural heirs of popular courts at the bottom level, holding the same authority and applying customary law prevailing in the communities they serve.

One of the most important criticisms about the law creating community courts (Law 4/92) is that it refers to customary law *only* in its preamble. There is no further allusion to it *within* the law itself. In addition, the law does not provide any room for appeal. It also sanctions the dissociation of customary law from the formal justice system and does not provide any avenues for the development of customary law. As a result, the formal and the customary law systems operate and exist as two separate and distinct realities, which work parallel to each other. This is obviously not conducive to an effective unitary Mozambican law. It is a task of paramount necessity and urgency to create legal entities that will enable citizens to resolve minor disputes within the communities; that will contribute toward the harmonization of the various judicial practices for the development and enrichment of norms of the customary law; that will consolidate various judicial systems into what may become a unitary and effective Mozambican law.

The court system in Mozambique still suffers from a lack of legal professionals. There are, more or less, four hundred law graduate professionals in the country, about 10 percent of whom are in the judiciary. The rest are in private practice, in public administration, or business in general. Additionally, legal resources in the shape of trained professionals are unevenly distributed across the country: about 90 percent of Mozambican lawyers are based in Maputo, the capital city. The Mozambican Bar Association has only recently been created and is still in the process of establishing a structure, protocols, and standards of professionalism. It was to remedy this situation that the Institute for Legal Assistance (IPAJ) was created by Decree 54/95 of December 13, 1995. Unfortunately the decree is nothing more than a repetition of the act that regulates the Bar Association, with the exception that IPAJ is conceived of as an "infra-bar association." Nongovernmental organizations have also been hiring law graduates or students who can render legal assistance. These organizations have undertaken a number of projects aimed at promoting human rights, including training paralegal personnel who do human rights work at the community level. However, a human rights culture does not come into existence overnight. It is a lengthy process that is the outcome of concerted and collaborative institutional, social, and legal efforts. Much remains to be done to establish a framework that can guarantee the effective legal protection of the interests of those citizens who have limited financial resources.

The Political, Economic, and Social Context

The Political Context

Elections

The 1990 constitution paved the way for a pluralist democracy, which enabled the emergence of political parties, as well as social associations and organizations. Act 7/91 of January 23, 1991, established the framework for the creation of political parties. As a result, more than fifteen political parties and independent candidates participated in the general and presidential elections of 1994—the first elections for a multiparty Parliament. The constitutional framework for the establishment of a multiparty democracy is irreversible. However, with the exception of the ruling party that was victorious in the 1994 elections, FRELIMO, and, to a certain extent, the major representative of the opposition, RENAMO (both of whom were signatories of the Rome Peace Agreement that brought war to an end in Mozambique), the recently created parties display serious structural problems that hinder their capacity to function. For instance, several political parties are composed merely of a small group of members who claim leadership of the party. These parties have no other members at the grass roots and no noticeable social presence among the electorate. Even RENAMO is still in a peculiar phase of its development, trying to transform itself from a guerrilla movement into an effective political party.

In December 1999, the country held the second general elections. This time, the electoral scenario was radically different. The Supreme Court, acting as Constitutional Council, approved two candidates for the presidential post. For the parliamentary elections, the two major political parties played the most important role in the process, as was the case in the earlier elections. RENAMO formed a coalition with some of the smaller parties and fought the elections as the RENAMO–União Eleitoral. This coalition offered the smaller parties the opportunity of parliamentary representation. In the first general elections, the international community had provided for a trust fund that allowed individual candidates and small political parties to compete in elections. (It is important to recall that the first general elections took place as the culmination of the peace process in the country, following the Rome Peace Accord signed in October 1992.) In addition, elections had taken place under the auspices of the UN peacekeeping operation as per the Rome Accord. In the second general elections, the cost was borne by the slim budgetary resources of the country. As a result, only the two major parties actually competed in the elections. Dissent and mistrust marked the second general elections. RENAMO claimed that the ruling party committed fraud in the electoral process. FRELIMO claimed that RENAMO had placed false ballots in the electoral kits and that people were caught in the act of placing those false ballots. At a certain stage, before the announcement of electoral results, RENAMO claimed itself victorious, but data conferred victory to other side. When the National Electoral Commission published the results, RENAMO appealed against these results in court. The court dismissed the appeal on the ground that it lacked material and positive corroboration to support the allegations.

The Impact of the Peace Accord

The Mozambican peace process that followed the Rome Accord is unique in terms of its character. It was marked by forgiveness, by placing a heavy stone over the atrocities and human rights violations of the past. In keeping with the spirit of this idea, President Machel personally met every one who was involved with or linked to oppressive colonial structures; these meetings were an opportunity for the public confession of crimes. Thousands of people attended these meetings where most of them reported crimes perpetrated against the civilian population. The idea, in the words of President Samora, was to liberate them from their past so that they could also be proud of being Mozambicans. Photographs of those who had committed these crimes were also displayed at their workplaces. The process, thus, was one of forgiving but at the same time one of curing the wounds and scars of oppression. The peace process clearly rejected former policies, in that it was not confrontational. The Amnesty Law covering crimes against state security and military crimes (Act 15 of 1992) is also true to this spirit.[13] It may be argued that such generosity can be interpreted as weakness, and an alternative solution, in keeping with contemporary political discourse, would be to focus on the issue of reparations. Yet, if we agree with this stand, one can, in the present, only *estimate* the *total* number of deaths caused by the war (one million) and the total cost in economic damages (US$10 billion). According to this perspective, issues such as identifying each person who was killed, when they were killed, and where they were buried would become irrelevant. This is a sensitive issue in the context of traditional cultural beliefs. People deserve to know where their relatives lie in eternal rest.

The peace process in Mozambique is an important event in the international history of harmonious conflict settlement. Since the signing of the Rome Accord, peace has reigned in the country. Peace is a precondition for economic development, stability, and poverty alleviation. It also contributes to the creation of an environment for the realization of human rights. The challenge is to consolidate democracy and the rule of law. However, consolidating democracy is a long and difficult task, particularly in the developing world where states' institutional capacities are weakened and a plural democratic culture does not exist.

The Economic Context

Mozambique is one of the poorest countries in the world, with a per capita income of about US$100. Recent economic indicators show a gradual and steady recovery of the national economy, which is moving at a 10 percent growth rate. According to UNDP sources, Mozambique is the fourth most populated among the fourteen member countries of the South African Development Community (SADC), but it has the lowest human development index. Life expectancy has decreased (to forty-two), in comparison with the first years of independence (forty-five for men and fifty for women). More than 70 percent of the population lives below the poverty line. War, severe droughts for several years, and floods are calamities that have made the situation more dire. Along with natural disasters, countless endemic diseases are responsible for taking the lives of many people. Malaria, cholera, and HIV/AIDS are major problems. The AIDS pandemic will kill thousands of Mozambicans in a short period of time. According to UNDP sources, the first case was recorded in 1986. In August 1999, government authorities estimated that an average of 600 to 700 people were infected daily with the HIV virus. This number is estimated to rise from 1.1 million people in 1998 to 1.9 million people in 2002.[14] The HIV/AIDS pandemic is also responsible for increasing the infant mortality rate and reducing life expectancy among the adult population.

Mozambique, today, is a country in transition from a socialist to a capitalist economy. This transition was flagged off in January 1987, after Mozambique had formally joined the IMF and the World Bank in September 1984. The destabilization caused by war and severe droughts had led to the collapse of the national economy. Industry was paralyzed because of a shortage of raw materials; sugar plantations and the textile industry were most severely hit. The crisis deepened in 1982–83 when aid and credit was cut off. After long negotiations with the IMF and the World Bank, the government adopted the rehabilitation program. However, the Mozambican government adopted the Economic Rehabilitation Program (PRE) without the formal approval of the IMF or World Bank, although most of its content had been negotiated with those institutions. This program is, in essence, structural adjustment "based on a package of 'de's: deregulation, devaluation, denationalization, decreased government deficit, decreased demand and deflation."[15] In 1990, a new component was added to the program—the social component. The program was then renamed the Economic and Social Rehabilitation Program (PRES).

The negative impact of these programs on the lives of citizens has been obvious. Mozambique moved from a situation where the market had nothing to offer and people had *some* money in their pockets to a situation where the market was doing well but people *could not afford to buy anything*. Basic social services like education and health were no longer subsidized by the state. Under the PRES, a special office was created with the aim of providing assistance to vulnerable people. The Gabinete de Apoio à Populaçao Vulneravel (GAPVU) rendered substantial relief to those in need, but it has been like a small drop of water in a hot desert. Privatization also put heavy pressure on the living standard of the majority of Mozambicans. The unemployment rate increased highly since many industrial units closed down or were privatized. In addition, IMF/World Bank polices led to the annihilation of national industries, especially cashew nut processing plants.

It is important to highlight that this structural adjustment program has been effective in curtailing the degradation of the national economy. However, the measures introduced by the program have resulted in an increase in the cost of life, creating a world of basic needs, which few among the population can afford. This significantly negates the positive impact of the program. Given that Mozambique has just emerged out of a devastating war, which lasted for sixteen years, it is also clear that the recent measures taken in order to revive the economy will have a limited impact on the lives of ordinary citizens.

The Social Context

Mozambican society is undergoing marked changes in its social and cultural values. One of most devastating consequences of war has been the erosion of social values, the destruction of basic elements of cultural identity and Mozambican citizenship. Atrocities that were common during the war and were responsible for the loss of lives have certainly eroded the ethical and moral fabric. Family values, such as respect for elders, were undermined when children were forced to commit atrocities against their parents, relatives, friends, and other people. Today the steady rise of the crime rate in all sorts of horrendous manifestations reinforces the fact that social values are in a state of deep crisis. This situation is compounded by the weakness of the state and law-enforcing institutions. In a recent interview with Ernesto Pedro Zunguza, a traditional chief at the Massinga District in Inhambane Province, I was told that the cause of the current high crime rate was the fact that soon after independence traditional institutions were marginalized. Ipso facto, popular control at the community level was drastically reduced. It was then possible to steal in the towns and hide the stolen products in rural villages. Zunguza also added that violent crime in rural settlements was growing due to a large consumption of drugs (*cannabis sativa*) among the youth population. Traditionally, only elders could take such drugs. In my view, this problem is only the visible part of the iceberg. It does indicate the presence of a complex problem that has not been properly addressed—the issue of the social rehabilitation of child soldiers, who are the youth of today, and the men and women of tomorrow. Consequently, values of African and social solidarity are today being replaced by individualistic and selfish principles like greed and the desire to make an easy fortune without work or sacrifice. A new type of hero now dominates society—the rich person. The means do not matter; but it is imperative that this objective be fulfilled as quickly as possible.

Corruption is another malaise affecting the social fabric. It is widespread to the point that a public agent *demands* gifts, often in the form of a significant amount of money. Corruption is not a new phenomenon; however, its ubiquity and the manner in which it manifests itself are truly alarming. The salary of a public servant is paid for by the contributions of taxpayers. But public servants still demand bribes from the public in order to fulfill their public duties. Corruption affects most sectors of the public service, including the court system.

The new and widespread culture of corruption is well captured by the popular saying "a goat only grazes from the grass around it." This pithy saying aptly describes the practice of officials, from the most junior to most senior levels, who misuse their public positions to obtain unlawful material or financial benefits. Officials often cause deliberate delays in rendering a simple service as a way of demanding bribes. Senior officials who are responsible for public service sectors covertly set up or engage in businesses, which operate in those sectors and are automatically favored in deals. Combating corruption requires a global plan involving the whole society. The government has recently adopted a plan to fight corruption through reforming the public sector. I argue that regulation and practice will counter the steady process of corruptive practices. Such an initiative thus requires detailed regulation of public authorities at all levels. State agents, the public, and civil society should know the full set of rights and duties of those employed by the state. In conclusion, the need to establish a culture of legality as well as a human rights culture in society is an urgent matter.

The judiciary is not uncontaminated by corruption. Yet, one has to recognize the efforts that have been taken to cope with the problem inasmuch as it affects the judiciary. Dozens of judges and justice officials have been expelled from the judiciary since the Superior Council of the judiciary was created. In all these cases, aggrieved parties had lodged appeals to the relevant authority—a disciplinary chamber of the Supreme Court comprising by three professional judges.

The judiciary is the last chain of law enforcement agencies. If corruptive practices do not work with police agents or public prosecutors, those who offer bribes resort to the judiciary as the last target of corruption. The parties willing to bribe the judiciary seek to obtain favorable decisions even when they have no case, to destroy evidence in the case, to halt the case, or to obtain a quick decision. The wide range of potential corruptible agents demonstrates that the problem is not restricted to the judiciary but is a problem of society at large. The 1997 Judicial Council session had addressed this problem as it applied to the court system, and the Chief Justice Mário Mangaze had made an important analysis on the phenomenon while addressing the Judicial Council.[16]

The Role of Human Rights Nongovernmental Organizations

Law 9/91 of July 18, 1991, regulates the right to freedom of association established by Article 76 of the constitution. The general principle that governs the formation of associations states in the first article that these associations will be nonprofitable and that their objectives will conform to the constitutional principles, to the moral, economic, and social order of the country, and that they shall not offend the rights of third parties or the public good. Currently there are more than two hundred different social organizations—national and international—operating in Mozambique. Included in this number are organizations of a professional nature. At the very outset, a special mention needs to be made of the Mozambican League of Human Rights and the Association of Human Rights and Development (DHD). Both organizations have been successful in the protection of the rights of citizens before the courts and the forces of law and order, mostly the police. They have been active in denouncing cases of abuse and violation of human rights as well as in offering training activities for paralegal activists.

The Human Rights League (LDH), the first to be established in the country, concentrates its efforts in seeking remedies for rights violations particularly when people from the less privileged sectors of society are the victims. The LDH has consistently denounced cases of the abusive use of power by the law enforcers, police and state agents. It has played a vital role in drafting a handbook for police training in the academy as well as the Code of Conduct for police officers. Police officers, professors at the police academy, and external consultants composed the drafting team in a project funded by the Danish Center for Human Rights. LDH has also created a paralegal network across the country that has enhanced its capacity to offer mediation, legal counseling, and legal representation for citizens. The Human Rights and Development Association has also made a seminal contribution to developing a human rights culture in Mozambique. Its operational field is training and disseminating human rights norms through an extensive network (Bandla). The DHD releases a monthly newspaper and is directing efforts to strengthen its capacity for attending to citizens' complaints. The Mozambican Association for Women in Judicial Careers (AMMCJ) directs its attention to the especially vulnerable groups of women and children. It focuses on cases of domestic violence. In the year 2000, the association dealt with 683 cases of domestic violence.[17]

Deserving equal mention are NGOs whose activities are geared toward the development of rural communities. An example is the Foundation for Community Development, which creates and revitalizes social infrastructure, including schools, that enable the rehabilitation of returnee communities. Also worthy of notice is the campaign for removing land mines, which works in tandem with the government to rid the land of mines so that people can farm with safety.

The collective scope of NGOs' work is wide-ranging. Their projects cover initiatives and activities relating to national reconstruction; the social and economic liberation of vulnerable groups like children, women, the disabled, and the elderly; actions for the strengthening and empowerment of communities for a sustainable development; actions aimed at combating hunger and poverty; and the development of the regions where they function. Yet, despite the significant achievements of these NGOs, there is not much cause for unqualified optimism. Aside from the international NGOs, the majority of local NGOs face serious financial resource problems. They also suffer from institutional problems, such as the lack of qualified personnel, which affects their performance.

There is thus an urgent need for redesigning and redefining the roles and objectives of NGOs. In fact, funding agents and donors have also been offering support, conditional upon the NGOs changing their purpose and objectives. In a situation where the state budget still depends heavily on foreign aid, NGOs also depend on international donors. The present context creates a stifling environment with regard to local initiatives. From my point of view, NGOs must offer solutions to develop internal resources so that they can be more proactive in funding themselves. It should also be mentioned that Mozambique's unique experiences of the peace process need to be shared with other peoples. A proper chronicling and publication of these experiences is definitely required. Social organizations constitute a powerful tool not only for economic rehabilitation, but also for the settlement of displaced people and refugees who were exposed to the war, for sustainable self-development, and for the progress of rural and urban communities. Their importance cannot be understated.

Conclusions and Recommendations

As discussed earlier, the legal framework in force in Mozambique establishes a wide range of human rights, namely, civil, political, economic, and social rights, fundamental rights and liberties as well as their respective guarantees. However, narrowing the gap between these fundamental rights and principles and their fulfillment and consolidation is a lengthy process. It is therefore necessary that every agent of the public administration be made aware of his or her sphere of responsibilities, powers, limitations, and duties, so as to avoid an abuse of the powers vested in that agent. Each citizen will also have to become conscious of his or her rights and duties to be able to observe and monitor their realization.

The protection of human rights in Mozambique is effected through the state law and the diverse systems of the unofficial law. A serious effort needs to be made to reform formal law, which has to be made more relevant to the sociocultural reality of Mozambique. There are several aspects of the positive law which are unjustifiably divorced from reality. Family law, especially as it pertains to the regulation of paternal authority over children, is a case in point, since, depending on the geographical region, either patrilineal or matrilineal systems have the customary hold. The succession law also calls for an urgent reappraisal. The Penal Code in force is another example. As mentioned, the code dates back to 1886 when a huge fire almost destroyed Lisbon. This incident operates as the historical rationale for the hard penalty (sixteen to twenty years' imprisonment) for the crime of arson. Again, it must be stressed that people often resort to setting houses (a house, here, would refer to a little reed-and-mud hut) on fire as a way of revenging a serious offense. This proves the irrationality of the hard penalty applied without distinction both in metropolitan Lisbon and in a rural setting in Mozambique.

Making the positive law conform to customary law in its variety of manifestations does not imply the codification of the customary law but, rather, the incorporation of its basic norms into the formal law. This may, in turn, ensure the expansion of legal assistance to a range of rights that are marginalized by the state legal system. For example, a wedding celebrated according to customary law, although socially recognized, will only be eligible for legal assistance if registered in the civil order. Such possibilities were made available to the people soon after the independence of Mozambique, but for some reason they were not adhered to or made accessible to citizens. As a result many married people are today single according to their official identity documents. The reform of the law should also include the restructuring of legal institutions. There is a need to reformulate not only the formal justice system, but also the institutions of informal law that apply and administer the customary law.

Education and training constitute the main ways of promoting and disseminating human rights. The proposed reform of the law should cover the way in which the law itself is taught in educational and training institutions. First of all, it may be appropriate to give human rights the status of an autonomous subject in the faculty of law at the Eduardo Mondlane University. Aside from just teaching the law, a legal education should enable students of law to gain a better understanding of the life of communities. There is a need to reorient the activities of students toward legal assistance and the defense of human rights. In addition, educational institutions should establish a closer relationship with social organizations in preparing curricula, holding seminars, and offering workshops and training courses on human rights. More regular meetings should be held with the involvement of NGOs and human rights activists in order to discuss specific aspects and common problems. Interuniversity contests in which simulated trials are held at the African continent level need to be encouraged.

The protection of human rights through courts needs to be reinforced. This will be achieved only when lawyers, judges, and public prosecutors master the pertinent legal instruments for human rights. Courts do apply relevant norms pertaining to human rights in concrete cases. But it is desirable that *all* legal professionals should invoke the norms of international and national human rights in their petitions. This would significantly contribute to an environment that is favorable to a human rights culture.

Yet, this in itself is not enough. It is also necessary that human rights education be extended to the national system of education. Every sector of civil society, religious groups, and the family, the basic cell of the Mozambican society—all need to be involved in this process. In Mozambique, such an aspiration cannot be realized only through the official medium of expression, Portuguese, but requires the use of local vernaculars as well. Relevant texts of excerpts of the constitution will have to be identified and translated into the local African languages that are spoken in Mozambique and disseminated in the communities where those languages are spoken.

It is the duty of the state, NGOs, and the civil society to empower people, especially the less favored groups—women, children, youth, and elders. Efforts in this direction will gradually enable people to enjoy equal opportunities in economic and social spheres in order to improve their quality of life.

Provided that human and material resources are allocated, rehabilitating physical infrastructure is relatively easy. However, healing the wounds and scars affecting the ethical and social fabric has long proved to be a difficult process. To maintain peace, stability, progress, and social justice, Mozambicans must engage in social reconstruction, regain their national culture and identity, and fully exercise their citizens' rights.

Corruption affects every sector of society. Everyone has a responsibility in combating corruption and preventing the further erosion of Mozambican identity. To achieve this purpose, a proactive attitude is required. To render effective the global plan to fight corruption through public sector reform, it is necessary that every citizen take part in the process. In addition, strengthening the state's institutional capacity to cope with organized crime and violence is the need of the hour. International assistance can be adequately used only if the domestic ability is first in place.

Social organizations need to combine efforts with other social groups within in the country, in the African region, and in other parts of the world. Cooperation needs to be fostered among NGOs working at the local level. There has to be better coordination at the local, national, and regional levels, based on the identity of social programs. These joint efforts must be consolidated and groups must set up twinning arrangements as a means of sharing experience, profitable use of resources, and institutional capacity-building for more active and effective interventions. The activities of NGOs that operate in the spheres of civil, political, economic, and social rights need to complement the efforts of the state and civil society. Although the Bretton Woods institutions (IMF and World Bank) are optimistic about economic indicators, the common citizen, who still lives in extreme poverty, cannot yet feel their impact.

The legal professions, namely those of judges, public prosecutors and lawyers, must be encouraged to develop professional associations in each country and to cooperate on a regional scale. There are already signs of initiatives being taken by lawyers in southern Africa who want to establish a regional professional association. A concerted effort is under way to integrate local judges in the Commonwealth Magistrate Judges Association (CMJA).

Finally, conditions are set for the establishment of a multiparty democracy, for the respect of human rights, economic development, and the prosperity of the people of Mozambique. However, one of the keystones of the democratic edifice is the political will to preserve the achievements realized until now. These must be crystallized through the relevant legal instruments as a testament to the peace that must prevail among humans.

Notes

1. Mozambique is a sub-Saharan country located in southern Africa and stretching along the Indian Ocean, with more than 2,000 kilometers of coastline on the east. It shares borders (in the north, northwest, west, and south) with Tanzania, Malawi, Zambia, Zimbabwe, South Africa, and Swaziland. Its total surface area is 799,380 square kilometers. The last census (1977) indicated that the population of Mozambique was 16,075,708. Recent projections made by the National Institute for Statistics, released in October 1999, point to a population of 16.9 million.[1] However, the distribution of the population is not uniform: 40 percent of this population

lives in only two provinces, Nampula and Zambezia, which cover only 22 percent of the total surface of the country.

2. According to the relevant article, the maximum awardable penalty was twenty to twenty-four years of imprisonment. Only the Military Code provided for capital punishment for serious crimes such as treason.

3. *Relatório do Comité Central da FRELIMO ao III Congresso* (1977), p. 44.

4. Samora Machel, "The Liberation of Women Is a Fundamental Necessity for the Revolution," in *Mozambique: Sowing the Seeds of Revolution* (London: Committee for Freedom in Mozambique, Angola, and Guinea, 1975).

5. Hans Abrahamson and Anders Nilsson, *Mozambique: The Troubled Transition from Socialist Construction to Free Market Capitalism,* trans. Mary Dally (Atlantic Highlands, N.J.: Zed Books, 1995), p. 84.

6. Joseph Hanlon, *Mozambique: Who Calls the Shots?* (Bloomington: Indiana University Press, 1991), p. 260.

7. Julius K. Nyerere, foreword, in *Destructive Engagement: Southern Africa at War,* ed. Phillys Johnson and David Martin (Zimbabwe Publishing House for the Southern Africa Research and Documentation Centre [ZPH/SARDC], 1986), vii.

8. See Luis Mondlane, "Access to Justice and Alternative Dispute Resolution," presented at "Building Justice, A Conference on Establishing the Rule of Law in Post-Conflict Situations," Vienna International Centre, 1998.

9. UNDP, *Human Development Report 2000,* p. 50.

10. On this commonly accepted proposition, see John Rawls, *A Theory of Justice* (Cambridge, Mass.: Belknap Press of Harvard University Press, 1971), p. 28.

11. A landmark case decided by the Supreme Court in its capacity as the Constitutional Council is the Islamic holidays case (Porcesso No. 1/96 CC, Acórdão do Tribunal Supremo de 27 de Dezembro de 1996). Parliament had adopted a law creating Islamic holidays. President Chissano held its promulgation and requested the Constitutional Council to examine whether the draft law was in accordance with the constitution. The court ruled that the draft legislation was unconstitutional on the ground that Mozambique is a secular state and for that reason there is a clear-cut separation between state and religious affairs. Consequently, by introducing religious holidays, the state is dealing with matters that fall within the religious sphere.

12. Albie Sachs and Gita Honwana Welch, *Liberating the Law: Creating Popular Justice in Mozambique* (London: Zed Books, 1990), pp. 125, 126.

13. This policy is also supported by the former amnesty law adopted in 1987 with regard to crimes specified in the Security Act.

14. UNDP, *Mozambique, Economic Growth and Human Development: Progress, Obstacles and Challenges.* National Human Development Report 1999 UNDP 2000. (Maputo: Southern African Research and Documentation Centre [SARDC], 1999), p. 69.

15. Hanlon, *Mozambique,* p. 123.

16. See the research project on the judiciary in Mozambique conducted by Boaventura Sousa Santos, *Conflito e Transformação Social: Uma Paisagem das Justiças em Moçambique,* a joint project of the Centro de Estudos Sociais da Universidade de Coimbra and the Centro de Estudos Africanos da Universidade Eduardo Mondlane.

17. Association for Mozambican Women Within the Judicial System, Report, 2001. Data collected from a special report made by Dr. Luisa Chadraca as a result of my request after interviewing her. The letter is dated April 10, 2001.

Chapter 7
Nigeria
Combating Legacies of Colonialism and Militarism

Chinonye Obiagwu and Chidi Anselm Odinkalu

This chapter examines the constitutional framework and mechanisms for legal protection of human rights in Nigeria. It highlights the current difficulties in enforcing human rights through the legal process and explores suggestions for improvement. The chapter comprises four sections. The first introduces the country and its political and constitutional history. The second discusses the current constitutional provisions and mechanisms for human rights protection. The third section examines formal institutional mechanisms, particularly, the judiciary. The fourth and final section deals with the social and economic context for protection of constitutional rights and the roles of civil society organizations. The prospects for improvement in the current transitional democracy in the country are highlighted in the conclusion.

Nigerian Political History and Systems

The Federal Republic of Nigeria occupies an area of 924,000 square kilometers. With a population of about 115 million, Nigeria is the most populous country in Africa. Its average population density of 107 persons per square kilometer is equally one of the highest in the continent. A major petroleum exporter, Nigeria is estimated to have earned over $300 billion from petroleum since the 1970s and remains the sixth largest petroleum exporter within the Organization of Petroleum Exporting Countries (OPEC).[1] The gross domestic product per capita in 1998 was estimated at US$310, compared to US$950 in 1980–1985, which is rather low for a resource-rich country, and below the average of US$315 in sub-Saharan Africa. In 1998 48.5 percent of the population lived below the poverty line and 37.2 percent lived in extreme poverty.[2] Adult literacy is 56 percent.[3]

The dominant religions are Islam, Christianity, and traditional religions. The official language, as a result of its colonial history, is English, but there are also over 250 languages of as many diverse ethnic groups. The dominant ethnic groups are the Hausa in the north, Ibo in the southeast, and Yoruba in the southwest, each with a population of over 10 million. The precolonial native polities had independent political, economic, cultural, and historic identities, but also had extensive diplomatic and trade links with each other. According to Jadesola Akande:

the institutions, people and cultures that eventually developed in the Nigerian region were the end products of long processes of accommodation and fusion of different strands brought in by different migratory groups. . . . As [they] began to settle down and consolidate in their present abode, they began to elaborate systems of governance which varied in style and complexity depending upon their geographical environment, available military technology, economic, spiritual and moral forces.[4]

The colonization of the Nigerian territory by the British imperial government interfered with the traditional political systems of the ethnic polities. By the late nineteenth century, the British government had introduced formal administrative structures in the colony. The territory was ruled under the Southern and Northern Protectorates with the colonial administrative capital territory in Lagos. In 1914, the British government amalgamated the protectorates, thus bringing all of the ethnic nationalities into one political union called Nigeria.

After the world wars, there was increased agitation by Nigerian nationalists for more political participation of the local population in governance. Gradually, the colonial government allowed the "natives" more franchise and more seats in the legislative houses of the colony. By 1950, the legislative house of the colony was dominated by Nigerians. The country eventually achieved political independence on October 1, 1960, and became a republic in 1963.

The colonial experience in Nigeria invariably affected its postcolonial legal structures. The legal system of the country, including its legal education and court systems, was rooted in the English common law. Nigeria's current legal and political structure has also been substantially shaped by the prolonged period of military rule in the postindependence period. Military governments ruled Nigeria for most of the period since independence. As of October 1, 2000, the country had been ruled for thirty-one years of the forty years of independence by military regimes. Prolonged military rule impacted heavily on the laws and institutions for the defense of human rights as the military regimes ruled by the force of arms with scant regard for the rule of law. On assuming power, successive military regimes usually abrogated the constitution and abolished the powers of the courts to inquire into any action or decision of the government.[5] Being unaccountable in this way, the military governments consequently perpetrated and encouraged public corruption and large-scale violations of the fundamental rights of the people of Nigeria. On May 29, 1999, following years of sustained local and international pressure, the military handed over power to a new civilian government under a new federal constitution with a bill of rights.

Legal Framework and Mechanism for the Protection of Human Rights

It is necessary for an understanding of the protection of human rights in Nigeria to highlight major landmarks in the constitutional history of the country. There are four stages. The first is the colonial period up to independence in 1960. The second stage is from independence to the first military intervention on January 15, 1996; the third, to the end of military rule on May 29, 1999; and finally, the stage of the implementation of the constitutional framework under the current elected civilian government.

The Colonial Period

The importance of this period in the constitutional history of Nigeria is underscored by the wide impact of colonialism on the postindependence legal and political systems. It seems a legal misnomer to speak of a "constitution" under the colonial regimes, because a constitution is, strictly speaking, the basic law of people developed by them for the social, political, and legal administration of their society. A colonial society cannot, therefore, develop a "constitution" per se. However, the term "constitution" is used loosely in this context to mean the fundamental or basic law for the arrangement of the political order.

The first constitution of 1914 established the formal colonial political structures and amalgamated the Southern and Northern Protectorates into the Nigeria state.[6] Laws were made for the colonies by the British imperial government and administered through the colonial administrators in Nigeria. The 1914 constitution established the legislative council, the executive under the governor general, and the judiciary. Under the judiciary, three classes of courts were established, namely the Supreme Court, the provincial courts, and the native courts. The Supreme Court was the highest within the colony, but its decisions could be appealed to the West African Court of Appeal (WACA), then serving British colonies in the West Africa region. Final appeals went to the Judicial Committee of the Privy Council sitting in London. The provincial and native courts were staffed by colonial district administrative officers who exercised both executive and judicial functions.[7] The legislative house, composed mainly of colonial administrators, had only advisory jurisdiction, as the power to make laws for the colony was in the imperial government of Britain.

In 1922, the colonial government introduced a new constitution to broaden the legislative house. Limited franchise rights and legislative seats were granted to the indigenous peoples. Of the forty-six seats in the Legislative Council, nineteen were elected from the local population and the others were colonial officials.[8] The political and legal structures remained as they were under the 1914 constitution.

Growing agitation in Nigeria and Britain for greater participation of colonized people in the affairs of the colonies, particularly on the heels of World War I, forced the colonial government to introduce a new constitution in 1946, which increased the number of legislative seats for Nigerians to a majority. This constitution also decentralized governance by dividing the country into northern, eastern, and western regions. The heads of the regional governments were elected from the natives. The division into regions was clearly along major ethnic groupings of Hausa, Ibo, and Yoruba. This also created the scene for ethnic political polarization of the country as well as internal ethnic strife between the majority ethnic groups and the minority groups within the same region.

The colonial government introduced new constitutions in 1951 and in 1954, though without major changes in the system of colonial governance. However, each constitution gave wider powers and jurisdiction to the regional governments, which also had their own constitutions. The 1954 constitution created the federal Supreme Court as a national appellate instance to replace the West African Court of Appeal which was about to become defunct. The old Supreme Court became high courts, which, together with magistrates, customary courts, and area courts were also created under the regional judiciaries.[9] The 1954 constitution effectively designed the basic structure of Nigeria's courts based on a bipolar model of federal (appellate) courts and regional (later state, and mostly) first instance courts.

Following intensified nationalist agitation and subsequent constitutional conferences between 1956 and 1959, the imperial government eventually granted the country political independence in 1960 with the enactment of the Independence Constitution of 1960. Toward independence, when the regional governments were introduced, the minority ethnic groups expressed fear of their domination by the majority groups within the regions and consequently agitated for separate regions. As will be seen below, the departing colonial government introduced the European Convention on Human Rights as Nigeria's national bill of rights in 1959 so as to provide constitutional security against marginalization of the minority ethnic groups by the majority groups.[10]

Postindependence Period Before the Military Coups

At independence, the first indigenous government headed by Alhaji Tafawa Balewa as the prime minister came into power on the platform of the Northern Peoples Congress (NPC), which won the 1959 general elections that ushered in the independence government. The political parties, and consequently the voting pattern, in the 1959 election were along ethnic lines. The parties were built around the three prominent political figures dominant in each of the three regions, namely, Ahmadu Bello in the north, Nnamdi Azikiwe in the east, and Obafemi Awolowo in the west.[11] Ethnic consciousness in politics was promoted and encouraged by the political leaders in order to maintain political control in their regions. The phenomenon of ethnic politics has remained in the Nigerian polity up to the present time.[12]

In 1963, a new constitution was introduced to consolidate the political independence and to turn the country into a republic. Despite its new status as a republic, the legal and political systems were still based on the colonial tradition and standards. This is particularly evident in the laws and the judicial systems, which were, and are still, dominated by the traditions of the English common law. For example, the rules of civil procedure, the laws of sedition, official secret, petition of rights, and so on, introduced by the colonial governments to suppress nationalist campaigns for self rule remain largely in force in the country.[13] After independence, the new regime that took over governance, and the subsequent military regimes, found these repressive colonial laws useful for their own political purposes and therefore retained and used them against political opposition.

Between 1964 and 1965, there was widespread civil unrest in many parts of the country following the general elections in 1964. Opposition political parties as well as the minority ethnic groups in the regions accused the ruling parties at the central and regional governments of rigging the elections and returning unpopular candidates. In the Western Region for instance, the civil unrest led to loss of thousands of lives. Consequently, the central government declared a state of emergency in the entire Western Region, and suspended some officials of the western regional government. This led to more crises and more loss of lives.[14]

The Period from the First Military Intervention to May 29, 1999

Following prolonged civil crisis that fell out of the 1964 elections, on January 15, 1966, a section of the military led by Major Chukwuma Nzeogwu staged a coup d'état and in the process assassinated the prime minister, Tafawa Balewa, and other prominent political leaders in the north and the west. However, no prominent Ibo politician was killed, and since Nzeogwu was Ibo, there was suspicion of an ethnic undertone to the coup. However, the leaders of the coup were unable to take control of the government. The then head of the army, Major General Johnson Aguiyi-Ironsi, who was not part of the coup plot, took over as the head of state.

Clearly, by then, there was general confidence in the army to redeem the crisis and restore public order and peace because what the army did was seen as a temporary and necessary measure to curb a failing law and order situation. In his inaugural address to the country, the then general officer commanding (GOC) of the Nigerian army disclosed that the armed forces had been invited to form "an interim military government."[15] In the case of *Lakanmi v. Attorney General (West)*,[16] the Supreme Court of Nigeria decided that the events preceding the "handover" of government to the military were not outside the contemplation of the constitution of the Federal Republic of Nigeria, 1963. While acknowledging that the manner of the cession of power to the military was unusual, the court excused it by resort to necessity. It ruled that being the succeeding military regime it was required to respect the constitution. Holding that the old constitutional order was still preserved in spite of the cession, the court continued: "[W]e venture to put the attitude of the Acting President and the Council of Ministers to the head of the army thus—'your men have started a rebellion, which we fear may spread; you have the means to deal with them. We leave it to you to deal with them and after this, return the administrative power of the government to us.' "[17] Thus, there was little or no apprehension from the civil population that the military would hold tight to political power after it had restored public order.

The new military government set up a ruling council, which promulgated several decrees abrogating the 1963 constitution and those of the regions.[18] However, in July 1966, there was another coup in which Aguiyi-Ironsi was killed, and Lieutenant Colonel Yakubu Gowon, a northerner, took over. Following the alleged ethnic undertone of the January 1966 coup and the July 1966 countercoup, there were ethnic uprisings in several parts of the country and the Ibos suffered heavy casualties in the north. Consequently, the military administrator of the Ibo-dominated southeastern region declared, on May 29, 1967, that the region had seceded from the Republic of Nigeria. The Nigerian military moved into the region to crush the secessionists, resulting in a thirty-month civil war that ended in January 1970. Over one million Ibos were massacred in the war, which also did extensive damage to the socioeconomic system of the country.

In 1975, General Gowon's government was overthrown in another coup and Major General Murata Mohammed became the head of state, but was assassinated shortly thereafter in an aborted coup on February 13, 1976. His deputy, Major General Olusegun Obasanjo, took power and organized a transition to civil rule that resulted in the establishment of the elected civilian government of Alhaji Shehu Shagari on October 1, 1979, under a new constitution. The 1979 constitution contained fundamental rights provisions similar to those in the 1960 and 1963 constitutions.

In December 31, 1983, the Shagari government was toppled in a coup d'état that brought in the military regime of General Mohamed Buhari. The new regime suspended the 1979 constitution and abrogated civil rights. On August 27, 1985, there was yet another coup bringing General Ibrahim Babangida to power. In 1993, after several aborted transitions to civil rule, the Babangida government held general elections but later cancelled the presidential result. Chief Moshood Abiola, a wealthy businessman and publisher from southwestern Nigeria, was widely believed to have won the annulled presidential election. He was later arrested and imprisoned by the military in 1994 and died in 1998 while in detention.

The annulment of the 1993 election by the military confirmed the apprehension of the civilian population that the military was not willing to surrender political power to a civil democratic government. There were widespread protests against the annulment across Nigeria and the government responded by deploying soldiers and tanks to the streets, killing more than three hundred civilian protesters. As the mass protest continued, the military leader, Ibrahim Babangida, was forced to hand over power to an Interim National Government (ING) composed of public servants and military officials. After just three months, on November 17, 1993, General Sanni Abacha, who was then head of the army, ousted the ING and took over power. The Abacha regime introduced draconian laws, abolished human rights provisions in the constitution, and unleashed a reign of terror on the country. The regime arrested, detained, or assassinated several human rights and prodemocracy activists, including Ken Saro-Wiwa, a minority rights activist, who with eight of his Ogoni kinsmen was killed. In 1995, General Abacha commenced a transition program to civil rule, but he manipulated the transition process to enable him to retire from the army to succeed himself as the civilian head of state. He cajoled all five registered political parties to adopt him as their joint and only presidential candidate in the election scheduled for September 1998. Happily for the Nigerian people, he died suddenly on June 8, 1998, of an undisclosed ailment. General Abdusalami Abubakar, Abacha's army chief, succeeded him as head of state. Following widespread local and international pressure for a quick return to civil rule, the Abubakar regime began a fresh transition program, which ended with general elections in February 1999. He handed power over to a civil government headed by Chief Olusegun Obasanjo, a retired general and the former military ruler.

Nigeria's military regimes were characterized by draconian decrees that infringed on the fundamental rights of citizens. The bill of rights was suspended by the first military decree in 1966 (the Constitution [Suspension and Modification] Decree No. 1 of 1966). Successive military regimes adopted this law to prevent the enforcement of fundamental rights in the country. The military regimes also enacted preventive detention decrees that gave powers to military and police officials to arrest and detain any person indefinitely. The decrees abolished the powers of the courts to review such detentions.

The impact of these measures on the protection of human rights in Nigeria is demonstrated by the decision of the Nigerian Court of Appeal in the case of *Wang Chin-Yao v. Chief of Staff, Supreme Headquarters*.[19] In this case, the court of appeal affirmed the decision of a high court judge refusing to hear an application for release of some persons detained without charge or trial on the ground that the ouster provisions in the state Security (Detention of Persons) Decree No. 2 of 1984, under which detainees were held precluded the court from exercising any jurisdiction. Speaking for the court of appeal, Justice Adenekan Ademola held that:

Section 4(2) of the decree suspended the whole of Chapter IV dealing with the usual rights to personal liberty, fair hearing, freedom of expression, freedom of movement, freedom of association, and such like rights. It has also removed the special jurisdiction of the State High Courts to adjudicate on such matters. It is my view also that the provision has the effect of suspending the issuance of the writ of *habeas corpus* without saying so. . . . It should also be noted that the abolition of the right of appeal from the High Court to the Court of Appeal is also taken care of by sub-section 2 of section 4 of the *Decree No. 2 of 1984.* . . . My view is that the combined effect of the provisions of *Decree No. 2 and Decree No. 13 of 1984* is that *on the question of civil liberties, the law courts must as of now blow muted trumpets.*[20]

In *Nwosu v. Imo State Environmental Sanitation Authority*, the Supreme Court of Nigeria described human rights litigation in the country under the military as a fruitless "journey of discovery." The court advised victims of human rights violations to rather pursue administrative remedies. In the words of Justice Salihu Modibbo Alfa Belgore writing for the Supreme Court:

in military regimes, decrees of the Federal Military Government clearly oust the court's jurisdiction, there is no dancing around the issue to find jurisdiction that has been taken away. Lawyers trained and groomed under the notion of civil liberties frown on ouster provisions in any act of parliament, so do the judges of similar background. But it must be remembered that the Armed Forces Ruling Council is not a parliament, neither does it pretend to be one. We have lived with their decrees (whether by Supreme Military Council or Armed Forces Ruling Council, in fact nomenclature is not relevant) for long enough now that there should be no doubt as to the meaning of their ouster provisions. Their decrees, they always emphasize for avoidance of doubt, are supreme even to the Constitution. *It is for that purpose that legal practice will attract more confidence if administrative avenues are pursued rather than journey of discovery* [sic] *inherent in court action in such matters.*[21]

Period Under Civil Rule from May 1999 to Present

The military regimes were also corrupt. They perpetrated and encouraged massive looting of public funds by government officials. The new civilian government in Nigeria has within one year recovered close to US$1billion from the family of the late General Abacha and from his associates stolen from public treasury and deposited in foreign banks in Europe and North America. Testimonies at the Human Rights Violations Investigation Commission (called the Oputa Commission after its chairperson, Justice Chukwudifu Oputa) revealed series of systematic and massive violations of human rights of Nigerian people by officials of the Abacha regime. The commission was set up in 1999 by the new government to investigate violations of human rights under the past military regimes.[22]

The civilian government of Chief Obasanjo came into power under the 1999 constitution, modeled after the 1979 constitution with a bill of rights in Chapter 4. Chapter 2 provides for the "Fundamental Objectives and Directive Principles of State Policies," containing statements of economic, social, and cultural rights, but these provisions are declared nonjusticiable by the same constitution.

Human Rights Provisions in the Nigerian Constitution

Origins: The Willink Commission

All constitutions in the country since independence contained bills of rights of similar provisions, the first being the 1960 Independence Constitution. The origin of these human rights provisions can be traced to the Minorities Commission headed by Sir Henry Willink. The commission was set up by the colonial government in 1957 to investigate complaints by the minority ethnic groups that the majority groups in an independent Nigeria would dominate them. The commission was asked to make recommendations on how these fears, if found genuine, could be allayed. The commission recommended the entrenchment of fundamental rights provisions in the Independence Constitution as a security for the minorities against discrimination. The commission noted that "while provisions of this kind are difficult to enforce and sometimes difficult to interpret, they should be inserted in the constitution because they define beliefs widespread among democratic countries and provide a standard to which appeal may be made by those whose rights are infringed."[23]

Despite the fact that the suggestion for the inclusion of a bill of rights in the Independence Constitution was made for the protection of the minority ethnic groups, there is no doubt that their provisions are for the benefit of all Nigerians. As Obafemi Awolowo, a leading lawyer and politician, said "the fundamental human rights [in the 1979 constitution] were ordained not for the protection of ethnic minorities as such but for the protection of the citizens at large against executive and legislative tyranny and excesses."[24]

The bill of rights in the independence and subsequent constitutions contained only civil and political rights and, with a few insignificant modifications, was a verbatim transplantation of the substantive provisions of the European Convention on Human Rights. As was the case with the constitutions of most new African states at the time of Nigerian independence, economic, social, and cultural rights were excluded from judicially enforceable rights. Professor Osita Eze explained the reason for the exclusion of these rights from the justiciable bills of rights thus:

The reason for the marked absence of socio-economic rights in African constitutions is often based on the fact that unlike political and civil rights which attempt to limit the encroachment of state and its instruments on human rights, they require state to provide material means for their enjoyment . . . since African countries are underdeveloped, it would be futile to encourage litigation based on infraction of socio-economic rights.[25]

Human Rights Guarantees in the Nigerian Constitution of 1999

The bill of rights in Chapter 4 of the 1999 constitution, covering sections 33 to 46, allows for the following rights.

Right to Life

Section 33 guarantees the right to life except in cases of execution of a capital sentence of a court.[26] In *Kalu v. State*, the Supreme Court of Nigeria affirmed the constitutionality of the death penalty.[27] The right to life may also be lawfully infringed in exercise of lawful arrest, or prevention of escape from lawful custody, or death resulting from use of lawful force for self-defense, defense of another person or property, or for suppressing a riot or a mutiny.[28] In the latter instances, the force used must be proportionate to the danger of the threat. The relations or dependents of a victim can claim compensation, despite the fact that the rights enforcement provisions in section 46 of 1999 constitution appear to be personal.[29]

Rights to Respect for the Dignity of One's Person

Section 34 requires that every person be treated with respect to the dignity inherent to the human person.[30] The Supreme Court has held that the right to humane treatment extends to prisoners as their convictions do not deny them constitutionally protected fundamental rights.[31] However, the same court appears to take the view that prisoners on death row may not enjoy this right. In *Kalu v. State,* the Nigerian Supreme Court pointed out that "inhuman and degrading treatment outside the inevitable confinement on death row gives rise to an enforceable right under the Constitution but it does not make the sentence illegal."[32] The provision also abolishes forced labor, slavery, torture, and degrading punishment.

Right to Personal Liberty

Section 35 guarantees the liberty and security of every person except in the circumstances permitted by law, namely, in execution of the sentence or order of a court, upon reasonable suspicion of commission of a crime, to prevent commission of a crime, for the education or welfare of a person under the age of eighteen, for medical treatment of infectious or mental disease, or for the purpose of extradition, or expulsion of an illegal immigrant.[33] This section also prohibits prolonged pre-trial detention or detention for a period longer than the maximum period of imprisonment prescribed for the offense. It also guarantees the right to silence; the right to be informed within twenty-four hours of arrest of grounds of arrest; the right to be arraigned within a reasonable time after arrest; and the right to compensation and public apology in the case of unlawful arrest and detention.

Right to Fair Hearing

Section 36 provides that "every person shall be entitled to fair hearing within a reasonable time before a court or tribunal constituted in such a manner as to secure its independence and impartiality."[34] This provision also prescribes the index for a fair hearing to include, in civil and criminal cases: right to public hearing and open decision; right to adequate legal representation of the person's choice; and right of appeal. In criminal proceedings, additional prescriptions include entitlements to: the presumption of innocence until guilt is proved; the right to be informed of details of charge in the language the accused person understands; adequate time and facilities for preparation of defense; and legal representation of the choice of the accused person. In cases of capital offenses, the court is under obligation to provide a lawyer for an unrepresented accused; right to adequate time and facilities to cross-examine prosecution witnesses; right to a free interpreter; right to access to the records of proceedings and judgment of the court; prohibition against retroactive legislation; prohibition against imposition of punishment not prescribed by law; prohibition against double jeopardy; right of silence during trial; and right not to be charged for an unwritten offense (this protects against criminal customary or religious offenses). These provisions apply to proceedings before all courts or tribunals, as well as bodies exercising administrative, quasi-judicial, or judicial functions.[35]

Rights to Privacy and Family Life

Section 37 guarantees the rights to privacy of communication, and life within a family.[36]

Freedoms of Thought, Conscience, and Religion

The rights to freedom of thought, conscience, and religion are guaranteed in Section 38.[37] This underlines the fact that Nigeria is a secular state as provided in section 10 of the 1999 constitution, which states that "The Government of the Federation or of a state shall not adopt any religion as State Religion" (section 38[2] and [3]). The constitution also prohibits the imposition of any religious instruction in schools. The recent introduction of *shari'a* criminal laws in some states in the north raises high constitutional issues with regard to these provisions.[38]

Rights to Freedom of Expression and the Press

Section 39 secures freedom of information and the right to receive and impart ideas and information.[39] Section 39(3) protects the confidentiality of sources of information.[40] The permissible limitations of this right include laws made to maintain the authority and independence of the courts, to regulate broadcasts and cinematography,[41] and to implement the Official Secrets Act,[42] a piece of colonial legislation whose compatibility with a constitutional guarantee of free expression is at best highly questionable. An access to information bill currently before the national legislature will expand the legal ambit of freedom of expression in Nigeria by circumscribing the permissible limitations under existing law.

Rights to Peaceful Assembly and Association

Section 40 provides that "every person shall be entitled to assemble freely and associate with other persons, and in particular, he or she may form or belong to any political party, trade union or any other association for the protection of his or her interest."[43]

Right to Freedom of Movement

Section 41 protects the right to freedom of movement, residence, and exit and entry into the country.[44] The right may be derogated in order to prevent a person standing criminal trial from leaving the country, or in the case of extradition of a citizen to face criminal trial or serve a prison sentence outside Nigeria. Under the immigration laws, foreigners are entitled to enter, reside in, or leave in Nigeria subject to administrative requirements for visas or resident permits.

One major corollary to the exercise of the right of entry to and exit from the country is the right of every citizen to his or her passport. It has been held in the case of *Olisa Agbakoba v. Director of State Security Services* that the right to obtain and keep a passport is an integral part of the right to freedom of movement, and therefore the seizure of a citizen's passport, except in circumstances permitted by immigration laws, infringed on this right.[45] In this case, state security agents seized the passport of the appellant at the airport on his way out of the country. He applied to court for the return of his passport and compensation. The trial court (High Court) dismissed the application on the grounds that a passport was a property of the government and could be confiscated or withdrawn at the pleasure of the government. The High Court relied on an inscription on the back cover of Nigerian passports that says the passport belongs to the government. On appeal, the Court of Appeal reversed the High Court and held that ownership of a passport, as an important document of international travel, is an indispensable right, and that the seizure of the appellant's passport inhibited his right to free movement.

Right to Freedom from Discrimination

Section 42 protects citizens from discrimination on the grounds of tribe, ethnic group, sex, place of birth, religion, political opinion, or circumstances of birth.[46] The section prohibits discrimination against anyone "in the practical application of any law in force in Nigeria or any executive or administrative action of the government." This provision has expanded the constitutional protection of women against discriminatory traditional or religious practices under customary and religious laws, as well as gender discriminations in employment by government. However, there are no clear provisions against discrimination on the grounds of mental or physical disability, or for reason of ill health or on ground that a person has an infectious disease such as HIV or AIDS. In a February 5, 2001, ruling, a judge of the Lagos State High Court excluded a seropositive plaintiff from attending to testify in her court case on the unfounded fear that HIV/AIDS was contagious.[47]

Rights to Property

Section 43 does not guarantee the right to private ownership of property, but merely protects the right to adequate compensation when private property is compulsorily acquired or damaged. There is no express guide-line for assessment of compensation, but the Court of Appeal held in the case of *Shell Petroleum and Development Company v. Farrah and Others* (1995) that the amount payable in compensation is the current market value of the affected property, including interest, damages and loss of earnings.[48]

Derogation from Fundamental Rights Provisions

Section 45 of the 1999 constitution provides circumstances under which the state could restrict the rights to private and family life, freedom of thought, conscience and religion, expression and the press, peaceful assembly, association, and movement. These rights may be derogated by "any law that is reasonably justifiable in a democratic society for the interest of defense, public safety, public order, public morality, or public health, or for protecting rights and freedom of other persons."[49]

Also the right to life and personal liberty can be lawfully restricted in periods of emergency or war, but the protection against retroactive legislation and imposition of sentence beyond legislative stipulations for offenses cannot be derogated from under any circumstances.[50]

Jurisdiction for Enforcement of Fundamental Rights

Section 46 of the 1999 constitution confers jurisdiction on the federal and state high courts to enforce the rights contained in the bill of rights. Pursuant to section 42(3) of the 1979 constitution, the then chief justice of Nigeria made special rules in 1980 for enforcement of the bill of rights in that constitution. These were published as the Fundamental Rights (Enforcement Procedure) Rules, 1980, and remain in force under and applicable to the 1999 constitution. The Fundamental Rights (Enforcement Procedure) Rules make provisions for speedier hearing of human rights cases than other civil cases by the courts. Under these rules, court cases for the enforcement of human rights go through a two-stage process reminiscent of the process for enforcing prerogative writs.[51] The first stage is an ex parte application for leave or permission to bring the proceedings. At this stage all the applicant needs to show is a prima facie case of a violation.[52] The court at this stage may also indicate any provisional or interim measures that it deems necessary for the protection of the subject matter of the litigation. If leave is granted, the proceedings can then be commenced within fourteen days of the date of granting of leave.[53] The rules provide for evidence in such cases to be taken predominantly by means of affidavits.[54]

Legal Aid

Section 46(4) of the 1999 constitution requires the National Assembly to make law to provide for financial assistance to any indigent citizen whose fundamental rights are violated, with a view to enabling him or her to engage the services of a legal practitioner. No such law has been made and no effective legal aid program exists. However, there is a Legal Aid Council (LAC) created under the Legal Aid Act of 1976[55] as amended by the Legal Aid (Amendment) Decree No. 22 of 1994. The LAC is mandated under these laws to provide legal representation to indigent persons, currently defined as persons with a gross annual income of not more than N5,000 (about US$37.88 at current exchange rates). This unrealistically low income threshold means that many Nigerians below the poverty line who are genuinely unable to afford legal service are statutorily excluded from legal assistance. The governing board of the council has recently recommended an upward review of this income threshold by 1,440 percent to N72,000 (about US$545.45), but this is yet to be adopted by the government. From its inception in 1976 until the beginning of 2000, the council had received 50,100 applications for legal aid, of which it granted 42,515, rejecting 7,585. In the same period, it completed 32,167 cases and by 2000 had a live caseload of 10,348 cases.[56]

Initially limited to providing legal assistance in capital cases or other serious criminal cases, the subject matter remit of the Legal Aid Council was extended by the 1994 amendment to include "cases involving the infringement of fundamental human rights as guaranteed under the 1999 Constitution of the Federal Republic of Nigeria."[57] It has a complement of forty-six salaried lawyers assisted by nine hundred other lawyers in private practice who work with it on a subsidized consultancy basis in casework across the thirty-six states of Nigeria and the Federal Capital Territory of Abuja.[58] Private practitioners who desire to work with the council apply to be listed on its register of consulting counsel and are assigned cases as and when necessary.

The legal aid scheme is also deficient because of the absence of the provision of legal aid during arrest and the interrogation of suspects. This is a serious omission in view of the right to adequate time and facilities recognized as part of the right to a fair trial in the Nigerian constitution and in international human rights law. The Legal Aid Act does not adequately fulfill the intention of section 46(4) of the constitution. It is grossly underfunded and lacks the required personnel complement to fulfill the demands placed upon it by law. The LAC's director-general admits that "at present, the Council does not have enough lawyers to provide a responsive customer service."[59] The work of the council is increasingly supplemented by informal or quasi-formal legal assistance schemes run by many Nigerian NGOs. However, the complementarity of the council and the NGO schemes is yet to be optimized in the absence of mechanisms for coordination and burden-sharing between them.

Economic, Social, and Cultural Rights

As noted above, Chapter 2 of the 1999 constitution contains provides for a number of economic, social, and cultural rights (ESCRs). Section 6(6)(c) prohibits judicial enforcement of the provisions of Chapter 2 but section 13 of the same constitution, itself part of Chapter 2, requires that "it shall be the duty and responsibility of all organs of government, and all authorities and persons exercising legislative, executive or judicial powers, to conform to, observe and apply the provisions of this chapter." The courts in Nigeria have held that section 6(6)(c) trumps section 13, finding the economic, social, and cultural rights in the Fundamental Objectives and Directive Principles of State Policy to be nonjusticiable.[60] This contrasts unfavorably with the situation in other African countries such as Ghana and Uganda with similar provisions whose courts have found means to provide judicial oversight of the implementation of Chapter 2 rights.[61] Some of the provisions of Chapter 2 include the "rights" to political participation (section 14[2][a]), security and welfare (14[2][b]), adequate shelter and residence (15[6][d] and 16[2][d]), protection from corruption and abuse of power (15[5]), equal opportunities (17[2] and 16[1][a]), social and economic development and equitable distribution of national wealth (16[1][c] and [2][a]), protection from exploitation of natural resources other than for the good of the community (17[1][d]), employment and adequate means of livelihood (17[3][a] and [b]), adequate medical and health facilities (17[3][c] and [d]), protection of children, young persons, and the aged against exploitation and neglect (17[3][f]), public assistance to persons in need and victims of crime(17[3][g]),[62] free and compulsory education (18[1] and [2]).

Human Rights Provisions Under the African Charter on Human and Peoples' Rights

Nigeria ratified and incorporated the charter into its laws in 1983 by virtue of the African Charter on Human and Peoples' Rights (Ratification and Enforcement) Act.[63] The charter contains civil and political rights as in the constitution, as well as a number of economic, social, and cultural rights. The latter include the right to work under equitable and satisfactory conditions (Article 15), right to health (Article 16), right to education (Article 17), right of the aged and disabled persons to special protection (Article 18[4]), right against the domination of a people by another (Article 19), right of a people to existence and self-determination (Article 20), right of a people to the benefit of their wealth and natural resources (Article 21), right to economic, social, and cultural development (Article 22), and right to a satisfactory environment (Article 24).[64] The human rights provisions in the charter are part of the Nigerian laws and can be enforced through any of the rules of procedure of the courts.[65] However, the Supreme Court held in *Gani Fawehinmi v. General Sanni Abacha* that the provisions of the charter cannot override those of the constitution.[66] It therefore appears that inasmuch as the constitution makes provisions similar to those in the charter for economic, social, and cultural rights but declared those rights as nonjusticiable, these rights cannot be judicially enforced by virtue of their being provided for in the charter. In other words, the charter, even though it has been domesticated, cannot introduce justiciable rights that the constitution has declared nonjusticiable. This means that where there is an application for judicial enforcement of economic, social, and cultural rights in the African Charter, the application could be challenged by the nonjusticiability provision in the constitution, as enforcing these rights would also mean enforcing Chapter 2 rights through the charter. However, it can be argued that the charter, being a statute of its own, stands on its own legs, and its provisions can be enforced without the ouster provision of section 6(6)(c) of the constitution. This issue has not yet been canvassed in Nigerian courts. There is, however, no doubt that the domestication of the African Charter, and hopefully its judicial interpretation and application, will assist in the development of the human rights law in Nigeria.

Human Rights Under the Military Governments

Although Nigeria is now under a civil constitutional government, it is important to highlight the problem of the protection and promotion of human rights under the past military regimes. This is not only because Nigerian society still suffers from the long-term effects of the military regimes, but also, more important, because most of the legal and institutional structures of those military regimes are still in place.

Successive military governments suspended and abrogated the fundamental rights provisions in the various constitutions that they overthrew. They did this in two ways. First, they would enact decrees suspending the part of the constitution that contained the bill of rights. (See the various Constitution (Suspension and Modification) Decrees, Nos. 1 of 1966, 1 of 1984, and 107 of 1993.) Second, they abrogated judicial review of acts done under any decree and prohibited powers of the courts to entertain complaints concerning the breach of fundamental rights by the executive.

For instance, section 1(2) of the Federal Military Government (Supremacy of Powers) Decree No. 12 of 1994 provided that:

(i). No civil proceedings shall lie or be instituted in any court for or on account of or in respect of any act, matter or thing done or purported to be done or pursuant to any Decree or Edict and if such proceedings are instituted before, on or after the commencement of this Decree the proceedings shall abate, be discharged and made void;

(ii). The question whether any provision of Chapter IV of the Constitution of the Federal Republic of Nigeria 1979 has been, is being or would be contravened by anything done or purported to be done in pursuance of any Decree shall not be inquired into in any court of law and accordingly, no provision of the Constitution shall apply in respect of any such question.

In spite of such an awesome ouster of court jurisdiction, some of the courts still managed to pronounce on the rights of the people. The attitude of the courts was to go beyond the ouster clause, in an attempt to see that what was called for under the decree was done properly and within powers conferred by the decree. And so, through their interpretative jurisdiction, the courts in a few cases upheld fundamental rights. For example, in the case of *Guardian Newspapers Ltd. v. Attorney General of the Federation,* the court of appeal struck down a media censorship decree that proscribed titles of the Guardian Newspapers because the proscription did not follow the procedure in the decree.[67] In *Okaroafor v. Miscellaneous Offences Tribunal,* the proceedings of a military tribunal were annulled by the courts because the tribunal did not comply with the trial time frame set by a military decree.[68] However, even when courts gave decisions for redress of violation of rights, it was difficult to enforce such decisions because the military regimes would not obey court orders.[69] They would simply ignore the court order or punish the judge who gave the order.[70] In one instance in 1995, the military administrator of Akwa Ibom State in the Niger delta suspended a State High Court judge by executive fiat and withdrew his police orderly and him from his official residence because the judge issued a garnishee order against the government in enforcement of a judgment obtained by a contractor against the state government. To protest this, lawyers in the Ikeja branch of the Nigerian Bar Association withdrew their services from the courts on July 17, 1995.[71]

International Human Rights Treaties and Norms and
Record of Nigerian Ratification

Nigeria, like other common law countries, has a dualist system with regard to the domestic application of international laws. An international treaty has to be ratified by the executive and domesticated by local legislation before it can be domestically enforceable. Section 12 of the 1999 constitution provides that "no treaty between the Federation and any other country shall have the force of law except to the extent to which such treaty has been enacted into law by the National Assembly."

Even if an international treaty or norm has not been domesticated, a judge is allowed by the common law rules of *stare decisis* to seek guidance from such a norm or from a comparative jurisprudence or authority where such a norm has been applied or interpreted. In *Ogugu v. State*, the Supreme Court held that:

It has long been the cardinal principle of our constitutional law that on account of the unique character and diversity of our constitution, the courts should always endeavor to find solutions to constitutional questions within the Constitution through its interpretation but the courts may seek guidance as persuasive authorities from the decisions of the courts of other common law jurisdictions on the interpretation and construction of the provisions of their Constitution which are in pari materia with the relevant provisions of our Constitution.[72]

By November 1, 2000, Nigeria had ratified the International Covenant on Civil and Political Rights (ICCPR); International Covenant on Economic, Social, and Cultural Rights (ICESCR); the Convention on the Elimination of All Forms of Racial Discrimination (CERD), Convention on the Elimination of All Forms of Discrimination Against Women (CEDAW); the Convention on the Rights of the Child (CRC); the Geneva convention relating to the status of refugees and its 1967 protocol; the Slavery Conventions of 1926 and 1956; and the four 1949 Geneva conventions and their additional protocols of 1977. With regard to labor rights treaties, Nigeria has ratified the Forced Labor Convention (No. 29), the Freedom of Association and Protection of the Rights to Organize Convention (No. 87), and the Right to Organize and Collective Bargaining Convention (No. 98).[73] In addition, Nigeria had signed, but not ratified, the Convention Against Torture and Other Cruel, Inhuman, or Degrading Treatment or Punishment (CAT) as well as the Convention on the Prevention and Punishment of the Crime of Genocide. On the African regional level, Nigeria has ratified and domesticated the African Charter on Human and Peoples' Rights and has signed but not ratified the African Charter on the Rights and Welfare of the Child, nor the optional protocols to the African Charter on Human and Peoples' Rights on the establishment of an African Court on Human and Peoples' Rights.

Nigeria has not submitted to any of the implementation mechanisms of the international treaties. Similarly, it has failed to ratify the Statute of the International Criminal Court, nor has it accepted the supervising mechanisms under the first optional protocol to the ICCPR, the optional protocols to the CEDAW and CRC, and under the CERD. Nigeria has also not ratified the second Optional Protocol to the ICCPR aimed at the abolition of the death penalty. On the contrary, Nigeria's constitution still upholds the death penalty,[74] though its use has been reduced since the new civilian regime assumed power in May 1999.

Constraints on the Legal Protection of Human Rights in Nigeria

Constraints on the legal protection of human rights in Nigeria include the deficiencies in the substantive provisions of the bill of rights and other laws, the inadequate procedural rules for enforcement of rights, the impact of prolonged military rule on the rule of law and institutions for protecting and upholding it, and the elitist nature of the legal systems in the country arising from its colonial antecedents.

Substantive Law Deficiencies

One major deficiency in the bill of rights in Nigeria is that the rights in Chapter 4 of the constitution have several clawbacks or grounds for derogation. For instance, the right to life can be limited for reasons of defense of persons and properties or for suppression of civil protests or arrests of suspects. The right to personal liberty may similarly be limited for the purpose of securing an individual's extradition or alien repatriation, or for effecting one's arrest on suspicion of having committed a capital offense. Another major deficiency is the nonjusticiability of the economic, social, and cultural rights in Chapter 2 of the 1999 constitution. The provisions on ESCRs are no doubt important in the enjoyment of civil and political rights. In a country with a predominantly poor population such as Nigeria, these rights are fundamental to the well-being of the average person and to the effective enjoyment of even the civil and political rights.

Another constraint on legal enforcement of human rights is the restriction of enforcement proceedings to the high court. The procedures of the high courts and other superior courts of record are complex and expensive, and the services of lawyers are required to litigate cases in these courts, unlike in the magistrate and customary/area courts of summary jurisdiction in which the procedures are simpler, cheaper, and less technical. Not many people can afford the cost of legal representation or of litigating cases at the high courts. The absence of an effective legal aid scheme means that many victims cannot afford to seek redress for the violations of their rights.

Technicalities and Deficient Rules of Procedure

A technical constraint on the legal protection of human rights is the statutory requirement of notice before action against government bodies. Several laws require that suits against government agencies be preceded by notice of the suit to the agency.[75] The pre-action notice rule limits access to the courts and restricts the principle of equality before the law. Most times in an action to forestall a violation by a government agency, the breach would have been completed before the expiration of the notice and the legal suit.

The Fundamental Rights (Enforcement Procedure) Rules of 1979 have not adequately achieved the legislative purpose of speeding up fundamental rights proceedings.[76] Under the rules, an applicant must first apply for leave of court and show prima facie proof of the breach of right complained of before he or she could apply to enforce the rights. This requirement of pre-action leave of court creates extra burden to human rights cases

Human rights cases, like other suits, are usually protracted for several months, sometimes even years, because the courts are congested. In Lagos State, for example, a high court judge has an average of one hundred cases in his or her daily cause lists, or more than five hundred cases weekly. The working facilities of the courts are deteriorating or not available. Judges still take notes of proceedings in longhand, and, in some cases, there is no electric power, or even stationery and other amenities in the court premises. An average suit for enforcement of human rights may take between one and two years to conclude at trial court, and two to three years on appeal to the court of appeal and about the same or longer period for a further appeal to the Supreme Court, assuming the parties have the money to proceed to the highest court.

Absence of a Culture of Respect for the Rule of Law

Perhaps the most enduring impediment to the protection of human rights in Nigeria under the military regimes, and even under the present civil government, is the absence of a culture of constitutionalism and the rule of law. In order to understand this phenomenon and the lingering impact of the prolonged military government on the protection and promotion of human rights in the country, it is important to discuss the problems as they existed under the military regimes. The phenomenon of impunity and unconstitutionalism under the military manifested itself in three major ways: unstable constitutional development, absence of a clear separation of powers, and disobedience of court orders by the regimes.

Successive military regimes stultified the development of constitutionalism in Nigeria by promulgating decrees that abrogated the application of the constitution, particularly its fundamental rights provisions. Every new regime modified or suspended the constitution and introduced draconian decrees. All eight military regimes that ruled Nigeria since independence have put the constitution on hold.[77] Three of them drafted new constitutions. Since independence, there have been six constitutions, in 1960, 1963, 1979, 1989, 1995, and 1999. The 1989 (Babangida regime) and the 1995 (Abacha regime) constitutions were not put in use because the transition programs they intended to usher in never came into being.

One obstacle to the legal protection of human rights in Nigeria under the military governments was the disregard of court proceedings and disobedience of court orders by the executive. A Supreme Court judge once referred to this attitude as "executive lawlessness."[78] In some instances, judicial summons and court orders were simply ignored. In other cases, the executive would simply disregard due process in carrying out action that affected the fundamental rights of citizens. For example, in 1990, the Lagos State government demolished Maroko settlement and displaced about 300,000 residents of the community. No proper statutory notices were given, and the demolition went on despite an application for injunction to stop the demolition pending at the Lagos High Court.[79] Also in 1995, the government demolished houses in the town of Aja, despite a court injunction restraining such demolition. The military governments set themselves and their actions far above the law of the land. They would not obey any rules, not even their own laws.

This phenomenon is still taking place in the new administration in the country. In reality, there has been little change now from the situation under the military in the attitude of law enforcement and security officials in dealing with the fundamental rights of citizens. The widespread civil conflicts arising from religious and ethnic differences result in violations of rights. Many state governments have introduced *shari'a* criminal laws with considerable negative impact on peace and security of the communities. Between February and October 2000, more than one thousand persons died from ethnic and religious conflicts in various parts of the country. The present civilian government, like its military predecessors, has failed or refused to create the atmosphere and opportunity for the diverse ethnic, religious, and other groups in Nigeria to dialogue and fashion out a universally acceptable political system for the country. Many civil society groups have consistently called for the convocation of a national conference of all ethnic nationalities in Nigeria to enable all groups to (re)negotiate a mutually acceptable political and constitutional structure of governance in the country.[80]

Access to the Courts

Another major constraint on the legal protection of human rights in Nigeria is the limit on access to the courts for the enforcement of human rights by the strict rule of *locus standi,* or the capacity to sue. Before a person can maintain a suit, he or she must disclose his or her personal interest in the matter, as was ruled in the case of *Adesanya v. President.*[81] There are two major obstacles posed by this strict interpretation of *locus standi.* First, a human rights NGO or an individual activist can not sue to enforce generic or group rights because it would be difficult to show under those circumstances a special interest in such a matter to meet the requirements of the *Adesanya* rule. The second obstacle is that individual victims who are required to disclose a sufficient personal interest in the matter rarely succeed because personal interest, defined as interest over and above that of the general public, is difficult to prove where the alleged violation also affects other members of the public.[82]

Judicial misconceptions of the decision of the Supreme Court in the *Adesanya* case have largely frustrated the enforcement of fundamental rights through public interest litigation.[83] It is commonly believed that the *Adesanya* case allowed for a single test for *locus standi* in all circumstances, namely, disclosure of personal interest over and above other persons affected by the injury. But it appears from the totality of the judgment in the case that this is not so. There may be room for a plaintiff to sue where he or she can disclose "legitimate interest" in the subject matter even though the injury he or she suffers is not different from the injury suffered by other persons. This may allow a group or an activist with professional interest in a subject matter to sue on that issue. This liberal interpretation of *locus standi* will encourage public interest litigation and therefore facilitate the development of public law in the country.

Constraints Arising from Colonial History

The colonial history of Nigeria, as is the case of many other former colonies in Africa, impacts considerably on the regime of the legal protection of human rights. First, the rules of evidence and procedure as well as several pieces of legislation introduced by the colonial government are still in force in Nigeria.[84] Most of these rules and laws have not been reviewed after several years of independence or modified to reflect the realities of postindependence Nigeria and the current demands of justice, even though their equivalent provisions in England have been amended and updated many times. Most of the rules of court were made when the quantity of litigation was small. By 1961, when the present rules of court were introduced, a Lagos High Court judge heard about six cases weekly. Today, the same court lists over up to five hundred cases in a week. Moreover, the court facilities are deteriorating. Because the rules (and the general law) have not kept up with the changes in society, law enforcement and the judicial processes have become overstretched and overburdened, the therefore unable to respond to the demands of the society.

Another colonial influence on the legal system is in the urban and elitist nature of the judicial process and the legal profession. Following the colonial political and administrative structures, postindependence facilities for legal enforcement are largely elitist, overly complex, and only available in urban areas. Nigeria's judicial structure divides each state into judicial divisions and magisterial or area court districts. The high courts, the magistrate, and area courts are in the judicial divisional headquarters, and these are usually the former colonial administrative centers. The federal courts, namely the federal high court and the court of appeal, are in a few state capitals, and the Supreme Court is in the federal capital, Abuja. As a result of the urban and elitist court system, legal practice has developed in the same manner. However, customary courts, which dispense customary laws, are in rural areas, but, as will be shown below, customary law itself contains elements that are not conducive to the protection of civil rights. The effect of the elitism of the legal profession is that legal and judicial processes are perceived as removed from the general population. The court processes are too complex and technical for the ordinary Nigerian to understand and trust, and the cost of legal services is too high for the average citizen.

Customary Laws and Human Rights

Nigeria's Evidence Act defines custom as "a rule which in a particular locality has, from long usage acquired the force of law."[85] There are, broadly speaking, two customary law systems in Nigeria. One is the Islamic/*shari'a* law predominant in the north where majority of the country's Muslim population lives, and the other is the scheme of indigenous bodies rules of customs and traditions of various ethnic groups, particularly, in the south and the middle belt. *Shari'a* law, which is rooted in the Koran, is applicable as the personal law of Muslims and non-Muslims who voluntarily submit to them either by conduct or contract. The rules of indigenous customary laws differ from one ethnic community to another. The court may enforce any aspect of custom if it is proved by evidence as an accepted rule of custom of the people concerned.[86]

The requirements for proof of customary law are contained in various high court laws of the states as well as the in federal Evidence Act. The major requirement (with a colonial antecedent) is that the custom must be compatible with the rules of natural justice, equity, and good conscience.[87] This compatibility test, otherwise better known as the "repugnancy test," comes from the English common law standard and is meant for judicial oversight over applicable rules of custom. In some cases, customary law contains rules contrary to acceptable human rights standards. For instance, the customs of some communities disallow the widow, daughters, and illegitimate children of a deceased man from inheriting his estate. Such custom has been declared unlawful by the superior courts.[88] The compatibility test helps to ensure that such rules of customs that are contrary to accepted human rights standards are excluded. However, the recent introduction of *shari'a* criminal law in some states in the north have reintroduced some forms of punishment such as flogging, stoning, and amputation that were earlier abolished as contrary to the constitutional rights against inhuman and degrading treatment or punishment.

Institutional Framework for the Legal Protection of Human Rights

The Judiciary: Structure and Independence

The courts and their judicial powers are defined in the constitution. The highest court is the Supreme Court, which sits in one chamber in the federal capital. Below the Supreme Court in the hierarchy is the Court of Appeal with ten divisions in different parts of Nigeria, each division overseeing a collection of contiguous states.[89] Then the federal and state high courts, and the customary or shari'a courts of appeal of the state, which are of coordinate jurisdiction in the hierarchy. Magistrates and area and customary courts are inferior courts created by laws of the different states.[90]

The jurisdiction of the Supreme Court, as the apex court, is defined in sections 230–236 of the 1999 constitution. It hears appeals from the Court of Appeal and has original jurisdiction only in respect of disputes between the federation and a state or between states. The Court of Appeal is defined under sections 237–248 of the 1999 Constitution, and hears appeals from the federal and state high courts, the Code of Conduct tribunal, ad hoc electoral tribunals, and the *shari'a* and customary courts of appeal. The federal high courts hear cases at first instance relating to federal revenue or federal government agencies. The state high court have unlimited jurisdiction, subject to the jurisdiction of the federal high courts. Under the 1999 constitution, the president appoints all justices of the Supreme Court, Court of Appeal, and the federal high court while state governors appoint judges to the high courts of the respective states on the recommendation of the National Judicial Council (a new centralized body for the judiciary).[91]

Under the military, however, there were no constitutional legislatures, and so the process of judicial appointments was haphazard at best. Consequently, military officials arbitrarily appointed judicial officers. There have been few changes in the judiciary under the new civilian regime from the situation under the military. Judicial officials appointed for political purposes or on political considerations have their tenure preserved under the current dispensation. The absence of an objective recruitment system for judges under the military also meant that there was no guarantee that capable and qualified persons were appointed. The 1999 constitution makes provisions for establishing proper safeguards for the independence and integrity of the judiciary in Nigeria at both federal and state levels.[92] Sections 291 and 292 deal with the tenure and removal, respectively, of judicial officers. Federal judicial officers retire mandatorily at seventy years while the retirement age for state judicial officers is sixty-five. Judges who have not attained the age of retirement may only be removed strictly in accordance with the procedure contained in these sections of constitution.

Independence of the Judiciary

The judiciary was not independent of the military regime. While advances have been made, the state of the judiciary under the current civilian government remains far from ideal. Under the military, the executive was responsible for the appointment, promotion, and discipline of judges. This responsibility is now exercised under the advice of the National Judicial Council (NJC), which itself is composed of mainly judicial officers and representatives of the Nigerian Bar Association.[93] Under the 1999 constitution (section 84 [1] and [4]), the remuneration of judicial officers of the rank of judges and above is determined by the Revenue Mobilization, Allocation, and Fiscal Commission and charged directly on the Consolidated Revenue Fund. The constitution makes the judiciary self-accounting, with the management of the recurrent expenditure of both the state and federal judiciaries centralized in the NJC. The NJC and its members have not been given supporting bureaucracy or skills to enable them to undertake this new role. Although this has standardized the salaries of judicial officers on or above the level of high court judges, the conditions of service of judicial officers, including salaries and working facilities, have deteriorated with the general decline in living standards in Nigeria. Judicial remuneration in real dollar terms in Nigeria between 1959 and 1998 declined, registering the most dramatic drop from a high of more than US$100,000 in 1978 to just over US $10,000 in 1998.

A 1998 study on judicial remuneration in Nigeria rightly found that:

During the 1960s and 1970s, the first 20 years after [Nigeria's] independence, Nigeria's GDP per capita averaged $820 per year in constant 1998 dollars. During the same period, Nigerian High Court judges were being compensated at an average rate of almost $100,000 per year in constant dollars. This was very adequate by any standard, not to speak of Nigeria, where it was over 100 times GDP per capita. . . . The reason for the collapse in real value of the judges' compensation is not far to seek: it is the collapse of the Naira [Nigeria's currency].[94]

These poor conditions have until recently discouraged good candidates or successful lawyers from making themselves available for consideration for judicial appointment. As a result, most judges are appointed from the civil service and government departments, especially from the Ministries of Justice. For instance, between 1996 and 1999, the Lagos State government appointed ten high court judges, all of whom were from the state ministry of justice or court registry or the magistracy.

Moreover, states remain responsible for the capital appropriations of their respective judiciaries and for the remuneration of their lower bench (magistrates, customary court judges, registry staff, and so on) as these are not chargeable to the Consolidated Revenue Fund. Magistrates, judges' assistants, and registry staff registrars are not covered by the constitutional provisions affecting the remuneration of judicial officers. Rather, they form part of the civil service scale of remuneration and conditions. Moreover, in the absence of adequate capital appropriations for the judiciary, the courts, their staff, and court users suffer a perennial shortage of the necessary working facilities such as courtrooms, books, typewriters, stationery, and files. Most litigants in the high courts are required to bring their own stationery for their cases. The lower bench, including the magistrates, area courts, and customary courts, are even worse off both in terms of remuneration and facilities. As a result of these conditions, there is much ineptitude and corruption among judicial officers. [95] Clerks, registrars, and even magistrates openly extort money from litigants. A panel of inquiry, set up in 1994 to recommend reform in the judiciary,[96] submitted a report in 1995 indicting many judges and magistrates of corruption, but there has been no response from the government. There is little or no continuing legal education for judicial officers in the country. The National Judicial Institute was set up for the continued training (and "retraining") of judicial officers,[97] but it has made little impact due to poor funding from the government.

National Human Rights Commission

The National Human Rights Commission was established on September 27, 1995, by the National Human Rights Commission Decree No. 22 of 1995 with a mandate to engage the promotion of and education on human rights and protection of victims. The commission receives complaints of human rights violations from individuals and NGOs and advises the government or concerned agencies on redress for such violations. The commission was established by the Abacha regime, and, clearly, this was little more than an attempt to launder his regime's image. Now, however, the commission is trying to reposition itself in the context of the new civilian regime to enable it to promote respect for human rights in the country.

Human Rights Violations Investigation Commission

On June 18, 1999, barely three weeks after being sworn in as Nigeria's first elected president in fifteen years and only its third elected leader since independence, President Obasanjo established a commission to investigate human rights violations committed by successive military regimes.[98] Established under the Tribunals of Inquiry Act, the Commission comprised seven members and a Secretary. It is headed by Chukwudifu Oputa, a respected retired justice of the Supreme Court of Nigeria. An amendment to the first instrument under which it was constituted designated this body as the Judicial Commission of Inquiry for the Investigation of Human Rights Violations (Oputa Commussion) and spelled out its mandate to:

- ascertain or establish the causes, nature, and extent of all gross violations of human rights committed in Nigeria between the 15th day of January 1966 (the date of the first military coup in Nigeria) and the 28th day of May 1999 (the date of the inauguration of the current civilian dispensation);
- identify the person or persons, authorities, institutions, or organizations which may be held accountable for such gross violations of human rights and determine the motives for the violations or abuses, the victims and circumstances thereof, and the effect on such victims and the society generally of the atrocities;
- determine whether such abuses or violations were the product of deliberate state policy or the policy of any of its organs or institutions or whether they arose from abuses of office by state officials or whether they were the acts of any political organizations, liberation movements or other groups or individuals;
- recommend measures which may be taken whether judicial, administrative, legislative, or institutional to redress the injustices of the past and prevent or forestall future violations or human rights abuses.[99]

Following its inauguration, the commission invited memoranda and petitions from the Nigerian public and received thousands of petitions. Beginning in October 2000, the commission began public hearings in five venues across Nigeria of the petitions submitted to it in order to collect evi-

dence and hear victims and witnesses. The commission is expected to report sometime in 2002.

The Bar Association

The Nigerian Bar Association (NBA) is the corporate body of all legal
practitioners in Nigeria. The association has branches in all the state capitals and subbranches in all the judicial divisions (see web site, www.nba.
org.ng). From 1992 to 1998, the NBA was in disarray after the Babangida
government attempted to impose a leadership on the association at its
biannual conference in Port Harcourt in 1992. A majority of the members
resisted this action, and, thus, the elections for the national executive did
not take place. Subsequently, the government issued a decree handing
over control of the association to the Body of Benchers, a pro-government
group made up of the attorneys general, the chief justice of the federation,
the chief judges of the states, select appellate judges, and senior advocates.[100] The decree was widely criticized by lawyers and was eventually
nullified by the Court of Appeal because it was inconsistent with the constitution.[101] The disbandment of the NBA had negative impact on the legal
profession in the country. In August 1998, the state chapters of the association organized a national meeting, and new officers were appointed. The
bar association is, therefore, gradually rebuilding itself from the ruin of
disbandment by the military regimes.

Before this crisis, the bar association had not really been in the forefront
in the legal defense of human rights, except for a brief period between 1988
and 1990, when the national leadership was under Alao Aka-Bashorun, a human rights advocate. During that period, the Nigerian Bar Association mobilized lawyers against the rampant executive disobedience of court orders,
and, in particular, it encouraged lawyers to boycott courts in certain states
where court orders were ignored. There were also human rights committees of the association whose members offered free legal support to victims
of human rights violations, initiatives that are now being resuscitated by
the current bar.

Other Associations of Lawyers

There are other bar associations to which Nigerian lawyers belong and
which have the capacity to engage in the legal protection human rights in
Nigeria. These include the African Bar Association (ABA), the Commonwealth Lawyers Association (CLA), the International Bar Association (IBA),
the International Federation of Women Lawyers (FIDA), and the Association of Nigerian Law Teachers. Within these associations, there are committees or sections on human rights and the rule of law. FIDA, for instance,

provides free legal counseling for women and children, and the IBA has a human rights institute that assists in developing the capacity of the local law community on human rights casework. Nigeria also has a quite vibrant community of public interest NGOs in which lawyers are vocal and dominant in the defense of the rule of law, constitutional government, and human rights.

There is great potential for lawyers' associations to be involved in the legal protection of human rights. As lawyers, they have the necessary skills and expertise and a better understanding of the legal mechanisms for defense of rights. But these have not been properly put in use in Nigeria. Under the military regimes, it was difficult to mobilize individual lawyers to offer voluntary service for the protection of human rights because of their fear of persecution or reprisal from the government. Lawyers who engaged in human rights work under the military regimes were branded antigovernment activists, and many were persecuted.

There is no legal training on human rights for lawyers and judicial officers. The curricula of law faculties and the Nigerian Law School do not have a single human rights course, though there may be a few passing references to international human rights instruments in the (optional) International Public Law courses. There is also no effective continuing education for practicing lawyers, except occasional workshops or conferences by the few human rights NGOs.

Social and Economic Factors in the Legal Protection of Human Rights in Nigeria

The Nigerian economy has been in recession since the 1980s, which has resulted in problems of unemployment, poor standards of living, and rising inflation. Invariably, this has affected the human rights regime in the country and access to the legal mechanisms for redress in cases of violations. Only very few people can afford the legal fees for the pursuit of legal proceedings to compensate for breached rights. Though filing fees for civil cases are quite low (about N1,000 or US$10, on average, to file a human rights claim at the high court), the cost of legal services is considerably higher. An average lawyer charges about N50,000 (US$500) to prosecute a personal liberty suit at the high court, and twice that amount for appeals. As noted above, the government's legal aid scheme is grossly underfunded and therefore nonfunctional. A few of the human rights NGOs do, however, provide some pro bono legal aid services, but these are inadequate.

The legal mechanism for the enforcement of rights has not been directed to the protection of economic, social, and cultural rights because of the widely held notion that these rights articulated in Chapter 2 of the 1999 constitution are nonjusticiable by virtue of section 6(6)(c). There is no doubt that the nonenforcement of ESCRs in Chapter 2 of the constitution renders the Chapter 4 rights merely academic because the civil and political rights in Chapter 4 cannot be fully realized by citizens if they are denied ESCRs. The nonjusticiability clause in section 6(6)(c) also calls into question the ample provisions of the African Charter on Human and Peoples' Rights on economic, social, and cultural rights, which have been domesticated in Nigeria. However, as noted above, the case of *Olisa Agbakoba v. Director of State Security Services,* demonstrates the interdependence and interrelatedness of all categories of human rights. As it was held in that case, even though there was express provision for justiciable right to a passport, the possession of a passport is a constitutional right of citizens, because without a passport the citizen cannot exercise his or her right of movement in and out of Nigeria. It, therefore, appears that the courts have hinted that certain "nonjusticiable" rights that are necessary for the enjoyment of "justiciable" rights are themselves enforceable so as to give meaning and effect to such rights.

It is important to note that corruption in both public and private sectors in the country impact negatively on the systems of protection of human rights. Public and popular corruption has resulted in increasing poverty in Nigeria, as in many other parts of Africa. A 2000 assessment on corruption in Nigeria concluded among other things that corruption was "pervasive in the public and private sectors and has become woven into the fabric of the society. Successive military dictatorships have tapped the nation's vast oil riches to fill their pockets and foreign bank accounts while crippling the economy and deepening the nation's underdevelopment."[102] Apart from slavery, poverty in the continent is perhaps the most vicious form of dehumanization of the people of Africa. Despite its huge natural and human resources, nearly a half of the 110 million people of Nigeria live on below one U.S. dollar per day. The widespread poverty is perhaps the clearest demonstration of the failure of governance in Nigeria. Consequently, people have gradually lost faith in the national government and pay more allegiance to ethnic, religious, and other subsocial entities that provide them some measure of hope. This has resulted in ethnic, religious, and regional consciousness, which itself is a main cause of civil strife and violence that have besieged Nigeria since independence.[103]

Status and Role of NGOs

NGOs first emerged in Nigeria during the nationalist struggle for independence but were at that time mainly political pressure groups, labor and humanitarian organizations. The emergence of NGOs for the promotion of human rights was a more recent phenomenon. The Nigerian Chapter of Amnesty International was the earliest human rights NGO to emerge in the country, but it existed mainly in the universities and had a more academic outlook. It was not until 1987, with increasing violations of the fundamental rights by the military regime of Ibrahim Babangida, that professional human rights NGOs began to emerge. The pioneer in this respect was the Civil Liberties Organization (CLO) set up in October 1987. It is still the largest human rights NGO in Nigeria. Historically, the increased military repression of human rights was an impetus for the emergence of human rights NGOs in Nigeria, but the result of such crusades was often arrests, detention, and the restriction of the jurisdiction of the courts.

By 1990, there were about fifty human rights and prodemocracy groups in Nigeria that specialized in general human rights, or in specific areas such as media rights, rule of law, popular political participation, environment, women's human rights, housing, labor, and children rights. One significant feature of most of these NGOs is that they are located in urban areas. There are two main reasons for this phenomenon. First, the social pattern of Nigerian society as inherited from colonialism encourages urbanism and urban migration. Almost every educated Nigerian lives or has his or her professional base in an urban town. The rural areas, therefore, are made up of mainly the very poorest, mostly illiterate or the retired and aged. Second, facilities for human rights campaigns, including the courts, media, public utilities such as telephone, electricity, and other resources are more easily found in urban areas than in the rural areas. However, since 1993, the environmental rights campaigns, particularly in the oil-producing communities, drew the attention of NGOs to the rural communities. Such campaigns have even given rise to many community-based NGOs. The Movement for the Survival of Ogoni People (MOSOP) and the Environmental Rights Action (ERA) effectively blazed the trail in this area, and there are currently about twenty NGOs in the Niger delta area where oil is produced, most of them purely community-interest organizations.

Under the military regimes, human rights NGOs fought for a return to democracy. They effectively mobilized local and international support for this purpose. The hanging in November 1995 of Ken Saro-Wiwa, the head of MOSOP, along with eight of his Ogoni kinsmen, drew the attention of the international community to the evils of military rule in Nigeria. With the establishment of civil democracy in May 1999, human rights NGOs are beginning to restrategize and reposition themselves to constructively engage with the new civilian regime. Many of them now engage in advocacy for law reform, human rights education, and good governance. Activists now carry out their work with little or no threat to their lives and liberty unlike the situation under the military regimes where many activists were regularly arrested, detained, or killed by the regimes.

Most NGOs rely on financial aid from foreign-based foundations and organizations for their work. There is little local mobilization of financial resources, and there appear to be three reasons for this. First, under the military regimes, there was a general fear of reprisal in being identified with supporting human rights activities. Second, the Nigerian economy has been in recession since the 1980s, and this has affected incomes and standards of living. Except for certain multinationals, particularly in the oil industries, only very few people or organizations can afford to support NGO activities. But, the most important factor has been that the NGOs themselves have not properly reached out to their local constituencies in order to widen their local resource base. The CLO, for instance, had only 15,000 members across Nigeria as of 1997, and most of these are university students and trade unionists. Nonetheless, the small local constituencies of NGOs have not affected their legitimacy and acceptance in the society. In fact, the civil society looks upon the NGOs, though often from a safe distance, for the promotion and protection of fundamental rights in the country, especially under the military regimes. For example, in 1992 when the Babangida regime cancelled the October presidential primaries of the two political parties and extended (for the second time) the transition period by one year, the human rights and prodemocracy NGOs organized themselves into a coalition called Campaign for Democracy with the aim of pushing for democracy in Nigeria. This coalition became the popular vanguard for democracy and rule of law, and despite the killing and detention of many of its members, it successfully led the massive campaign (particularly after the annulment of the June 12, 1993, election) which eventually forced Babangida out of office.

The human rights and prodemocracy NGO community remained in the forefront of the struggle against the military, and the community suffered heavily for that. Many human rights and pluralism advocates who remained in the country during the Babangida and Abacha eras (1985–1998) were imprisoned, and some of them disappeared or were assassinated. The population continued to look up to the NGOs as the alternative voice, as the military effectively silenced, coopted, or intimidated all other pressure groups in the polity including the trade unions, professional associations, and religious organizations. To this extent, the NGO community has wide local constituency and legitimacy. Under the present civilian regime, the population looks upon the NGOs as the credible opposition to check the excesses of the government. As noted above, all the major security structures, personnel, and laws of the military regimes have not been reformed or changed in the new civil regime.

Undoubtedly, there is a need for the NGO community to mobilize more support both domestically and internationally to ensure that they keep up the pressure on the present government to respect human rights. It has also been suggested that by offering alternative visions and choice to the Nigerian people in electoral contests, civil society activists should aspire to active political power so as to consolidate the gains of their struggle in government.

Conclusion

The phenomenon of colonial rule and military intervention in governance in Nigeria had considerably impeded the social and economic development of the country and consequently the regime of human rights protection. The absence of popular political participation and the lack of public accountability of the military regimes had encouraged corruption and mismanagement of the public wealth. The result is the increasingly deteriorating economy, which itself results in other social problems and conflicts in the country. Rising ethnic militia and vigilante groups, which considerably contribute to the increasing level of violence across the country, can be traced to the high unemployment rate. Public utilities are nonfunctional, and the facilities of governance are overstretched. The current government has announced its intention to deal with these problems through campaigns against corruption, punishment for those granted impunity in the past, and privatization of utilities. But it has not demonstrated sufficient political will to decisively deal with these problems. There are still wide violations of human rights, especially extrajudicial killings by the police, and also impunity, as the perpetrators of these violations are not brought to book. The new government has not distanced itself from the structures and systems of the past military regimes, and, as was the case when the colonial government handed power over to the independent government, these structures and systems may be used by the new and subsequent regimes for their selfish political agenda.

As demonstrated above, it is clear that the military incursion into governance in Nigeria inhibited the legal protection of human rights and resulted in massive violations of rights. It also discouraged law reforms and law development. Consequently, the legal and judicial systems could not progress at the same rate as the demands made on them by the increasing population. The enthronement of civil government in Nigeria in 1999 was a major step toward better possibilities for the legal protection of rights. The recently elected civilian government no doubt provides a better opportunity and environment for legislative and good governance advocacy by the civil society groups. Unlike in the past under the military, the constitutional institutions of governance are now in place, and public officials are more accessible to the population. There is now a better climate for advancing the regime of human rights through education, advocacy, and law reform at federal and state legislatures. A number of civil society organizations have initiated law reform programs with the legislature. Such initiatives include the Freedom of Information Bill,[104] bills to review the criminal laws, to criminalize gender-based violence, to abolish sedition laws, and to repeal decrees of the past military governments. However, there is still little or no improvement in the area of access to the courts and the procedural problems of the courts. Greater empowerment of the civil society and increased awareness and civic education on issues of human rights and good governance are required to ensure popular participation in governance and to strengthen the institutions of democracy in Nigeria. It is important to reform the legal systems and justice sectors and to properly empower the citizenry and retrain the legal community to effectively position them to protect and defend rights of citizens in the new democracy.

Notes

1. Casals and Associates, *Nigeria: Anti-Corruption Assessment, Executive Summary* (Alexandria, Va.: Casals and Associates, 2000), p. 1.

2. *Human Development Report: Nigeria 1998* (Lagos: United Nations Development Program, 1999), p. 3.

3. *Nigeria Country Strategy Paper* (London: Department for International Development, 2000), p. 2.

4. Jadesola Akande, *The Constitutions of Nigeria: How Democratic in Democracy and Law* (Lagos: Federal Ministry of Justice, 1991), p. 54.

5. Civil Liberties Organization, *Human Rights in Retreat: A Report on the Human Rights Violations of the Military Regime of General Ibrahim Babangida* (1993), pp. 12–24, 95–111; Constitutional Rights Project, *Nigeria: The Limits of Justice* (1993), pp. 40–57. For a comparison of the methods used by successive military regimes in Nigeria to undermine constitutional government, see Chidi Anselm Odinkalu, "The Management of Transition to Civil Rule by the Military in Nigeria, 1966–1996," background paper prepared for the Workshop on the Nigerian Democratization Process and the European Union, Centre d'étude d'Afrique noire, Bordeaux, 1996.

6. It is usually called the Lugard Constitution after the then governor general, Sir Frederick Lugard. Cited and discussed in Udo Udoma, *History and the Law of the Constitution of Nigeria* (Lagos: Ibadan, Malthouse Press, 1994), pp. 36–87.

7. This was a sort of "political justice" system. Legal practitioners were allowed to appear only in the Supreme Court, and not in the provincial or native courts. See section 33(i) of the Provincial Court Ordinance, Lugard Constitution, in Udoma, *History and the Law*, p. 46.

8. See B. O. Nwabueze, *A Constitutional History of Nigeria* (Enugu: Fourth Dimension, 1982), p. 38.

9. Area courts still exist in northern Nigeria. For a fuller description and analysis of these courts see Anselm Chidi Odinkalu, *Justice Denied: Area Courts in the Northern States of Nigeria* (Lagos: Kraft Books/CLO, 1993).

10. See D. C. Holland, "Human Rights in Nigeria," *Current Legal Problems* 15 (1962), p. 145; S. A. de Smith, "Fundamental Rights in the New Commonwealth," *International and Comparative Law Quarterly* (1961), p. 83.

11. Ahmadu Bello was the leader of the Northern Peoples Congress (NPC),

which controlled the north; Nnamdi Azikiwe was the leader of the National Council of Nigerian Citizens, (NCNC), which dominated the eastern region; and Obafemi Awolowo was the leader of the Action Group (AG), which dominated the western region.

12. See Okwudibia Nnoli, *Ethnic Politics in Nigeria* (Enugu: Fourth Dimension, 1983), chapters 2 and 3.

13. See, for example, *Director of Public Prosecution v. Chike Obi* (1961) 1 All NLR 234. Also, see *Ransome Kuti v. Attorney General of the Federation* (1985) 1 NWLR (Pt. 5) 1, on the discussion by the Supreme Court on the Petition of Rights Law, which had prohibited suits against the government except with the permission of the attorney general. This was an extension in Nigeria of the imperial immunity to civil suits in England.

14. See Biko Agozino and Unyiere Idem, *Nigeria: Democratizing a Militarized Civil Society,* Occasional Paper Series No. 5 (London: Center for Democracy and Development, 2001), pp. 43–45.

15. Subsequent military regimes in Nigeria also professed to be corrective and temporary. Addressing the Conference of Attorneys General in Abuja, Nigeria, on September 9, 1991, General Babangida, then president, put forward what he called the "custodian theory of military intervention in our body politic," in which he justified occasional military intervention in Nigerian politics as necessary from time to time in order to restore sanity in national politics. He argued that such intervention was justifiable provided it was "temporary and corrective."

16. SC 58/69 of April 24, 1970, [1974] *East Central State Law Reports*, 713.

17. Ibid. The regime promptly nullified the effect of this decision through the Federal Military Government (Supremacy and Enforcement of Powers) Decree 28 of 1970, which declared the takeover of government.

18. In particular, the Constitution (Suspension and Modification) Decree No. 1 of 1966. This body was called the Supreme Military Council under Major General Aguiyi-Ironsi as the head of state and commander in chief of the armed forces.

19. Gani Fawehinmi, ed., *Nigerian Law of Habeas Corpus* (Lagos: Nigeria Law Publications, 1985), p. 437.

20. Ibid., pp. 446–447, paragraphs E-F, emphasis added.

21. *Nwosu v. Imo State Environmental Sanitation Authority* (1990) 2 NWLR (Pt. 135) 688, 727, paragraphs C-E, emphasis added. The legislative and executive powers of the Federal Military Government of Nigeria are vested in one ruling body called by various names by the various, successive military regimes. Under the present military government, the ruling body is the Provisional Ruling Council (PRC), which succeeded the Armed Forces Ruling Council (AFRC) as it was called in the previous administration. In the military regimes before 1985, the supreme law-making body was known as the Supreme Military Council (SMC). The PRC appoints military administrators to govern the states. The executive and legislative powers at the state level are vested in the military administrator.

22. See Sony C. Onyegbula, "Human Rights Violations Investigation Commission: The Journey So Far," *Democracy and Development*, 2 (2000), p. 31.

23. *Report of the Commission Appointed to Enquire into the Fears of Minorities and Means of Allaying Them* (Cmnd. 505) (London: HMSO, 1958), p. 97; quoted in J. D. Ojo, *The Development of the Executive Under the Nigerian Constitution 1960–81* (Ibadan: University Press, 1985), pp. 114–115.

24. Ibid., p. 116.

25. Ibid., p. 118.

26. Corresponding to sections 17, 20, and 30 of the 1960, 1963, and 1979 constitutions, respectively.

27. [1998] 13 NWLR 531; (1999) 2 CHRLD 337.

28. The version of this provision in the 1960 and 1963 constitutions contained an exception to right to life where the deprivation of life was for the purpose of preventing commission of a crime. This provision was too widely abused by the police and other law enforcement agencies and was dropped in the 1979 constitution.

29. See the case of *Aliu Bello v. Attorney General of Oyo State* (1986) 2 NSCC 1257; (1986) 5 NWLR 828. In this case, a prisoner whose appeal against his conviction and sentence was pending at the court of appeal was executed on the recommendation of the Oyo State attorney general. His relations sued for compensation. The Supreme Court declared the execution unconstitutional and illegal, awarded damages. See also *Mohammed Garuba and Eleven Others v. Attorney General of the Federation* (unreported), Suit No. ID/599/90, where the Lagos High Court awarded compensation to the relatives of seven persons unlawfully killed by the police at Oko Oba, Lagos State.

30. Sections 18, 21, and 31 of the 1960, 1963, and 1979 constitutions, respectively.

31. See *Ogugu v. the State* (1994) 9 NWLR (Pt. 366), p. 1. See also *Peter Nemi v. Attorney General of Lagos State* (1996) 6 NWLR (Pt. 452), p. 42.

32. (1999) 2 CHRLD 337, 339.

33. Sections 20, 21, and 32 of the 1960, 1963, and 1979 constitutions, respectively.

34. Sections 21, 32, and 33 of the 1960, 1963, and 1979 constitutions, respectively.

35. See the cases of *Garba v. University of Maiduguri* (1986) 1 NWLR (Pt. 18) 550 and *Akintemi v. Onwumechili* (1985) 1 NWLR (Pt. 1) 68.

36. Sections 33, 32, and 34 of the 1960, 1963, and 1979 constitutions, respectively.

37. Sections 34, 33, and 35 of the 1960, 1963, and 1979 constitutions, respectively.

38. For an account developments regarding the introduction of *shariʿa* in the northern states of Nigeria and its implications for constitutional rights, see J. Kayode Fayemi, "Sharia: Democracy and the Constitutional Reform Agenda in Nigeria," *Democracy and Development* 2 (2001), p. 21.

39. Sections 34, 35, and 36 of the 1960, 1963, and 1979 constitutions, respectively.

40. See *Tony Momoh v. Speaker, Federal House of Representatives* (1982) NCLR 105 where it was held that a person is entitled to refuse to disclose his or her source of information.

41. The National Broadcasting Council Regulation for licensed electronic media houses stipulates the type of programs and the timing of programs to broadcast, with greater restriction on foreign content and religious programs.

42. This act restricts government officials from disclosing information about their office, which creates a censor on official information.

43. Sections 25, 26, and 37 of the 1960, 1963, and 1979 constitutions, respectively.

44. Sections 26, 37, and 37 of the 1960, 1963, and 1979 constitutions, respectively.

45. (1994) 6 NWLR (Pt. 351) 475.

46. Sections 27, 38, and 39 of the 1960, 1963, and 1979 constitutions, respectively.

47. *Ahamefula v. Imperial Medical Centre*, Ruling of the High Court of Lagos State, Ikeja Division, February 5, 2001 (unreported).

48. (1995) 3 NWLR (Pt. 382) 148.

49. The 1960 and 1963 constitutions permitted only derogation from the rights to personal liberty, fair hearing, and freedom from discrimination during emergencies. The 1979 and 1999 constitutions extended the derogated rights and grounds of restriction.

50. Section 45 (2) of the 1999 constitution.

51. See generally Clement Nwankwo and Melissa Crow, *Guide to Human Rights Litigation in Nigeria* (Lagos: Constitutional Rights Project, 1994).

52. Fundamental Rights (Enforcement Procedure) Rules, 1980, Order 1 Rule 2, Reprinted in Nwankwo and Crow, *Guide to Human Rights Litigation in Nigeria*, p. 74.

53. Ibid., Order 2, Rule 1(2).

54. Ibid., Order 2, Rule 2.

55. Chapter 205, Laws of the Federation of Nigeria 1990.

56. U. A. Hassan Baba (director-general), "Report on the Operation of the Legal Aid Council of the Federal Republic of Nigeria," presented to the Annual General Conference of the Nigerian Bar Association, Abuja, August 21–25, 2000, p. 6 and appendix A.

57. Ibid., p. 6.

58. Ibid., p. 8.

59. Ibid., p. 13.

60. See *Archbishop Olubunmi Okogie and Seven Others v. Attorney General of Lagos State* (1981) 1 NCLR 218.

61. In Ghana, the Supreme Court held that they "are mandated to apply them in their interpretative duty, when they [fundamental objectives and directive principles of State policy] are read in conjunction with other enforceable parts of the Constitution." Per Bamford Addo J.S.C. in *New Patriotic Party v. Attorney General*, [1996–97] *Sup. Ct. of Ghana LR* 728, 745. See also the decision of the Constitutional Court of Uganda in *Salvatori Abuki and Obuga v. Attorney General*, 3 *Butterworths Hum. Rts. Cases* 199 (1998). The latter approach is also favored by the courts in India. See the decision of the Indian Supreme Court in *State of Kerala v. Thomas* [1976] SCR 906, 993.

62. On the view that the emerging concept of victimology is admitted within this provision, see Anselm Chidi Odinkalu and Uju Roseline Chiemeka, "Victimology and the Criminal Justice System in Nigeria," *Journal of Human Rights Law and Practice* 3 (December 1993), pp. 115, 129–130.

63. Chapter 10, Laws of the Federation of Nigeria, 1990.

64. For a description and analysis of economic, social, and cultural rights in the African Charter, see Chidi Anselm Odinkalu, "Analysis of Paralysis or Paralysis by Analysis? Implementing Economic, Social and Cultural Rights Under the African Charter on Human and Peoples' Rights," *Human Rights Quarterly* 23 (2001), p. 327.

65. See *Ogugu v. State* (1996) 6 NWLR (Pt. 316), 1, pp. 30–31, per Mohammed, CJN.

66. (2000) 6 NWLR (Pt. 660) 228.

67. (1990) 5 NWLR (Pt. 398) 703.

68. (1995) 4 NWLR (Pt. 387) 59.

69. See for instance *Ojukwu v. Governor of Lagos State* (1986) 5 NWLR (Pt. 18) 15.

70. For an extensive survey of instances of disobedience of court orders by the military regimes in Nigeria, see Civil Liberties Organization, *Executive Lawlessness in the Babangida Administration*, 1992.

71. See Constitutional Rights Project, *Human Rights Practices in Nigeria, January 1995 to June 1996* (Lagos: Civil Liberties Organization, 1996), p. 87.

72. *Ogugu v. State* (1994) 9 NWLR (pt. 366), 27–28.

73. Despite the fact that Nigeria has ratified these treaties, nonetheless, the military regimes have enacted decrees to curtail certain labor rights. In 1993, after the annulment of the June 12 election and on the heels of labor's demand for the resuscitation of democracy, the military rulers enacted three decrees to disband the leadership of the Nigerian Labor Congress (NLC), the National Union of Petro-

leum and Natural Gas Workers (NUPENG), and Petroleum and Natural Gas Workers Senior Staff Association.

74. See section 33(1) of the 1999 constitution. See also *Onuoha Kanu v. State* (1998) 13 NWLR (Pt. 583) 531, where the Supreme Court upheld the constitutionality of capital punishment.

75. See *Nigeria Ports Authority v. Construzioni Generali Fasura Cogefa* (1974) 9 NSCC 622.

76. See *Tafida v. Abubakar* (1992) 2 NWLR (Pt. 230) 521 at 522, where the court said that the legislative goal of the fundamental rights enforcement rules was to achieve speedier disposal of fundamental rights cases than ordinary civil suits.

77. The regimes, named after their military head of state, were the Ironsi (January–July 1966), the Gowon (July 1966–1975), the Murtala (1975–1976), the Obasanjo (1976–1979), the Buhari (1983–1985), the Babangida (1985–August 1993), the Abacha (November 1993–June 8 1998), and the Abubakar (June 1998–May 29, 1999).

78. See Kayode Eso, J.S.C., in *Ojukwu v. Governor of Lagos State.*

79. Civil Liberties Organization, *Executive Lawlessness,* p. 5.

80. See Agozino and Idem, *Nigeria.*

81. (1982) 1 NCLR 231.

82. For a critique of the Nigerian jurisprudence on access to courts and *locus standi,* see Tunde Ogowewo, "The Problem with Standing to Sue in Nigeria," 39 *Journal of African Law* 9 (1995).

83. Tunde Ogowewo, "Wrecking the Law: How Article III of the Constitution of the United States Led to the Discovery of a Law of Standing to Sue in Nigeria," 26 *Brooklyn Journal of International Law* 527.

84. Under the Judgment Enforcement Rules established under the Sheriffs and Civil Process Act, Chapter 407, Laws of the Federation of Nigeria, 1990, the consent of the attorney general is required for execution of any judgment against the government. The effect of this law is that, unless the government willingly consents, no judgment can be executed against it.

85. Evidence Act, Chapter 112, Laws of the Federation of Nigeria, 1990, section 1.

86. Eze Onyekpere, *Justice for Sale: A Report on the Administration of Justice in the Magistrates and Customary Courts of Southern Nigeria* (Lagos: Civil Liberties Organization, 1996), p. 51. See generally, T. O. Elias, *The Nature of African Customary Law* (Manchester: Manchester University Press, 1956).

87. Evidence Act, section 14(3).

88. See *Mojekwu v. Mojekwu* (1997) 7 NWLR (Pt. 512) 283. See also *Muojekwu v. Ejikeme* (2000) 5 NWLR (Pt. 657) 402.

89. The divisions of the Court of Appeal are sited in Abuja, Benin, Calabar, Enugu, Ibadan, Ilorin, Jos, Kaduna, Lagos, and Port Harcourt.

90. For a description of Nigeria's courts, see Gani Fawehinmi, *Court Systems in Nigeria: A Guide* (Lagos: Nigerian Law Publications, 1992).

91. Section 153 (1)(i) of the 1999 constitution. The powers of the National Judicial Council are defined in paragraph 21 of part 1 of the third schedule to the 1999 constitution. Under this provision, the body is empowered, *inter alia,* to advise the president and state governors with respect to the appointment, tenure and discipline of judicial officers of the level of high court judge or above.

92. Chapter 7 of the 1999 constitution, which deals with the judiciary, covers sixty-six sections (230–296).

93. The National Judicial Council is comprised of the chief justice of Nigeria, most senior Supreme Court justice, the president of the court of appeal, five retired

justices of the Supreme Court, the chief judge of the federal high court, five out of the thirty-six chief judges of the state high courts appointed by the chief justice of Nigeria, one Grand Kadi and one judge of state *shari'a* and customary courts of appeal, respectively, five representatives of the Nigerian Bar Association, and two lay members. The council has the power to recommend the appointment or discipline of judicial officers to the federal or state governments and has fiscal control of the judiciary in Nigeria. Thus, the 1999 constitution, unlike its predecessors, has established the centralized control of the judiciary in Nigeria.

94. Philip Ostien, "A Study of the Compensation of Nigerian Judges Since Independence," *Current Issues in Development* (July–December 1998), pp. 3–4.

95. See Joseph Otteh, *The Fading Lights of Justice: An Empirical Study of Criminal Justice Administration in Southern Nigeria Customary Courts* (Lagos: Civil Liberties Organization and Copenhagen: Danish Centre for Human Rights, 1995), pp. 39–49; Onyekpere, *Justice for Sale*, pp. 52–67.

96. The Eso Panel is named after its chairman, Justice Kayode Eso, a retired Supreme Court justice.

97. See Adenekan Ademola, "From Continuing Education to a National Judicial Institute," *Commonwealth Lawyer*, 5 (1993), pp. 29–42.

98. Instrument Constituting a Panel for the Investigation of Human Rights Violations Under the Tribunals of Inquiry Act, (Chapter 447) Laws of the Federation of Nigeria, 1990, Statutory Instrument 18 of 1998.

99. Amendment of Instrument Constituting a Judicial Commission of Inquiry for the Investigation of Human Rights Violations, Statutory Instrument of October 4, 1999.

100. Legal Practitioners (Amendment) Decree 21 of 1994.

101. *Williams v. Akintunde* (1995) 3 NWLR (Pt. 381) 101.

102. Casals and Associates, *Nigeria: Anti-Corruption Assessment*, p. 1.

103. See Said Adejumobi, "Citizenship, Rights and the Problem of Conflicts and Civil Wars in Africa," *Human Rights Quarterly* 23 (2001), pp. 148–170.

104. "Legislature Pledges Speedy Enactment of Freedom of Information Act," *Media Rights Monitor*, 4 (December 1999), p. 1.

Chapter 8
Rwanda
Building Constitutional Order
in the Aftermath of Genocide
Bibiane Mbaye Gahamanyi

The Afronet/Interights meeting in Lusaka, Zambia, 1995, defined the legal protection of human rights as "the whole process of using the law, to demand and enforce these rights." In Africa, it has been observed that very little use is made of courts and tribunals and the law in general; and this failure to use the law is even more marked where the protection of human rights is concerned. Most often, other forms of struggle have been used against human rights abuse, such as denunciations through the media, demonstrations, and even civil disobedience. There seems to be, at best, a resignation toward or, at worst, a mistrust of the courts, which are viewed as belonging to the "system." The bench, like all the machinery of government, is perceived as at the beck and call of the executive. In general, Africans do not believe in the independence of the judiciary and, thus, in the impartiality of their judgments. This, combined with the problem of access to the courts, would explain why their use has yet to enter into the cultures of the African people. This state of affairs both results from and contributes to the democratic deficit experienced by our countries and encourages impunity and lack of accountability. The overall objective of the study conducted by Interights and Afronet was to establish a state-of-the-art report and to identify the causes of the nonuse of the courts, with a view to proposing solutions to promote the legal protection of human rights.

Following a brief overview of the Rwandan political landscape and a chronological review of the principal political events that have marked Rwanda's history from independence to the present day, the first part of this chapter will examine the constitutional and legislative frameworks, as well as the Rwandan judicial system. This part will focus on the prescriptive and structural frameworks in Rwanda. The first section will review the various constitutions of the Rwandan Republic. The second section will pay particular attention to the Basic Act, which is currently in force. A third section will briefly explain the main features of the Rwandan legal system, especially in terms of its origins, its sources, the place of customary law, and the place of international conventions on human rights. The fourth section on the Rwandan judicial system will present the organization of the judicial system, the training and makeup of judicial personnel, and the working of the judicial system.

The second part of this chapter focuses on the Rwandan sociopolitical environment that produced Rwanda's Basic Act. I begin this part by examining the genealogy of the genocide of the Tutsis and the massacre of opposition Hutus in 1994. The influence of the various historical, external, economic, and political factors, as well as the nature of the first republican governments will be examined. The second section will focus on the transition government in place from 1994 to the present day. The third section involves the role and status of nongovernmental organizations (NGOs) for human rights (or working in a human rights–related area of development). Finally, in the last part, I assess the constitution and its enforcement thus far and suggest ways in which Rwanda might better meet the challenge of human rights protection and promotion.[1]

Thumbnail Sketch of Rwanda

Rwanda is a small country (26,000 square kilometers) located in the central-eastern region of the African continent, landlocked and bordering on Uganda in the northeast, Tanzania in the east, Congo (formerly Zaire) in the west, and Burundi in the south. With about three hundred inhabitants per square kilometer, Rwanda has the highest population density in Africa. Until recently, most of the population has lived in mostly rural areas. However, after the genocide in 1994, efforts have been made to resettle people in villages (*imidugudu*). This option seems to be the most appropriate way of relocating survivors, those refugees returning from exile, and other displaced persons, while ensuring their security and access to the infrastructures needed to accompany the expected development. The Rwandan people are made up of three socioethnic groups that speak the same language and share the same geographic area. The Hutu group is the largest in number, followed by the Tutsis, and finally the Twa, who are a small minority.

Principal Political Events

When Tutsi elite, who were up to then favored by Belgian colonial authorities, started agitating for independence in 1959–60, those authorities and the Catholic Church began playing the two main "tribes" against each other and turned their preference to Hutus. Hatred campaigns against Tutsis were launched and resulted in the first Tutsi people massacres. After the deposal of the *mwami* (Tutsi king of Rwanda), the Rwandan Republic was founded on July 1, 1962, under the leadership of Grégoire Kayibanda, former secretary of the head of the Rwandan Church and the chairman of PARMEHUTU (Party for the Emancipation of the Hutu People). Following guerrilla actions launched from abroad by Tutsi refugees in 1963–64, a wave of repression occurred against Tutsis within Rwanda, which resulted in massacres of Tutsis and a new wave of Tutsi refugees. In 1973 there were massacres of Tutsis in urban centers and an exodus of survivors to neighboring countries. The military coup d'état by the chief of staff, Major Juvénal Habyarimana on July 5, 1973, led to the establishment of the Movement for National Revolution and Development (MRND), a single party in which all Rwandans were deemed to be members.

Civil war broke out when the Rwandan Patriotic Front (RPF) began its attacks on October 1, 1990. In response, the government adopted a new constitution in 1990 that recognizes the multiple-party system, and the Arusha Peace Agreement was signed between the government of the Rwandan Republic and the RPF in 1992–93. But resistance to the implementation of that agreement resulted in the assassination of President Habyarimana on April 6, 1994, which marked the beginning of the genocide of Tutsis and the massacre of opposition Hutus and other members of civil society known as moderate Hutus. The genocide continued until the RPF took Kigali on July 4, 1994, but that resulted in a massive exodus of Habyarimana government officials and Hutu populations to Zaire and Tanzania. A National Union Government was established under the auspices of the RPF in November 1994.

Today, the majority of the refugees from the mass displacements of 1959, 1964, 1973, as well as 1994 have returned to Rwanda. Cohabitation, marked by mistrust, fear, resentment, and vengeance, but also hope and surpassing of oneself, has already begun. In the space of six years, Rwanda has experienced famine, civil war, assassinations of almost all of the leaders of its political opposition and civil society, genocide, and massive movements of the population. The instability of such a situation, in a particularly difficult economic and political context, aggravated by the massive presence of arms in the country as well as armed groups left over from defeated armies or militias in the region, makes the protection of human rights in general a difficult undertaking or at least an enormous challenge.

Prescriptive and Structural Framework for the Legal Protection of Human Rights in Rwanda

Rwanda's Past Constitutions

A brief review of Rwanda's previous constitutions and their main features, with a view to presenting the country's constitutional culture, serves as a prelude to the examination of its current constitution. Since gaining independence on July 1, 1962, Rwanda has adopted four separate constitutions, the constitutions of 1962, 1978, 1991, and its current Basic Act.

The Constitution of November 24, 1962

The 1962 constitution was adopted in the historical context of "social revolution," and its main achievement was the abolition of the monarchy and its privileges and the foundation of the republic. This constitution emphasized the exercise of power by the population through a parliamentarian regime. The president of the republic was controlled by and accountable to the National Assembly, which could use a vote of no confidence to end his or her term in office.

Another important feature of the 1962 constitution was that it forbade any "communist" activity or propaganda.[2] Not only did the provision of the 1962 constitution violate the freedoms of speech and association, but it also showed the prominence of the Church, which was the mainspring of both the new political order and the constitution. Forbidding communism in the constitution shows how powerful the Church was. The official justification of the hatred against communists or the preference for the capitalism was that communism supposedly denied the existence of God, and thus the Church has good grounds for strongly opposing communism. Moreover, it also revealed the limitations of the Rwandan "social revolution" that had pledged allegiance, in an "unnatural" union,[3] with the colonial/neocolonial powers of the Western bloc. It should be remembered that among the dominant features of the late 1950s and the 1960s were the opposition between the Eastern and Western blocs, the cold war, decolonization, and the assistance that socialist and communist countries provided to various liberation movements around the world. Third World anticolonialists and nationalists were particularly receptive to Marxist revolutionary discourse, which spoke to their expectations of social justice and freedom.

While it claimed to recognize the rights enumerated in the Universal Declaration of Human Rights, the 1962 constitution also expressly provided that the exercise of certain rights was limited by Rwandan law and regulations (Article 13[2]).[4] In other words, the terms of the exercise of these rights were determined by the law and the creation of regulations. As a result, the executive authorities who could make regulations could abuse the rights covered by the Universal Declaration extensively.

The 1962 constitution was revised twice. The first revision, on June 12, 1963, modified Article 52 of the constitution which provided for presidential election by universal suffrage. The amendment aimed to confirm the president of the republic—already appointed at the time of the promulgation of the constitution—in his position until the holding of an election by universal direct suffrage. The second revision, on May 18, 1973, instituted "democratic socialism" as the official economic system and strengthened the office of the president. The length of the presidential term in office was increased from four to five years; also, the limitation for the president to exercise more than three successive terms of office and the age limit (sixty years) for candidates in presidential elections were abolished. This amendment reflected the desire of the first president of the Rwandan Republic Grégoire Kayibanda to cling to power; after eleven years in power, his goal was, apparently, to be president for life.

The multiparty system that had been established was replaced by a de facto one-party system.[5] PARMEHUTU, a party representing only Hutus, was the single party allowed to operate. Other parties, including UNAR (Rwandan National Union), RADER (Democratic Assembly for the Republic), and APROSOMA (Association for the Social Progress of the Masses), were dissolved and their leaders were exiled, imprisoned, or killed.[6] Politics became increasingly intertwined with ethnicity between 1962 and 1973. There were no Tutsis in the government, the territorial administration, or the army.

The Constitution of December 20, 1978

Following the military coup of July 5, 1973, the new authorities suspended thirty-one articles of the constitution, including the articles setting out the constitutional requirements for laws. After the coup, the president then ruled by decree and was not subject to any control.

The MRND, commonly called the "Movement," was formed on July 5, 1976. Every Rwandan was a member from birth. It was the only political framework in the entire country and no political activity could be undertaken outside of the Movement.[7] Before the adoption of the new constitution, the International Covenant on Civil and Political Rights, the International Covenant on Economic, Social, and Cultural Rights, and the Convention on the Elimination of All Forms of Racial Discrimination were ratified by Decree 8/75 on December 12, 1975. However, the race convention was adopted with a reservation to Article 22, dealing with the procedure of the International Court of Justice for settling disputes between states on interpretations or applications of the convention. Unfortunately, as will be discussed below, the judicial system and the state organization were such that none of these treaties was respected.

The 1978 constitution differed in a number of important ways from the constitution of 1962. Organizationally, it officially established the following:

1. a one-party system;
2. a presidential regime headed by a single person;
3. a nearly complete lack of accountability of the president of the republic;
4. the condition that only an MRND candidate could run for president; and
5. unlimited consecutive presidential terms of office.

It eliminated the direct application of the Universal Declaration of Human Rights in domestic law and thus limited the scope of human rights guaranteed by the previous constitution. However, under the new constitution only laws could determine the exercise of these rights and freedoms, which were thus no longer subject to the limitations established by regulations.

The Supreme Judicial Council was formed. It had to be consulted before the president of the republic could appoint or remove magistrates. It should be noted, however, that the president was the chairman, the minister of justice was its deputy chairman, and the president appointed other members of the council. In addition, before being submitted to the council, applications were sent by the Ministry of Justice to the president's office to be completed and criticized. After that, the council had only to ratify the choices made by the president's office. Finally, the 1978 constitution eliminated the Supreme Court.

The MRND essentially became the state party. In the initial drafts of the constitution, party organs had been institutionalized, following the model of Zaire and its single party, the MPR. This constitution clearly reflected the influence of the Zairian model of government organization, and the personal influence of Mobutu, the Zairian head of state and mentor to Rwanda's President Habyarimana.

To speak of a constitutional culture in Rwanda is something of a misnomer, because such a culture is essentially nonexistent. Habyarimana's regime remained at a low level of institutionalization. A Belgian jurist who was, at one point, very close to President Habyarimana, stated that "[t]he second Republic and its constitution were Juvenal Habyarimana."[8] The keynote speeches of the president and the bylaws of the Movement became more important than the constitution and the laws. Thus, the ethnic and regional quota system, which applied to all sectors, was not established in any of the laws, but rather it was established by one of the keynote speeches of the president and in the bylaws of the MRND.[9]

The Basic Act: Composition and Significant Features

Rwanda's current constitution, known as the Basic Act, was adopted on May 5, 1995, by the Transitional National Assembly.[10] It consists of several texts, including the 1991 constitution, the Arusha Peace Agreement, the RPF's Declaration Relating to the Establishment of Institutions of July 17, 1994, and the Protocol Agreement concluded by all the political forces except the MRND on the establishment of national institutions, signed on November 24, 1994. Where the texts conflict, the latest text prevails.

The 1991 Constitution

After the RPF launched the civil war in 1990, the Kigali regime came under increasing pressure from international donor countries and the internal opposition to make democratic reforms. One of the reforms the regime undertook as a result of this pressure was to write a new constitution. The 1991 constitution was meant to guarantee democracy, eliminate the one-party system, and show a commitment to human rights. It established a virtually unlimited multiparty system; the only constraint on this new system was that monarchists remained banned (Article 7). Other important aspects of the 1991 constitution included:

1. The creation of the position of prime minister. Thus, under the new constitution there was no longer a single person leading the country. Rather, power was divided between the president and the prime minister (Article 35).
2. Article 40 limited the president to a maximum of two five–year terms in office.
3. Judges were to elect the Supreme Council of Judges, which overturned the earlier practice of appointment by the executive.

This constitution took steps toward judicial independence, but the principle of irremovability of judges, the best single guarantee of judicial independence, remained unknown in Rwanda. According to some analysts, Rwanda's failure to adopt the principle of irremovability of judges can be explained by the shortage of trained judges and by the need for flexibility in order to allow trained judges gradually to replace untrained ones. Additionally, under the 1991 constitution, the Supreme Court was still not reinstated.

The Arusha Peace Agreement

International and domestic pressure increased for the Rwandan regime to initiate peace talks. Because it needed external financial and military assistance, the government reluctantly agreed to negotiations. Later events demonstrated that neither the government nor *Akazu* (close family members of the president and his wife) intended to apply these agreements. Rather, they needed time to acquire the means to drive off the RPF and murder the remaining Tutsis and Hutu opponents. It took two years, starting in 1991, to complete the negotiations and to sign the various texts of the Arusha Agreement. The agreement was finalized in 1993 and entered into force on August 4 of that year.

The Arusha Peace Agreement consists of six texts, namely:

1. the Nsele Cease-fire Agreement of March 29, 1991, Between the Government of the Republic of Rwanda and the RPF, as amended in Gbadolite on September 16, 1991, and in Arusha on July 12, 1992;
2. the Protocol of Agreement Between the Government of Rwanda and the RPF on the Rule of Law, signed in Arusha on September 18, 1992;
3. The Protocol of Agreement Between the Government of Rwanda and the RPF on Broad-Based Power Sharing during a transition period, signed in Arusha on October 30, 1992, and January 9, 1993;
4. the Protocol of Agreement Between the Government of Rwanda and the RPF on Repatriation of Refugees and the Resettlement of Displaced Persons; signed at Arusha on June 9, 1993;
5. The Protocol Agreement Between the Government of Rwanda and the RPF on the Integration of the armed forces of both parties, signed on August 3, 1993; and
6. the Protocol of Agreement Between the Government of Rwanda and the RPF on Miscellaneous Issues and Final Provisions, signed in Arusha on August 3, 1993.

The agreements are highly detailed, and as such, they may lack the flexibility that would make them durable. Due to mutual distrust, both sides wanted the agreements to include as many safeguards as possible. The Arusha agreements superseded many of the articles in the 1991 constitution dealing with the organization of government and division of power. However, the preamble of the constitution and the sections dealing with certain formal aspects of the republic—its territorial organization, official languages, mechanisms for popular input, definition, form, seals and emblems, and anthem—were retained by the Arusha agreements.

The constitution's chapter on public liberties was also fully maintained. The provisions protecting liberties and fundamental rights were already reasonably good. However, the authoritarian and racist nature of the regime, together with the absence of any opposition with the power to challenge actions of the state or its officials, severely limited the exercise of these rights. It appeared that any improvement could only come from a change in the political will and would be linked to the reorganization of government and a power sharing arrangement.

Nsele Cease-Fire Agreement.   Only one article of the Nsele Cease-Fire Agreement, Article 5, is relevant to this discussion. Article 5 outlines the accepted basic principles to end the hostilities, and the peace agreement provisions, which govern the transition to a democratic regime, are based on these principles. The principles, defined in sections 1, 2, and 3 of Article 5, are:

1. the establishment of the rule of law, based on national unity, democracy, pluralism, and the respect for human rights;
2. the formation of a national army integrating government and RPF forces; and
3. broad-based power sharing in the transitional government.

All later negotiations and agreements were based on the acceptance of these three principles by both sides in the conflict, and, thus, this is the defining text of all the peace agreements. The other texts deal with the means of enforcing the principles defined by Article 5.

Protocol Agreement on the Rule of Law.   The primary causes of Rwanda's civil war were ethnic or racial and regional discrimination, the control of the government by a minority (Hutus from the north in general and those from *Akazu* in particular), and, lastly, weak, if not nonexistent, institutions and opposition parties. This protocol agreement was intended to deal with these problems.

The agreement is divided into chapters on national unity, democracy, pluralism, and human rights. The first articles of the agreement recognize the equality of all citizens before the law, guaranteed equal opportunities, and prohibited all forms of discrimination.[11] The fourth article establishes the right for refugees to return home and recognizes this to be an inalienable right.[12]

Article 6 acknowledges the Universal Declaration of Human Rights and the African Charter on Human and Peoples' Rights as the basic principles of democracy. However, while recognizing civil and political rights as part of the Basic Act, economic, social, and cultural rights are described as "programmatic," leaving it up to the government to implement policies to promote these rights.[13] This clearly violates the principles of the African Charter on Human and Peoples' Rights which places the two categories on equal footing.

A full chapter of the agreement is devoted to human rights. The principle of the universality of human rights is reaffirmed in Article 14.

Article 15 provides for the establishment of an independent National Human Rights Committee. This commission is mandated to investigate human rights violations and to initiate legal action.

Protocol Agreement on Broad-Based Power Sharing.   This protocol agreement defines the institutions required for the transition, institutes specialized committees, and organizes the executive, the legislature, and the judiciary. This component of the Arusha Peace Agreement is the most detailed of all the texts. The eighty-eight-article agreement lays out the conditions for power sharing and institutional operation. It develops a political code of ethics, which is to be binding on all political groups involved in the transition, and outlines the governmental transition program.

The protocol provides for the creation of certain specialized committees to develop a legal framework for the transition and beyond. The National Unity and Reconciliation Committee is charged with studying ways to promote reconciliation. The Legal and Constitutional Committee was established to try to harmonize previous legal texts with the peace agreement, particularly focusing on the protocol on the rule of law, and to draft a constitution that will govern the country after the transition. Finally, an Election Committee was created to prepare for and organize elections.

The executive power in the power-sharing protocol is laid out in Article 4, which states that "the executive power is exercised *collectively* through the decisions of the Council of Ministers, the President of the Republic and the Government." Articles 5 through 12 drastically reduce the president's powers from those enjoyed by the president under earlier systems. Under this protocol, the president ratifies the decisions of the Council of Ministers with no power of veto, meaning that if, within a period of ten days from the receipt date, the president does not sign the presidential decrees approved by the Council of Ministers, the prime minister has the power to approve the decision through a ministerial order.[14] Additionally, the president of the republic sanctions and promulgates the laws adopted by the National Assembly, again with no veto power. If the president refuses to promulgate a law, the chairman of the National Assembly can do so after a period of ten days.

Another important limit on presidential powers is that, under Article 12, the content of the president's speeches is to be determined by the Council of Ministers. It should not be forgotten that presidential speeches in Rwanda had been perceived as more important than the laws of the republic (widely broadcast and familiar to all, in the past they were considered to be "watchwords"), and the president of the republic had used the public media excessively.

The Council of Ministers and the prime minister have expanded powers.

The prime minister even has the power in "exceptional circumstances," to proclaim a state of emergency or martial law, following a decision of the Council of Ministers and consultation with the Office of the National Assembly and the Supreme Court.[15] According to this provision, the Office of the National Assembly and the Supreme Court are to be merely "consulted," and it does not mention the need for their approval or judgment. The Office of the National Assembly is made up of the chairmen of the commissions. Furthermore, the prime minister can, by decision of the Council of Ministers, request the dissolution of the Transitional National Assembly.

However, the real power is placed in the hands of the Council of Ministers, the head of which is the prime minister. The council's decisions are generally made by consensus, though a two-thirds majority of the members present is sufficient. There are a few specific issues for which consensus is required—amendment of the agreement, declaration of war, and issues relating to defense and security. The composition of the transitional government is outlined by this protocol. Articles 55 through 58 divide up positions between political parties.

The power-sharing protocol lists the recognized courts and bans the use of special courts. The Supreme Court is restored and its duties, composition, and procedures for appointing the president and vice president of the court are laid out in the protocol. Article 80 contains provisions on the Political Code of Ethics and establishes the National Unity and Reconciliation Committee to monitor compliance with the code. The Supreme Court is given the power to exclude, at the request of the committee, any political force found guilty of violating the provisions of the Political Code of Ethics under the transitional regime.[16]

Articles 60 to 79 contain the provisions establishing the Transitional National Assembly, which shares legislative power with the transitional government. The Transitional National Assembly votes on laws while the government issues decrees in case of emergency or when the assembly is not in session. All officially recognized parties that have signed the Code of Ethics and committed themselves to abiding by the principles of the Protocol Agreement on the Rule of Law, supporting the peace process, and avoiding any sectarian practice or violence are to be represented in the Transitional National Assembly.[17] Each of the parties participating in the government coalition is to have the same number of seats in the assembly. The National Assembly has numerous tools for controlling the government, including the power to take a vote of no confidence, which would result in the resignation of a particular minister, or even possibly the entire government.

The Protocol Agreement on the Repatriation of Refugees and the Resettlement of Displaced Persons.   The Rwandan government's refusal to allow refugees to return home was one of the main causes of the 1990 war. Therefore, it was critical both to allow their return and to find ways to ensure that the returning refugees and displaced populations are protected. Additionally it was necessary to make their return as orderly as possible in order to avoid disturbances that could undermine the peace process. Article 1 of the protocol on refugees and displaced persons recognized that "the return of Rwandan refugees to their country is an inalienable right and a factor of peace, national unity and reconciliation." The protocol defines the basic principles of this right and requires the government to facilitate access to unoccupied lands.[18] The protocol calls for the organization of these development sites and provides for economic assistance and the reintegration of their populations into the Rwandan economy. The protocol also guarantees equal opportunities and the equitable distribution of aid and access to employment, placing a special emphasis on language training.[19] Language training is particularly important because many of the returning refugees have grown up speaking languages not spoken in Rwanda.[20] Another important element of the protocol is that, though the refugees' rights to recover their property have been recognized, it was recommended that, for the sake of national harmony and reconciliation, those refugees who had been outside of the country for more than ten years should not claim their property if it had been occupied. This recommendation demonstrates the desire to respect the competing rights of all people, which is particularly difficult in practice. In recognition of the experiences and practical realities of the refugees' lives, Article 7 allows for citizens to have dual nationality.

The Protocol Agreement on the Integration of the Armed Forces.   This protocol agreement was intended to establish a truly national army for the first time in the history of the Republic of Rwanda, to ensure equal opportunities for all ethnic groups and to avoid the domination of the army by one group, as had been the case with the Hutu-dominated army. The high command of the Hutu army had been almost exclusively made up of people from the region around Ruhengeri and Gisenyi, which was the home of President Habyarimana. Under the protocol, all the members of the Council of the High Command of the Army were to be appointed directly by the Council of Ministers, whereas the general officers, field officers, and company officers were appointed and promoted by the Council of Ministers on the recommendation of the High Command of the Army (Articles 20–22). As part of the effort to build an army that is loyal to the entire country, this protocol provides that the military and the police will receive civic and political training.

Protocol of Agreement on Miscellaneous Issues and Final Provisions.   This part of the Arusha Agreement organizes the state security services and supplements the other protocols with its general provisions. The first section of chapter 1 relates to security services. The issue of the reorganization and training of communal police services, the public prosecutor's office, and prison guards and wardens was highlighted. Article 1(C)(1) stipulates, for example, that the public prosecutor's office should be "reorganized in depth" and opened up to all Rwandans. This provision provides some insight into the arbitrariness that formerly prevailed and the exceptional prerogatives and partisan behavior of the public prosecutor's office under the previous government.

Section 2 describes the different state security services, detailing their structure, their guiding principles, and their coordination. This section also provides for the participation of the Rwandan Patriotic Front in the exercise of power at all levels of the government and the protection of the fundamental freedoms of Rwandan citizens. Article 15 of the last chapter, on general provisions, makes it compulsory for the transition government to ratify all international human rights instruments that Rwanda has yet to ratify and remove all reservations that Rwanda had expressed regarding those already ratified. Article 17 on public freedoms and fundamental rights confirms the supremacy of the principles of the Universal Declaration of Human Rights over those of the Rwandan Constitution. This final chapter also designates the Transitional National Assembly as the institution responsible for interpreting the Peace Agreement and states that only the interpretation of that body will be official. Thus, its interpretation is political and not judicial.

The RPF Declaration of July 17, 1994, on the Establishment of Institutions

Unfortunately, things did not develop in the way anticipated by the Arusha Agreement. In its attempt to retain the power it was about to lose, the former single party (the MRND), led by President Habyarimana, did not respect its commitments under the Arusha Agreement and resorted to extreme violence: genocide of the Tutsis and the extermination of Hutu opponents, individuals in the civil society who did not pay allegiance to *Akazu*, and so-called moderate Hutus.

The RPF again took up arms and, after taking Kigali, expressed its intention to continue to abide by the substance of the Arusha Agreement. This declaration of July 17, 1994, reaffirmed the RPF's commitment to the principles of establishing the rule of law, forming a national army open to all Rwandans, and power sharing in the transition government (Article 1).

The new government modified the power-sharing arrangement of the peace agreements in response to the new political realities. The declaration established the post of vice president of the republic, to be held jointly with a cabinet post (Article 2). The declaration also provided for the army to be represented in the National Assembly and gave the president broader powers than those set out in the Arusha Agreement. The president could now initiate a ministerial reshuffle and remove the prime minister from office, subject to the approval of the National Assembly. If the Council of Ministers was unable to make a decision, the decision-making power would fall to the president. Moreover, given the role played by Rwanda's Armed Forces in the genocide, and despite the appeals made by the Rwandan Patriotic Army (RPA) command, the old army forces were no longer to be integrated into the new army according to the terms provided for in the Protocol Agreement on the Integration of the Armed Forces. Integration was to be carried out by selecting only the members of the Rwandan Armed Forces that had not compromised themselves by participating in the genocide. The president of the republic was to be chosen by consensus by the RPF Political Bureau, while the process for appointing the prime minister did not change from the process described in the Arusha Agreement.

The Protocol Agreement Between the Political Powers

This protocol confirms the partnership between the RPF and the other Rwandan political forces. It adopted the RPF's July 17 declaration and distributed assembly seats evenly among the participating parties (thirteen seats each).

The fundamental law is far from being as concise as might be desired in a constitution. The details of this law could act as obstacles to achieving its principles and may increase the likelihood that acts of the government will be found to be unconstitutional. Additionally, in order to adapt the fundamental law to the new realities of the country, the new legislature introduced several amendments, making the application of the fundamental law even more complicated and perhaps damaging the normative force of the constitution. Moreover, these amendments were carried out without the requisite consultation of the population.

The Basic Act Revision of January 18, 1996

In order to adapt the Basic Act to the new realities of the country, the new legislature introduced several amendments, which were initially grouped together under this law that entered into effect a year and a half after the beginning of the transition.

After the genocide, the judicial system was virtually paralyzed by the lack of qualified personnel. To enable it to begin functioning again, the government relaxed Article 31 of the protocol on power sharing, which had required superior court judges to hold a bachelor's degree in law and granted a special dispensation to judges of courts of first instance and appeal courts, which allowed people who were not Bachelors of Law to serve as judges on these courts. The only judges not affected by this relaxation of requirements were the presidents of the superior courts and the appeal courts. In the same vein, a special dispensation was introduced in Article 38 of the same protocol in order to organize the first meeting of the High Council of Judges.[21]

The government also modified the Protocol Agreement on the Integration of the Armed Forces to ensure the operation of military tribunals and to organize jurisdictional privileges within the military command. In addition, the revision allowed military courts to judge civilians accused of aiding and abetting the military in the genocide and other crimes, such as destruction of property and pillaging. However, the decisions handed down by these military courts could be appealed to the Highest Court of Appeal, which can be construed as an application of the principle of "oneness of acts" that makes it possible to judge acts of different natures that make up the same crime, but the judgment of civilians by military courts presents definite dangers for the civilians' rights.

The government also modified Article 12 (2) of the 1991 constitution to allow for the retroactivity of the law in cases "where an exceptional public danger threatens the existence of the nation." The new government also added a provision stating: "Acts and omissions which were not punishable at the time they were committed may be investigated and judged if they were considered criminal in the light of the general legal principles recognized as such by the law of nations." This provision was intended to cover acts of genocide and crimes against humanity committed between 1990 and 1994. In 1996 an institutional act was adopted to deal with these crimes.[22]

Rwanda's Legal System: Origin and Main Characteristics

Until independence, Rwanda's legal system was the colonial law of the Belgian Congo, which had been extended to Rwanda and Burundi, territories then under Belgian control. The Colonial Charter created two categories of rules, created and maintained as two separate systems.[23] The written law applied to Europeans and to "Europeanized groups" of the indigenous population, while "indigenous custom" governed relationships among most local people. The practical breakdown of these categories was essentially race-based (that is, between blacks and whites). In reality, however, the indigenous population was governed both by the customary law and the texts enacted by the colonizer in cases in which the colonizer wanted to make changes in the lifestyle of Rwandans. For instance, customary marriage was considered valid and legally recognized, except that polygamy was expressly banned.

After independence, the written law inherited from the Belgians was applied to all Rwandans and it is these same inherited texts that form the framework of Rwandan law today.[24] Thus, the National Assembly has the power to legislate either on the initiative of the government or on its own. However, the population is not sufficiently consulted on the process of law adoption, nor are the observations of the various constituent groups (the civil society) taken into consideration. A case in point was the adoption of the Institutional Act on the Organization of the Prosecution of Offenses Constituting the Crime of Genocide or Crimes Against Humanity, committed on or after October 1, 1990, the details of which I will explain below.

Customary and Written Laws

In Rwanda, as in many African countries, there are tensions between written and traditional laws, especially regarding individual and family law. This tension is particularly acute in issues of individual status, lineage, and inheritance.

According to Article 98 of the 1991 constitution, written law should prevail over customary rule; custom is only to complement written law. In practice, however, some courts have given preference to custom in an attempt to alleviate the potentially harsh effects of the law, particularly regarding affiliation and inheritance.[25]

Part of the tension comes from the different paradigms of written family law and customary law. The most common cases involve affiliation and paternity suits for children born of polygamous customary marriages. Polygamy was abolished in 1950, but customary marriage was recognized until 1988, when the individual and family law was adopted, a situation which contributed to a certain confusion in peoples' minds. Furthermore, customary law has maintained a certain "passive resistance" to change,[26] which means that certain things are perceived as profoundly rooted in a cultural identity that cannot be changed without causing harm. Affiliation is just one example. In Rwandan customary law, every child born of a lawfully married woman is the child of his or her mother's husband, whatever the circumstances. This remains valid even if the husband is absent for several years, or even if the child is of another color than the two spouses, which goes well beyond the simple presumption of paternity professed by modern law.[27] Written law has changed this, and has introduced the notion of the adulterine child, which is viewed as harmful by some in Rwandan society.

Customary law approaches marriage as the result of a formal understanding between two families, rather than a relationship between two individuals. Such agreements are public, and the persons who are considered to be the wisest members of the family, community, or neighborhood act as negotiators. The same persons settle the separation process if the couple ceases to get along. Even today, the great majority of the population, particularly in rural areas, continues to use this traditional process, where marriage and divorce is concerned, as it is more accessible to the society than the family code. While these traditional practices facilitate social cohesion, they are problematic in that they do not treat everyone equally; men are often privileged. Moreover, because of the inaccessibility of the formal legal system, the advantages it can provide do not benefit most of the people. For example, when couples separate, the children often remain with their father's family, because in this patriarchal society children belong to the father, and mothers seldom have the material resources needed to raise children on their own. The child support to be paid by the father provided for in the family code is rarely paid and, when it is, is grossly insufficient for raising a child.

Finally, it is unfortunate that many customary practices have been left by the wayside, especially in matters of criminal law and public law, where no reference is made to the precolonial organization of society. Some ideas of punishment and compensation that are not found in Rwanda's modern laws might be useful in the current situation in Rwanda. For example, under customary law, when one person harmed another, the official reaction was not necessarily to punish the crime or offense of the person who violated society's rules. Rather, the emphasis was on reparation or *icyiru* to the community or the person whose rights had been harmed.[28] This type of sanction applied for most crimes other than murder and treason, which were punishable by death.

Religious laws such as Muslim law (*shariʿa*) are not taken into consideration by Rwandan legislation or custom. Recently, however, new jurisdictions inspired by customary law have been created to hear and determine crimes of genocide. These are a revised form of the *gacaca* institution[29] a traditional system of justice involving local people in trying the accused when the disputes were not submitted to the authorities. Arrangements were made by family chiefs (*abatware bʿimiryango*), those family friends or neighbors perceived as wise to the satisfaction of both parties through arbitration. Arrangements often included payment of icyiru by the guilty. It should be noted that murders could never be brought before *gacaca*.

Today, in response to the serious cases posed by the genocide, the Rwandan government has decided to innovate by setting up a participatory justice system that can pronounce sentences of imprisonment and impose community service. Rwanda is faced with the following dilemma: on the one hand, the need to do justice and put an end to impunity, and, on the other hand, the impossibility of doing justice and the problem of what to do with the potentially massive numbers of prisoners after their condemnation. The sections to follow will illustrate the lack of means of the Rwandan justice system and the magnitude of the task at hand. The accused number is in the hundreds of thousands (there are currently 120,000 prisoners awaiting trial), and they have the right to be judged equitably and without undue delay. In the three years since the justice system was set up, it has been able to judge only a tiny fraction (some 2,000) of these cases. Moreover, the International Criminal Tribunal for Rwanda, set up by the United Nations with much greater means than the Rwandan government, has only been able to hand down five decisions at a cost of US $140 million.[30]

Thus, the idea of reestablishing the gacaca tribunals in order to deal with crimes of genocide was born. Contrary to the old gacaca, they will have considerable popular involvement at all administrative levels from the smallest body (cells) to the prefectorial level. Twenty elected arbitrators will sit in the *gacaca*. Among them, five persons will be elected as coordinators to lead the debates and record discussions and judgments. The judgments handed down may be appealed at the next higher level (from cells to communes and from communes to prefectures), and will be enforceable by the law enforcement authorities. The judgments of prefectorial *gacaca* will be final.

Rwandan citizens and certain international organizations have proffered both much criticism and favorable comments on these jurisdictions. After the methods of law enforcement and the mechanisms of these tribunals become better known, a proper, in-depth analysis can be made of them, but for the time being we reserve judgment on these tribunals due to lack of sufficient information.

Status of International Conventions

Rwanda is among those countries that, in order to promote their international image, have ratified a large number of international conventions and have also not attracted much negative attention by placing a lot of reservations on the conventions they have ratified. According to Luc Sindjoun, this kind of policy has been part of the "state's system of seduction" aimed at the international community.[31] Nonetheless, the Additional Protocols to the International Covenant on Civil and Political Rights were not ratified, and, moreover, Rwanda placed reservations on Article 9 of the Convention on the Prevention and Punishment of the Crime of Genocide, regarding the competence of the International Court of Justice at The Hague to settle disputes or interpret the convention. This reservation is however automatically revoked by Article 15 of the Protocol of Agreement between the Government of the Rwandan Republic and the Rwandan Patriotic Front on Miscellaneous issues and Final Provisions, but the additional protocols referred to above have still not been ratified.

Since 1992, Article 6 of the convention on the rule of law incorporates international human rights instruments, specifically the Universal Declaration of Human Rights and the African Charter on Human and Peoples' Rights, which, therefore, are part of the Basic Act. Officially, the direct effect of all the international instruments ratified by Rwanda is accepted, even if they are not incorporated into domestic law, if, however they can be enforced immediately without requiring enforcement measures or adaptation to domestic legislation. Thus, in Rwanda, in the purest tradition of constitutional law, judges are obliged to "enforce the provisions of conventions when these are enforceable in all cases brought before [them]."[32] In cases where the texts require the creation of a framework or the adoption of enforcement measures, it remains that provisions of domestic law contrary to the rights guaranteed by these international instruments should not be enforced and in the event that they are, the state will be accountable. However, in practice, it is difficult to find jurisprudence to confirm the doctrine on this specific point.[33] In Rwanda, perhaps more than anywhere else, international law has an "inhibiting" effect.[34] Indeed, international standards are complex and unfamiliar to judges and lawyers and reveal, as we shall see below, the limits of professional training of Rwandan judicial personnel, although their short-term training programs increasingly stress the importance of knowledge of international standards.

Rwanda's Judicial System

Organization of the Judicial System

Based on the Belgian/French model, Rwanda's judicial system is made up of the following branches: the courts and tribunals, the public prosecutor's offices, and the judicial administration and resource management section. The administration and resource management section are under the authority of the Supreme Court in the Department of Courts and Tribunals.

Courts and Tribunals.   The canton courts are the lowest courts, followed by the courts of first instance, the courts of appeal, and, finally, the Supreme Court at the top of the pyramid.[35] Rwanda has 143 canton courts, 12 magistrate courts, and 4 appellate courts.

Canton courts have original jurisdiction over civil matters involving sums up to fifty thousand (Rwandan francs [FRW] 50,000, about US$150) and disputes governed by customary law. There is one canton court in each administrative district. The courts of first instance deal with disputes involving amounts of more than FRW 50,000 (US$150) and most criminal matters. They also handle issues of preventative detention and hear appeals of judgments made by the canton courts. Each prefecture has at least one court of first instance. The courts of appeal hear appeals of trial judgments made by courts of first instance.

The Supreme Court consists of the following departments:

1. The Department of Courts and Tribunals, which is the administrative section and manages magistrates' careers and the operation of courts and tribunals.
2. The Court of Cassation, the final court for appealing judicial decisions. It does not rule on the merits of cases, but rather interprets the law applied in the case. It also has original jurisdiction over cases involving the highest authorities of the state.
3. The Constitutional Court, which examines the constitutionality of laws and decrees before they are promulgated.
4. The State Council, an administrative court that hears challenges to the legality of regulations and decrees of administrative authorities. It is also consulted as an adviser on legislative or regulatory bills.
5. The Auditor General's Department, which oversees the government's accounts and state-owned enterprises on behalf of the National Assembly.

The Public Prosecutor's Office.   The public prosecutor's office is responsible for judicial investigations. It investigates crimes, identifies the perpetrators, and brings them before the court for judgment. There are twelve public prosecutor's offices, each of which is linked to a magistrate court and four offices of the director of public prosecutions (DPP), which serve the four appellate courts. The judges are appointed by the Supreme Council of Judges, while the prosecutors, from the public prosecutor's offices up through the director of public prosecutions are appointed by the Council of Ministers.

Judicial Staff Training.   Rwanda's judicial system has never had a professional staff that was sufficiently trained to carry out its responsibilities. For example, many magistrates have had no legal training. At the same time, young law graduates have been, on occasion, discouraged from becoming judges.[36] In 1993, out of 708 magistrates, only 45 were jurists whose degree of qualification was unknown.[37] This weakness was corrected by the Arusha Agreement, which required high court magistrates to hold at least a bachelor's degree.

After the genocide and the massacres, the situation became even worse.

In April 1995, only 253 judges or prosecutors remained in the entire court system.[38] It was not possible to respect the minimum training requirements imposed by the Arusha Agreement for fear of completely paralyzing a judicial system that was already barely functioning. As a stopgap emergency measure, the Ministry of Justice organized intensive three-month training programs. Seven hundred people were trained and appointed to the judicial system in 1995 alone. They began working as magistrates, judicial police inspectors, registrars, and typists.

In view of the legacy of the genocide, there was a great deal of emphasis on training judicial police in Rwandan law, international standards, arrest procedure, investigation, and detention.[39] The government hopes that the jurists graduating from the university each year will, over time, fill the shortage of qualified personnel. In addition, the government has increased the salaries of the judicial staff in a move to attract and retain qualified staff.

Judicial Officers

The term "judicial officer" refers to those individuals accredited by the Ministry of Justice to defend persons accused of crimes before the courts. In the absence of a bar association or any other form of oversight, these justice proxies are not necessarily expected to be jurists or to obey any professional code of ethics. Moreover, their accreditation depends only on the good will of the Ministry of Justice. The formation of a bar association had not been permitted in Rwanda due to the totalitarian nature of the regimes in place before July 1994, which did not tolerate any institutions that might challenge them. A law establishing a bar association has recently been passed. However, due to the rather small number of lawyers (less than sixty in the whole country), the law on the foundation of a law society recognized what it calls "judicial defenders," and it regulates their training and their mode of operation. Judicial defenders can counsel and represent accused persons before courts of first instance. Judicial defenders are paralegals.

Operation of the Judicial System

Rwanda has always lacked the political will to build sound and independent judicial institutions. Unsurprisingly, staff without the training or skills for their positions have, therefore, worked in whatever manner was best for them, usually to the detriment of the plaintiff. The general rule has been to gain as much from a position as possible before being replaced. In addition to the lack of qualified personnel, one need only see the tiny, rundown premises allotted to even the highest jurisdictions, such as the Court of Cassation, to be convinced of the low priority given to the creation and promotion of strong and independent judicial institutions.

Additionally, it should be noted that French is only taught in Rwanda in secondary school, and thus the magistrates who have received only primary school education or one or two years of secondary education do not speak or read French. Most legal texts and documentation are in French, and French is used in the training seminars organized by the Ministry of Justice. Thus, many magistrates cannot use legal texts or benefit from the training seminars.

As already indicated, war and genocide have made this situation worse. Buildings and records were destroyed, many qualified personnel died, and the government's coffers were emptied. In the immediate aftermath of the war, the judicial system was no longer operational due to lack of staff,[40] equipment, and funds. However, the Arusha Agreement, which aimed to build a nation based on the rule of law, required all magistrates of the high courts to hold at least a bachelor's law degree. When the negotiations leading to the adoption of the Arusha Agreement took place they were not intended to manage a postgenocide situation, which is why after July 1994 some provisions stressing guiding principles seem to contradict the actual situation.

The first arrests and imprisonments related to genocide and crimes against humanity were carried out by the RPF military. The military was gradually replaced by the gendarmes, who were authorized to make arrests. In most cases, the files of the accused only consist of statements written by the military. The state has not had the means to follow judicial procedure. Though most of the prosecutor's offices started operating only in 1996, efforts were made to regularize the detention of those already in prison and to ensure that the detention of new arrestees conformed to the law. This has been a particularly important development, because it is during the preliminary investigation, when the accused is under the authority of the public prosecutor that most human rights violations occur. It should be recognized that the preliminary investigation takes place in an extremely difficult context, because not only does the DPP lack adequate resources, but also the entire atmosphere is one of suspicion, insecurity, and prejudice.[41]

In this context, some judicial and legislative reforms were necessary to adapt to the new situation after the genocide. These reforms include a law establishing provisional modifications of the Penal Procedural Code (PPC) relating to arrests and detentions, adopted by the Transitional National Assembly on May 26, 1996.[42] This law, which is retroactive to April 6, 1994, aims at regularizing arrests and detentions carried out since that date. It authorizes the extension of detention and deprives the accused of his or her right to appeal the detention decisions. The law was a temporary and exceptional measure necessitated both by the nature and scope of the violence and by the destruction of Rwanda's judicial infrastructure (the measure was to last three years, ending July 17, 1999). Furthermore, for the dispute over genocide, there is a provision for a procedure for the pretrial release of individuals found to deserve provisional or final liberation. The task of deciding who should be liberated has been entrusted to the Sorting Committees, which formed at the prefecture level, are made up of representatives of the Ministries of Defense, Interior, and Intelligence, and the director of public prosecutions.

The most glaring weaknesses of Rwanda's judicial system include:

1. The canton courts were essentially not operational in early 1996.[43]
2. Several thousands of illegally arrested people (i.e., people arrested using procedures that did not comply with the law) were still detained in central prisons or administrative district or prefecture jails.
3. All courts lack adequate and skilled personnel.
4. Most of the offices allocated to the courts are cramped, dilapidated, and inadequately furnished. The roofs leak in a country where it rains nine months of the year. Records are kept in a haphazard manner. Despite the purchase of motorcycles, there is insufficient transportation for the investigative staff. There are neither telephones nor electricity in most offices.
5. Only an OMP (Officer du Ministère Public) can deliver an arrest warrant, and this can only be done after the OMP has personally questioned the accused. Until 1996, there was only one OMP per prosecutor's office. A single person simply cannot question the many hundreds of people suspected of participating in the genocide in any given magistrate court district. In 1996, the OMP was replaced by judicial police inspectors, who can interrogate suspects and deliver warrants for arrest against them.
6. Due to the enormity (quantitatively and qualitatively) of the genocide and crimes against humanity, there is a tendency to trivialize minor crimes in order to avoid adding to the backlog of work for the prosecutor's office. Therefore, "amicable solutions" are encouraged. Even property violations committed during the genocide are considered civil cases and subjected to amicable settlements under the authority of local administrators.
7. For ordinary crimes, unrelated to the genocide, regular hearings are compromised by understaffing. Judges, therefore, increasingly resort to using emergency laws, allowing cases to be provisionally decided by a single judge, rather than a panel of judges.
8. By 1996, the Supreme Court, which had been reinstated, still had

inadequate office space. Two of its departments, the Court of Cassation and the State Council, had small, run-down offices, and the other sections were temporarily housed in the offices of the Kigali Appellate Court.
9. Legal documentation is scarce.
10. Not a single tribunal owned a vehicle in early 1996.

Nonetheless, judicial institutions have been gradually reestablished, and there have been several notable developments. The special courts have been abolished. The Supreme Court has been reinstated and a bar association has been created. A Supreme Council of Judges has also been established. Its members are elected by fellow magistrates and the council is responsible for the appointment and assignment of magistrates. Additionally, the operation of courts and tribunals is now overseen by the Supreme Court, which is expected to significantly reduce the executive's control over the judiciary.

Institutional Act on the Organization of the Prosecution of Offenses Constituting the Crime of Genocide or Crimes Against Humanity, Committed on or after October 1, 1990

The law on legal proceedings relating to genocide is extremely important to the development of the legal culture of Rwanda. This law, promulgated on August 30, 1996, governs the indictment of people charged with genocide or crimes against humanity. It is an attempt to reach a compromise between the need to put an end to impunity and the political need for national reconciliation. The law, which is extremely controversial, as was to be expected, given the circumstances, consists of seven chapters. The first chapter defines the crimes covered by the law.

The second delineates the time period and defines the four designated categories of crime dealt with in this law. The law covers crimes committed between October 1, 1990, and December 31, 1994. Similar types of crimes committed after this period are to be governed by the penal code, according to the general law on genocide and crimes against humanity. This distinction is explained by the fact that any acts of genocide committed after 1994 are not considered to have been sponsored or encouraged by the government. Consequently, although all instances of such crimes are considered just as serious as those committed during the 1990s, they cannot be dealt with in the same manner.[44] The first category includes "the planners, organizers, instigators, supervisors and leaders," people representing the political, civil, military, or religious authorities, murderers who showed particular zeal in the killings or excessive malice, and those found guilty of acts of sexual torture. There can be no reduction of sentences handed down for people found guilty of this category of crimes, and they are systematically sentenced to death. The second category concerns the perpetrators or accomplices of premeditated homicides. The third category involves those found guilty of other serious human rights violations. The fourth category covers property violations.

The third chapter of the law lays out the procedures for confession and guilty pleas and allows for the reduction of sentences for those who admit their crimes. The amount of the reduction depends on whether the person confesses before or after trial. However, no sentence reduction is allowed for defendants who are accused of crimes in the first category.

Chapter 4 establishes the sentences for each of the categories. Upon a finding of guilt, criminals in the first category are sentenced to death. A guilty finding for the second category of crime leads to life imprisonment with the possibility of sentence reduction if the defendant confesses. If the accused confesses before trial, the life sentence is reduced to from seven to eleven years, whereas, if the person confesses after being convicted, the sentence will be twelve to fifteen years in prison. For the third category, the court will impose the sentences prescribed in the penal code. Such sentences will be reduced to one-third the prescribed length if the accused confesses before trial and to one-half upon confession after trial. In both cases, the sentences handed down take the duration of pretrial detention into consideration. For the fourth category, civil reparations are encouraged; if the accused is sentenced to a prison term, the sentence is suspended.

Chapter 5 deals with the courts that will hear these cases. It establishes special courts within the magistrate and military courts. There will be several of these special courts, including one that will be made up of juvenile court judges to hear only cases involving minors. Chapter 6 establishes the procedures for appeals. A ruling of the court of appeal can only be appealed if, after having been acquitted by a tribunal, the appellate jurisdiction hands down a death penalty. In such cases, the defendant is allowed to appeal to the Court of Cassation, which will render a final judgment on the merits of the case. This is an exception because ordinarily the Court of Cassation does not rule on merits, but only on form, and reverses decisions that it deems affected by irregularities, in which case the decision returns to a court of appeal for a new judgment on merits. Here, a case may be tried on merits by three different jurisdictions, first the court of first instance, then the court of appeal, and, if the latter hands down a death sentence, the Court of Cassation may be appealed to and may decide on the merits of the case in the last instance. Finally, the last two chapters are devoted to damages and final provisions.

While a person who is found guilty of murder will be sentenced to life in prison under Rwanda's penal code, this law allows that a person who committed murder with the intention of participating in genocide will be sentenced to only seven to eleven years, provided that he confesses. Genocide survivors have voiced their opposition to this law, which they find too lenient. At the time it was passed, there was a debate about whether there should be public education campaigns about the law. Human rights organizations expressed their concern that such campaigns should have taken place before the passage of the law and that there should have been time for a national debate on the subject. The fact that almost no one confesses or enters a guilty plea, and that witnesses continue to be murdered, has escalated the controversy over the wisdom of mercy for those who participated in genocide.

Sociopolitical and Economic Environment

The prescriptive and structural framework described above implies that the political evolution of Rwanda is similar to that of many other African countries: the institution of a one-party system, the constitutionalization of a military regime, and the adoption of a strong presidential regime. Ethnic politics and the gap between legal theory and reality are all too common in Africa. The first two republics of Rwanda established and maintained a system of Hutu supremacy and the concomitant exclusion of Tutsis from government. The principles that instituted the supremacy of some and the exclusion of others were based on race,[45] and on what Donald L. Horowitz calls "struggles over belonging."[46] Indeed, according to those in power, who reproduced many colonial theories, Hutus were "authentic Rwandans," while Tutsis were considered to be foreign, not only to Rwanda, but also to the whole Bantu family, and probably to Africa. This system of supremacy and exclusion is not explicit either in the constitution or in the laws of the period.

The Hutu-Tutsi Conflict

Since independence, political life in Rwanda has been largely defined by decolonization and the Hutu-Tutsi conflict. The Hutu-Tutsi conflict is among the most violent domestic conflicts ever experienced in Africa. Most conflicts in Africa have the appearance of ethnic or religious conflicts, although other factors can have the same effect, or ethnicity can be a consequence rather than a cause. They are the result of the dominance of one individual or group and the exclusion of others, and they are aggravated by the difficult context of building a nation in the aftermath of colonization. In Rwanda, as in other countries, the historic context, external factors, economic factors, and issues of governance, in combination, have led to the conflict between those in power and those seeking greater social justice.

The Historic Context

In Rwanda, references to history are constant, and the current violence is often said to be rooted in history. A brief review of Rwanda's various periods is necessary to understand the events and dynamics that led to the 1994 crisis and created the current situation.

Ancient and Colonial Rwanda.   In what is now Rwanda, power was exercised at the highest level by the Tutsi *mwami* (king), and in some regions and at certain times by Hutu kings, or Abahinza. The mode of government was organized such that three governors, *abatware*,[47] each had authority over a single geographical territory. They had separate yet interdependent powers, and thus a balance was maintained because they all needed each other. In principle, any of these governors could be either Hutu or Tutsi; however, in general, they were distributed as follows: *Umutware b'ubutaka*, or the governor of the land, was Hutu and dealt with problems involving agriculture and farmers, *umutware w'umukenke*, a Tutsi, was in charge of pastures and herders as well as their livestock, *umutware w'ingabo*, who could be Tutsi or Hutu according to personal merit, usually based on recognition of bravery, was the chief of the army. Thus, Hutus and Tutsis were included and both groups had recourse in the event of a problem or an abuse of power by any of the authorities.[48]

In Nduga, central Rwanda (under the direct authority of the *mwami*), the majority of the governors or other authorities were Tutsis, while in the north and west, Bushiru Bugoyi, Bukunzi, and Busozo were independently ruled by the *Bahinza*. They merely had to pay tribute to the *mwami* and participate along with the other regions in defensive wars or invasions led by Rwanda. Most of the leaders of these latter regions were Hutus. It should be noted, moreover, that membership in any Hutu or Tutsi group was not static but dynamic, and that changes in membership and social status were common, especially in central Rwanda.

Similarly, the social system differed according to region. In central Rwanda, the *buhake* system was a patronage contract between an owner of cattle and a person who wanted to own cattle. The latter had to carry out certain social services in exchange for one or several heads of cattle that the owner turned over to him. In the north, there was a *bukonde* system, whereby big landowners lent portions of farmland to those who had none in exchange for various agricultural services. In these systems, both partners owed each other assistance and allegiance but remained free to break the bonds of *buhake* or *bukonde* and change partners. In general, *bukonde* was practiced by big Hutu landowners and buhake by big Tutsi herders. However, this did not prevent Tutsis from also being farmers and Hutus from also raising livestock. *Buhake* was abolished in 1954 by the *mwami*, but *bukonde* continued to be practiced even after independence.

When the German, Dutch, and Belgian colonizers and missionaries arrived in the late 1800s and early 1900s, they applied their own conceptions of race and society to Rwanda. Though they found a people speaking the same language and sharing the same culture within the same social organization,[49] they categorized Rwandans into three distinct ethnic groups that they believed originated from different racial stock and distinct geographical areas. Hutus were said to be Bantu, Tutsis to be Hamitic, and Twas to be Pygmies. The colonizers' supposedly scientific theories were highly speculative, even fantastic. Some Europeans even believed the Tutsis to be of Tibetan origin.[50]

Starting around 1925, the Belgian government took over the administration of Rwanda. They installed Tutsi governors, deposed all the Hutu *batware*, and replaced them with Tutsis.[51] The Belgians viewed the *mwami* as a dangerous figure because of his power and therefore removed him.[52] The traditional administrative and organizational structures that had guaranteed social cohesion were destroyed. The Belgians created the positions of chief and deputy-chief, which concentrated political and administrative power at the regional level. Most importantly, these functions became hereditary. Hutus were thus permanently excluded, and a Tutsi monopoly was created.[53]

The Tutsi chiefs were closely controlled by the Belgian administration and enjoyed no real decision-making power. They were, in other words, no more than instruments of oppression in the hands of the colonizer. Those who rebelled were simply deposed. Forced labor, or *uburetwa*, began during this period,[54] and Tutsi administrators were required to provide the laborers. The Belgian policy of placing administrative power solely in the hands of the Tutsis alone led to a societal division based on racial categories and to the creation of an aristocracy of Tutsis.

In this context, the Hutu elites, educated in Catholic missions, formed the PARMEHUTU (Party for the Emancipation of the Hutu People) in the late 1950s as part of their struggle for social justice. The Tutsis, who were trying to free themselves from the colonizers' authority, formed the UNAR party (Rwanda National Union), which tried to bring Hutus and Tutsis together in the struggle for Rwanda's independence. Around this time, the colonial authority and the Church, two longtime allies, made an abrupt about-face; they began supporting the PARMEHUTU in its struggle and trying to undermine the Tutsis who had provoked them by demanding independence and forming relationships with other African nationalist movements.[55]

As a result of the opposition between colonial authorities and Tutsi chiefs, anti-Tutsi campaigns were mounted by the end of the fifties followed by violence against all Tutsis. In this highly charged atmosphere, the United Nations organized a referendum on the abolition of the monarchy. PARMEHUTU won the referendum, which UNAR boycotted. The Hutu's "Social Revolution" was under way. They ousted the *mwami* in particular and the Tutsis in general from power. Labeled as oppressors, Tutsis were driven away, stripped of their possessions or murdered. Hundreds of thousands of Tutsis left Rwanda, and tens of thousands were massacred. Those who survived and remained in the country after independence were considered second-class citizens and were continuously subjected to systematic violence and discrimination. The history taught in Rwandan schools until the 1980s had been shaped to match the racial theories introduced by the colonizers.[56]

Hutu Republics.   The Social Revolution did not end the injustice suffered by Rwandans prior to independence; rather, it simply inverted and aggravated it. Following the colonial model, the first two republics, lasting from 1962 to 1994, were based on racism and exclusion. Rwandans, especially the educated elite, appropriated the supposedly scientific theories of racial distinctions that had been imported by the colonizers.

The government of the First Republic, with the assurance of a government that enjoys the support of a large majority and the backing of the former colonial power, claimed the state identity for itself. In other words, Rwanda became a Hutu country. Power was finally in the hands of those viewed as the real children of the country. Rule by the Hutu *rubanda nyamwinshi* (majority) became synonymous with legitimacy. Being a Tutsi became a defect, an original sin. The Second Republic, established in 1973, did not question this belief. Nonetheless, during the Second Republic, the massacres of Tutsis ceased, though a policy of systematic discrimination persisted against Tutsis in all sectors of socioeconomic life. The Tutsis who fled Rwanda in 1959 were still not allowed to return home because, the government claimed, the country was too small and crowded. The founding myth of the two republics was Hutu supremacy based on the 1959 Social Revolution. Therefore, under the colonizers and during the first two republics as well, for a total of seventy-five years, Rwanda's leaders ruled the country according to a racial policy, first pro-Tutsi and later pro-Hutu.

As in many African nations, the difficulty of building a nation-state and uniting the people of Rwanda was linked to two particular aspects of colonization. The first was the colonizer's divide and rule strategy. The new modes of government perverted or destroyed traditional institutions, created illegitimate institutions, and installed chiefs charged with safeguarding the interests of the colonizers. This is what caused the ethnic divisions in Rwanda. Second, hasty decolonization and the lack of political maturity of the population made it easy for new leaders to manipulate the people. In the case of Rwanda, the population was not prepared at all. Health and education, for example, were completely in the hands of European missionaries. This monopoly, coupled with the missionaries' moral authority, explains the Church's power and role in Rwanda. Additionally, because the Belgians had intended to unite Rwanda-Urundi (as it was then called) with Congo, as of 1962, there were no urban centers, little infrastructure, and no university-trained Rwandans to form a future elite.

External Factors

The role played by Belgium in the violent decolonization and the establishment of a racist government in Rwanda is now well known. France later replaced Belgium in the painful history of modern Rwanda. Both powers not only supported false racial theories on the origin of the two main groups in Rwanda, but they also became directly involved in the violence, massacres, and genocide that befell Rwanda. Belgium, as the tutelary power, participated in the violence from 1959 to 1962; it sent in paratroopers under the command of Colonel Guy Logiest to "assist the Social Revolution" led by Hutus.[57] Belgium was later the principal supporter of the First Republic. Even today, extremist Hutus still receive support from Belgian Christian-Democrats.[58]

French support for the Habyarimana regime was initiated by President Valery Giscard d'Estaing in the 1970s and increased under President François Mitterand. Despite the notorious public atrocities committed by this regime, especially in its final years, France continued to provide massive and unconditional support until after the beginning of the genocide, thus propping up a criminal regime until the very end. The Habyarimana regime also enjoyed support from Switzerland and the United States.[59] Despite assassinations and the rampant abuse of power, Rwanda had a good reputation internationally. It was considered democratic because the ethnic majority was in power. Despite bureaucratic waste, corruption, and embezzlement, Rwanda continued to enjoy its good image, primarily because it seemed to be doing better than its neighbors, particularly Mobutu's Zaire, Uganda under Idi Amin and Milton Obote, and Julius Nyerere's "African socialism" in Tanzania. Lastly, Rwanda was seen as a paradise for foreign aid workers. The continuing international support made it easy for Rwandan authorities to treat the country as their personal property and to ignore the resentment of excluded groups.

In 1989, some Belgians began to recognize what was happening in Rwanda and timidly started denouncing abuses. However, Swiss, American, and French authorities continued to ignore the growing tensions. The French refusal to see the problem had particularly serious effects. France openly supported the Habyarimana regime in the years leading up to the civil war and continued to provide assistance during the war. It provided Rwanda's army with funding, arms, and training. It also trained the now infamous *interahamwe* militia,[60] shelled the RPF troops, and helped hundreds of participants in the genocide escape from justice.[61] Finally, it contributed to destabilizing the country over the long term, particularly through Operation Turquoise, hastily organized on the eve of the military victory of the RPF.[62] This French humanitarian military operation, which delimited a "humanitarian safe zone" on the border of what was then Zaire and Rwanda, allowed populations including militias, the defeated army, administration, and government to flee with all the state apparatus out of Rwanda.

This foreign support not only legitimized the Rwandans' racist acts in their own eyes, it also provided them with the economic and political means to accomplish their aims. I can illustrate the role of the United Nations simply by noting that Canadian General R. Dallaire, who commanded the MINUAR I United Nations peacekeeping troops stationed in Rwanda, sent a written message in January 1994 to the Secretary-General of the United Nations, Boutros Boutros-Ghali, informing him that, "one ethnic group was preparing to exterminate the other, and was also preparing an action against the MINUAR soldiers to shock them and make them leave Rwanda."[63] Despite this information, he merely asked for authorization to make the necessary verifications, identify the arms caches, and, if necessary, use force to protect civilians in danger. Boutros Boutros-Ghali (current secretary-general of the Organisation Internationale de la Francophonie— an international organization of French-speaking countries) and Kofi Annan, who was then in charge of UN peacekeeping operations and who succeeded Boutros Boutros-Ghali in the position of Secretary-General of the United Nations, did not reply. The genocide of the Tutsis began four months later in April 1994. The assassination of ten Belgian peacekeepers was committed in the first three days. Following that, MINUAR effectively pulled out of Rwanda in a hasty retreat.

Economic Factors and Governance

Economic factors and governance are closely related because the failure of economic management in African countries is linked to a personalized mode of political management by an extroverted clique through a patronage network. Everything works, in other words, through "membership and personal loyalty."[64] This is also valid elsewhere in Africa, but especially in

Rwanda, where the region of origin and the membership in a specific "ethnic" group determines virtually everything in people's lives. The ethnicization and regionalization of state structures was implemented methodically and sometimes with extreme violence.

Another connection between economic management and governance is the fact that maintaining power through repression requires a great deal of financial resources. In Rwanda, the government created a presidential guard endowed with exorbitant powers and privileges and established paramilitary groups. The cost of arming, training, and maintaining more than 20,000 militiamen required funds which could only be mobilized at the expense of other sectors of the national economy. In the absence of substantial sources of income, international aid was diverted. Sometimes alliances were struck with international drug-dealing and money-laundering networks.[65] Rwanda's militia was largely made up of unemployed youth from the capital, suggesting that poverty and the precariousness of people's lives create a population vulnerable to this kind of violence and manipulation.

Rwanda's major sociopolitical features before 1994 can be summed up by four key words: Hutuism or Hutu power, regionalism, authoritarianism, and Christianity.

Hutuism or Hutu Power.   Rwanda's political life has been marked since the First Republic by the emergence of Hutuism. Hutuism is an ideology intended to reinforce the power of Hutus and to exclude all others, even to the point of their elimination.[66] The spread of the ideology is probably the main achievement of the First Republic. The colonial theory whereby Tutsis were regarded as foreign invaders was reproduced, and the link was made between ethnic majority and democratic majority. In other words, there was a willful confusion between the notion of ethnic majority and that of democratic majority. The Second Republic reinforced this ideology and added to it with conceptions of regionalism and authoritarianism.

Hutuism led to the genocide of Tutsis and the massacre of moderate Hutus in 1994 because it identified all Tutsis, and even all Hutus who did not prescribe to it, as enemies to be mercilessly eliminated. Considered traitors to their race, the moderate Hutus were subjected to the same treatment as the Tutsis. Not surprisingly, the propaganda glorifying the Hutus and demonizing the Tutsis was absolute and elaborate, and the official media played a considerable role. It should be noted that national positions and statements made within various international bodies or authorities were ambiguous. The Rwandan genocide was unanimously condemned, but the racist ideology behind it was not. In fact, under the pretense of not taking sides between Hutus and Tutsis, they avoided condemning the cause of the genocide. This international response to Hutuism is a harmful attitude that reduces people to generalizations, in effect accepting that Hutus, because they are Hutus, must believe in Hutuism and are necessarily enemies of Tutsis, and vice versa. However, this ignores the reality that thousands of Hutus rejected Hutuism and were killed because of their refusal to adhere to this racist ideology. This attitude is not only harmful in that it reinforces the tenets of this criminal ideology, it is also off base. It is the same as saying—according to the sort of simplified schema of African sociopolitical relations favored by some—that Hutus, simply because they are Hutus, are proponents of Hutu Power and automatically enemies of the Tutsis and vice versa. Hutuism should be clearly condemned just like Nazism or any other form of institutionalized racism.

Regionalism. As explained above, the northern, southern, and central regions of Rwanda have had different political histories. The latter two regions were directly under the administration of the *mwami* of Rwanda, while northern Rwanda was autonomous and resisted the power of the Rwandan kings. For Hutu northerners, the southern Hutu populations are often seen as Tutsis,[67] while central and southern Hutu populations consider northerners uncivilized. At the start of the Second Republic, the population of each region and each ethnic group was tallied and a quota system was devised. This system was purported to ensure that each group was proportionately represented in education, employment (including in the private sector), and particularly in the army. However, these quotas were actually intended to perpetuate the supremacy of the northern Hutu populations in all sectors. In any case, the quotas were not respected.[68] For example, there was not a single Tutsi in the army or in the territorial administration.

Authoritarianism. Rwanda is a classic model of authoritarianism. All of the standard elements are present: the absence of any process for the popular legitimization of the state, the centralization of power, the absence of political involvement by the general population, the disenfranchisement of large segments of the population, the dominance of development over all other goals, an oppressive culture, and the abusive use of force.[69]

The MRND, the only legal party, controlled and disseminated the state ideology. By Habyarimana's decree, each Rwandan was a member of this party from birth until death. The society was divided into party entities, the smallest being the cell, or *nyumba kumi*, which means, literally, "ten houses." Each cell had a chief, through whom it linked up with the other cells to form larger groups. The party groupings were all linked in ever larger bodies, covering the entire country. No one could escape the "Movement" because it controlled everything. Everyone knew his or her place.

One could not travel from one place to another in Rwanda without authorization from the administrative authorities. The authorization to move from one region to another was generally refused, unless the person had employment-related reasons for requesting permission to move. Some commentators claim that the Rwandan government under Habyarimana had the tightest administrative control over its population of any country in the world, other than some of the communist bloc countries.[70] It should be noted that the party was not, in theory, political. The word political was avoided; rather, the party was called a "development institution."

Christianity.   The Church has contributed to the creation of the ethnic myths of Rwanda: the Tutsis as Hamitic aristocrats, the race of lords who came to colonize and organize the local peoples, and the Hutus as the authentic Rwandans, a simple, hardworking, and virtuous people who liberated themselves from the Tutsi invaders. The Church had control over education, health, development projects, and many sectors of the economy.[71] It was the moral guarantor of the system, from the smallest administrative unit to the largest. Indeed, the parish priest was always a member of the town council, and the archbishop of Kigali, head of the Rwandan Church, was a member of the MRND Central Committee.

As early as 1959, the priests were already preaching against Tutsi "communists," and they never issued any official condemnation against the widespread persecution and massacres of Tutsis. Within the Rwandan clergy, the same kind of discrimination and persecution was evident, but, again, the Church did not respond. Similarly, in 1994, the Church was clearly positioned alongside the regime. Perhaps this helps explain why, in such a highly Christianized country,[72] the population felt no compunction about turning churches into mass graves.

Together, these four ingredients—Hutuism, regionalism, authoritarianism, and the Church—led the country to genocide. The totalitarian racist regime had no alternative for staying in power than attempting to reconstitute "Hutu nationalism," which had been weakened by regionalism and the economic difficulties resulting from control by a predatory elite. Sadly, this old trick worked, as it had at the end of each earlier regime in Rwanda. Tutsis were the scapegoats and paid dearly. The end of colonialism witnessed the first massacres of Tutsis and sealed the alliance between the Belgian authorities and the Hutus. At the end of the First Republic in 1973, Habyarimana claimed to restore order and security for all after the pogroms and manhunts organized against Tutsis.[73] And, finally, in 1994, the Habyarimana regime ended with the massacres of moderate Hutus and the genocide of Tutsis.

The Transitional Regime, 1994 to the Present

In 1994, as the massacres and genocide started, the RPF took up arms again. It captured Kigali in July 1994, and, during that same month, an RPF-led coalition took power in the country. The devastation of the country at this time was almost unimaginable; half of the population had fled the country. With the assistance of France, the former Rwandan Army was rebuilding itself in Zaire and Tanzania under the protection of Mobutu and the United Nations.[74] The public coffers had been emptied by those fleeing the country. The political class had been decimated, the judicial system destroyed, and the social fabric had imploded. Hundreds of thousands Rwandans had taken part in the massacres. Hundreds of thousands of others were slaughtered or barely survived attacks by their neighbors. Others found themselves torn between the two sides of the societal divide. There were more than 500,000 orphans. Ethnic divides had never been so strong. In this painful context, all the people had to find a way to live together, justice had to be administered, security restored, and the country rebuilt, all while working toward national reconciliation.

The transitional government maintained the spirit of the Arusha Agreement. It instituted power sharing and attempted to establish the rule of law. However, the new government did introduce a few modifications to the agreement, in order to adapt to the new situation. In particular, it made the head of the armed forces the vice president, and the RPF took the ministerial posts that had been allocated to the now-disqualified MRND. Because it was formed after the military victory of the RPF, which is primarily made up of Tutsis, the new government was seen by the Western media as a Tutsi government. This is a misrepresentation. Hutus hold numerous important positions. The RPF has shown its willingness to work with other political parties to rebuild and run the country.

In the current postwar context, Rwanda's army (RPA) plays an important role. Though the majority of the army is Tutsi, any Rwandan is free to join the RPA and make a career in the military. This includes members of the former Rwandan Armed Forces (Ex-FAR) who have proven that they did not participate in the massacres. Some Ex-FAR members have already enrolled and have retained their ranks, thus establishing Rwanda's first multiethnic army.

The government has had to face many challenges all at once, including poverty, a paralyzed justice system, underdevelopment, and the desperate need for national reconciliation. Moreover, even in the most favorable conditions, the defeat of an authoritarian regime on the battlefield does not necessarily mean that the victorious insurgents will be able to ensure a transition to democracy.[75] The challenges have been particularly great in Rwanda, where people distrust each other, ethnic mechanisms come into play at every turn, the population does not know and has no reason to trust the new politicians, and the sentiments that led to the genocide remain. Many have questioned the political will to punish the authors of genocide. In legal terms, the basic principles have been established and reasonably well respected.[76] Independent institutions must still be built in order to implement these principles, a massive task that is unlikely to be completed within the five-year deadline set by the RPF for organizing elections.

In light of the general context, the organization of presidential and legislative elections were deferred and the five-year initial transition period was extended by four years. An electoral commission was set up in order to prepare for elections, the law establishing it was passed by the National Assembly in November 2000, its bureau has been appointed, and it is setting up its operating framework. Moreover, the election of territorial government authorities has already begun with the election of district officials, and the electoral campaign for the communal elections is underway.

The Status and Role of Human Rights Organizations

Rwanda has had a rich and varied civil society. Most associations or NGOs are involved with development projects and are either cooperative or church-based organizations. The government allowed or even encouraged these associations to the extent that they were associations concerned only with development, were not politically active, and were, on the contrary, in the service of the authorities. It should be remembered again that everyone belonged to the MRND. These associations, although they were not officially part of the MRND, were infiltrated and closely controlled by the Movement. As for those associations with ties to the churches, they represented no danger due to the ties between the religious and state authorities. Starting around 1990, human rights organizations began to appear. The most well known of these are the Rwandan Human Rights Association (ARDHO), the Association of Volunteers for Peace (AVP), the League for the Promotion of Human Rights (LIPRODHOR), Kanyarwanda, the Association for the Defense of Liberty (ADL), and Ibuka, which was created after the genocide.

Like many human rights organizations in Africa, these NGOs are young and financially dependent on donor countries of the North. Some are politically partisan, even thought to have been created by the government, while others have been linked to internal and external opposition. Few have the means to pay full-time staff. Nonetheless, these NGOs have some experienced members who know the environment well and are able to do important work. Some play a crucial role by systematically denouncing abuses, preparing reliable reports on the human rights situation in Rwanda, or leading human rights training campaigns. However, they do little in terms of providing legal assistance and have not undertaken any legal actions on their own. Recently, some of the human rights groups have announced that they intend to provide legal assistance to the victims of genocide and to those accused of participating in the violence.

The members of these organizations were particularly targeted by the Habyarimana regime and were among the first victims of the massacres. However, the NGOs report that they now have normal working relationships with the transitional government. Permission to visit prisoners is easily arranged, and it appears that human rights activists are allowed access to all jails, without exception. The new authorities have facilitated human rights education campaigns and local authorities frequently participate. Relationships with NGOs of the North are generally limited to training and funding. According to local NGOs, the UN Human Rights Mission and the International Criminal Tribunal do not work with them in any way.

Conclusions and Recommendations

The Basic Act is difficult to manipulate. It consists of six different texts adopted at different times and is subject to revision in view of the postwar and postgenocide situation. It is intended to apply only during the transitional period. During the transition, a constitutional committee is to draft a new constitution, which will be subject to approval by referendum. In the current situation, there is a tendency to minimize the importance of crimes not related to the genocide. This tendency, essentially an attempt not to overwork magistrates or exacerbate the overcrowding in the prisons, may increase the level of crime in the country.

Serious liberty violations continue, generally linked to the extraordinary social situation and to the deep trauma that this society has experienced so recently. They are also the result of the serious shortage of equipment and trained personnel, the legacy of decades of totalitarian and racist regimes; again, the latent problems of property and people's security impede normalization. They also stem from the need to administer justice while working toward national reconciliation and unity. Reconciliation requires not only justice, but also the ability to pardon and the possibility of tolerance. Unquestionably, Rwanda faces enormous difficulties in the short term.

The human rights provisions contained in the Basic Act can reasonably ensure the equitable management of Rwanda in the current situation. However, as in any country, the decisive factor for effective protection of constitutional liberties will be the political will to protect them. Effective legal mechanisms and procedures, while necessary, are insufficient for the legal protection of human rights, if the political will to respect such rights is not there.

Rwanda is confronted with three major challenges. The first is to establish a state based on the rule of law. As in any totalitarian state, power was concentrated in the hands of a very few people, rather than being divided among different groups and different branches of government. The provisions contained in the Arusha agreements on the rule of law and power sharing and those of the 1991 constitution will assist in the establishment of a system based on the separation of powers. The new regime has clearly chosen to move toward the rule of law and judicial institutions are gradually being established. Four important steps have been taken already: the elimination of special courts, the reinstatement of the Supreme Court, the creation of an elected Supreme Council of Judges, and the creation of a bar association.

The second major challenge facing the new regime is that of judging those accused of genocide and crimes against humanity, thereby putting an end to the culture of impunity and sending a strong deterrent signal. From a prescriptive and institutional standpoint, the Institutional Act on the Organization of the Prosecution of Offenses Constituting the Crime of Genocide or Crimes Against Humanity, committed on or after October 1, 1990, enables the judicial system to begin to move through this process. Groups of genocide survivors expressed their dissatisfaction with the law and the fact that some of the law's provisions seem too lenient toward criminals. Nonetheless, given the enormity of the challenge facing the courts, it may be better to have imperfect justice than no justice at all. One can argue, therefore, that authorities should not be blamed for piling up 120,000 prisoners in Rwandan prisons. Having 120,000 prisoners means having 120,000 living people suspected of participation in genocide, which in itself is encouraging, as they could have been killed in vengeance or speedily judged by special courts. The legal cases will take a long time and will cost a great deal of money. Even for a country with a normally functioning judicial system, trying all the alleged perpetrators of a genocide with such massive participation would be a gigantic task. It is feared that the enormity of the legal challenge may hinder the government in its attempt to normalize the society and may destroy any chance for the establishment of the rule of law.

The third and most important challenge is peaceful cohabitation between Hutu and Tutsi groups. The Basic Act does not specifically address this issue, but it is critically important. The population has committed genocide against one of its component groups.[77] In this postgenocide context, the people must find a way to live together again.

This division and the need for cohabitation between Hutus and Tutsis should be taken into consideration, and cohabitation should be politically and constitutionally organized. For example, organizing an administration for the country that would explicitly take into consideration the various components of Rwandan society in order to reassure all parties regarding their share of power. The peaceful cohabitation between Hutus and Tutsis is a prerequisite for economic and social reconstruction, national reconciliation, and the development of a legitimate state. In other genocide contexts, a solution based on the physical separation of the parties has sometimes been possible; the creation of Israel after the Holocaust and of Armenia after the genocide of Armenians by the Turks are two examples of this possible solution. Such a solution—either dividing Rwanda into two countries or creating a homeland outside of Rwanda for either group—is not a realistic option. The only solution is to create a political framework, guaranteed by the constitution, that would protect both groups and enable them to accept a single national identity. All the difficulty lies here. The case of Rwanda calls for innovation; the usual democratic models may not function in such a context, as they sometimes fail in ethnically diverse societies. For example, it is probable that in the current situation, elections would lead to an ethnic vote. Rwanda's problems will not be fixed by some miraculous solution, but rather through the painstaking search for the best path toward the reconstruction of the Rwandan nation.

Perhaps the new constitution should not, in applying the principle of power sharing, take into account only political parties, but rather the various communities that form Rwandan society. These ethnic and multiethnic communities have not been organized as such, because Rwandan society has been perceived as rather homogeneous on the surface. This homogeneity, however, has been shattered, and it is perhaps necessary to recognize the fact formally and to organize the various societies that would share power between them. The terms of such community organizing would need to be carefully drawn up. Special attention would need to be given to the group(s) threatened with extermination or extinction or exclusion during the period of time required to end this risk forever.

Notes

1. In order to best understand the specificities of Rwanda and make up for the lack of documentation (as a result of the war, many documents and archives were misplaced or destroyed), it was necessary to conduct interviews with judges, Justice Ministry personnel, lawyers, members of Parliament, members of the Armée Patriotique Rwandaise (Rwandan Patriotic Army), and activists from human rights organizations.

2. Filip Reyntjens, "Rwanda," in *Constitutiones Africae* (Brussels: Bruylart, 1992), p. 11. "Communist" should be understood here to mean "nationalist."

3. Unnatural because it was supposed to be a social and class rooted fight for equality, social justice, and freedom, and therefore against any form of domination of a people over another people.

4. Article 13, section 2. See also Reyntjens, "Rwanda," p. 12.

5. See M. Mubashankwaya, "Le Rwanda depuis 1959: Evolution politique, économique et sociale," Ph.D. diss., Université de Provence, Aix, France, 1971.

6. See P. Tabara, *Afrique: La face cachée* (Paris: La Pensée Universelle, 1992).

7. Reyntjens, "Rwanda," p. 18.

8. Ibid., p. 24.

9. A collection of the speeches exists; research is under way to have them republished. The quota system will be discussed below.

10. JORR, No. 11, June 1, 1995.

11. Articles 1 and 3, JORR, No. 15, August 15, 1993, p. 1280.

12. One of the causes of the war was that the movement had denied the Tutsi refugees the right to return. President Habyarimana had even gone so far as to declare this before the United Nations General Assembly, a declaration that met little protest. See the interview with President Habyarimana in *Jeune Afrique*, no. 1474, May 4, 1989.

13. Article 9, JORR, No. 15, August 15, 1993, p. 1281.

14. Article 9, JORR, No. 15, August 15, 1993, p. 1281.

15. See Articles 18, 10, and 76, JORR, No. 15, August 15, 1993, pp. 1295 and 1319.

16. As indicated in Articles 80, 81, and 82, JORR, No. 15, August 15, 1993, pp. 1230–31, this Ethics Code reiterates the ban on incitement to violence, all forms of violence, and discrimination, while encouraging the promotion of liberties and human rights, through political training and the respect for democracy.

17. Discrimination is repeatedly banned in the protocols, suggesting both that discriminatory practices are widespread and that there is a strong determination to combat it.

18. See Articles 2 through 7, JORR, No. 15, August 15, 1993, pp. 1325–27.

19. See Articles 12 through 34 and 42 through 45, JORR, No. 15, August 15, 1993, pp. 1329–36.

20. Rwanda will therefore have Kinyarwanda, French, and English as official languages.

21. For the first meeting of the High Council of Judges (HCJ), the revision authorizes the president of the Supreme Court to appoint fourteen of the council members. Under the Arusha Agreement, HCJ members were to be elected by panels of judges, but the latter could be constituted only after the appointment by the HCJ of the judges who were supposed to constitute it. The High Council of Judges that was supposed to elect the senior members of the bench first had to be appointed by a Supreme Council of Judges.

22. See the Institutional Act on the Organization of the Prosecution of Acts of enses Constituting the Crime of Genocide and Crimes Against Humanity, committed on or after October 1, 1990. JORR 8/96 of 30/08/96.

23. The 1908 law was made applicable in Rwanda by the 1924 law on the government of Rwanda-Urundi.

24. For example Rwanda's penal code has existed only since 1977 and the individual and family codes, since 1988. Before these codes were promulgated, codes from the Belgian Congo were applicable.

25. Charles Ntampaka, "Individuals and Families," vol. 1 of Rwandan Law Manuals, unpublished document, 1993, p. 1.

26. See ibid., pp. 1–12.

27. In modern continental law, there is a presumption of paternity in the fate of the mother's husband. In the Rwandan customary law it is not a presumption it is a "certitude."

28. *Icyiru* has often been translated as "fine," but the actual concept is quite different. *Icyiru* may be directly paid by the culprit to the victim in the form of property, but may also be in the form of community service, according to the nature of the harm caused. *Icyiru* may be imposed either on the guilty person or on the person's family as a form of reparation and a public recognition of the harm.

29. Unfortunately, as the institutional law establishing the *gacaca* jurisdictions has only recently been passed by the National Assembly, I have not had access to the references or the text of this law, which has not yet been published in the *Official Bulletin*. According to a member of the ad hoc committee that participated in the preparatory work, the *gacaca* will not be functional before June 2001.

30. Figures provided by the "The Proposed New Gacaca Tribunals in Rwanda," background paper, Danish Centre for Human Rights, Copenhagen, January 2000, p. 12.

31. Luc Sindjoun, "Les nouvelles constitutions Africaines et la politique internationale: contribution à une économie internationale des biens politico-constitutionels" *Afrique* 22 (2000), pp. 37–46.

32. Abdelkader Boye, "L'application des règles du droit international public dans les ordres juridiques internes," in *Droit International Bilan et Perspectives,* vol. 1, ed. Mohammed Bedjaoui (Paris: Pédone/UNESCO, 1991), pp. 301–11.

33. We do not have any jurisprudence to illustrate this, but the judges, lawyers and members of parliament we interviewed were unanimous on the subject. On the same subject, see also Ntampaka, *Individuals and Families,* p. 4.

34. On the inhibiting effect of international law, see A. Boye, "L'application des règles," pp. 304–5.

35. The Supreme Court, which was suppressed by the 1978 constitution, was restored by the Basic Act (Arusha Agreement) and is governed by Institutional Act No. 07/96 of June 6, 1996. This law spelled out the organization, operation, and functions of the Supreme Court.

36. The bachelor of arts degree, as it exists in the Rwandan system, is a university degree obtained after four successful years of studies and is equivalent to a master's degree in France. Of the seven hundred Rwandans who hold a B.A. in law, only about forty were on the payroll of the judicial authorities. For an analysis of the situation of Rwanda's judicial system, see Vincent Nkezabaganwa, "Situation judiciaire au Rwanda: Un constat amer" (Kigali: Final Appellate Court, 1992).

37. Alphonse Marie Nkubito, "Le rôle de la justice dans la crise rwandaise," in *Les crises politiques au Rwanda et au Burundi,* ed. André Chaoua (Paris: Karthala, 1995), p. 282. Nkubito was a human rights activist until his appointment as attorney general during the last years of the Second Republic, and, in 1994, as minister of justice in the first extended National Union Government.

38. See United Nations High Commissioner for Human Rights Field Operations in Rwanda, "L'administration de la justice au Rwanda après le génocide," UN Doc. HRFOR/JUSTICE/ JUNE 1996/97, Appendix L.

39. The training materials consisted primarily of a trilingual compilation (Kinyarwanda, French, English) of Rwanda's legislation on arrest and detention procedures and a trilingual manual on "Les poursuites pour crimes de génocide et crime contre l'humanité: Fondements juridiques." These materials were created by a Belgian NGO, Réseau des Citoyens, in collaboration with Rwandan jurists.

40. In 1995, Rwanda had only forty magistrates, only one of who was licensed in law.

41. As reported by Réseau des Citoyens, "[t]he population is divided into two categories; those who defend the dead and those who defend the prisoners." The former believe that the judicial police inspector (JPI) is "one who has been trained and given a motorcycle to free the criminals while the latter argue that he is one who arrests innocent people." Participation in the genocide is denied by 95 percent of those accused. See Réseau des Citoyens, "Overview of Rwanda's Judicial System—December 1995," p. 17.

42. See the January 18, 1996, revision of the Basic Act and the Institutional Act on the Organization of Legal Prosecution of Offenses Constituting the Crime of Genocide or Crimes Against Humanity, committed on or after October 1, 1990.

43. To our knowledge, out of 143 canton courts, only 4 were operating.

44. See "Raporo y'Inama y'Abaperezida yongeye gusuzuma uniushinga w'itegeko rigenga imitunganyirize y' ikurikirana ry'ibyaha bigize icyaha cy'itsembatsemba n'itsembabwoko cyangwa ibyaha byibasive inyoko muntu," Inteko Ishinga Amategeko (Report by the Bureau of Committee chairmen which examined the bill establishing the organization of prosecutions of genocide or crimes against humanity, National Assembly), No. 1112/AN/1996. This document exists only in Kinyarwanda.

45. I use the term "race" because the differentiation between Rwandan Hutus and Tutsis is often based on biological criteria (race) and not cultural criteria (ethnic origin). For example, one group is said to be tall and the other short, one is supposed to have fine features and the other "Negroid" features. For further details on these racial distinctions, see Dominique Franche, "Généalogie du génocide rwandais. Hutus et Tutsis: Gaulois et francs? » *Les Temps Modernes* (May–June 1995), pp. 1–57.

46. See Donald L. Horowitz, "The Challenge of Ethnic Conflict: Democracy in Divided Societies," *Journal of Democracy* 4:4 (October 1993).

47. This is a noun derived from the verb *gutwara,* meaning to govern.

48. For further details on the sociopolitical system of ancient Rwanda, see Pancrace Twagiramutara, "Conflits ethniques en Afrique: Le cas du Rwanda, Ethnicité-Démocratie-Développement," in *Séminaires du Codesria* (Nairobi, November 1992), pp. 16–18. See also Alexis Kagame, *Un abrégé de l'ethno-histoire du Rwanda,* vol. 1 (Butare: Universitaires du Rwanda, Collection Muntu, 1972–75).

49. There is no evidence of any violent or nonviolent conflict between the Hutus and the Tutsis before colonization. The two groups had little interaction until then.

50. For a list of these writings and an overview of these theories, see Gérard Prunier, *The Rwanda Crisis, 1959–1994: History of a Genocide* (Kampala: Fountain Publishers, 1995).

51. See, for example, Tabara, *Afrique, La face cachée,* p. 72. Tabara was appointed deputy chief by the colonial authority and was an important figure during this period of Rwanda's history.

52. The *mwami* in power when the Belgians took control, Yuhi Musinga, was deposed and exiled to Zaire, where he remained until his death. His son, Charles Rudahigwa, returned to Rwanda and eventually convinced Rwandans of his legitimacy. He became a leader in the struggle for social reforms and later for independence. He died in 1959 after receiving an injection from a Belgian doctor. The cause of his death was never fully explained; there was no autopsy and it was suspected that the Belgian government was responsible for his death.

53. See Twagiramutara, "Conflits ethniques," pp. 16–18, and Tabara, *Afrique, La face cachée,* p. 72.

54. Forced labor was primarily used to build the country's infrastructure, but in-

digenous labor was also freely used in the Belgian colonizers' private enterprises. Tabara describes the case of the owner of a timber company who regularly used laborers to cut wood under the forced labor program.

55. At that time, the label most often applied to Tutsis changed from "aristocrats" to "communists."

56. For more details on the falsification of Rwanda's history, see J. P. Chrétien, *Le défi de l'ethnisme au Rwanda et au Burundi, 1990–1996* (Paris: Karthala, 1997). See also Tabarra, *Afrique, La face cachée.*

57. See also Guy Logiest, *Mission au Rwanda* (Brussels: Didier-Hatier, 1988).

58. On this subject, see Léon Saur, *Influences parallèles: L'internationale démocrate chrétienne au Rwanda* (Brussels: Luc Pire, 1998).

59. Rwanda receives more Swiss aid than any other country.

60. The militia trained by the French in the Bigogwe camp massacred thousands of Bagogwe, a people that was largely assimilated into the Tutsi community.

61. French assistance to Rwanda was explained by its fear of anglophone expansionism as the core of the RPF came from Museveni's English-speaking Ugandan National Resistance Army.

62. Regarding this operation, it should be noted that certain communes in the "humanitarian safe zone" had the highest rates of elimination of Tutsis in the whole country. In addition, it is well known that these communes were used as a refuge for those responsible for the genocide, their army and their militias, which were thereby able not only to escape justice, but also to regroup and reorganize.

63. See the Belgian parliamentary study on Rwanda. I personally heard General Dallaire tell his story on the Canadian television show *Le Point;* the episode also featured A. Destexhe, a Belgian senator, and the authors of a number of documents on the Rwandan tragedy.

64. Kumar Rupesinghe, ed., *Conflict resolution in Uganda* (Oslo: International Peace Research Institute, 1989).

65. It is common knowledge that the Habyarimana regime produced drugs in the forest of Nyungwe.

66. See the Hutu's Ten Commandments, published in *Kangura,* a newspaper that was closely associated with the government. *Kangura,* no. 6, December 1990.

67. The majority of those referred to as moderate Hutus were from central or southern Rwanda.

68. For more details on the ethnic and regional quotas, see Twagiramutara, "Conflits ethniques."

69. See Issa G. Shivji, "State and Constitutionalism: A New Democratic Perspective," in *An African Debate on Democracy,* ed. Issa G. Shivji (Harare, Zimbabwe: SAPES Trust, 1991), pp. 27–54.

70. Prunier, *The Rwandan Crisis,* p. 77.

71. For example, major grocery stores and woodworking shops in Kigali and small backcountry towns were run by the general store of the White Fathers (the term does not refer to white Europeans in general, but the congregation of the White Fathers who were missionaries in Africa).

72. More than 90 percent of the population is Christian.

73. Interestingly, the massacres of 1973 were limited to the cities and to the educated populations. The peasants did not take part in the violence.

74. According to an inquiry carried out by D. de St. Exupéry of the French daily *Le Figaro,* France appeared to have violated the arms embargo decreed by the United Nations and continued to arm the former Rwandan armed forces.

75. Horowitz, "The Challenge of Ethnic Conflict," p. 22.

76. Given the context and the limited means even the overpopulated prisons may be seen as a partial victory of the rule of law over the instinct of vengeance. These prisoners cost Rwanda $20 million annually.

77. One of the peculiar aspects of the genocide in Rwanda was that its organizers tried to bind Hutus together through their participation in the violence. All Hutus were to participate, and many of those who refused to kill paid with their lives. Others risked everything attempting to save Tutsis. The orders to kill were, however, obeyed by huge numbers of people, though often reluctantly.

Chapter 9
South Africa
The Interdependence of All Human Rights

Lucrecia Seafield

South Africa is a large country, situated at the foot of Africa. Its population is the second largest in Africa, making the country home to approximately 43 million people. The population of the country is divided into different racial groups, and twenty-two official languages are recognized. The country has a diversity of cultures and religions. The republic has a hybrid governance structure with strong powers vested in the central government and some federal characteristics, with provinces having limited legislation-making functions.

The country has one of the largest and most diverse economies in Africa. Although formerly heavily dependent on gold and the mining industries, the economy is now a broad-based one, with manufacturing comprising a large sector. Despite this relative economic prosperity, South Africa is a country of vast extremes. A recent report by the United Nations Development Program ranks South Africa as the third most unequal country in the world, surpassed only by Brazil and Guatemala. The massive inequalities in income and wealth translate into extensive poverty.

The infrastructure distribution within the country is divided along racial lines; the provision of infrastructure in white areas is at par with first world standards and equivalent to that in the five most developed countries in the world. This is in sharp contrast to the black communities, where the situation is akin to that of some of the least developed Third World countries. This contrast between the Third World and First World is one of South Africa's more striking features.

Unemployment is very high and of a structural nature. For the 25.6 million adult population, the South African economy only provides employment opportunities for 9.6 million people. Some of the factors influencing the unemployment rate are the high illiteracy rate and the lack of technical skills among the majority population group. More than three million people have no formal education at all, and 90 percent of this group is black.

Just over half of the population lives in rural areas. A recent study found that 68 percent of the total rural population lives in abject poverty. Very little profit-based agricultural activity takes place in rural areas and subsistence farming is limited. The incidence of illiteracy and lack of basic resources is compounded in such areas. The relaxation of influx control over the last few years has resulted in rapid urbanization and the expansion of informal settlements. These informal urban settlements are associated with all the social problems typical to these types of settings.

The socioeconomic setting characterizing the South Africa of today has been significantly shaped by the policies of apartheid and the political reforms of the last few years.

Historic Background

The Khoi and San originally inhabited South Africa. In 1652, the Dutch East India Company came to the Cape, intent on establishing a permanent fort to supply fresh produce for their ships en route to and from the East. This fort, however, in the long term provided a basis for colonialization.

During the period of competing interests and the scramble for territories among the colonial powers, the British invaded the Cape to prevent it from falling into French hands. The initial British occupation had little impact, and by 1830 the colony was handed over to the Batavian Republic.

In 1806, the British once again secured the Cape from French occupation. This second period of colonial occupation saw a more hands-on approach to local affairs. By then, discrimination on the basis of color was already deeply entrenched and the new colonial power's sense of racial superiority prevented it from making any radical reforms. The abolishment of slavery in the Cape in 1833 was regarded as a major concession. However, a Master and Servant Ordinance that was passed in 1841 perpetuated white control.

The most significant development in the nineteenth century was the discovery, in 1886, of the world's richest goldfields in the country. This discovery and the subsequent discovery of diamonds ensured that the country became a valuable imperialist possession. This economic development thus gave new impetus to the British imperialist design.

In 1906, the British government decided to grant limited political autonomy to the various provinces that existed then, under what was termed "responsible government." In 1909, a draft constitution for the unification of the four provinces was submitted to the British Parliament. This constitution was adopted without any amendments. On May 31, 1910, the Union of South Africa, a subgoverning dominion within the British Empire, came into being. The 1909 Constitution of the Union of South Africa introduced a sovereign parliament along the lines of the Westminster model. This constitution makes no mention of individual rights and, in line with the Westminster tradition, does not contain a bill of rights.

During the years between the formation of the union and the elections of 1948, South Africa began to legalize the segregation of blacks and whites that had always been inherent in society. Various pieces of legislation were passed during this phase with an underlying motive of segregation. Some of the most notable pieces of legislation passed were the Mines and Work Act,[1] the Native Land Act,[2] and the Native Urban Areas Act.[3]

In 1948, the National Party came to power. Once in power, the National Party began its implementation of a calculated and systematic political and socioeconomic plan aimed at marginalizing the black community. A barrage of legislation that qualified and extended racial discrimination in the private, political, and social spheres was passed in quick succession.[4]

All these pieces of legislation brought the social experiment of apartheid to fruition. The institutionalization of power in the hands of the white minority and the processes of racism permeated every aspect of the individual's personal, political, and societal life. This process was also accompanied by an economic policy aimed at the creation of a large working class and an industrial capitalist class. The intersection between race and class was not an accidental product of the whole process, but was the outcome of a deliberate policy aimed at ensuring that the wealth of the country remained in the hands of the white minority.

During this period, black people resisted these attempts to exclude them from the mainstream of political, social, and economic activity in the country. In 1955, and as a result of black resistance, the National Congress of the people adopted the Freedom Charter. The Freedom Charter set out the basis for a democratic society. It was fundamentally based on the principle of a united South Africa based on equality and universal franchise.

Notable during the protest action during this period was the incident of the Sharpeville shootings in 1959. Large numbers of people were brutally massacred in a peaceful protest against the passage of laws that restricted their movement. The government declared a state of emergency and detained several of the leaders of the African National Congress (ANC) and the Pan African Congress (PAC). These organizations represented the legitimate voices of the oppressed. The incident necessitated a change of strategy on the part of the liberation movements. It now became clear that the racist regime was not going to yield to the legitimate demands of the people and that mere peaceful resistance was not going to bring about the desired change in governance. This led many leaders to flee the country and set up military wings in exile.

This incident also had a ripple effect in the international arena. Serious calls for economic sanctions were made at the United Nations. Due to criticism leveled at the apartheid regime at the Commonwealth Conference, South Africa also withdrew its participation from this international forum.

Internally, the aftermath of Sharpeville saw the intensification of the implementation of a policy of state control. The General Law Amendment Act (1963) introduced and granted the police the powers to detain individuals without trial. In 1959, the promotion of the Bantu Self-Government Act led to the establishment of several homelands with limited degrees of self-government. The act established a system of homelands based on ethnicity. This homeland policy led to the forced relocation of millions of black South Africans. It is impossible to accurately detail the nature, impact, and extent of the suffering resulting from the callous disregard for human life and dignity caused by this process.

The constitutional change in 1984 brought the Tri-Cameral Parliament into being. The government announced certain measures aimed at extending the franchise to Indians and coloreds and granting these groups limited political powers. These measures, however, only represented cosmetic changes; they were aimed at the exclusion of the African population. The government made it clear that it was attempting to restructure apartheid rather than to dismantle it. Antiapartheid forces mobilized themselves against the implementation of these constitutional changes. The United Democratic Front (UDF) and the National Forum were founded in 1983. The UDF called for the rejection of the apartheid state and a boycott of the Tri-Cameral Parliament.

Popular protest intensified during this period and a virtually permanent state of emergency was declared. This led to the detention, without trial, of thousands of people including many children. Even as the principles of parliamentary sovereignty were adhered to, the infringement on basic human rights continued unabated. International condemnation against the system increased with the United States and most Commonwealth and European nations speeding up their campaigns of disinvestment and sanctions.

Discontent with government policies was now also starting to be witnessed in the business community. The 1980s saw the stagnation of the economy and a rising unemployment rate. Capital productivity declined markedly and by the mid-1980s gross investment was barely above replacement levels. Loans granted by the World Bank were called in without renewal and as a result the rand collapsed.

It was during this time that discussions around a prospective South African constitutional and political system began to intensify. In 1986, the government instructed the South African Law Commission to investigate group and human rights.[5] The ANC in 1988 also produced its constitutional guidelines for a democratic South Africa.[6]

All constitutional orders devised from the period of 1910 until 1994 excluded the majority of people from meaningful participation in South African political and economic life. According to all the constitutions of this period, the South African Parliament was sovereign. The courts had no power to question the content of the legislation and could only enquire into the procedure through which this legislation was passed.[7] The constitution did not contain a bill of rights and was not subject to any superior authority. The courts had to apply apartheid and security legislation irrespective of how discriminatory and unfair it might be.

The law and the institutions whose task it was to uphold and implement these policies were, at all times, blind to the ordinary South African's experience of the apartheid state. Within their confines, however, there were a number of lawyers and judges that attempted to protect the individual against the greater power of the state. This, however, did not hold true for the majority of judges and lawyers. It is, therefore, not surprising that victims appearing before the Truth Commission questioned the role of the judiciary and the legal profession in the protection of fundamental rights and lobbied for the legal profession to explain its actions during the apartheid era. Bishop Desmond Tutu, chairperson of the Truth Commission, echoed the view that certain judges colluded with the policies of apartheid, when these very judges should have been the last bastion against the inroads made by the state into the few rights people still held.

Process Leading up to the Adoption of a New Constitutional Order

The first public announcement that South Africa was on the road to democracy was made in February 1991 by then president F. W. De Klerk. Among the steps announced was the lifting of the ban on bodies such as the African National Congress, the Pan African Congress, and the South African Communist Party (SACP), the release of a number of political prisoners, and the lifting of emergency regulations.

Within weeks after the ban on the liberation groups was lifted, negotiations began in earnest. These negotiations were aimed at removing obstacles to the creation of a climate that would allow the participation of all concerned parties in the negotiated settlement. A meeting between the government and the ANC led to the adoption of the Groote Schuur Minutes. The Groote Schuur Minutes represented the first formal meeting between the ANC leadership and the government. The minutes provided for the establishment of a working group, given the task of making recommendations for the release of political prisoners. Specific areas identified were: the definition of political offenses in the South African situation, time scales, advice on norms and mechanisms for dealing with the release of political prisoners, and the granting of immunity with regard to political offenses to those within and outside South Africa.

The Pretoria Minutes followed the Groote Schuur Minutes. These meetings could be regarded as the real beginning of a peaceful negotiated settlement in South Africa. The ANC suspended its thirty-year-old arms struggle in the interests of moving speedily toward a negotiated settlement. The government recommitted itself to the Groote Schuur Minutes and the working group's reports on political offenses were accepted by both parties. The next few months saw the talks getting deadlocked on various issues. The main bones of contention were the interpretation of armed action and the failure of the government to grant indemnity to returned exiles. The negotiations culminated in the signing of the D. F. Malan Accord in Cape Town on February 12, 1991.

In May 1991, the nationalist government repealed most of the legislation that had been the basis of apartheid. Political violence, however, continued to pose a major threat to the democratization process, and members of civil society viewed this as an initiative to set up structures that would deal with this volatile situation. Largely as a result of initiatives on the part of civil society, the Peace Accord was signed on September 14, 1992. The aim of the Peace Accord was to establish a code of conduct and mechanisms to achieve the common purpose of bringing an end to political violence. The Peace Accord was seen as a major step in the creation of a political climate conducive to initiating the formal negotiation process.

However, it was the Convention for a Democratic South Africa (CODESA) that was the body that served as the catalyst for arriving at a negotiated settlement. The working groups designated for this process considered the following issues: the creation of a climate for prepolitical participation; general constitutional principles and the composition of a constitution-making body; original arrangements and an interim government; the future of the independent homelands; and, last, time frames for the implementation of the decisions reached. The negotiation process was complex, difficult, and marked sometimes by withdrawals and boycotts. Appreciation should be expressed for the foresight, endurance, and tenacity of those involved in the process. Their commitment to the process helped avoid an escalation of political discontent that could have resulted in a bloodbath which the country could not afford.

The second plenary session of CODESA took place on May 15 and 16, 1992. Although some of the working groups had reached a consensus on a number of issues, they were deadlocked on several very important ones. There was major disagreement on the following issues: whether the future system of government should be federal or unitary, the economic policy to be adopted, and participation of political minorities in executive and legislative structures.

Bilateral meetings between the ANC and the National Party as well as other parties ensured that the major impediments to a negotiated settlement were removed, paving a way for renewal of the multiparty talks. The progress made in these bilateral meetings ensured that when the parties met on April 1, 1993, the deadlocks which had ended CODESA II were largely resolved.

The multiparty talks resumed in March 1993 to seek a negotiated settlement for South Africa's political problems. Negotiations took place under the structure of the Negotiating Council. Within the council, decisions were taken on the basis of sufficient consensus and these decisions were subject to endorsement by the Plenary Session, a body consisting of the leaders of the various political parties represented on the Negotiating Council and nine representatives from each party. After several breakthroughs as well as deadlocks, a draft constitution was eventually agreed upon on December 6, 1993.

The fourth constitution of South Africa was passed by Parliament on September 22, 1993 (Act 200 of 1993). It was amended by Parliament on March 3, 1994, by Act 200 of 1994 and on April 26, 1994, by Act 3 of 1994. It came into operation on April 22, 1994, the day on which the first national democratic election was held.

The Interim Constitution was adopted in a process that was largely undemocratic. Only the leaders of a number of political parties and groups, many of them without proven support, agreed on the provisions of this constitution. A mechanism had to be devised for the creation of a final constitution which allowed for the greater participation of legitimate political parties and civil society. The process for the adoption of a final constitution is set out in Chapter 5 of the Interim Constitution. According to the Interim Constitution, the Constitutional Assembly was required to draft and approve a final constitution.

In terms of the provisions of section 71, the constitutional text has to comply with the set of thirty-three constitutional principles in the Interim Constitution. These principles broadly guarantee a democratic form of government, separation of power, a state in which there is equality before the law, and a respect for internationally accepted human rights with an independent judiciary to enforce these rights.

The Constitutional Assembly in line with the constitutional provisions drafted and approved a draft final constitution. The process leading up to the adoption of the final draft were participatory in nature and individuals, interest groups, and nongovernmental organizations made submissions pertaining to most of the sections in the constitution.

The Constitutional Court was given the task of determining whether all the constitutional provisions complied with the constitutional text. The court, in its first certification hearing, held that several provisions did not comply with constitutional principles.[8] The constitution was eventually certified by the Constitutional Court and adopted by the National Assembly on the October 11, 1996.[9]

Constitutional Framework for the Protection of Human Rights

The constitution creates a new sovereign and democratic state based on the principles of nonracialism and nonsexism, equality, and the protection of human rights (section 1). It establishes a judicial, legislative, and executive authority based on the principles of the separation of powers.

Parliament consists of the National Assembly and the National Council of Provinces (section 42[1]). The National Council of Provinces' objective is to ensure that the interests of the provinces are taken into account in the formulation of national legislation and policy (section 42[1] [4]). Legislative authority is vested, at the national level, in Parliament as set out in section 44.

Executive authority is vested in the president, who exercises and performs his or her powers subject to, and in accordance with, the constitution.[10] Judicial independence is guaranteed by the judicial powers vested in the courts in section 165.

In addition, the constitution also creates a number of state institutions to support democracy such as the public protector, the Human Rights Commission, the Commission for the Promotion and Protection of the Rights of Cultural, Religious, and Linguistic Communities, the Commission on Gender Equality, the auditor general, and the Electoral Commission (Chapter 9).

Most of the rights and freedoms that South Africans enjoy are set out in Chapter 2 of the constitution. The majority of these rights are the traditional and conventional first generation rights such as the rights to equality (section 9), human dignity (section 10), life (section 10), freedom of opinion, expression, and privacy (sections 14–16), rights related to free political activity (sections 17–20), and rights related to the protection of private property (section 25).

The rights of detained, arrested, and accused persons are set out in section 35. This section stipulates all the due process rights afforded to individuals, but also places a constitutional responsibility on the state to provide an individual with legal representation of his or her choice, to minimize the potential for injustice. Legal representation is to be provided at state expense and the accused has to be informed of these rights (section 35[2]).

The chapter on fundamental rights does not extend a similar right to legal representation in civil matters. It affords individuals the right to have a justiciable dispute settled by a court of law or any other tribunal but does not confer an obligation on the state to provide legal representation. However, section 28, that deals with the rights of the child, grants children the right to a legal practitioner, assigned to the child at state expense in civil proceedings (section 28[h]).

Equality is one of the fundamental values underpinning the constitution. Section 9 guarantees the right to equality before the law and equal protection by the law. It also provides for measures to be taken for the protection and advancement of groups previously disadvantaged by unfair discrimination. The wording of this section makes it clear that the constitutional drafters intended to render equality before the law a reality. It thus embraces a concept of equality that includes both procedural and substantive equality. The equality provisions are also applicable to noncitizens.[11]

The struggle for democracy in South Africa was for the attainment of political rights and social justice. Black people rose against the apartheid regime in protest against their exclusion from the political process and the denial of basic social rights, which resulted in the horrendous social and economic position they found themselves in. To deny the existence of any rights other than those associated with civil liberties and political freedoms not only creates the impression of equality and justice, it also leaves the socioeconomic inequalities unredressed. It was, therefore, important that the constitution express these aspirations and values of the majority of the people.

The South African constitution to a large extent recognizes the interdependence and the interaction of social and political rights. The bill of rights specifically includes the following socioeconomic rights: the right to a healthy environment (section 24); the right of access to land (section 25[4], [5]), secure tenure (section 25[6]), and land restitution (section 25[5]–[9]); the rights of access to adequate housing and protection against arbitrary evictions and demolitions (section 26); the rights to access to health care, food, water, and social security (section 27); and the right to education (Section 29).

The constitution contains certain rights for children such as basic nutrition, shelter, basic health care services, and social services and the right to be protected against maltreatment, neglect, abuse, and degradation (section 28[1][c] and [d]).

Reasonable legislative measures have to be adopted to ensure the progressive realization of these rights. It is therefore evident that there is an acceptance that these rights are not immediately enforceable. The limited justiciability and reporting procedures provided for in terms of these rights constitutes a major constitutional breakthrough and, at least on paper, renders the indivisibility of rights a reality in the South Africa.

All the rights contained in the bill of rights are subject to the limitation clause (section 36). The constitution sets out a general test for the limitation of rights. All the rights in the constitution can now only be limited by a law of general application to the extent that such limitation is reasonable and justifiable in an open and democratic society based on human dignity, equality, and freedom. The section sets out the various factors that the court should take into account to determine whether a limitation is justified. Provision is also made for the suspension of certain rights during a state of emergency (section 37).

Application of the Constitution

In a number of cases decided under the interim constitution, the courts held that there is no single and uniform answer to the question of whether an alleged breach of fundamental rights can be found in an action between individuals and private entities or whether the bill of rights provisions are only enforceable in cases between individuals and the state organs. An answer to any such case will depend on the nature and extent of the fundamental rights and their underlying values and the context in which the alleged breach of the right takes place.[12]

The Transvaal Supreme Court, however, came to an opposite conclusion in the matter of *Du Plessis and Others v. De Klerk and Another,*[13] a matter relating to an action between individuals. The court held that the provisions of Chapter 3 of the constitution do not have horizontal application and that the defendant could not involve the right to freedom of expression as a defense in a civil action for damages for defamation. Following application for leave to appeal, the court *a quo* referred the matter to the Constitutional Court to make a determination as to whether the provisions of Chapter 3 of the constitution are applicable to any relationship other than between persons and legislative and executive organs of state.[14] The majority of the court found that the provisions of Chapter 3 (of the Interim Constitution) are not generally capable of application to any relationship other than that between persons and legislative or executive organs of government at all levels.

In the minority judgment, Judge Kriegler acknowledged the jurisprudential concerns regarding the horizontal application of the provisions of Chapter 3 but held that the framers of the constitution had the intention of ensuring that the bill of rights was not only aimed at combating the repressive use of state power and that the state is no longer the only powerful institution in society. The provisions apply to all law without any qualification. He held that some of the rights in Chapter 3 lend themselves to direct horizontal application while Chapter 3 was indirectly horizontally applicable with respect to other rights.

The final constitution attempts to remedy this confusion. Section 8(1) states in no uncertain terms that "the Bill of Rights applies to all law, and binds the legislature, the executive, the judiciary and all organs of state." Section 8(2) goes further and makes the bill of rights specifically applicable to natural and juristic persons with the provision that the extent of its applicability in this sphere depends on the nature and content of the rights and the duties imposed by the rights.

Standing to Enforce Fundamental Rights

The law generally requires a litigant to personally have a direct and material interest in the relief sought. This restrictive approach has had an effect of curtailing the rights of people who might otherwise be entitled to bring an application to court. Certain exceptions were subsequently made to this restrictive approach. In *Wood v. Odangwa Tribal Authority*,[15] the court allowed a group of church leaders to claim and interdict on behalf of an undefined group of persons who feared that they would be summarily detained and subjected to punishment on account of their political affiliations. The application of this exception was limited only to matters relating to the protection of life, liberty, and physical integrity. Representative organizations have also on occasion been granted standing.[16]

The constitution provides for a more expansive concept of standing in regard to the enforcement of fundamental rights. Section 38 grants the following categories of persons the right to apply to a competent court for appropriate relief, where there is infringement or a threatened infringement of a right:

1. A person acting in his or her own interest
2. Anyone acting on behalf of another person who is not in a position to seek such relief in his or her own name
3. Anyone acting as a member of or in the interest of a group or class of persons
4. A person acting in the public interest
5. An association acting in the interest of its members

In *Ferreira v. Levin NO and Others*,[17] the court held that in constitutional cases, the constitution requires that a broad approach be used for a *locus standi*. A prerequisite for the applicability of this section is that the case must rest on an allegation that the rights in the bill of rights have been infringed.[18]

International Law

Customary international law has always been considered part of South African law. Despite the acknowledgment of the applicability of customary international law, the South African courts have generally been reluctant to resort to it. The whole system of governance was based on a total disregard for international law, and earlier governments demonstrated this disregard for international laws, norms, and values, by directly violating them.

The bill of rights now expressly directs courts to be guided by public international law. Section 39 compels courts to consider international law where applicable and provides for discretion in the application of foreign case law. In *The State v. Makwanyane and Another*,[19] a case that was decided under the Interim Constitution, the court in considering the applicability of public international human rights law held as follows:

> In the context of section 35(1), Public International Law would include non binding as well as binding law. Both may be used under this section as tools of interpretation. International agreements and customary international law provides a framework within which chapter 3 can be evaluated and understood and for that purpose decisions of tribunals dealing with comparable instruments such as the United Nations Committee on Human Rights, the Inter American Court of Human Rights and the European Court of Human Rights, and in appropriate circumstances reports of international agencies such as the International Labour Organization may provide guidance as to the correct interpretation of particular provisions of chapter 3.

With regard to the application of foreign case law, the courts, although acknowledging the important persuasive value of comparative case law, cautioned against the wholesale application of such precedents and warned that we have to be aware of the different context in which foreign constitutions were drafted. *Qozeleni v. Minister of Law and Order* is a case in point.[20]

Section 232 incorporates customary international law, which is binding in the law of South Africa, unless it is inconsistent with the constitution or an act of Parliament. Courts now have to apply the provisions of customary international law where it is not in conflict with the law or the constitution.[21] Parliament has the power to ratify treaties, and domestic effect can only be given to human rights treaties after the adoption of legislation to this effect (section 231[4]).

Since January 1993, the country is party to a host of international agreements. The following conventions have been signed since then: the 1984 Convention Against Torture and Other Cruel, Inhuman, or Degrading Treatment or Punishment; the 1952 Convention on the Political Rights of Women; the 1957 Convention on the Nationality of Married Women; the

International Covenant on Civil and Political Rights; the International Covenant on Economic, Social, and Cultural Rights; and the International Convention on the Elimination of All Forms of Racial Discrimination.

The following human rights treaties have been ratified: the ICCPR (on civil and political rights); the convention on racism; Convention on the Rights of the Child; the 1979 Convention on the Elimination of All Forms of Discrimination Against Women; the 1979 Convention and Protocol Relating to the Status of Refugees; the OAU Convention Governing Specific Aspects of Refugee Problems in Africa; and the African Charter on Human and Peoples' Rights. The UN convention on economic, social, and cultural rights has not been ratified.

Customary Law

Customary law was recognized as a supplementary legal system which could be applied at the court's discretion to particular cases. Legislative recognition of customary law was consolidated in the Black Administration Act (Act 38 of 1927). This piece of legislation was an attempt to introduce a new and more rational structure to address black legal affairs. The application of customary law was permitted in disputes where all the parties were black persons and if it was not in conflict with the public policy or the rules of natural justice.[22]

Section 39(3) recognizes customary law with the proviso that it be exercised in a manner that is consistent with the bill of rights. By recognizing customary law and at the same time subjecting it to the bill of rights, the constitution has brought about a potential head-on confrontation between two opposed principles—an individual's right to equality and a group's right to pursue the culture of its choice.

Recognition of customary law and practices is essential in that the de facto situation is that customary law governs the domestic affairs of three-quarters of the South African population. This has been the situation in reality, notwithstanding the fact that there was no official recognition of this system of law.

The conflict between the chapter on fundamental rights and customary law of succession has recently been brought to the attention of the appellate division in the matter of *Mthembu v. Letsela and Another*. The issue in dispute was the principle of primogeniture in succession. This rule was also given legislative recognition.[23] It was argued that this rule is grossly discriminatory against black women and girls, as it excludes them from participation in intestate succession, while it does not visit the same disability on eldest sons or anybody who is not black.[24] Notwithstanding the obviously discriminatory impact of this rule, the court upheld its constitutionality and held that it could summarily dismiss an African institution without reference to its essential purpose and content. In *Moseneke v. Master of the High Court*,[25] the constitutional court had the opportunity to consider some of the provisions of the Black Administration Act relating to the winding up of a black person's estate. The court held that it was painful that acts of this nature still survived at all. It held that the specific sections under scrutiny imposed differentiation on the grounds of race, ethnic origin, and color.

In an important development, customary marriages were given recognition by the promulgation of the Customary Marriages Act of 1998. The South African Law Commission is also working on various projects related to the harmonization of common law and indigenous law.[26]

Muslim Law

Muslims constitute about 1.1 percent of the total population excluding the sixty-nine former TBVC states, in contrast to Christians who account for approximately 66 percent.[27] Despite having been granted freedom to practice their religion since 1804, Muslims have not been able give legal effect to their personal law.

The constitution creates a secular state. Freedom of religion, belief, and opinion is protected (section 15), and legislation can be adopted to recognize religious marriages and systems of personal and family law. Section 15(3), however, makes clear that such legislation must comply with the provisions of the constitution.

Various Islamic bodies have reached a consensus on the recognition of Muslim personal law, but are still struggling to resolve two main issues: (1) Who would be responsible for the application of Muslim personal law—the ordinary courts, family courts, or the special courts presided over by Muslim judges? and (2) Should Muslim personal law be covered by a bill of rights?

In the judgment of *Rylands v. Edros*,[28] the court held that the recognition of marriages entered into in accordance with Islamic law was no longer per se contrary to public policy,[29] and it gave recognition to the contractual relationship arising from such marriages. It held that the underlying values of the fundamental rights provision are the principle of equality, the principles of tolerance and diversity, and the plural nature of our society. It is these principles that now should inform our courts in determining what constitutes public policy and the *boni mores* of society. The South African Law Commission's Project 59 is also currently looking at the recognition of Muslim marriages and related affairs.

The Court Structures

The effectiveness of a bill of rights depends on the nature and extent of the control exercised over compliance with its provisions. Judicial control over the compliance with the provisions of the constitution is a notable feature of the South African Constitution. Judicial authority is vested in the courts, which are to be independent, impartial, and subject only to the constitution and the law (section 165).

Chapter 8 details provisions for the Constitutional Court, the Supreme Court consisting of the appellate division, provincial and local divisions, and the area of operation, and any other court as prescribed by legislation. The following courts have been established by enabling legislation: lower courts comprising district magistrate's courts with limited criminal jurisdiction and small claims courts with limited civil jurisdiction; regional magistrate's courts with limited criminal jurisdiction; courts of chiefs and headmen with limited jurisdiction; and special courts, including the labor, land claims, competition appeals, consumer, electoral, small claims, and divorce courts.

The Constitutional Court is the highest court in constitutional matters. The Interim Constitution specifically proscribes the Supreme Court of Appeal from having any jurisdiction in constitutional matters. The removal of the appeal courts jurisdiction on constitutional matters was prompted by a number of factors, not least of all the fact that the institution of the constitutional courts was intended to bring about a clear break from the past. There was a feeling that the existing court structure and hierarchy were tainted with the baggage of the previous regime and strong arguments were advanced for the creation of a totally new structure that embodied the principles and the value system of the new dispensation.

The final constitution, however, grants jurisdiction to the appeal court in constitutional issues, but the constitutional courts remain the courts of final instance in constitutional matters.

The high court is the court in the final instance in any matters save for those matters that fall within the exclusive jurisdiction of the constitutional court. The high court is vested with inherent jurisdiction in civil and criminal matters.

Lower courts may be given jurisdiction over constitutional matters by national legislation provided that they may not enquire into or rule on the constitutionality of any legislation or the conduct of the president (section 170). In *Qozeleni v. Minister of Law and Order*,[30] the court held the view that it was inconceivable that magistrates could not enforce Chapter 3 of the constitution in the courts where the majority of the people have contact with the court system. It was held that lower courts had a broad constitutional jurisdiction in terms of the Interim Constitution. This decision, however, was overturned by a full bench decision in the matter of *Port Elizabeth Municipality v. Prut NO.*[31]

This position is radically different from that of other countries such as Canada. There, the Supreme Court held that as per the provisions in the Canadian Charter of Rights and Freedoms any competent court could grant an appropriate remedy for the violation of a right in the charter, including all trial courts.[32]

Procedural Matters

Rule 17(1) of the Rules of the Constitutional Court makes a provision for direct access to the Constitutional Court in instances where urgency can be proven, or if the matter is of such public importance that the delay necessitated by the use of the ordinary procedures would prejudice the public interest or prejudice the ends of justice and good government.[33] The Constitutional Court has on numerous occasions refused to appropriate the role of a court of first instance.[34]

A matter can only be referred from the Supreme Court to the Constitutional Court if a constitutional issue has been raised in the proceedings in the high court, the matter in which the issue was raised has been disposed of, and if the court is of the opinion that the constitutional issue is of sufficient public importance to require a ruling by the Constitutional Court. In *Zantsi v. Council of State, Ciskei,* it was held that the underlying purpose of these requirements are "to restrict the jurisdiction of the Constitutional Court and to ensure that the Court does not anticipate a question of constitutional law in advance of the necessity of deciding it and never to formulate a rule or constitutional law broader than is required by the precise facts to which it applies."[35]

As per Rule 4(13), the registrar of the court is required to refer an unrepresented accused for assistance to the Human Rights Commission, legal aid, or a law clinic. In the event of the party failing to secure legal assistance from these institutions, the registrar is obliged to assist the party in the preparation of his or her case.

The normal rule with regard to awarding costs in a matter is that the cost order follows the outcome of the proceedings. The constitution, however, adopted the principle of awarding cost on the basis of equity and fairness.[36] This approach is to be welcomed in that the threat of a substantial cost order could deter potential litigants from instituting an action, notwithstanding the fact that they might have a valid claim.

Appointment of Judicial Officers

In the past, judges were almost exclusively appointed from the ranks of senior advocates and presiding officers in the magistrate courts were appointed from the ranks of prosecutors. The executive made appointments. Almost all these appointments were white males. There was only one black judge in the country up to April 1994. Some black magistrates were appointed in the former black independent states and the self-governing territories. The appointment of judicial officers has therefore understandably always been a controversial issue in South Africa.

The constitution makes significant changes to the method of appointing judges, by the creation of the Judicial Service Commission (section 178). The functions of this commission are to make recommendations regarding appointment and removal from office and it may advise the national government on any matter relating to the judiciary and the administration of justice (section 178[4]–[5]). The commission is chaired by the chief justice and consists of stakeholders in the legal profession including the minister of justice, representatives of the National Assembly and the National Council of Provinces, and persons appointed by the president as head of the executive.

Since 1993, magistrates are appointed in accordance with the Magistrates Act 90 of 1993 and its regulations. This act established the Magistrates Commission to attend *inter alia* to the appointment of magistrates. Magistrates are therefore no longer appointed subject to the rules of public service and, as such, are no longer civil servants.

Constitutional Court judges are appointed for a nonrenewable term of twelve years and other judges hold office until they are discharged from active service in terms of an act of Parliament. The salaries, allowances, and benefits of judges may not be reduced.

The efforts of the judicial and magistrates' commissions have, in recent years, accomplished some representativity in terms of race and gender into the ranks of the judiciary. There have also been some attempts to ensure that the bench represents the diversity of society. The degree of representativity still falls short of what is required to make the judiciary more representative of the majority of black South Africans. The appointment of black women to the judiciary should be regarded as a priority.

There are moves afoot to create a single judiciary. This will entail the implementation of the same procedures for the appointments of magistrates and judges.

National Machinery for the Enforcement of Human Rights

The responsibility for the promotion, protection, and fulfillment of human rights rests on the state (section 7[2]). In order to fulfill this mandate, the constitution has created a number of public institutions to support and give practical effect to the constitutional democracy. These institutions are the public protector (section 182), the Human Rights Commission (section 184), the Commission on Gender Equality (section 187), the Commission for the Promotion and Protection of the Rights of Cultural, Religious, and Linguistic Communities (section 185), the auditor general (section 188), the Electoral Commission (section 190), and an independent authority to regulate broadcasting (section 192).

The independence of all these institutions is constitutionally guaranteed (section 181[2]) and they are protected from interference by any person or organ of state (section 181[4]). All government and state departments must assist these institutions and protect their independence and impartiality. All commissions are obliged to table an annual report to the National Assembly (section 181[5]).

Members of these institutions are appointed by the Parliament on the recommendation of the National Assembly. The criteria for the appointment of members to these commissions are set out in section 193. Civil society may be involved in the recommendation process. Members are appointed for a fixed period and may only be removed from office on grounds of misconduct or incompetence. The National Assembly must make a finding to this effect and adopt a resolution for the removal from office of any member (section 194[2]).

While Chapter 9 creates a number of institutions, only two of these institutions are essentially given the task of the promotion and protection of all the rights in the bill of rights. These are the Human Rights Commission and the Commission on Gender Equality. However, the functions of the other institutions have an indirect impact on the promotion of human rights and must be acknowledged to this extent.

Human Rights Commission

The interim and final constitutions provide for the establishment of a National Human Rights Commission. The Human Rights Commission was established in 1995, in keeping with the Human Rights Commission Act (no. 54 of 1994).

The functions of the commission are: to promote the observance of human rights; to develop an awareness of fundamental rights among all people; to recommend progressive measures for the promotion of fundamental rights in all organs of state at all levels; to investigate complaints of human rights violations; and to advise government on all levels on the steps necessary to ensure the implementation of human rights. The final constitution also gives the Human Rights Commission the additional responsibility of monitoring the realization of socioeconomic rights by all organs of state (section 184[3]).

The commission has wide powers of investigation which include the power to subpoena witnesses and the power of search and seizure. Other organs of state are obliged to render reasonable assistance to the commission.

The Commission on Gender Equality

In order to ensure the effective participation of women in all spheres of society and to work toward the eradication of gender discrimination, the drafters of the constitution thought it wise to establish a gender commission. The Commission on Gender Equality was established in consonance with the provisions of the interim and final constitutions and the Commission on Gender Equality Act (no. 39 of 1996).

The object of the commission is to promote gender equality and to advise and make recommendations to Parliament or any legislator with regard to any law or proposed legislation that affects gender equality and the status of women.

Other Transitional Institutions

The Interim Constitution further provides for the establishment of two transitional commissions: the Truth and Reconciliation Commission and the Commission on the Restitution of Land Rights (section 122).

Truth and Reconciliation Commission

The issue of how to deal with human rights violations of the past is a vexed and complicated one. Strong voices from various parties supported the prosecution of individuals that committed human rights violations against the people of the country in the prenegotiation phase. A number of political parties were strongly opposed to this position and promoted the principle of the granting of amnesty to perpetrators of human rights violations. This was one of the major issues on which various parties were deadlocked during the negotiations. The attempt to seek a solution was not made any easier by the fact that the transition to a democracy in South Africa took place as a result of a negotiated settlement and that the previous regime was to remain part of the Government of National Unity.

In the spirit of compromise and negotiations, and in the final hours of the negotiation process, the political parties agreed that the best process

for reconciliation would be the granting of amnesty to human rights violators. A "postamble" to the Interim Constitution with the following wording
was then accepted:

In order to advance such reconciliation and reconstruction, amnesty shall be
granted in respect of acts, omissions and offences associated with political objectives and committed in the course of the conflicts of the past. To this end, Parliament under this Constitution shall adopt a law determining a firm cut-off date,
which shall be a date after 8 October 1990 and before 6 December 1993, and providing for the mechanisms, criteria and procedures, including tribunals if any
through which such amnesty shall be dealt with at any time after the law has been
passed.

In compliance with the provisions of the postamble, the Truth and Reconciliation Commission was created by the Promotion of National Unity
and Reconciliation Act no. 34 of 1995. This act was later referred to as the
TRC Act. The objectives of the TRC Act were: (1) To provide reparations
and rehabilitation to victims of gross human rights abuses and to establish
as complete a picture as possible of the causes, nature, and extent of the
gross violations of human rights; (2) to facilitate the granting of amnesty to
persons who made full disclosure of all relevant facts relating to acts associated with a political objective, and who complied with the requirements of
the TRC Act; (3) to restore the human and civil dignity of victims by giving
them an opportunity to relate their account of the violations of which they
were victims; (4) to compile a comprehensive report of all the activities
and findings of the commission, and to make recommendations on measures to prevent the future violation of human rights.

Seventeen commissioners were appointed to implement these objec-
tives. Three subcommittees were further established: the Human Rights
Violations Committee, the Amnesty Committee, and the Rehabilitations
Committee.

The Commission on the Restitution of Land Rights

People dispossessed of their land on the basis of racial discriminatory
practices between 1914 and 1994 are entitled to claim for restitution of their
rights to such land. The Land Rights Act provides for the restitution process
and sets up the mechanisms to deal with such claims. A quasi-judicial commission on land rights has been instituted to investigate the merits of any
claim, to mediate and settle disputes, and to perform such other functions
as may be contemplated. A land claims court has been instituted to adjudicate on conscientious land claim cases and to make policy recommendations on the implementation of the land reform policy.

The Legal Profession

The South African legal profession is traditionally split between the attorney (side-bar) and advocate (bar) professions. There are also different statutory regimes regulating the two groupings in the profession.[37] Members of the attorneys' profession practice as members of the Law Society. Membership in the Law Society is compulsory and takes effect immediately after admission. Unlike attorneys, advocates are not legally obliged to become members of the Association of Advocates.

Until recently, attorneys could only appear in the lower courts and advocates could appear in all courts. The Right of Appearance in Court Act (no. 62 of 1995) granted attorneys who complied with the criteria the opportunity to apply to the Registrar of the High Court for the right of appearance. An advocate may not accept an instruction from a member of the public without an instruction (brief) from an attorney, irrespective of whether the advocate is a member of one of the constituent bars of the General Council of the Bar.[38]

The associations of the legal profession are still, to a large extent, polarized on racial and ideological lines. Statutory bodies historically have not enjoyed the confidence and support of a significant number of the members of this profession. This has led to the establishment of nonstatutory bodies such as the National Association of Democratic Lawyers (NADEL) and the Black Lawyers Association (BLA). The aim of these organizations is to work toward the transformation of the legal system and the judiciary.

A recent study indicated that the legal profession remains a patriarchal and male dominated profession, notwithstanding the increase in the number of women in the profession.[39] This male domination is especially evident in the governing bodies of the profession.[40]

Legal Aid Board

The Justice Department further provides legal services to indigent persons through the Legal Aid Board, which was established according to the terms of the Legal Aid Act of 1969. The principle objective of the Legal Aid Board was initially to provide legal aid to indigent persons who had passed the means test. The constitution has now changed the criteria (Legal Aid Amendment Act of 1996) and the board now has to meet the constitutional obligation of providing legal services to arrested, detained, and accused persons where substantial injustice would otherwise result. The emphasis of the constitution is on a fair trial, not on indigence.

Since its inception, the board has been funded almost exclusively by money appropriated by Parliament. Until recently, the board had made little impact because it had a ridiculously low budget, applied restrictive bureaucratic procedures, and was regarded with suspicion by the majority of the population. However, in the late 1980s and early 1990s, the budget of the scheme was increased and the Legal Aid Board became more proactive in the delivery of legal aid services. It also established a pilot project Public Defender Office.

The Legal Aid Board provides legal aid in criminal and civil cases. The board discharges aid mainly through the judicare system, but the board has also established a number of cooperative schemes with legal aid clinics at universities. It is also currently in the process of setting up justice centers throughout the country discussing proposals for joint access to justice initiatives with NGOs.

Other State Departments

South Africa probably has one of the largest prison populations in the world. As per the Human Rights Watch World Report: South Africa: Human Rights Development, on April 30, 2000, the prison population was 172,271. The country was notorious for its treatment of prisoners. Information about deaths in prisons, assaults on prisoners, and a general disregard for the rights of prisoners were among the issues often raised about South Africa at international forums. Section 35[2] of the constitution grants prisoners extensive rights.

In 1991, the Prison Service was renamed the Department of Correctional Services. In 1993, a white paper on the policy of the department was released, which provided a new framework based on human rights principles. This policy document was reviewed by NGOs and an alternative white paper was formulated. A Correctional Service Act was adopted[41], largely in line with the constitution as well as international human rights obligations.

Like other government departments, Correctional Services is also in a process of transformation. A Transformation Board has been established, comprising members of the department, the Parliamentary Standing Committee on Correctional Services, and NGOs.

The Correctional Services Act was further amended to make provisions for the establishment of the Judicial Inspectorate, the appointment of an inspecting judge, and the Independent Prison Visitors Program.[42] The Judicial Inspectorate is an independent body responsible for the investigation of the prison department, the monitoring of prison conditions and the treatment of prisoners, and the inspection of dishonest and corrupt practices in prisons.

Ministry of Safety and Security

The South African Police Services are well known for their abuse of human rights and their brutality toward ordinary citizens. The number of people killed and tortured by the police during the period of apartheid is not yet known. Recent revelations before the Truth and Reconciliation Commission demonstrate the extent of police brutality during the apartheid period. The Interim Constitution (section 222) and the Police Services Act (no. 68 of 1995) provide for the establishment of an Independent Complainants Directorate under civilian control to investigate any misconduct of members of the police service. The ICD considers complaints or allegations relating to: deaths of persons in police custody, the involvement of members in criminal activities, and police conduct or behavior that is prohibited by the police regulations or a failure to comply with the code of conduct.

The act also makes provisions for the establishment of community police forums at the local level. All these mechanisms are aimed at ensuring greater accountability of the police force and the participation of members of civil society in the activities of the police.

The NGO Sector

The South African NGO sector emerged out of opposition to the apartheid system. Organizations were engaged in various activities from services, education programs, advocacy, and lobbying initiatives. They shared one common objective, and that was to replace the apartheid regime. During this period, the relationship of the NGOs toward the government was clear: the NGOs were part of the opposition camp.

The transition period placed a different demand on NGOs and there was a definite need to reconceptualize their role. The human rights sector in the main has supported a collaborative approach to government since there was an honest belief that the new government was committed to the protection and promotion of human rights.

Over the past decade, a number of law-based human rights NGOs have been founded.[43] These organizations are making an important contribution toward the legal protection of human rights. They provide services in the following areas.

Advice and Legal Representation

The Legal Resources Center (LRC) focuses mainly on public interest law cases and has achieved significant decreases in human rights violations in this respect. Legal assistance and advice office work are also undertaken by Lawyers for Human Rights (LHR), the National Institute for Public Law (NIPILAR), and BLA. Whereas the LRC's litigation work is much more focused on precedent setting litigation, these organizations provide legal assistance of a more general nature in areas such as labor law, pensions, children's rights, and women's rights. These organizations also provide legal support to a number of advice offices. Most university law centers have law clinics. The purpose of these clinics is to provide service to the public and to provide law students with practical legal training. These clinics are often staffed by law students.

Training

Along with supporting paralegals with advice and referrals, some of these NGOs also provide paralegal training. LHR, Community Law Center and National Paralegal Institute have implemented a structured training course for paralegals.

The Legal Education Center of the Black Lawyers Association (LEC) has, over the years, undertaken legal education projects intended to provide training, confer professional skills and expertise, and create opportunities for historically disadvantaged communities. The LEC annually presents training programs in trial advocacy and seminars on important human rights issues. The organization also subsidizes the salaries of candidate attorneys to assure their access to the legal profession.

NGOs have also implemented training with state structures such as the Department of Safety and Security, the Department of Correctional Services, and the Department of Home Affairs.

Education

The South African Street Law Program has been incorporated in a number of universities. Street Law coordinators implement and run these programs throughout the country. The Street Law Program is designed to be taught to people who have no background in law. A number of other education programs have been introduced to teacher training colleges and community and educational organizations.

Lawyers for Human Rights is currently running a human rights education program. The objective of the program is to create a human rights culture and to inform people of their rights and mechanisms for the enforcement thereof. The program also contains modules on democracy. Through the efforts of this organization, human rights have been incorporated into the official curriculum of the Practical Law School for candidate attorneys.

Community organizations such as advice offices, churches, women's groups, and agricultural unions also conduct various education programs. Educational materials have been developed on various issues, such as the constitution and the bill of rights, public institutions, land rights, and the rights of women, children, refugee, prisoners, and farm workers. The Community Law Center at the University of the Western Cape has just completed an extensive training manual on socioeconomic rights. Education programs in international law and procedures are implemented by organizations such as Hurisa.

Advocacy Monitoring and Lobbying

Since 1994, a number of organizations have developed very good advocacy and monitoring skills. This mainly holds for the bigger and urban-based NGOs. A number of NGOs now have a strong parliamentary presence,[44] and NGOs have made a valuable contribution toward the legislation and policy formulation process.

The Human Rights Committee (HRC) and National Association of Democratic Lawyers have, over the years, been monitoring the human rights situation in South Africa and have made their findings available to all relevant pressure groups. They have also monitored public institutions and the Constitutional Court. This organization has also been active in monitoring various parliamentary committees on a regular basis.

A number of NGOs work on specific issues such as socioeconomic rights, rights, and rights of children, prisoners, women, refugee, and people living with HIV/AIDS.

Some of the most notable achievements of the efforts of NGOs are the welfare campaign that led to a revision of government policy and the increase of the child support grants. The Open Democracy Campaign successfully persuaded the Parliamentary Committee to extend the provision of the act to cover privately held information and to reconceptualize the provisions relating to whistle-blowers. The efforts of the Treatment Action campaign that led to pharmaceutical companies' withdrawal from a court action in which they challenged certain of the provision of the Medicine Act is also demonstrative of the strong advocacy and lobbying skills of civil society in general. This was a critical step toward establishing a framework for ensuring that medicines could be provided on a more affordable basis.

Evaluation of the Implementation of the Constitution

The legal system and the administration of justice through the judicial process had, for decades, been used as instruments of oppression, with their major objective being the denial of the basic human rights of the majority of the people. Consquently, people lost faith in the system that administers justice and in the law itself. The new constitutional dispensation heralds the end of this oppressive system and ushers in a governmental system based on respect for human rights.

The final constitution is in several aspects a progressive piece of legislation, intending not only to redress the wrongs caused through the long-standing policy of apartheid but also to promote social and economic regeneration for the majority of South Africans.

The South African Constitution is based on a foundational premise that recognizes the right to equality and the right of everyone to equal protection and benefit of the law. The bill of rights not only protects civil and political rights but also articulates the state's responsibility to work toward the progressive realization of socioeconomic rights.

The constitution also guarantees most internationally recognized rights and principles of justice, these being: equal protection and benefit of the law; the rights of an accused person to be heard before a competent and impartial court; the right to legal defense and access to legal representation if the interests of justice so require; the right of appeal; presumption of innocence; and the right to be tried speedily and fairly.

The creation of an independent judiciary and the installation of a Constitutional Court as the upper guardian for the protection and enforcement of human rights are aimed at ensuring full judicial review. The constitution also sets up a multitude of national human rights enforcement mechanisms such as the Human Rights Commission, the public protector, the Gender Commission, the Land Commission, and the Truth Commission, thus providing a stable base, in addition to the theoretical underpinning, for a comprehensive framework for the protection of human rights.

Key legislation has been passed, to give effect to the constitution and the bill of rights. The Promotion of Access to Information Act (no. 2 of 2000), the Promotion of Administrative Justice Act (no 3 of 2000), the Promotion of Equality and the Prevention of Unfair Discrimination Act (no. 4 of 2000), the Prevention of Illegal Eviction from and Unlawful Occupation of Land Act (no. 19 of 1998), the Maintenance Act (no. 99 of 1998), the Domestic Violence Act (no. 116 of 1998), the Recognition of Customary Marriages Act (no. 120 of 1998), and the Refugee Act (no. 130 of 1998) are some of the legislations worth mentioning.

With the adoption of the constitution, a clear role has been established for public international law in the field of human rights. A number of key international documents have been adopted by the government to ensure that we as a country are in line with the norms and values of the international community.

The constitution describes itself as supreme law, which provides the people of South Africa with a means "to heal the divisions of the past and establish a society based on democratic values, social justice and fundamental human rights." The question that now begs consideration is the extent to which these objectives have been achieved.

The Constitutional Court has demonstrated a great degree of independence and, as custodian of the bill of rights, has handed down a number of judgments that went against majority opinion, such as the abolition of the death penalty and the declaration of corporal punishment for juvenile offenders as unconstitutional.[45] In these judgments the court confronted some of the major issues of the day in a manner that instills the concept of judicial independence and impartiality in our legal system. The viewpoint of the Constitutional Court on this issue has been clearly stated in *The State v. Makwanyane.*

If public opinion were to be decisive, there would be no need for constitutional adjudication. The protection of the rights could then be left to Parliament, which has a mandate from the public and is answerable to the public for the way its mandate is exercised, but this would be a return to parliamentary sovereignty, and a retreat from the new legal order established under the 1993 Constitution. By the same token the issue of the Constitutionality of the death penalty cannot be referred to a referendum, in which the majority view will prevail over the wishes of the minority. The very reason for establishing the new legal order, and for vesting the power of judicial review of legislation in the courts, was to protect the rights of the minorities and others who cannot protect their rights adequately through the democratic process.[46]

In other cases the court elected to adopt a technical approach to the matters that came before it. In *The State v. Vermaas; State v. Du Plessis,*[47] the court had the opportunity to address the content of the right to legal representation and to determine the broad principles applicable to such a determination. The court refused to make a ruling as to the applicant's right to legal representation and instead held that the judge in each case was better placed to determine whether the applicant was, in fact, entitled to legal representation and whether the denial of such representation would result in substantial injustice. This was a unique opportunity for the Constitutional Court to set down these guidelines.

Another decision of the Constitutional Court that is open for criticism is the matter of *The Azanian People's Organization v. the President of the Republic of South Africa.*[48] The Constitutional Court also upheld the constitutionality of the amnesty provision in the Promotion of National Unity and Reconciliation Act. The Constitutional Court refused to apply international standards and rather adopted the approach that all the parties to the negotiation forum agreed upon amnesty and Parliament was free to decide on the ambit of the amnesty provisions. It thus upheld the decisions of the state, notwithstanding the fact that these decisions resulted in grave injustice to the victims of human rights violations. This approach goes against recent developments on crimes against humanity in international law and the approach to impunity.

The court also had the opportunity to give effect to the socioeconomic rights provisions in the bill of rights. In the certification judgment the court confirmed that socioeconomic rights have the same status as civil and political rights in the constitution. The court held socioeconomic rights were compatible with the doctrine of separation of powers and were no less justiciable than any other rights.[49]

In *Soobramoney v. the Minister of Health, KwaZulu Natal,*[50] the court was called on to give effect to the right to access to health care services and access to emergency medical treatment. The court held that the provincial authority had shown that it did not have the resources to provide all patients with the type of medical treatment requested by the client. The court made it clear that it will be slow to interfere in rational decisions taken in good faith by those whose responsibility it is to deal with the issues under consideration. The rationale applied in this decision is in contrast with a decision of the Cape Division of the High Court in *B v. Minister of Correctional Services.*[52] Whereas budgetary constraints were relevant, the lack of funds could not be an answer to a prisoner's constitutional claim to adequate medical treatment. According to the constitution, prisoners are entitled to higher levels of medical care than ordinary citizens.

In the recent groundbreaking judgment of *Grootboom,* the court reviewed the housing policy in a particular province.[52] It found that the policy did not make provisions for an accelerated program of housing for the most needy. Also, it did not make provisions for the housing department to implement such a policy. The court issued an order regarding monitoring the implementation of such a program. This decision provides a window of opportunity for litigation on socioeconomic rights.

To date, most of the cases under the bill of rights were brought by groups attempting to protect business interests through enforcing the provisions of the constitution. Contrary to expectation, the court has not been inundated with human rights issues relating to the equality provision, customary law, issues affecting women, and so on. The great flow of litigation around issues that affect most people and could lead to a decisive change in their daily conditions still has to be brought to this court. Save for the Legal Resources Center, very few NGOs have instituted legal action in the Constitutional Court. NGOs have, however, played an important role in terms of filing *amicus curiae* briefs.[53]

Popularizing the decisions of the Constitutional Court is a problem. The impact of this court and the contribution it has made in the development of a human rights culture are lost to most South Africans. Law reports are technical, costly, and not accessible. The public at large is unaware of the role and functions of the court.

Access to the court is problematic. The financial resources required to bring a matter to the Constitutional Court are so high that it is beyond the means of many South Africans to institute litigation in this forum. While some bodies, such as the Foundation for Human Rights, provide funding for precedent-setting matters on constitutional and human rights litigation, such funding is very limited.

The importance of the Constitutional Court can only be further assessed in terms of the extent to which its decisions are implemented by lower courts and other governmental departments. To date, there are numerous complaints that important decisions are not implemented by magistrates in the more remote areas.

The extent to which a legal system guarantees, promotes, and protects the interests of a society is unfortunately not solely judged by the manner in which its highest courts discharge their duty, but ultimately depend on how justice is being dispensed at the level where the majority of citizens interface with the judicial system. The levels to which human rights are guaranteed in these forums will become evident in later discussions.

The last few years have seen the establishment of important public institutions charged with the promotion and protection of human rights. These new institutions, although created by the constitution and supported by the state, have to function in an independent and impartial manner. These institutions are in a somewhat unenviable position in that they are situated somewhere between the state and the NGO sector. There are numerous expectations of the institutions from both civil society and government and these tensions have to be managed.

There are divergent opinions on the role of these institutions in promoting a human rights culture. Although they have done a great deal of work, it is difficult to evaluate their impact. The creation of a human rights culture and the concretization of democratic gains is a long-term process. What cannot be disputed, however, is the fact that all these institutions have in some way contributed to the formation of the human rights landscape in the country.

All these commissions have implemented programs in terms of their respective mandates. Most of these organizations have undertaken investigations in critical human rights areas. The findings of these investigations have been made public. Reports with recommendations, based on the findings of investigations of a serious nature, have been submitted to the National Assembly. The South African Human Rights Commission (SAHRC) has also submitted its second report on measures taken by government departments toward the realization of socioeconomic rights as demanded by section 184(3) of the constitution. It is, however, unclear what significance is attached to the findings and recommendations of these institutions. There is no identified body that has the explicit task of addressing the considerations of these reports and monitoring the implementation of the accepted rec-ommendations of the reports. Thus, while it is not clear how much weight is attached to these annual reports, they are discussed once a year in the National Assembly.

The success of these bodies depends to a large extent on the resources allocated to the structure. To date, the government has imposed real fiscal constraints on these institutions, severely hampering their ability to deliver on their mandates.[54]

The impartiality and independence of these institutions are constitu-tionally guaranteed and enforced in the enabling legislation. To date, there are has been no indication that the government has in any way inter-fered with their functional independence. There is, however, a problem concerning the manner in which these bodies are funded, which con-tributes to a perception that their independence is in some way compro-mised. At present, funding is being channeled through the Department of Justice. There have been calls from various institutions and the public that such institutions should have access to funding channeled directly through Parliament.

A study to assess the knowledge of the general public on human rights indicated that there is a significant lack of awareness of the public institu-tions. Reporting on their findings, the researchers point out that bodies such as the South African Human Rights Commission, the Public Protec-tor, and the Commission for Gender Equality are seldom mentioned in the context of questions asked about human rights.[55] This indicates that more resources should be allocated toward an awareness program on the role of these institutions. It also indicates that the institutions have not yet estab-lished a record of being vocal enough in the execution of their mandates. A number of NGOs are implementing education programs on the role and functions of these institutions but there is still much work to be done in this area, especially in the rural areas.

The next few years will be crucial for the government's land reform process. The pressure on the government to deliver in terms of its land re-form and redistribution program is high and to date it has not been able to meet the target set in the Reconstruction and Development Program for the redistribution of 30 percent of the land. In fact, statistics indicate only 1.06 percent of this target has been met.

The Commission on Land Restitution, together with the land claims court, has to ensure that restitution of land rights takes place. NGOs such as the National Land Committee have often questioned the commission's capacity to facilitate the land reform and restitution process. This is espe-cially problematic given that the policy is market-based and relies on the policy of willing buyers. At the heart of the land debate is the constitu-tional compromise that protects private property.

The recent development relating to land reform in neighboring Zimbabwe has provided an impetus for discussions on the land reform process. It has also ensured that land reform remains a priority on the national agenda. There is a growing consensus that there is a need to review current legislation and policies on land. The crucial question is whether the nascent democracy can accommodate a major shift on land policy and whether there is the political will by all stakeholders—and especially those who still occupy 85 percent of the land—to address the core problem relating to land.

The Truth and Reconciliation Commission differs in many respects from the other commissions. Not only was it a commission set up for a certain period but it was also well funded. There was tremendous public interest and awareness on the work of the commission. The TRC work was suspended in October 1998 but several amendments to the legislation were passed to allow the Amnesty Committee to complete its work.

In October 1998, the TRC released its first five-volume report to the president. Public opinion on the extent to which the commission has succeeded in its mission differs considerably. In evaluating the TRC, one has to ascertain the extent to which it has been able to achieve the objectives that were defined in the legislation.

There can be no doubt that the TRC process and reports provide an invaluable account of the past. Many of the atrocities of the past have been publicly disclosed and the processes sensitized millions of South Africans, and in particular the white community, to what really happened in the past. Lack of awareness as a justification for denial has therefore effectively been annihilated. The public hearings in which victims recalled their experiences were extremely cathartic and contributed toward a process in which the dignity of victims could be restored.

The manner in which the Amnesty Committee reaches its decisions is, however, open for criticism. The TRC Act specifically stated that amnesty would only be considered for violations committed with a political objective and where full disclosure has been made (section 20). It then goes further to set out the criteria to apply in determining whether an act was committed with a political objective (the Nougaat principles). The extent to which the Amnesty Committee applied this criterion in arriving at a decision is debatable. A cursory glance at some of the decisions makes one wonder whether the process was not in essence political horse-trading. Granted, there have been some very good decisions, but most of these were in high profile cases where families were in a position to employ some of the best legal brains in the country. It is sad that even in processes such as these one must wonder if the maxim "we are all equal but some of us are just more equal" is not true indeed.

The biggest test for the Truth Commission is the manner in which it will deal with the issue of reparation to victims and whether there will be any prosecutions of those who did not avail themselves of the amnesty process. The expectations for reparations are high and many victims are pinning their hopes on the commission to compensate for the suffering and loss caused. The TRC process took away the right of victims to pursue justice through the courts and to obtain compensation through judicial means. Victims went to the TRC because they believe that the state will make good its constitutional promise and comply with its statutory duty to provide reparation. It will be sad if the following statement by Archbishop Njongonkulu Ndungane is proven to be correct:

> Those who took their cases to the TRC have been failed three times; firstly, by the apartheid system, secondly, by the fact that in appearing before the commission they have forfeited their right to the use of the existing justice system and, thirdly because promises of restitution by this government have so far been proven hollow. As we fail to keep our promise of gravestones, monuments, heroes acres, bursaries for victims and their children. . . . As we fail to provide emotional, medical and social support, so we fail the world at large.[56]

The TRC report recommended that prosecutions be considered where amnesty was not sought. A special unit has been set up in the office of the national prosecutor to investigate possible prosecutions. It is hoped that this unit will institute some prosecutions; history has taught us that a people's quest for vengeance and justice does not disappear.

Access to the Law

The right to legal representation for specific categories of persons is provided for in the constitution and various other pieces of legislation. The Legal Aid Board has been given the task of complying with the provisions of legal assistance. The SAHRC and Commission on Gender Equality also have legal units to assist people whose rights have been violated; both institutions can also institute strategic litigation. The rules of the constitution also require the registrar to assist a party who is unable to obtain assistance; the registrar may render assistance in preparing the papers required by the rules or, if directed to do so by the president, request an advocate or attorney to assist the party. According to the Supreme Court, indigent litigants can apply to the court to sue or defend a lawsuit *in forma pauperis*, whereupon an attorney or an advocate will be appointed to act in this capacity.

The limited resources of the Human Rights Commission make it impossible for it to render legal assistance on the scale that is required. This institution should not be an alternative to the Legal Aid Board but should rather use its resources to make an impact on cases where some systemic patterns of human rights violations can be identified. The *in forma pauperis* proceeding is very seldom used to provide legal assistance to the poor. This is the result of the pathetically low means test and because most legal practitioners have forgotten or tend to ignore this provision of the rules of court.

The rationale for the provision of legal representation at state expense is aimed at ensuring that issues such as poverty, illiteracy, social standing, and gender do not obstruct or impede an individual's right to a trial that is procedurally and substantially fair. The limited extent to which the judicial system has up to now been in a position to ameliorate the effects of such factors and to render the justice system more accessible and fair is apparent from the fact that the majority of people are still being denied access to legal representation.

Very little was done to establish the financial and administrative structure for the realization of the fundamental right in section 25(3)(e) of the Interim Constitution, entitling the accused to be provided with legal representation. This led the Constitutional Court in *State v. Vermaas* to the following remark:

Every month countless thousands of South Africans are criminally tried without legal representation because they are too poor to pay for it. They are presumably informed in the beginning, as the section requires them peremptorily to be, of their right to obtain that representation free of charge in the circumstances, which it defines. Imparting such information becomes an empty gesture and a mockery of the Constitution, however, if it is not backed up by mechanisms that are adequate for the enforcement of the right. The Constitution will surely not brook an undue delay in the fulfillment of the promise made by it about fundamental rights.[57]

Although one of the problems is the lack of funding,[58] the availability of financial resources on their own will not remedy the situation. The whole concept of the provision of state funded legal aid needs to be restructured.

The Legal Aid Board has traditionally provided legal aid by using private lawyers. The fees for such services are paid according to the Legal Aid Board's tariff. This process of implementation is very costly notwithstanding the reduced rate. This reduced rate has an impact on the quality of services and the Constitutional Court has also observed that state legal aid does not attract the best lawyers. At the National Legal Aid Forum, which took place in January 1998, consensus was reached that the judicare method of delivery should be drastically scaled down and replaced with the delivery of services by salaried employees in legal aid clinics, advice offices, and public defender offices.

The system of salaried lawyers attached to justice centers is now being further explored. It has already been proven that the utilization of funds for the establishment and operation of pilot projects such as the public defenders system and community legal clinics are more cost-effective and better placed to provide the necessary services. The salaried lawyer system also has drawbacks, such as the use of young inexperienced lawyers and high caseloads, that could have a negative impact on the provision of legal services.

There is no legal basis on which the distinction regarding the provision of legal services to an accused person and a litigant in a civil matter is based. Both parties should be afforded the opportunity to have their rights protected with the assistance of a legal representative. The concentration of resouces has also given rise to perceptions that state resources are mainly used to protect the rights of the criminal and that victim support is not regarded as a priority.

The Legal Aid Board primarily provides assistance in criminal matters and in certain civil matters. Besides these traditional areas of operation, the potential for human rights litigation and areas such equability, land, labor, and family law litigation will require the provision of adequate resources. The board, as noted, is having a problem with financial resources. The expansion of its services will only result in a cutback of the provision of legal services in criminal cases, which is surely not the intention. The only manner in which the board can make an impact in all these areas and provide required services is through the establishment of the offices referred to above.

The provision of legal services should be extended to surpass the conventional mode of legal aid. The present legal aid system does not cover the preliminary work such as advisory service and mediation. This type of work could have a preventive and educational role. Much costly litigation can be avoided if persons have access to legal advice. Most NGOs and advice offices are in a position to intervene and mediate in matters, thus preventing litigation.

Any access to justice initiatives should take into consideration the differences between rural and urban communities. In urban areas, the educational standard is usually higher and the higher economic standard makes the legal recourse more accessible. Not only are most rural dwellers unaware of the existence of state aided legal systems, the high rate of illiteracy and poverty means that people are unaware of their basic rights and of the mechanisms that exist for the enforcement of these rights. Most of the administrative centers for the provision of legal aid are situated in urban areas which are hundreds of kilometers away for people living in rural areas, and transport is in most instances unavailable or extremely costly.

The state-funded legal aid scheme has up to now been unable to address this need of the rural community. Access to justice in the rural communities has to be extended to include the provision of primary legal services, education, and information. The advancement of social justice involves overcoming major social, economic, and legal obstacles. Illiteracy and lack of legal knowledge render legal services illusory.

The paralegal movement could provide models for addressing the needs of rural communities. Most of these offices, in addition to providing access to justice, also concentrate on human rights and literacy training programs in the most remote villages.

Court Structures

The courts are the public face of the justice system. It is in the courts that the public witnesses the system in action. Of central concern, therefore, is the establishment of a court structure which commands the respect, support, and acceptance of all South Africans, so as to render the whole system truly legitimate. In *State v. Baleka and Others*, it was stated: "The court exists for the protection of the rights of the community, individuals as well as the public. Its foundation is the law itself but all its legitimacy depends on the trust of the community. No legal system can afford that this confidence is undermined."[59]

The state has a huge expectation to live up to, if the South African system of justice administration is to successfully take root in society. The system must be able to cope with the needs of the people who have perennially been denied access to resources and education, while at the same time, it must meet the needs of some of the biggest corporations in Africa and the world.

The state courts are generally still structured in the European tradition, based on the legal culture of Roman-Dutch law, and are not able to comply with the demands of the constitutional dictates. The procedures in the formal court structure are complex. The chances of an undefended litigant or accused successfully defending his rights are very limited. There is a need to simplify the procedure and demystify the law.

The use of indigenous languages is not a priority in the court system. Given that English and Afrikaans are respectively the home language of only 15.5 percent and 8.68 percent of the population, the reliance on these two languages is unacceptable. The use of interpreters has been problematic due to the fact that official court interpreters are not properly trained. Many miscarriages of justice have resulted from interpreters misunderstanding or misrepresenting testimony.

The court procedure allows limited participation of lay people. Assessors are now allowed by law but there is a lack of resources to implement this service. The assessor system allows for people to be judged by their peers and can ensure that the diversity of society is brought into the legal system.

Access to justice requires that matters are dealt within a speedy, efficient, and less costly manner. At present the South African court system is characterized by inordinate delays, loss of court files, and ineffecient processing of cases by all the role players, including the court. A better system of court management has to be introduced to improve the efficiency of the courts.

One of the basic requirements for an efficient justice system is the provision of a facilitative infrastructure. Skewed resource allocation means that many of the courts that operate in predominantly black urban and rural areas have extremely poor infrastructure. In addition to providing court buildings, it is imperative that the most basic of services such as electricity, water, and communication facilities be made available to each and every court. A normal complaint from prosecutors and magistrates is that they are required to work in an environment where there is constant change and development, without having access to the necessary resources such as reports of recent judgments, law journals, foreign case law, and international conventions and treaties.

Traditional courts present a paradox: on the one hand, they are often very conservative and patriarchal in nature; on the other hand, many people are familiar with their processes, and these customary courts frequently place a greater premium on negotiations aimed at maintaining social cohesion. That the apartheid regime to a large extent discredited the customary courts is not disputable. But this does not mean that these courts are without merit. They provide a much cheaper, and in some instances more effective, solution and are less punitive in nature. This is all the more reason to believe that these courts will continue to exist. There are, however, major difficulties in reconciling this court system with the formal system. One major area of difficulty is reconciling the informal court structure with a developing human rights culture, especially in the area of gender relations.[60]

The consequence of attempting to integrate the informal courts into the state court system must be fully considered. There is a need for a comprehensive canvassing of popular opinion.

The Legal Profession

South Africa has a dire shortage of lawyers who can serve those who cannot afford the services of private practitioners. The shortage of lawyers working in the area of human rights is the result of a combination of factors, including lack of access to universities, lack of access to the legal profession, lack of training of lawyers in human rights, and lack of interest on the part of members of the profession to work in the area of human rights.

The South African education system has been notorious for its quality of education and inaccessibility. For those who were able to qualify for entry into universities, the excessive fees at these institutions made it almost impossible to complete a three-year degree, not to mention a four-year degree (such as a B.Proc.) or a five-year LL.B. degree. Most students had to depend on bursaries from private companies and these entities only allocated bursaries to a few black students. The few graduates who are able to finish their academic career face another stumbling block of securing articles that are a necessary requirement for admission to the legal profession. A great disparity exists between the numbers of those who qualify academically and those who obtain articles. Given the problems of lack of opportunity and access, a significant percentage of the law graduates will not be able to secure articles of clerkship in the attorney's profession and will therefore not be able to enter into the profession. Given the historic imbalance in the country, there is no doubt that the worst affected graduates would be those from the historically disadvantaged black universities.

Among the thorniest issues relating to access to the profession are admission exams and vocational training. Both law societies and bar councils insist on an admission exam, while organizations representing lawyers who were marginalized under the apartheid regime are adamant that the present system of examination presents a barrier to entry to the profession and must go. All role players agree that some minimum standards of proficiency should be met.

The split in the legal profession impacts the role of all these associations in the transformation phase and, in certain instances, even retards the process. The agreement on a process aimed at unifying all the professional bodies in the legal profession is to be welcomed. *Justice Vision 2000* suggests the possibility of integration of the profession and the creation of a single controlling body for the profession. In *Justice Vision 2000*, it is suggested that, in order to achieve the goal of having a representative group of people enter the legal profession, policies should be developed which support uniform standards for entry into all branches of the profession and alternative ways of entering the profession.

Training for lawyers in the in the area of human rights law is particularly important. A great number of lawyers obtained their qualifications long before the adoption of the current constitution, at a time when human rights was an issue that was frowned at. The full-time practical school run by the Association of Law Societies includes a section on human rights in its training program, but this course has only been standardized as recently as the beginning of 1995.

The role of lawyers in the observance of human rights extends beyond the courtroom. There is an obligation on lawyers to ensure that laws are demystified and that the ordinary citizens are empowered with the knowledge to access the institutions that administer justice. Lawyers have to ensure that the constitutional protection of human rights becomes a reality in order to lead the country to the society envisaged by the constitution.

The legal profession must take stock of itself. It needs to look at its composition, its structure, its strengths, and its pitfalls. It needs to develop a profession that is accessible and reflects the diversity of the South African society, promote a legal profession that is accessible and affordable to the broader segment of the South African population, and take the necessary steps to ensure the formation of a unified body that reflects the interests of the various sectors in the profession and addresses the needs of such a diverse society.

Parallel to the role of the traditional practitioners and lawyers, in the protection of human rights, is the role of the paralegals. It is believed that there are some 1,200 paralegals in South Africa. Paralegals have, to date, been able to provide legal services to millions of people in areas where lawyers seldom venture. There appears to be some consensus that paralegals constitute an important sector in the provision of legal services and that they should be formally recognized.

The fact that formal recognition might be given to paralegals has its own inherent problems. Paralegals are not governed by any professional body. The National Community Based Paralegal Association is the representative body for this sector. The NCBPA is currently trying to address some of the problems relating to the recognition and accreditation of paralegals, such as a uniform curriculum for training, codes of conduct, ethics, and vocational training.

The Paralegal movement performs a valuable service but is now facing financial difficulties. A number of advice offices have been closed down and many others are under threat of closure. This problem needs to be addressed and alternative funding resources need to be established. This sector is donor funded and receives no official recognition or support from the state.

Human Rights Education

The bill of rights can only become a reality if people are aware of it and its role, and if they possess the knowledge of how to exercise these rights. It is also important for those in positions of power and authority over others to know the content of a bill of rights and the limitations it places on the exercise of any power.

After the adoption of the constitution, the Constitutional Assembly embarked on a national constitution awareness and education campaign. Various trainers were trained and a number of workshops were conducted throughout the country. The Constitutional Assembly also organized People's Forums in all the major areas, where large numbers of people could debate the content of the bill of rights. Different forms of the media, specifically, radio and television, were used to popularize the constitution. Through these programs a million copies of the constitution were made available to the public.

In addition to this initiative by the state at the national level, a number of

NGOs and community-based organizations are conducting human rights programs. Some of these programs are of a general nature and others are on specific human rights issues such as children's, women's, and prisoners' rights. The target groups for these training programs are state officials, educational institutions, and community organizations.

These programs were initially implemented on an ad hoc basis and with very little coordination between the various NGOs and state institutions. There are a number of initiatives under way aimed at ensuring greater cooperation between the various role players. The formation of the National Human Rights Education Forum to coordinate the various activities is one such initiative.

Very few education programs reach rural communities. The main agent for implementing these projects in rural areas is the paralegal movement. Although the paralegals are attempting to implement some programs, lack of resources constrains the extent to which they can provide a human rights education.

Until recently, very few organizations used creative ways of conducting human rights education training programs. In the last few years, the methodology has changed considerably and has been adapted to meet the needs of the various communities.

Radio is a popular medium that can be used to reach all segments of society. Community radio stations are mushrooming in the country. These radio stations broadcast programs of local and regional interest and in the local languages. Because these radio stations are very popular and reach a large number of listeners, they could be a potentially important vehicle to convey information on human rights.

A lot of work has been done in this area, but very few studies indicate the success of the programs and the methods used. No information is available about how many people these programs actually reach. There is a need to evaluate the impact of human rights education in the country. The relevance of some of these programs to their target communities also needs further consideration.

Nongovernmental Organizations

NGOs are currently fulfilling a crucial role in strengthening the democratization process. They also serve as watchdogs with respect to the government. This is a role that most human rights NGOs have struggled to come to terms with. Most human rights NGOs were quite comfortable with just exposing human rights violations. This schizophrenia, created during the transformation phase, led many NGOs to redefine their role and purpose. Human rights NGOs, in general, have, over the last few years, been struggling to restructure and reestablish themselves. Some have survived this period of tribulation but many are still in the process of reestablishing themselves.

Human rights organizations before 1993 functioned mainly as service providers. Their resources and time were spent on the provision of legal defense to victims of the system. Except for some public interest litigation that required a more proactive and creative approach, most of the work done in this area was run-of-the-mill litigation of the kind offered by most attorney firms. This was, however, needed at that particular time in history and is still very much required today. Although most human rights organizations realize that they have to move away from the provision of conventional legal services, this is a long-term process that can only take place if the state takes the necessary steps to provide legal services.

The possibilities of challenging the legislature, administrative practices, and the acts violating the provisions of the constitution pose new challenges and opportunities for NGOs. Although some big NGOs have been able to make use of the opportunities provided on this level, these initiatives have not yet filtered through to the community organizations. Community-based organizations can fulfill a crucial role in ensuring that the delivery of services takes place. There is need to strengthen the capacity of organizations on the ground.

The incorporation of international human rights in the constitution opens up new possibilities for NGOs to explore. To date, South African NGOs remain aloof to participation in forums such as the African Commission. Participation in these forums is still a very individualistic activity and there is a need for NGOs to define their role in such bodies and in other international bodies. Lack of knowledge of international law remains a problem. Various training programs have created some awareness of international law and its relevance. There is, however, a need for more specialized training courses.

Most NGOs conduct human rights education programs in some form or another. These activities are often ad hoc and lack a long-term planning and coordinated approach. It makes more sense for all these bodies to coordinate their activities. The lack of networking and cooperation among NGOs is a major problem.

NGOs in South Africa work in exciting times. Yet, at the very moment of opportunity, there are a number of threats to the future of NGOs. The consolidation of the democratic process has not brought an enabling environment for NGOs. South African human rights NGOs remain largely dependent on foreign funding. These NGOs have been more fortunate than those in most other developing countries in attracting aid by the mere association with the antiapartheid struggle. Now, however, South African NGOs are under financial pressure as a result of new priorities of foreign donors and the fact that funding is increasingly being channeled to the government in the form of bilateral aid. Strategies for fund-raising are largely underdeveloped and attempts are only now being made to develop good fund-raising skills and to attract funds from local donors. The adoption of the Non-Profit Organizations Act in 2000 and the amendments to the tax law that allow for tax deduction for donors of public benefit organizations can go some way in improving the funding base of NGOs. However, it remains to be seen whether local donors regard the role of the human rights sector as sufficiently important to make NGOs beneficiaries of their social commitment programs.

Due to the decrease in funding, NGOs are not in a position to provide competitive salaries. These financial constraints have resulted in the migration of skilled personnel to the public and private sectors. This has left many NGOs in a crisis situation, trying to develop leadership and attempting to ensure the continuous provision of services. These crises have placed an enormous strain on NGOs that ultimately affects the quality of the services provided.

Conclusion

The provision of a new constitutional order that enshrines a bill of rights is an appropriate start, but it is only a start and not an end. History has taught us that a bill does not automatically lead to success. To make a bill of rights work is a difficult issue. The government has adopted the right framework. Delivery in terms of this framework is now required.

The effective realization of the aims and objectives of the bill of rights along with its legislative provisions depends on factors such as awareness of the rights contained in the document, access to the law, and the ability to enforce these rights. All these factors are, in turn, dependent on the external environment. Overall political, economic, and social stability is indispensable for the creation of an institutional framework favorable for the protection of human rights.

It will be decades before the black people of South Africa can free themselves from the shackles of apartheid. The vast majority are living in conditions of abject poverty. Poverty has a direct relevance to the democracy and a sustainable human rights culture. What do the rights to legal representation, housing, education, and health mean if people do not have the means to access these rights? The government has an obligation to ensure that these rights are met, but with limited state resources, civil society has a role to play in order to ensure that these resources are channeled in the right direction.

Rights in constitutions and the law, by themselves, have limited relevance to the majority of South Africans who still suffer as result of the structural subordination that continues to exist. Unless the issue of structural subordination is faced, equal rights will be little more than a hollow slogan for the great majority of the people in South Africa. There is a need to deliver substantive effective equality for all.

Racism, gender discrimination, and xenophobia remain major stumbling blocks, notwithstanding the major initiatives that have been undertaken to eliminate them. The increase in crime has resulted in a backlash against the constitution; people are now blaming the ills of society on the bill of rights and are calling for the reinstatement of capital punishment. A balancing act between the dictates of the constitution and being tough on crime is required.

The improvement of the economy is a *sine qua non* for the effective exercise and promotion of human rights. The government's economic policy, with its key objectives being the reduction of the external debt, privatizing of state assets, and downsizing of public services, has, to date, resulted in a decrease in social spending. The development of the economy through private investment has not reaped dividends, as the investment is just not forthcoming and unemployment and poverty are increasing. Money has to be generated to enable the government to implement policies that can redress social and economic ills. Poverty and unemployment have to be reduced for stability in the country. Failing this, the country might yet again face a popular revolt.

Education is essential in the exercise of rights. Because of illiteracy, many people do not know what their rights are; even when armed with this knowledge, they lack the information on how to access these rights. The process of human rights education is going to be long and fraught with a number of difficulties. This process, however, is essential for the development of a rights culture.

The drafting and adoption of the final constitution is the one area in which the government has delivered on its promise. It now remains to be seen whether the government will implement the provisions of the constitution within the time limit set by the people of the country. The present era has been dedicated to the implementation of legislation and policy, the next few years will therefore be crucial in ensuring that all the paper rights become real.

Recommendations

Overall

These recommendations are made on the basis that there is general acceptance and agreement that the responsibility for the provision of legal services for the protection of human rights ultimately rests on the state. Although the Justice Ministry and the government have repeatedly underscored their commitment to the provision of legal services, this is a long-term objective. This commitment could diminish with time depending on the political situation and the demands on the government. It is, therefore, important that advocacy lobbying and monitoring of the developments continue.

To this extent, these general recommendations are offered: (1) continued advocacy to persuade the state to meet its constitutional and wider obligation to provide legal services; and (2) the policy document released by the Department of Justice aimed at discharging this obligation must be adopted and implemented.

More specific recommendations concerning access to legal representation include: restructuring the Legal Aid Board; establishment of more legal aid clinics; responding to the specific needs of vulnerable groups such as women and children; increasing the number of lawyers; reviewing the legal cost, contingency fees, and special fee arrangements; providing for compulsory pro bono legal services by practicing attorneys; and Supporting and recognizing paralegals.

Human rights NGOs and private practitioners should provide legal services in the areas where it is appropriate to do so. To this end, the following are recommended: support for more attorneys to enter the legal profession; continued support for constitutional and specific interest litigation focusing on civil and political rights and the realization and enforcement of socioeconomic rights from the donor community; provision of training programs on human rights issues for legal practitioners; implementation of a mechanism to ensure that lower courts implement the decisions of the Constitutional Court; and ensuring that a program of judicial education is put in place for judicial officers.

The Legal Profession

Recommendations for improving the legal profession include: reviewing entry qualifications for attorneys; providing financial and other support for candidate attorneys to obtain articles of clerkship; including a compulsory course on human rights in the academic training program of law graduates at all universities; providing continuing and ongoing training programs for legal practitioners on human rights; and the unification of the profession.

Access to the Courts

To improve access to the courts, these recommendations are offered: building and renovating court structures in previously disadvantaged communities; extending small claims courts to all areas; simplifying court procedures; using plain language in court; using professional interpreters; promoting the use of all official languages in the courts; managing courts more efficiently; establishing advice and information desks at courts; creating greater public awareness about the role, function, and procedures of the court; and integrating the informal courts system.

Department of Justice

Improvements in the Department of Justice could be made through review of the employment, promotion, training, and salary structure of the department; recruitment practices that ensure a representative department in terms of race and gender; restructuring the Justice College; judicial training for all officers of the court; a rules board to enquire into the adversarial and inquisitorial procedures with the aim of expanding the inquisitorial procedure; restructuring the court system; and restructuring the attorney's profession.

Public Institutions

Implementation of more public awareness programs about the public institutions created by the constitution and increasing state support for these institutions are recommended.

A specific parliamentary committee to deal with public institutions should be appointed and internal and external monitoring mechanisms should be established to ensure implementation of the institutions' recommendations.

Human Rights Education

Human rights education should be included in the formal school curriculum and as a compulsory component in adult literacy training programs. Human rights education programs should be rationalized in state institutions; coordinated among NGOs; offered through different media, such as radio, television, and print; and developed to address the needs of the huge illiterate population; and human rights education materials should be developed in specific areas such as socioeconomic rights.

International Law

Lawyers, state officials, and paralegals should receive training in international law. NGOs should be trained in reporting to international and regional bodies and have greater participation in regional and international human rights forums. State compliance with international law should be monitored.

Notes

1. This act was passed in 1913 and imposed a color bar in the labor industry.

2. Act of 1913, which ensured segregation in regard to land ownership.

3. Act passed in 1923 which provided for residential segregation.

4. For more detailed information, see Mike Robertson, ed., *Human Rights for South Africans* (Cape Town: Oxford University Press, 1991).

5. Working Paper 25, Project 58 of the South African Law Commission, 1989. The minister of justice required the commission to investigate and make recommendations on the definition and protection of group rights within the context of the constitutional dispensation and the possible extension of the existing protection of individual rights. This created the impression that the government intended to protect minority interest at a time when it became apparent that the change was inevitable. The white paper however went further than what the government intended. The commission clearly came out in favor of the protection of individual rights.

6. Reproduced in the 1989 *South African Journal on Human Rights* (hereafter *SAJHR*). These constitutional guidelines were based on the Freedom Charter. In the guidelines, the ANC was quite clear on the need for a justiciable bill of rights.

7. *Harris v. Minister of the Interior* 1952 (4) SA 769 and *Collins v. Minister of the Interior* 1957 (1) SA 531.

8. Certification of the Constitution of the Republic of South Africa 1996 (10) BCLR.

9. Certification of the amended text of the Constitution of the Republic of South Africa 1997 (1) BCLR (CC); Act 108 of 1996.

10. *President of the RSA and Others v. SARFU and Others* (1999) BCLR 175 (CC). See also *President of the RSA v. Hugo* 1997 CCT 11/96.

11. *Larbi-Odam v. Member of Executive Council for Education* 1996 (12) BCLR 1612 (B).

12. *Mandela v. Falati* 1995 (1) SA 251 (W); *Potgieter and Another v. Killian* 1995 (2) BCLR 1498 (N); *Balaro and Others v. University of Bophuthatswana* 1995 (4) SA 197. *Gardener v. Whitaker* 1995 (2) SA 672 (B).

13. 1994 (6) BCLR 124 (t).

14. 1996 (5) BCLR 658 (CC).

15. 1975 (2) SA 29 (4).

16. *National Education Crisis Committee v. State President of the Republic of Society* (unreported case no. 16736 I 86); *African National Council (Border Branch) and Another v. Chairman Council of State of the Republic of Ciskei* 1992 (4) SA 434.

17. *Ferreira v. Levin NO and Others* 1996 (1) SA 984 (CC).

18. *Maluleke v. MEC Health and Welfare* 1999 (4) SA 364.

19. *State v. Makwanyane and Another* 1995 (3) SA 391 (CC); 1995 (6) BCLR 665 (CC).

20. 1994 (3) SA 625 (E).

21. See, however, John Dugards, "Abduction: Does the Appellate Division Care About International Law?" *SAJHR* 12 (1996) 324, and the judgment in *State v. December* 1995 (1) SACR 438, where the Appellate division ignored the international customary law that prohibits a state from exercising its police powers in a territory of another.

22. Section 1(1) of the Law of Evidence Amendment Act 45 of 1988.

23. Regulations for the Administration and Distribution of Estates of Deceased Blacks promulgated under Proclamation R 200 of 1987 in terms of the Black Administration Act 38 of 1927.

24. *Mthembu v. Letsela and Another* 2000 (3) SA 867 (SCA), p. 9.

25. 2001 (2) BCLR 103 (CC).

26. See SALC, Projects 108, 90, and 93.

27. Muslims are a minority in South Africa. The composition of the South African population is described by the South African government website (http://www.gov.za) in the following manner: "Almost 80% of South Africa's population adheres to the Christian faith. Other major religious groups are the Hindus, Muslims and Jews. A minority of South Africa's population does not belong to any of the major religions, but regard themselves as traditionalists or of no specific religious affiliation" (http://www.gov.za/yearbook/2001/landpeople.html#religion).

28. 1997 (1) BCLR 77 (C).

29. See *Ismail v. Ismail* 1983 (1) SA 1006, where such marriages were held as contrary to the public mores.

30. 1994 (3) SA 625.

31. 1996 (4) SA 318.

32. *R. v. Mills* (1985) 29 DLR 161 (SCC).

33. The rules and procedures to be adopted in bringing a matter to the Constitutional Court as published in the *Government Gazette* GN RS GG 16204, January 6, 1994.

34. *Hekpoort Environmental Society v. the Minister of Land Affairs* 1998 (1) SA 34.

35. *Zantsi v. Council of State, Ciskei, and Others* 1995 (4) SA 615 (CC).

36. *Ferreira v. Levin NO and Others* 1996 (1) SA 984 (CC).

37. Matters regarding the admission of attorneys are provided for in the Attorneys Act 53 of 1979. Matters regarding advocates are dealt with in the Advocates Admission Act 74 of 1964.

38. See *Society of Advocates of Natal v. De Freitas and Another* 1997 (4) SA 1134 (N); *General Council of the Bar of South Africa v. Van der Spuy* 1999 (1) SA 577 (T)

39. Law Society of South Africa, *LSSA Race and Gender Survey,* study commissioned by the Law Society and implemented by the National Association of Democratic Lawyers.

40. A policy document, *Justice Vision 2000,* published by the Department of Justice, focuses on the transformation of the legal profession. The main challenges identified were the lack of representavity of the profession; a largely inaccessible legal profession; the rationalization of the legal profession to bring the structure of the legal profession, and the laws which regulate it, into line with the new constitutional dispensation. This was also one of the main topics on the agenda of the first National Consultative Forum on the Administration of Justice in 1994 and has been the subject of continuing consultation since then. In November 1999, the Policy Unit of the Department of Justice convened a National Consultative Forum on Legal Practice. The purpose of the forum was to solicit the views on the structure, the qualification for admission to, and the regulation of the legal profession. This consultation was part of the process in drafting the Legal Practice Bill (the third draft has since been published for discussion).

41. The Prison Act was renamed the Correctional Services Act No. 8 of 1959.

42. Proclamation dated February 20, 1998, of the Correctional Service Amendment Act no. 102 of 1997.

43. For example, the Legal Resources Center (LRC), Lawyers for Human Rights (LHR), Black Lawyers Association (BLA), Black Sash, Community Law Center, the National Institute for Public Law (NIPILAR), Street Law, National Community-

Based Paralegal Association, Human Rights Institute of South Africa (HURISA), Center for Applied Legal Studies (CALS) at the University of the Witwatersrand, Center for Human Rights and the Community Law Center at the University of the Western Cape, and Women's Legal Center.

44. National Land Committee, Gay and Lesbian Coalition, Disabled People of South Africa, Environmental Monitoring Group, South Africa Catholic Bishops Conference, Black Sash, Women's Legal Center, South Africa Council of Churches, and Institute for Democracy in South Africa, among others.

45. *State v. Makwanyane and Another* 1995(3) SA 391 (CC); 1995(6) BCLR 665 (CC); and *State v. Williams and Others* 1995 (3) SA 632 (CC); 1995(7) BCLR 861 (CC).

46. *State v. Makwanyane and Others* 1995 (1) LRC 269.

47. 1995 (7) BCLR 851(CC).

48. 1996 (4) SA 671(CC)

49. In regard to certification of the constitution of the RSA 1996 (4) SA 944.

50. 1997 (12) BCLR 1696 (CC).

51. 1997(6) BCLR 787.

52. *Government of the Republic of South Africa v. Grootboom* 2001 (1) SA 46 (CC).

53. In *CASE* [Community Agency for Social Enquiry] *and Another v. Minister of Safety and Security* 1996 (5) BCLR 609, CALS and the Freedom of Expression Institute filed an amicus brief arguing that Section 2(1) of the Indecent and Obscene Photographic Matter Act constituted an impermissible limitation of freedom of expression. In *Brink v. Kitshof* CALS filed an amicus brief arguing that Section 44 of the Insurance Act violated women's right to equality. In *Du Plessis v. De Klerk* 1996 (5) BCLR 658, CALS and the Freedom of Expression Institute filed a brief arguing that the common law principles of defamation should be subject to the constitution. In *State v. Makhananye,* 1999 (6) BCLR 665, LHR, CALS, and the Society for the Abolition of the Death Penalty filed a brief on the constitutionality of the death penalty.

54. "Human Rights Body Strapped for Cash," *Mail and Guardian* October 10, 1996.

55. Community Agency for Social Enquiry (CASE), "Assessing Knowledge of Human Rights Among the General Population and Selected Target Groups," August 1998. This study was commissioned by the European Union Foundation for Human Rights (EUFHR).

56. *Saturday Argus* (Cape Town), April 29, 2000.

57. In *State v. Vermaas* 1996 (1) SACR 528, the Constitutional Court held that it is aware of the financial constraints but that the state needs to boost allocations to the legal aid fund.

58. 1988 (4) SA 703.

59. Sandra Burman and Wilfred Scharf, "Creating Peoples Justice: Street Committees and Peoples Courts in a South Africa City," *Law and Society Review* 24, no. 3 (1990).

Chapter 10
Sudan
In the Shadows of Civil War and Politicization of Islam

Siddig A. Hussein

The Sudan gained independence from the joint-colonial rule of Britain and Egypt (commonly known as the Anglo-Egyptian Condominium) on January 1, 1956. The Sudan is a vast country with a total area of almost a million square miles, inhabited by diverse ethnic and tribal groups. The most important division is between southern and northern Sudan. The south is inhabited by a myriad of indigenous African tribes, the principal among them are the Dinka, the Nuer, the Shiluk, and the Baria. Islam and Arabic culture are less influential in the South than in the north. The majority of southerners are Christians or followers of traditional African religions, and they speak different local dialects. Although the political leadership of the north identifies itself more with Arabic and Islamic cultures, northerners are not homogeneous either. The Beja in the east, the Nubians in the Northern State, and the Nuba in southwestern Sudan are some of the diverse tribal groups that inhabit northern Sudan.

Since independence, the Sudan has spent thirty years under military rule and only twelve under democratically elected governments. There have been three military regimes, which ruled from 1958 until 1964, 1969 until 1984, and 1989 until today. The three democratically elected governments, established in 1956, 1964, and 1985, each came to an abrupt end with a military takeover. Besides the problem of political instability, the Sudan has been torn apart by a civil war that started in 1955 and has continued on until today, except for an eleven-year truce. The said truce instated by the Addis Ababa Peace Agreement in 1972 came to an abrupt end with the declaration of Islamic laws in 1983.

The division between the north and the south is a direct product of British colonial policy in the Sudan.[1] Since independence, this division has been perpetuated by unequal economic development, a hardening of the class structure, and politics driven by the desire for power.

The weakness of the democratically elected governments and the vulnerability of the country to military coups must be analyzed within the socioeconomic context of underdevelopment in general, and within the characteristics of the Sudan in particular. The Sudan is largely an agrarian and nomadic society. The bases of political commitment are largely traditional. In such a situation a person affiliates to a particular party mainly for its association with a particular tribe, ethnic group, religious sect, or region. The country's two major political parties, the Umma and the National Unionist Party (NUP), are based on religious allegiances and draw their support from followers of the Ansar and Khatmiyya sects of Islam, respectively. Both sects adhere to a traditional, conservative form of Islam and are especially popular in the rural areas of northern Sudan. As the actual or potential beneficiaries of a multiparty system, the Umma and the NUP have always supported democracy.

Both the Ansar and the Khatmiyya are widely followed religious sects whose existence and influence are not coterminous with the suspension or dissolution of their political organizations. The versions of Islam dominant among followers of the two sects and advocated by their political organizations are relatively tolerant. In many respects, these two sects, along with many other Sufi brotherhoods, represent the main current of popular Islam in the Sudan. It is a political idiosyncrasy of the Sudan that it is the state itself that has perpetuated religious totalitarianism, often in the face of opposition from these two traditional religious parties. This idiosyncrasy sharply contrasts with experiences of neighboring states where populist Islam is identified with movements advocating an activist militant brand of Islam antagonistic to the state and the official religious establishment.[2]

The concept of a constitution in the context of the Sudan is peculiar enough to deserve explanation. Ordinarily, the word "constitution" carries with it an assumption that it will, in some way, include a bill of rights. However, there is no bill of rights incorporated into the constitutional decrees by which the government ruled the country from 1989 until June 30, 1998. A constitution devoid of a bill of rights is a structure without a soul and does not add to the legal tools for the protection of human rights. From this standpoint, therefore, there is, for the time being, no real constitution in the Sudan. Nonetheless, judging by past experience, this state of affairs is not the end of the vicious circle of military and parliamentarian succession to power in the Sudan. The think tanks of the present regime know this very well and it was the idea of one of these organizations that the 1998 constitution be promulgated as a step toward democratic reform.[3] This is not to say, however, that upon return to democracy the rule of law in the

Sudan will be the idealized juridical artifact of a human rights Eden articulated by the UN human rights treaties. As explained in the concluding paragraph of this chapter, socioeconomic factors do impose limitations on what can be achieved through law and the constitution.

In the Sudan, there have been two alternative forms of governance—military dictatorship and parliamentary democracy. Which of the two forms of governance will ultimately prevail is a question whose answer must be sought in the socioeconomic reality of the Sudan. One hopes that liberal democracy will prevail, as, on the face of it, liberal democracy is much more conducive to the protection of human rights.

This chapter endeavors to survey the constitutional and legal protection of human rights in the Sudan under the various regimes since the Sudan gained independence. The chapter discusses (1) the constitutional and legal framework of human rights protection, (2) the institutional framework comprising the judiciary and the legal profession, and (3) the political, social, and economic context within which the legal system operates.

Constitutional and Legal Framework

Immediately upon taking control of the Sudan in 1899, the British administration began establishing a legal and constitutional framework for governance of the country. That same year, Great Britain and Egypt signed an agreement on the administration of the Sudan. The agreement consolidated all legislative, executive, and judicial powers into the hands of a governor general of the Sudan.[4] Although a Penal Code and a Criminal Procedure Act were enacted the same year, the country continued to be governed under martial law.[5]

Section 23 of the Criminal Procedure Act empowered the governor general to confer on any military officer serving in the Sudan and qualified to sit on court martial all or any of the powers of a first, second, or third class magistrate. The colonial administration relied heavily on military officers for the administration of civil and criminal justice. In 1905, the power of the governor general to appoint extralegal professionals was extended, allowing him to confer judicial powers on any other public servant.[6]

The absolutist and authoritarian character of colonial governance displayed at the outset of the administration gradually eased. The willingness of the administration to abide by the rule of law and to lay a foundation for a legal order eventually led to the creation of an extensive legislative network of rules and procedures regulating all aspects of civil life. In 1929, the colonial administration successfully reformed and consolidated the legal and judicial system of criminal and civil justice comprising substantive and procedural laws that were to continue in effect long after independence.

The gradual movement toward the rule of law culminated in 1953 in the issuance of a Self-Government Statute, a document that laid the foundation for the governance of the Sudan after independence.[7] The Self-Government Statute was the starting place for the development of a democratic constitution. Chapter 2 of the statute, entitled "Fundamental Rights," provided for the right to freedom and equality (Article 5), freedom from confiscation of property and arrest (Article 6), freedom of religion, opinion, and association (Article 7), the supremacy of the rule of law (Article 8), the independence of the judiciary (Article 9), and the right to a constitutional remedy (Article 10).

The Self-Government Statute made the judiciary the guardian of its rules and gave it jurisdiction to hear and decide any matter involving the interpretation of the statute or the enforcement of the rights and freedoms guaranteed by Chapter 2 (Article 82). Even before the promulgation of the Self-Government Statute, the colonial administration had recognized freedom of association and protected the right to organize trade unions. The Regulation of Trade Disputes Ordinance of 1949 and the Trade Union Ordinance of 1949 paved the way for the de facto and de jure existence of trade unions.

The Trade Disputes Ordinance paved the way for recognition of freedom of association and protection of the right to organize. Industrial action taken in anticipation or furtherance of a trade dispute was protected from liability for simple criminal and civil conspiracy (section 4[1] and [2]) and immune from actions for breach of contract or interfering with the trade, business, or employment of some other person (section 6) and tort liability in general (section 4[1] and [2]). However this immunity from common law liabilities left trade unions vulnerable to statutory liability under the Sudan Penal Code 1925 (section 143), which made it a criminal offense for a government employee to stop work in agreement with one or more such employees.

The fundamental rights and freedoms guaranteed by the Self-Government Statute were accompanied by procedures aimed at ensuring that the rights were respected in practice. Following the promulgation of the Self-Government Statute in 1954, the Civil Justice Ordinance of 1929 was amended to regulate the jurisdiction conferred upon the High Court by Article 82 of the statute in matters involving the interpretation of the constitution. Under Civil Justice Ordinance Amendment Order 26 (1954), the court could entertain applications submitted by any person for the determination of any constitutional question if the person had a right or interest which would be directly affected by the outcome (section 4). However, if the court believed that the applicant was claiming any specific relief other than a declaration upon the question submitted, the court could reject the application (sections 5 and 6). If the court accepted the application, it issued its findings in a declaration on the question submitted (section 5[6]).

As mentioned above, the Self-Government Statute was the prototype for democratic constitutions in the Sudan. Later constitutions and the characteristics of the legal and constitutional regimes of parliamentary democracy are discussed below.

Constitutional and Legal Framework in Times of Democracy

The Transitional Constitution of 1956, promulgated by the democratically elected government in power at the time, guaranteed the same rights and freedoms protected by the Self-Government Statute. The Transitional Constitution was in force for only two years before being suspended, following a military takeover on November 17, 1958. The coup d'état brought the first democratically elected government to an end, and set the precedent for military usurpation of power that was to become a pattern in years to come. From the first day of the coup until the end of October 1964, the country was ruled under a state of emergency. The state of emergency was finally lifted by an agreement between the junta and the political parties in the country after a popular uprising against the junta on October 21, 1964. The agreement, known as the National Charter, was the prelude to reinstatement of parliamentary democracy and the newly amended Transitional Constitution. The political parties and the junta agreed on the following:

- the setting of common freedoms, including freedom of the press, freedom of speech, and freedom of organization and association;
- the lifting of the state of emergency and the repeal of all laws limiting liberties in areas where there were no security risks;
- making the independence of the judiciary and the independence of the university more secure; and
- the release of all political detainees (those extrajudicially detained) and of civilians serving prison sentences in political cases.

A transitional government was to rule the country in accordance with the Transitional Constitution of 1956 until free general elections could be held, which was to be no later than the end of March 1965.

On the basis of this agreement, the Transitional Constitution, as amended in 1964, was promulgated as "an instrument consisting of a fundamental law by which the Sudan [was] to be governed and by which there [would] be established a Constituent Assembly for the making of a permanent constitution."[8]

The 1964 Transitional Constitution reiterated the fundamental rights

recognized by its precursors. It guaranteed freedom and equality before
the law and prohibited discrimination against any Sudanese person on the
basis of birth, religion, race, or sex in regard to public or private employment or in the admission to or exercise of any occupation, trade, business,
or profession (Article 4). Likewise, it guaranteed freedom of conscience
and the right to freely profess religion and freedom of expression, association, and assembly (Article 5).

The Transitional Constitution also provided that "no person may be arrested, detained, imprisoned or deprived of the use or ownership of his
property, except by due process of law" (Article 6). It guaranteed all persons the right of access to the courts for protection or enforcement of any
of the rights conferred by the constitution, and confirmed the power of
the courts to make all such orders as may be necessary and appropriate to
secure the enjoyment of any right (Article 8). The independence of the judiciary was expressly guaranteed (Article 9), and its role as the custodian
of the constitution was reiterated.

The Transitional Constitution remained in effect until May 25, 1969. In
1969, a junta, led by Jaafar Numeiri, took over and suspended the constitution, thereby ending the second democracy.

The third period of democratic constitutionalism began in the aftermath
of the April 6, 1985, popular uprising that ousted Numeiri's regime. Once
again, major political parties and the trade unions drafted a new Transitional Constitution. The Transitional Constitution of 1985 came into effect
on October 10, 1985, as the fundamental law by which the Republic of the
Sudan was to be governed. Like the 1965 Transitional Constitution, it provided for the establishment of a Constituent Assembly that would be responsible for drafting a permanent constitution. The major political parties once
again negotiated and ratified a charter committing themselves to multiparty
democracy and the rule of law. Entitled "The Charter for the Defense of Democracy," this document was ratified on November 11, 1985, by representatives of all the political parties, except the National Islamic Front. NIF did
not give reasons at the time. In retrospect, "NIF did not see the charter as a
comprehensive reconciliation initiative nor a bill of unanimous constitutional mandate. The charter was an instance of political maneuver by rival
forces and NIF was not called to sign the charter since NIF was in a different
polar to which hostility was nurtured by the Left and the Umma Party both
looking at NIF as ally of the defunct regime."[9] NIF does not see that omission
to sign the charter or its subsequent complicity in the 1989 military coup as
expression of objection to democracy in principle. The signatories to the
charter committed themselves to the following principles and actions:

- multiparty democracy based on the rule of law, independence of the judiciary, and respect for human rights;

- total rejection of any movement toward military or civilian dictatorship, or weakening of the democratic system of governance, whatever the justifications;
- to undertake and abide by any contingency measures necessary to fight back any attack against the democratic system;
- to blacklist any foreign power or country that recognizes, supports, or maintains any dictatorial regime in the Sudan;
- declaration of the Sudanese people that they are not bound by any loan, credit, or aid agreement, nor by any treaty concluded by a dictatorial regime purporting to act on behalf of the Sudan; and
- the transformation of their alliance into a popular army for restoration of democracy, when necessary.

Compared to its predecessors, the bill of rights in the Transitional Constitution of 1985 was relatively comprehensive. Under the title "Principles of State Policy," the Transitional Constitution also introduced a set of principles to guide state policy including:

- the system of governance is multiparty democracy and the law shall protect parties abiding by the ethics and principles of democracy;
- the state shall endeavor to enable citizens to participate fully in public affairs;
- the judiciary is independent and no legislative or executive authority shall interfere with or oversee its work;
- the state shall guarantee the independence of universities and freedom of thought and scientific research;
- the civil service shall be independent, neutral, and subject only to the rule of law;
- the state and every person, whether corporate or natural, public officer or private citizen, shall abide by the rule of law, as applied by the courts; and
- the independence and neutrality of the publicly owned media and equality of opportunity of access to the media.

In addition to the fundamental rights and freedoms copied from its precursors, the Transitional Constitution of 1985 introduced a clearly defined set of civil rights, including:

- the right to liberty and personal security, and the prohibition of extralegal arrest, detention, or imprisonment;
- the right to assemble peacefully and to conduct processions in accordance with the rule of law;
- the right to choose a domicile and to move freely within or outside the country, subject to restrictions imposed by law;

- the right of litigation and of recourse to a court of competent jurisdiction;
- state action shall be subject to judicial review;
- the right to privacy and inviolability of the home;
- the presumption of innocence, the right of the accused in a criminal case to a prompt and fair trial, and the right to defend oneself, including the right to appoint counsel; likewise, the accused is guaranteed protection from inducements, oppression, torture, or the infliction upon himself or herself of any cruel or degrading punishment;
- the prohibition of retroactive laws (Article 27); and
- the guarantee to every person of the right to apply to the Supreme Court for the protection or implementation of any of the rights established by the constitution (Article 32).

The constitution also reiterated that the Supreme Court was the guardian of the constitution and guaranteed the jurisdiction of the Supreme Court to issue decrees and judgments, and follow up implementation thereof, in any matter pertaining to:

- the interpretation of the constitution and laws;
- the review of constitutional matters and constitutionality of laws; and
- the protection of the fundamental rights and freedoms guaranteed by the constitution.

The Transitional Constitution of 1985 placed some limits on fundamental rights and freedoms. Persons indicted for corrupting economic, political, or social life or undermining previous constitutional government could not challenge the constitutionality of a law depriving them of the rights to free expression and association, personal security, freedom from extrajudicial detention, assembly and demonstration, freedom of residence and movement, and protection against retroactive laws.

Furthermore, all the rights and freedoms set out in the constitution could be restricted by legislation protecting public security, morality, health, or the security of the national economy (Article 33). With the exception of the right to litigation, all rights and freedoms stated above could also be suspended by a declaration of a state of emergency (Article 134).

The head of state, in consultation with the Council of Ministers, could make such a declaration in case of grave and immediate danger threatening the security of the state, any part of the state, or national unity. After the declaration of a state of emergency, the Constituent Assembly was required to renew or terminate the state of emergency within fifteen days (Article 134[2]).

On April 2, 1987, a new article was added to the Transitional Constitution, obligating the state to realize the objectives articulated by the original National Charter of 1964.

Characteristics of Democratic Legality

It is a main premise of this chapter that the democratic constitutional development of the Sudan to date is significant, and not only as history. Experience has shown that this democratic constitutional tradition is evolving toward greater protection of rights. Over time, this tradition has become the ultimate test of the validity and legality of acts taken by government, the state, or private individuals, even if such acts were taken under military rule when the constitution had been suspended. From this perspective, military usurpation of power becomes, in itself, an act of constitutional treason for which the perpetrators must be held accountable when things revert to constitutional normality. The courts of the Sudan had, until 1989, by their conduct accepted this premise of constitutional legality and the supremacy of constitutional authority over authority backed up only by military might. Thus, the army officers who staged the coup d'état of May 1969 against the democratically elected government of the time were tried following the reinstatement of the democratic order sixteen years later.[10]

Ironically, the new prosecutors indicted the officers for offenses created by the draconian state security laws the military regime had enacted. The fact that these security laws were enacted after the commission of the act of usurping power did not help the defendants, because they were barred by the 1985 Transitional Constitution from protesting ex post facto laws (Article 32[2]). In 1991, the current military regime, perhaps conscious of the possibility of such legislation backfiring, abolished all political and economic crimes in the Penal Code of 1983 and the State Security Act of 1973. The regime also introduced statutes of limitations in the Criminal Procedure Act of 1991. These newly introduced time limits may ultimately block the prosecution of persons presently involved in the violation of human rights.

In sum, the development of the democratic constitutional tradition, from democratic period to democratic period, is the most appropriate way to analyze the framework of human rights protection in the Sudan. The legal system during the episodes of military dictatorship is also worth investigating for the more immediate purpose of formulating plans of action. These may include monitoring rights and freedoms likely to be under attack, preemptive protection of persons and groups at risk, legal documentation of human rights violations for time to come, and networking.

The ongoing development of a democratic constitutional tradition is also evident in the continuity of the legal order. This continuity is reflected in the continued binding force of international conventions to which the Sudan has become a party, procedural and substantive statutory law that basically has survived unchanged, as well as the continuation of customary law in various parts of the country. These elements, integral parts of the constitutional and legal framework, are examined below.

The democratic constitutional tradition of the Sudan has other characteristics that are worth examining. Some of these characteristics are dictated by political instability and expediency, though others are not. The first is that all of the democratic constitutions to date were meant to be transitional constitutions, promulgated in the hope that the democratic institutions envisaged by these constitutions would eventually draft and ratify a permanent constitution for the Sudan. This is, of course, a wish that has not yet been fulfilled. Because of their transitional nature, these constitutions did not carefully lay out fundamental rights and freedoms, and were much more detailed on issues of the governance and institutions of government.

Those rights and freedoms that are recognized in the democratic constitutions of the Sudan are all civil and political rights. Economic, social, and cultural rights are not protected in these constitutions. Therefore, from the perspective of some social groups, such as women, these democratic constitutions adopt a traditional and narrow concept of equality. The main shortcomings of such a concept are that:

- it simply assumes that such rights as are guaranteed for men will also be guaranteed for women;
- it does not contemplate particular forms of special protections that women may need; and
- it ignores the preexisting social and economic inequalities that need to be remedied.[11]

The promulgation of the transitional constitutions was expected to be followed by a comprehensive revision of the laws in order to bring them in line with the constitution. Unfortunately, parliamentary governments have sometimes jealously preserved laws passed by their military predecessors. Equivocation on the repeal of repressive laws was one of the factors that kept the last democratic government from becoming stable.

To conclude this section, reference must be made to the dichotomy of right and might exhibited by the succession of parliamentary and military regimes in the Sudan. The civilian, democratic constitutional governments have enjoyed popular solidarity and promoted the respect for democracy. The military has proved ruthless in its drive for political power through the barrel of the gun. In a disturbing development, it appears that some political parties in the country have begun to arm their supporters, following the lead of the army.

Constitutional Framework Under Authoritarian Regimes

Since independence, forms of associational life and fundamental rights and freedoms have been suspended on three separate occasions. The state confiscated the property of political parties and trade unions on all three occasions, in which there was a transition from parliamentary rule to military rule. The length and severity of each of these transitional periods varied. Throughout the two years that followed the military takeover of November 1958, trade unions remained banned and no political associations were allowed to operate, and fundamental rights and freedoms remained suspended. In 1960, a new restrictive law on trade unions was enacted, only to be rejected by the unions. Otherwise all rights remained suspended throughout the reign of the military regime.

Likewise for the first two years after the May 25, 1969, coup, when the country was governed by draconian Presidential Orders I–IV. These orders stifled all rights, disbanded trade unions, associations, and political parties, confiscated their property, and indiscriminately imposed the death penalty or life imprisonment for any form of opposition to the regime. These presidential orders were incorporated into legislation that was to last until 1985. Section 17 of the State Security Act of 1973 and of the State Security Act of 1981 were verbatim repetitions of the relevant articles of the Presidential Orders II and IV respectively. The Penal Code of 1983 incorporated a consolidated enactment of these sections of the State Security Acts. This section of the Penal Code set punishment of death or life imprisonment for any person who instigates, organizes, participates in or encourages participation in an unlawful strike, work stoppage, or mass resignation with the purpose of opposing the legitimate political authority, harming the national economy, obstructing the running of a public service or utility, or does any act which is intended or is likely to harm the national economy (section 98[b], [c]).

Moreover, the Penal Code of 1983 criminalized and made punishable with death or life imprisonment a myriad of other acts, some of which, in a democratic society, are considered as the lawful expression of opinion or the exercise of freedom of organization (section 96). Thus, the Penal Code of 1983 criminalized committing or aiding in the commission of any act intended to undermine the constitution, the government, or government authority (section 96[a]); and Possessing, preparing, or participating in the preparation of any document, publication, or recording involving any material critical of the regime or inviting rebellion or organization of opposition against the regime or the state (Section 98[k]).

The State Security Acts of 1973 and 1981 also made it a criminal offense, punishable with imprisonment for a term not exceeding ten years, for any person to establish, constitute, or join any society, body, organization, or political party other than the state-sponsored party, the Sudanese Socialist Union. Along with the State Security Acts there were other repressive laws consolidating the grip of the one-party state over all aspects of economic, social, and political activity. For example, the 1974 Exercise of Political Rights Act made the nomination and election for any public or union office a privilege to be enjoyed only by persons trusted by the regime and its political organization. Similar restrictions existed for entry into the civil service.[12] It is significant that these repressive laws remained in effect throughout Numeiri's regime.

A legal and constitutional order, consonant with notions of human rights, could not practically coexist with such repressive laws of this sort. It is ironic, however, that, along with these laws, the regime promulgated in 1973 a permanent constitution of the Sudan that remained in force until the demise of the regime in April 1985.

On June 30, 1989, a junta once again toppled the democratically elected government in the Sudan. The junta's first constitutional decree, issued on June 30, 1989, suspended the 1985 Transitional Constitution, disbanded Parliament, and dissolved the government, the Council of Ministers, and the State Council.[13]

The second constitutional decree, issued the same day, disbanded all political parties, confiscated their property, prohibited the formation and operation of political parties, disbanded all trade unions and federations, and confiscated their property as well.[14] The junta amended the second constitutional decree two days later, closing down all nongovernmental press associations and newspapers, annulling the registration of all nongovernmental organizations and societies, and declaring a state of emergency throughout the Sudan.[15]

This decree also empowered the president of the Command Council of the junta, or any person authorized by him, to issue emergency orders and take emergency measures. An emergency regulation, issued the same day, authorized the president of the Command Council to establish additional reserve or private volunteer forces to carry out any duties assigned to them.[16]

More orders followed that implemented these provisions of the second constitutional decree and the emergency regulation. Emergency Order 8/1989, which is still in effect, confers police powers on members of the armed forces. Emergency Order 9/1989 authorizes the president of the Command Council, or any person authorized by him, to issue an arrest warrant for any person who allegedly threatens the stability of the regime. The same order authorized the commanders of military areas to arrest any person believed to threaten the regime's stability. Emergency Order 10/1989 confers these emergency powers of arrest on the commander of the State Security Bureau. Act 27/1989, issued on July 6, 1989, gave the president of the Command Council, any person authorized by him, military governors, and the governor of Khartoum the power to form special courts. These courts consist of three army officers or other individuals of competence and trustworthiness. The president of the Command Council, or a person authorized by him, also has the power to establish courts to hear appeals of decisions of the special court. A decade later, the legal and political framework established by these emergency measures and orders has not changed.

Following the ratification by the president of the republic of the Constitution of the Republic of the Sudan 1998 on June 30, 1998, the Constitutional Decree 2 of 1989 and the Emergency Regulation of 1989 are now presumably defunct. However, the state of emergency continues, supported by the two new pieces of legislation. The first is the Emergency and Protection of Public Safety Act of 1997.[17] This is an enabling instrument, giving the president of the republic the power to declare a state of emergency subject to the rules of the act. The second is the Emergency and Protection of Public Safety Regulation, which came into effect on January 14, 1998.[18] This regulation is a replica of Constitutional Decree 2 of 1989 and the Defense of the Sudan Act of 1939.[19] The regulation also replaces the 1989 Emergency Regulation.

Upon declaration of emergency, the Emergency Act of 1997 empowers the president of the republic, the state governor, or a delegate to issue orders and take the following measures:

- to confiscate land, premises, stores, and goods, in the public interest, with the right to compensate the owners of confiscated property (section 5[c]; the 1998 emergency regulation [section 37] prohibits institution of any claim for damages save with prior notification of the justice minister; the period of notice is at least twelve months from the date compensation becomes due, and the finance and national economy minister has the right to prolong to any length the said period);
- to seize property, stores, premises, and goods suspected of being held or used in violation of the law, pending completion of investigation or judicial decision (section 5[d]);
- to ban or restrict the activity and movement of persons, things, and means of transport or communication, in any place, at any time, and subject to any conditions (sections 5[e]); and
- to detain persons believed to be a threat to political or economic security (section 5[h]).

Similarly, the 1998 emergency regulation bans all forms of political opposition to the government of the junta (section 29). It also prohibits work stoppages (section 30), and empowers the competent authority to order the employees of any public utility to resume work (section 33).

The 1998 regulation authorizes the police, the security services, or the army to search any premises, buildings, or means of transportation without judicial warrant (section 6). It empowers the competent authority (defined as the president of the republic, the state governor, or a person authorized) to inspect and intercept postal deliveries (section 18), impose a curfew (section 14), order preventative detention for a period decided by the competent authority (section 15), and restrict the place of residence and the movement of any person (section 16). The emergency regulation also restricts the transport of publications, correspondences, letters, or any written material and authorizes censorship (section 19). The regulation gives the police, the military, and the security forces the power to interrogate any person at any time or place (section 26). It also allows them to close down theaters, cinemas, and any other recreation facilities in order to maintain what the competent authority perceives as public order and tranquility (section 21).

Finally, the 1997 Emergency and Protection of Public Safety Act empowers the president to establish private courts and to determine the jurisdiction of such courts and the investigation procedures to be followed by such courts (section 6). There is no limit on this. According to the Emergency and Public Safety Act of 1997 (section 6[1]), the mandate of the special courts shall prevail in case of contradiction with the due process prescribed by the criminal procedure law.

Characteristics of Authoritarian Legitimacy

Under the banner of revolution, authoritarian regimes try to legitimize something that is inherently illegal and inhumane. From this perspective, unwarranted detention, search, or the confiscation of property become legitimate, simply because the political sovereign enacts legislation making it legitimate. This travesty of justice and legality collides with international standards of human rights and the presuppositions of humanist philosophies of law. Despite this obvious contradiction between authoritarianism and principles of legality, nonetheless, authoritarian regimes sometimes have constitutions of one sort or another. This section examines the type and extent of human rights that might survive in a climate of repression of the sort that I have described in the preceding pages. The Permanent Constitution of the Sudan of 1973, promulgated by the Numeiri's regime on May 8, 1973, guaranteed several rights of citizenship and dealt explicitly with issues of religion (Article 16).

The constitution recognized Islam as the religion of the majority of

Sudanese, and stated that Christianity "is the religion of a large number of people and that divine religions and sacred spiritual beliefs shall not be insulted or belittled" (Article 16[a]). Under Article 16(d), the state held that the followers of all religions and spiritual beliefs were equal. Additionally, the constitution banned the exploitation of religion for political purposes (Article 16[e]). Article 38 prohibited discrimination on the basis of religion. Article 47 guaranteed the freedom of religion, worship, and practice of rituals.

The 1973 constitution was much more pluralistic on the issue of religion than other Sudanese constitutions, either before or since. There was no counterpart to Article 16 of the 1973 constitution in the Transitional Constitution of 1985. Article 4 of the 1985 constitution read "*Shari'a* law and custom shall be the main sources of law, and non-Muslim family affairs shall be governed by the laws of their allegiance," and, except for the word "basic" in place of "main," was a verbatim reenactment of Article 9 of the 1973 constitution. The 1973 constitution also guaranteed numerous social and economic rights, including: the right to development (Articles 18 and 21), the right to education (Articles 20 and 53), freedom from hunger and thirst (Article 21), social security (Article 24), free health care (Article 54), the right to work and equal employment opportunity (Articles 36 and 56), the protection of childhood, motherhood, and working mothers (Articles 26, 27, and 55), cultural and artistic development (Article 25), and the eradication of illiteracy (Article 29).

Moreover, the 1973 constitution provided a facade of civil and political rights, such as:

- the right to private property (Articles 33 and 34),
- the right to equality (Article 38),
- freedom of residence and movement, subject to the law (Article 34),
- the right to privacy, subject to the law (Articles 42 and 43),
- the right to participate in public life and occupy public office, subject to the law (Article 46),
- freedom of conscience and expression within the limits of the law (Article 48),
- freedom of religion, worship, and practice of rituals (Article 47),
- freedom of the press (Article 49),
- freedom of peaceful assembly and procession, in accordance with the law (Article 50),
- freedom to form trade unions, federations, and associations, in accordance with the law (Article 51),
- freedom from forced labor, except for a military or civil contingency, or as part of a legal punishment as prescribed by law (Article 52),

- the right to legal representation, including the right to freely choose a lawyer (Article 63),
- the right of an accused to a prompt and fair trial (Article 64),
- freedom of accused persons from torture, coercion, or inducement, and the nullity of all evidence obtained through such means, the legal accountability of persons involved in such actions, and the right of the victim to compensation (Article 65),
- freedom from arrest or detention, except as provided by law (Article 66),
- the right to release on bail (Article 67),
- the right of the accused to hear and confront witnesses, and the right to have defense witnesses summoned before the court at the expense of the state and to select defense lawyers, provided that the state shall avail legal aid at its own expense if a person accused of a serious crime is unable to afford legal fees (Article 68),
- the right to the presumption of innocence and freedom of the accused not to incriminate himself or herself (Article 69),
- freedom from retroactive incrimination or punishment (Article 70),
- freedom from double jeopardy, except in cases provided under the law (Article 71),
- freedom from cruel and inhumane treatment or punishment (Article 72),
- the right to life, except when a death sentence has been imposed by a competent court (Article 73), though the death penalty could not be imposed upon a minor nor upon a pregnant or suckling woman (Article 75).

Article 58 of the 1973 constitution gave every person aggrieved by any piece of legislation the right to ask the Supreme Court to annul such legislation for infringing on the rights and freedoms guaranteed by the constitution. Additionally, the 1973 constitution provided that legislation could only restrict the rights and freedoms guaranteed by the constitution in accordance with the constitution (Article 79). It only allowed such restrictions where they were necessary for the respect of the freedoms and rights of others or for the security and welfare of the people (Article 79).

Compared with its democratic counterparts, the 1973 constitution provided a much more comprehensive bill of rights. The incorporation of social and economic rights into the constitution was innovative and has now been replicated in the new authoritarian constitution of 1998. However, the facade of legality in the 1973 constitution should not blind the observer to the myriad of repressive laws that existed alongside the constitution throughout the reign of the regime. This paradox of constitutionality on the one side and repression on the other can be explained by two factors. The first is that the plurality suggested by the bill of rights was far removed from the political reality of authoritarianism ruling at large. Issuance of a constitution does not by itself guarantee respect for human rights. A constitution derives authoritativeness and sanctity from the social and political power of interest groups that may be brought to bear on the government if its rules are violated. The 1973 constitution was promulgated after the regime had ruthlessly wiped out potential opposition from both the left and right of the political spectrum. The second relates to the fact that the constitutional rights and freedoms enumerated above were subject to the laws in force. The laws in force at the time were too repressive to allow any meaningful realization of these constitutional rights. The aggrieved parties could not challenge the constitutionality of laws authorizing extrajudicial arrest, invasion of privacy, or restriction of movement because the constitution itself made these rights subject to the law.

However, even despite their superficiality, the civil rights and freedoms listed above proved too much for the tolerance of the single-party state. In May 1975, the Numeiri regime amended the 1973 constitution. This amendment applied retroactively and introduced the following restrictions into the 1973 constitution.

- Article 41, providing for freedom of movement, was replaced by a new Article 41 which empowered the legislature to identify classes of persons who could be preventively detained or placed under house arrest or whose movements could be otherwise restricted.[20] The legislature could also determine the period of detention or movement restrictions, the cases in which it could be renewed, and the manner in which the detainee could be heard, and the cases where such a hearing could not be followed. Article 66 was amended, stripping persons arrested, detained, or restricted to their residence of the right to know the charge against them and to protest arbitrary arrest or prolonged detention (Article 2).
- Articles 81 and 82 were amended to give the president unfettered powers to take such actions and make such decisions as he saw fit (Articles 3 and 4).
- Article 196 was amended to allow for the establishment of martial courts, state security courts, and any other courts (Article 5).
- The state security courts were given the jurisdiction to hear cases of high treason (Article 5). High treason, as defined by Article 220 of the 1973 constitution, was an offense, not against the state, but against the regime. Therefore, any person who acted to undermine the regime, its constitution, or its political and economic system could be charged with high treason.

The 1973 constitution possessed features that were to be repeated in a 1998 constitution. These are (1) expanded statement of economic, social, and cultural rights generally phrased as state policy directives and technically injusticiable, (2) relatively narrow statement of civil and political rights making them subject to preexistent laws, and (3) rights and freedoms are prerogatively conceded and may at any time be rescinded by the authoritarian regime because the social and political power of the beneficiaries to protest had been systematically undermined prior to the promulgation of the constitution.

These characteristics of authoritarian legitimacy contrast with pluralistic politics and legality of democratic rule. The contrast is the basis for the thematic structure of this chapter wherein the constitutions of 1973 and 1998 are discussed together.

The present military regime has only just promulgated the 1998 constitution. Until the constitution was passed the country was ruled under authoritarian proclamations called constitutional decrees. Decrees 1 to 12 built on each other. Constitutional Decree 13 heralded by the state media as a step toward constitutional legality was issued on December 24, 1995, and replaced other decrees, with Decrees 1 and 2, dealing with the imposition of the state of emergency, unaffected. Decree 13 did not include any substantive rights; rather, its main focus was the organization of the federal government and the relationship of government organs to each other.

In its description of the powers of the president, Article 9 of Constitutional Decree 13 provided that an aggrieved person could apply to the Supreme Court for redress of any presidential act that infringed upon "the human rights provided for by the constitution." This remedy was impossible to achieve because the constitution referred to did not exist at the time.

Article 25 gave the same right of action against any such act by the federal Council of Ministers, a state government, or federal or state ministers. The decree also provided for a right to challenge the constitutionality of any law enacted by the federal parliament, a state parliament, the president of the republic, or a state government for transgressing "constitutional human rights" (Article 68).

Upon promulgation of the Constitution of the Republic of the Sudan in 1998, Constitutional Decrees 1–13 were all repealed. Constitutional Decree 14, which deals with the implementation of the peace agreement, remained in force alongside the new Constitution of the Republic of the Sudan and will expire at the end of a transitional period, which will be determined when the Southern States hold a referendum to decide to unite with or secede from the sixteen other newly created states of a federal Sudan.[21] The peace agreement was produced in the English edition of the 1998 constitution, but it is not organically part of it and has been chopped off the official Arabic-English edition of the 1998 constitution. The agreement stipulated that the referendum shall commence in four years' time, but the starting date from which the calculation of this limitation run is not made clear and it is certainly not the date of signature of the agreement. The agreement did not provide any guarantees to secure adherence to its terms and conditions. No wonder it subsequently faltered and is now defunct.

The phrases "constitutional human rights" and "human rights provided for by the constitution" from the constitutional decrees have been replicated by the phrases "constitutional rights" or "rights protected by the constitution" (Articles 34, 46, and 105). The language is significant. The phrases do not clearly support a right of action with respect to violations of human rights that are provided for under Sudanese law or international conventions rather than by the constitution. The question therefore arises whether this emphasis on the textual origin of rights is meant to exclude actions for violations of human rights provided for by the International Covenant on Civil and Political Rights and the Covenant on Economic, Social, and Cultural Rights, both ratified in 1985 by the Sudan, and thereby incorporated into Sudanese municipal law.

The system of government provided for in the 1998 constitution is a one-party system (Article 140). Starting June 30, 1998, the tenure of the incumbent president is five years and that of the national assembly is four years. It is envisaged by Articles 36–41 of the 1998 constitution that the Sudan shall have a president to be elected by the people at the end of this transitional period. In this and other respects, the new constitution does not substantially differ from the authoritarian 1973 constitution, particularly in the emphasis placed on social and economic rights and the subjection of constitutional rights and freedoms to the laws in force. The bill of rights enshrined in the 1998 constitution includes the following provisions:

- the state undertakes to develop the national economy and to try to achieve affluence, bounty, and justice among its states and regions (Article 8);
- social justice and care for the elderly and the disabled (Article 11);
- eradication of illiteracy and mobilization of support for this effort (Article 12);
- promotion of public health, sports, and the protection of the environment (Article 13);
- care for children and youth (Article 13);
- care for the family and the emancipation of women in the family and public life (Article 15);
- right to life, freedom, and safety of all persons, and freedom from slavery, forced labor, humiliation, or torture, in accordance with the law (Article 20);

- right to equality and the prohibition of discrimination on the grounds of race, sex, religious creed, or wealth (Article 21);
- right to nationality, as regulated by law (Article 22);
- freedom of movement under safeguards of the law (Article 23);
- freedom of conscience and religious creed, as articulated by law (Article 24);
- freedom of thought, expression, and information, as articulated by law (Article 25);
- freedom of association and organization, as regulated by law (Article 26);
- the right of communal, cultural, lingual, and religious communities to practice their culture, language, and religion and to bring up their children thereunder (Article 27);
- right to acquire property and to the security of earnings, subject to the law (Article 28);
- freedom of information, inviolability of correspondence and privacy, subject to controls provided by law (Article 29);
- freedom from detention, except in accordance with the law (Article 30);
- the right to litigation, subject to procedures and rules of law (Article 31);
- the right of the accused to the presumption of innocence, a prompt and fair trial, defense, choice of counsel, and the right not to be tried for acts that were not defined as crimes at the time they were committed (Article 32);
- reservation of the death penalty as punishment for only the most serious crimes. No one under eighteen shall be sentenced to death (neither the constitution nor the Criminal Law Act and the Criminal Procedure Act 1991 [sections 33 and 193 respectively] make clear whether maturity is relevant at the time of commission of the crime or at the time of trial). No one over seventy shall be sentenced to death or executed if sentenced earlier and having attained the age of seventy prior to execution. The exception of *hudud* and *qissas* stressed by Article 33 of the constitution means that these *shari'a* punishments shall be applied and carried out irrespective of age. Pregnant and suckling mothers are not immune to the death sentence but, according to Article 33, shall not be executed save after two years of lactation.

Like the 1973 constitution, the 1998 constitution makes all rights and freedoms subject to the law. The author of the 1998 constitution in this respect uses phrases such as "as regulated by law," "under safeguards of law," and "save upon permission by law" without differentiation. The drafting commission for the 1998 constitution had proposed that all rights and freedoms be guaranteed "in accordance with the due process of law." However, in the final version this phrasing was replaced by the phrases noted above. The 1998 constitution recognizes social and economic rights only as principles and policies to guide the state, rather than as justiciable constitutional rights (Article 19).

Provisional and Emergency Measures

The 1998 constitution empowers the president of the republic, the governor of a state, or if either of them is absent, the national or the state assembly, to issue provisional orders having the force of law, provided that such orders not affect constitutional freedoms, sanctities, and rights (Articles 90 and 98). Under the 1998 constitution, the president may declare a state of emergency in accordance with the constitution (Articles 131 and 132). The president also possesses parallel power not actually subjected to the constitution to declare a state of emergency under an enabling law already discussed. As the law stands there appears to be two frameworks of emergency powers: (1) a statutory framework already discussed which endows the president unfettered powers, and (2) a constitutional framework which is the subject of this paragraph. It is up to the president to choose. Upon declaration of a statutory emergency all or any of the rights and freedoms in the constitution may be suspended. The 1998 constitution itself does seem to condone this statutory intrusion. The enabling statute was enacted prior to the constitution. Upon coming into effect, the 1998 constitution Article 140(5) categorically asserted the continuity of all laws in force prior to promulgation of the 1998 constitution. Furthermore, Article 140(5) of the 1998 constitution provides that until the issue of new measures in accordance with the provisions of the constitution all laws shall continue. Hence the enabling statute and the regulation made under it have survived promulgation of the constitution unabated.

Although no right is protected from being suspended under the statutory emergency, the 1998 constitution provides that there shall not be under a constitutional emergency "infringement of the freedom from slavery or torture, the right of nondiscrimination only for race, sex, or religious creed, the right and sanctity in litigation or the right of innocence and defense" (Article 132[a]). Article 131(1) authorizes declaration of the state of emergency "upon the occurrence or approach of any emergent danger, whether it is war, invasion, blockade, disaster, or epidemic as may threaten the country or any part thereof or the safety or economy of the same."

Article 131(2) of the 1998 constitution provides that the declaration of the state of emergency shall be submitted to the National Assembly within fifteen days of its issue. When the assembly is not in session an emergency meeting shall be convoked for the purpose. It is the president of the republic who is supposed to call the assembly for this emergency meeting

(Article 75[3]). Article 131(3) provides for the contingency when the assembly approves the declaration of the state of emergency but is silent on the power to reject the declaration of emergency. In effect a declaration of the state of emergency will continue for at least one month without legislative approval even though the assembly is in session. If the assembly is not in session and the president does not wish to call an emergency session, the state of emergency may continue open-endedly. In this respect the new Constitutional Court has decided that the declaration of emergency made by the president on November 12, 1999, was constitutional even though it was not submitted to the assembly within fifteen days in violation of Article 131(2). The reason, in the words of the court, is, "It was impossible to submit the declaration of emergency to the assembly because the president had dissolved the assembly prior to the declaration of emergency."[22] However the court also stated in principle, "the declaration of emergency is of the issues that the courts do not intervene with."

As to the statutory emergency, section 4 of the Emergency and Protection of Public Safety Act 1997 in comparison empowers the president to issue a declaration of emergency in certain cases, such as invasion or blockade, eminent grave danger that threatens national unity, or safety of the country or any part thereof, economic crisis, or war, rebellion, or insurgency.

Section 4(2) of the act provides: "in accordance with the constitution every declaration shall be submitted to the National Assembly within thirty days from its issue to decide what it sees with respect to such declaration." And yet Section 4(3) of the act provides that the declaration of emergency shall remain in effect until it has expired or until the president has decided to lift the state of emergency. Section 4(2) of the act is of no practical effect for two reasons; first, Section 4(3) of the act preempts any meaningful intervention by the legislative authority since the state of emergency shall continue to its full term or until it has been lifted by the president, and, second, the scope of emergency measures that can be duly taken under the act is already determined by the Emergency and Protection of Public Safety Regulation of 1998. Section 1 of the regulation provides that it shall come into effect upon signature by the president. It was signed on January 14, 1998. It appears that the law and the constitution are equivocal on the power of the legislative authority to reverse a declaration of a state of emergency or a provisional order and on the duration of such emergency or provisional measures. This equivocation is in sharp contrast to the provisions proposed by the drafting commission, which would have limited the length of time a state of emergency could be in effect without legislative approval to fifteen days.

Article 105 of the constitution provides for the establishment of a Constitutional Court to hear claims for protection of freedoms, rights, and sanctities guaranteed by the constitution. The court has already been established.

It consists of seven judges under the presidency of former chief justice Gelal Ali Lutfi. It is my view that the court is inherently incapable of protecting constitutional rights and freedoms for a number of reasons.

The Constitutional Court is a special court, a body independent from and parallel to the judiciary. It constitutes a break with a long established tradition of the constitutional court that had been a circuit of the Supreme Court of the Sudan. Under the traditional system any six judges of the then sixty judges of the Supreme Court could constitute an ad hoc constitutional court to consider any constitutional issue or petition. The referral of a constitutional petition or any particular circuit was, under the old system, an internal affair to be conducted by the judiciary. The risk of external influence was relatively minimized because of the vast number of potential constitutional judges and the difficulty to forecast the identity of the judges who would adjudicate on a petition. Under the old system a decision of the constitutional circuit of the Supreme Court in a constitutional issue was deemed to represent the stance of the judiciary on such an issue. As a matter of practice the judiciary was the custodian of the constitution. The present Constitutional Court is made up of seven judges to be appointed by the president of the republic with the approval of the National Assembly. It is these same seven judges who would always adjudicate upon every constitutional petition as custodian of the constitution. The establishment of the court and its endowment with custody of the constitution dealt a severe blow to the independence of the judiciary and constitutional legality in the Sudan. Constitutional legality was backed up by the bulwark of a judiciary. Now it is backed by seven judges in a Constitutional Court that is separate from the judiciary. The establishment of the Constitutional Court is in effect an encroachment upon the mandate of the judiciary to have full jurisdiction over all matters of a justiciable nature.

Access to the Constitutional Court by the aggrieved is only allowed after the person making the complaint has exhausted all other remedies through administrative and executive organs (Article 140[5]).

The mandate of the Constitutional Court is equivocal and does not spell out a power to review the constitutionality of laws. Article 34 of the constitution provides that the Constitutional Court may according to due process exercise the power to annul any law or order that contravenes the constitution and restore the right to the aggrieved or compensate him for damage sustained. However in the Arabic text Article 34 stresses that the court shall exercise this jurisdiction *bil'ma'aroof*, which could mean benevolent pursuance as opposed to binding judicial decision making.

The ability of the Constitutional Court or any other court to protect constitutional rights and freedoms is bound to be weakened by the lack of clarity of the words and phrases which the 1998 constitution sometimes uses. The constitution abounds in ambiguity with phrases such as "religious creed" as opposed to religion, "sanctity of nationality" instead of right to nationality, the right to democracy in "the leadership of the organization" instead of the right to democracy, and the right to "affiliate in" political organizations instead of the right to freedom of association and organization. Both the Arabic and English texts were prepared by a group of three, Hassan al-Turabi and two academic lawyers. Nonconformism with constitutional terminology is believed to be Turabi's influence but could also be attributed to lack of acquaintance with the language of constitutional discourse.

Continuity of the Legal Order

The experience of the Sudan has shown that the legal order does not aways change in lockstep with political change. Although authoritarian written constitutions proved coterminous with the regimes that promulgate them, democratic constitutional norms do not fade away simply by suspension of a democratic constitution in the aftermath of a military takeover. Likewise statutes may outlive the regimes that enact them. Yet, legislation is not the sole means by which to provide continuity in the legal order. International treaties, once ratified, become part of national law, and subsequent governments are bound by them. Likewise, judicial precedents continue to mold the attitude of the courts toward legality and justice, although they may have been decided under the shadow of a liberal constitution. However, continuity of the legal order may also retard movement toward legality and respect for human rights, as democratic regimes are sometimes reluctant to ease the repressive laws inherited from their military predecessors. I examine these factors below.

International Conventions

The position of human rights in a country is adversely affected by the status of ratification by that country of relevant international conventions. But, equally the ratification of international conventions does not automatically alleviate the state of human rights to the level of international standards. Ratification even though important is only a first step toward bringing municipal determination and administration of rights to the level of international standards. The Sudan has become a party to the following human rights treaties:

- the International Covenant on Economic, Social, and Cultural Rights;
- the International Covenant on Civil and Political Rights;
- the International Convention on the Elimination of All Forms of Racial Discrimination;

- the Convention on the Rights of the Child;
- the Slavery Convention and the Supplementary Convention on the Abolition of Slavery, the Slave Trade, and Institutions and Practices Similar to Slavery;
- the Convention Relating to the Status of Refugees and Protocol thereto;
- the Convention Against Torture and Other Cruel, Inhuman, or Degrading Treatment or Punishment (signed but not ratified) (Article 90[4]);
- the Geneva Conventions of 1949;
- five fundamental and seven other ILO Conventions (Article 34).

This poor ratification record is *inter alia* a product of a rigid legislative system that militates against automatic incorporation of international treaties. Under the democratic tradition of the Sudan, no treaty, agreement, or convention with any other country or countries, or any decision made in any international convention, association, or other body has effect in the Sudan unless it is ratified and affirmed by Parliament.[23] The extent to which the judiciary of the Sudan has used international conventions and incorporated them into municipal law is explained below.

Common Law

Under the democratic constitutions, Sudanese courts exercised their role as the guardians of the rights and liberties of citizens. As early as 1958, the Court of Appeal, then the highest court in the country, established that "courts have jurisdiction to review the act of an administrative authority wherever the latter is invested with a legal authority to determine questions affecting the rights of subjects."[24]

The courts were called upon to decide at what point the exercise of the right of free expression and free opinion, guaranteed by Article 5(2) of the 1964 Transitional Constitution, was limited by the prohibition of sedition in the Penal Code. The constitutional jurisprudence from this period is as valid today as it was at the time the judgments were delivered.[25]

The role of the judiciary as guardian of the constitution stirred controversy in 1965 and 1966. In late 1965, for example, the Constituent Assembly amended Article 5 of the Transitional Constitution to exclude members of the Communist Party from Parliament. Article 5 was the article that had guaranteed freedom of expression, opinion, and association. The amendment read as follows:

1. The following proviso shall be added at the end of sub-article (2) of Article 5: "provided that no person shall perform or seek to perform any act in furtherance of communism, whether local or international, or perform or seek to perform any act to overthrow the government."
2. The following new sub-article shall be added after sub-article 2 of Article 5: "(3)

Every association whose aim or means constitutes a contravention of the proviso to sub-article (2) shall be deemed to be an unlawful association and the Constituent Assembly may enact any legislation which it shall deem to be necessary for the implementation of the provisions of that proviso."[26]

This amendment was contested by members of the Communist Party who had been elected as members of Parliament. They petitioned the High Court to declare the amendment unconstitutional because it infringed on a fundamental right guaranteed by Article 5(2) as it stood before the amendment.[27] The court concluded that the amendment was unconstitutional because the Transitional Constitution was the fundamental law and, as such, had supremacy over all other laws, as provided in Article 3 of the constitution. The court quoted, with approval, Kotaro Tanaka, then chief justice of the Supreme Court of Japan,

Fundamental human rights were not created by the state, but are eternal and universal institutions, common to all mankind and antedating the state. . . . Fundamental human rights, derived from natural law, are written into the constitution, and the constitution provides the court with power to review any Act violating those rights. The Supreme Court is popularly called the guardian of the constitution and it is, in fact, not unreasonable to regard the Supreme Court as a bulwark of human rights.[28]

Following the reinstatement of democratic rule for the third time in the history of independent Sudan, the courts again resumed their role as custodian of fundamental rights and freedoms enshrined in the democratic constitutions. In February 1986, the family of the late Islamic reformer Mahmoud Mohamed Taha petitioned the Supreme Court to declare the trial, judgment, and execution of Taha to be unconstitutional, and therefore null and void. The Supreme Court declared on November 11, 1986, that the 1983 trial and execution of Taha were null and void because: "The trial and appellate courts had acted against express provisions of the law, assumed legislative powers and created the criminal offense of apostasy, which was not part of the indictment and was not defined as a criminal offense by the laws in effect at the time the acts in question were committed." The trial and execution denied the accused his right to be heard. The Supreme Court stressed that "the right of the accused to be heard before condemnation is an eternal principle adhered to by all human societies as a sacred principle of natural law that, to be binding, does not need to be reinforced by express provisions of law."[29] The Supreme Court did not have the opportunity to review the death sentence, as required by law, and, therefore, the execution was premature.

In April 1987, in a case arising from a contradiction between the internal rules of a trade union and the provisions of the Employees Trade

Union Act of 1977, the Registrar of Trade Unions suspended the activity of the trade union concerned. The Khartoum Court of Appeal reversed the decision, stating that "[t]he International Covenant on Economic, Social and Cultural Rights, Article 8, confers upon trade unions the right to function freely, which . . . includes a trade union's right to formulate its constitution and internal regulation without interference from authorities. . . . This covenant has been part of the Sudanese law since the Transitional Government ratified the said convention by statute in 1985."[30]

Quoting Articles 1, 2, and 4 of the International Labor Organization Convention 87,[31] the court concluded that administrative authorities should not interfere with the internal affairs of the trade unions, and that such authorities were prohibited from dissolving or suspending the activities of trade unions. The court, thus, avoided interpreting the statute by finding that the legislature could not have intended to enact a law that was contrary to international law on trade unions.

Moreover, in times of democracy, the courts have protected the right of litigation and unrestricted access to the courts. In 1989 the Supreme Court was called upon to examine the constitutionality of section 4 of the Eviction from Public Premises Act of 1969. This section, inherited from the government's dictatorial predecessor, stripped courts of jurisdiction over disputes of orders or actions under the act. Deciding the case during the third period of democracy, while the 1985 Transitional Constitution was in effect, the Supreme Court declared that section 4 of the act was unconstitutional and, therefore, null and void.[32]

During this same period, the courts also established that they had jurisdiction to review and, if necessary, reverse government terminations of public employees on the grounds of "public policy," "public interest," or "interest of the service."[33]

The above judicial decisions reflect a stance in sharp contrast with the judicial docility demonstrated in times of authoritarian rule. For example, section 4 of the Eviction from Public Premises Act of 1969 gave rise to a series of litigations, beginning in 1978. The Supreme Court that decided in 1989 that section 4 was unconstitutional had considered the same question in 1978, during Numeiri's dictatorship. On that occasion, the Supreme Court decided that, because the 1973 constitution did not provide for a right of litigation, the deprivation of the plaintiffs' right to apply to the courts for judicial review was not an encroachment upon a constitutional right, but merely a denial of a legal right. In the opinion of the Supreme Court, prohibiting the courts from reviewing orders or acts taken under the Evictions Act was not, therefore, a transgression of a constitutional right. The Supreme Court then decided, on the basis of this logic, that section 4 of the act was not unconstitutional.

The court rejected the plaintiffs' argument that the right of litigation is a fundamental right, enshrined in natural law and principles of constitutional law and, as such, ought to be implied by the court, which was the argument the court ultimately accepted in 1989.

At this time, however, the Supreme Court dismissed this argument, stating that courts should not widen the scope of legislative provisions by extrapolating from natural law or comparative jurisprudence. According to the court, to do so would endow the courts with a legislative power that was not theirs.[34] Once again, in 1992, under the current military regime, the Supreme Court demonstrated that it had returned to its docile role. The court silently overlooked its 1989 decision and reinstated the law as it had been under Numeiri's regime, concluding that the courts have no jurisdiction to review acts or orders made under section 4 of the Evictions Act.[35] The Supreme Court neither disclosed its reasoning for this decision nor explained why it had resurrected a defunct law.

Public employment is another area of litigation in which the courts lack consistency. Following the military takeover of June 30, 1989, extensive purges of civil servants and other public employees were carried out on an unprecedented scale. The Public Service Appeals Board (PSAB, a tribunal established in 1972 to hear individual employment-related grievances of public employees) quickly announced that it had no authority to hear the complaints of those dismissed in the purges. The president of the tribunal declared that "dismissal of public employees under Section 24 of the Public Service Act of 1973 [dismissal in the public interest] and Section 26 of the Public Service Pensions Act of 1975 [dismissal in the interest of service] are not within the mandate of the tribunal, and the latter has no jurisdiction to entertain them."[36]

Furthermore, the courts have not dared to question or interpret the provision of Constitutional Decree 3 of 1989 that prohibits the courts from directly or indirectly reviewing sovereign action (Article 11). They also have not questioned the provision of Constitutional Decree 2 that prohibits the courts from directly or indirectly reviewing any order or decision made under either the decree or the Emergency Regulation of 1989 (Article 9[a]). Sudan Chief Justice Gelal Ali Lutfi directed all courts that they must abide by the wording of the ousting provisions and should not deal directly or indirectly with cases of dismissal of public employees carried out in accordance with powers of emergency.[37] The dual stance of the judiciary does not refute the thesis of continuity of the legal order. The data suggest that the jurisprudence of repression, like the jurisprudence under democratic regimes, is capable of reproducing itself whenever the political system changes. Moreover, it is important not to underestimate the lengths to which the authoritarian regimes may go in order to hammer the courts into obedience and docility. Mass dismissal of judges, occupational harassment, the establishment of rival special courts endowed with extensive judicial powers, and the appointment of laymen in appellate judicial ranks are measures that have been extensively used to date by the present regime.[38]

Legislation

Statutory law regulating various aspects of social, economic, and political life in the Sudan has remained virtually unchanged throughout the changes at the political and constitutional levels. Some of these laws are, by their nature, repressive. Others, though regulating functional social and economic roles, contain provisions that adversely affect human rights. I examine some of these laws in more detail below.

State Security Legislation.   Following consolidation of colonial rule and the establishment of legal institutions, civil administration and the rule of law gradually replaced martial law. However the authority to declare a state of emergency and rule through emergency powers was institutionalized as well. The Defense of the Sudan Act of 1939 empowered the head of the state to declare a state of emergency in the case of any event that, from his point of view, constituted an immediate threat to the Sudan, to public safety, or the life and welfare of the society.[39] This act remained in effect until 1997.

The head of the state could, under a state of emergency, issue regulations for the court-martial of any person, confiscate property, and amend and/or suspend any law. He could also suspend chapters of the Code of Criminal Procedure dealing with arrest, detention, the powers and jurisdiction of the courts, and the process of investigation, appeal, and review.[40]

Emergency powers conferred by the Defense of Sudan Act were subject only to provisions of the act itself and were not affected by the provisions of any other law. The Emergency and Protection of Public Safety Act of 1997 replaced the Defense of the Sudan Act of 1939, reenacting essentially the same emergency powers. State Security Laws were also enacted in 1967 and 1973. The State Security Act of 1973, enacted on June 27, 1973, consolidated previous statutes and created a Code of Political Crimes and a parallel system of state security courts to try such crimes. The 1973 act was repealed in 1985, following the fall of Numeiri's regime.

The present regime has not enacted a code of political or security crimes. However, the Emergency and Protection of Public Security Regulation of 1998 and its predecessor, the Emergency Regulation of 1989, fulfill the function of such a code. The present regime also enacted the National Security Act of 1990. The National Security Act is virtually a replica of a democratic predecessor, the National Security Act of 1988. Both acts were intended not to provide a code of political security crimes, but rather to regulate the state security force. The National Security Act was amended in July 1999 and again on October 10, 2000. The 1999 amendment reduced the maximum period of detention from seven months and three days to two months and three days. The 2000 amendment reneged on this and restored a general power of detention for two months further, extendable indefinitely, all without approval by the judiciary or the attorney general (section 31). The 2000 amendment also introduced a new power of detention in cases which from the point of view of the director of the State Security Bureau cause social panic or threaten security, safety of the people, public peace, and in cases of terrorism or dissemination of subversive ideologies (section 31[1] and [2]). In such cases the director is authorized to detain any person for three months, which, subject to no specific reasons, is extendable by his decision for another three months, and thereafter, if the director deems it necessary, he may submit the matter to the State Security Council to decide thereupon. Section 9 of the act authorizes the state security forces to spy on, investigate, search, summon, interrogate, and detain any person or seize property in accordance with the act. Section 31 of act confers the powers of the police under the Code of Criminal Procedure and the Police Act on members of the security forces.

The 1999 act intended to make extension of detention for a second month subject to approval by the prosecution attorney if there exists against the detainee proof of committing a crime against the state. Under the 1990 act the bureau did not have to give reasons for extension of detention up to seven months and three days. Likewise, the 1999 amendment has introduced under section 32 a right of the detainee to know the reason behind his detention, right to communicate with his family if this will not prejudice investigation, right to be treated humanely, and right not to be detained on a charge with a crime for which he has been acquitted by a competent court. The section also requires the special prosecution attorney to inspect detention centers to insure compliance with the law. The 1999 amendment was introduced at a time when the Hassan al-Turabi faction within the government was encouraging followers of other political parties to join in an internal struggle within the politburo for easing the grip of power to make this participation possible. Turabi believed this to be a condition for continuity of the triumph of his Islamic revolution. Every military regime in the Sudan, he believes, has a period of validity after which it expires and it would be unwise to entwine the fate of political revolution with that of such a regime. Differences over this strategy *inter alia* led to internal strife later to expel Turabi from the government and politburo.[41]

A judge, appointed by the chief justice, is supposed to supervise orders of preventative detention under the national security legislation (sections 31 ff.). The judge may review applications by detainees against prolonged or arbitrary detention, approve extension of detention, or release the detainee. The right of victims of violations of human rights to sue state security culprits is curtailed as a result of procedural immunities that for lack of impartiality and transparency are tantamount to impunities. Members of the national security force and those recruited by the force as informants may not be prosecuted or sued without prerogative permission of the director of the State Security Bureau (section 33[g]). Members of the security forces and their informants brought for trial before an ordinary court for acts relating to performance of official duty are tried in camera (section 33[c]). The October 2000 amendment has omitted right of compensation against the state for acts of the security forces previously stated under the 1999 act. The omission is adverse because action against the state not subject to procedural immunity was the resort for victims who cannot sue the direct wrongdoer impuned.

Labor Law. A return to parliamentary democracy has not meant a reversal of authoritarian trade union law. Many of the repressive features which exist today were established by previous political regimes, whether military or parliamentarian. The following is a brief list of some of the repressive features with regard to trade unions:

- The right to establish trade unions has always been restricted and now engineers, doctors, accountants, lawyers, and other professionals are not allowed to form trade unions of their own choice under the Employees Trade Unions Act of 1992 (section 4).
- The choice of unionization base has always been subject to interference by governments and is now predetermined by the state. Since the act of 1992, trade unions have been compelled to organize on an establishment basis (section 9[1]). This means that every union has to be based in an employment unit, be it a corporation or organization, rather than an industry. Trade unions' internal affairs are subject to supervision and control by administrative authorities (sections 11–18).
- The government can dissolve or suspend trade unions by administrative decree (sections 36–39, 14[2]).
- Trade unions' right to organize is unprotected and the right to strike has always been restricted. Strikes were now expressly prohibited under the Emergency Regulation of 1989 (section 35).[42]

Urban Planning and Public Peace Laws. Urban planning laws have always endowed administrative authorities with the power to forcefully evict people from shantytowns and then demolish them. The existing Land Disposition and Urban Planning Act of 1994, for example, empowers the governor of Khartoum and the planning committees to evict people from residences and condemn and demolish buildings within the state of Khartoum (sections 22–32). There are provincial and district planning committees and the Central Planning Committee for the state of Khartoum. The courts can review orders made under the Land Disposition Act only with regard to the amount of compensation to which a plaintiff is entitled. Other measures taken by the governor under the Land Disposition Act are viewed as sovereign actions and are not subject to judicial review.[43]

The Khartoum Public Order Act of 1996 is typical of statutes that have frequently been invoked by state authorities since the introduction of *shari'a* rules in September 1983. The underlying philosophy and implications of the Khartoum Act, more than its content, are questionable. What happens to civil rights, the right to privacy, and other personal freedoms when attempts are made to enforce moral standards by law? Furthermore, the fact that the law is administered by special public order courts and enforced by a special police force, the public order police, complicates matters even further. Public order courts do not adhere to the due process of law or respect the accused's right to defend himself, and they follow summary procedures even in serious accusations that may end up with a long prison sentence or an instantly carried out sentence of lashing that subsequent appeal will do nothing to cure. The right of appeal is restricted only to one designated Supreme Court judge. Public order courts, although first instance magisterial courts, are thus empowered to pass judgments that can only be challenged through a single tier appeal to the said judge of the Supreme Court. The public order police are ruthless and poorly disciplined in respect to rights. Members of the force may act in plainclothes and carry loaded machine guns in the fulfillment of their duties. The Public Order Act empowers the governor of any state to issue any order which from his point of view is necessary for the maintenance of public peace and public morality. The governor of the state of Khartoum has under this power issued orders banning all women from working between 6 P.M. and 6 A.M. in the capital in complete disregard to provisions of the federal Labor Code of 1997 which regulate this matter. The order still in effect is being challenged before the Constitutional Court.

Procedural Laws.   Procedural rules to protect constitutional rights were codified in 1954 and remained unchanged until 1972. The 1972 legislation was short-lived and did not have any practical impact worthy of investigation. Then in 1974, the legislature consolidated the rules for judicial review of administrative actions and of the constitutionality of laws into Chapters 2, 4, and 5 of Part 7 of the Civil Procedure Act of 1974. The rules then remained unchanged until the beginning of 1996. On March 14, 1996, the legislature enacted the Constitutional and Administrative Justice

Act. The 1996 act consolidated the rules of administrative and constitutional review previously embodied into the Civil Procedure Act of 1974. The Constitutional and Administrative Justice Act did not make any significant changes to the rules of procedure.

Many of the main features of Sudanese constitutional and administrative procedural law have remained constant since they were first codified in 1954. These characteristics include:

- Unlike civil law countries, the Sudan has a single system of judicial review of administrative and constitutional action. The same courts that hear cases between private citizens also hear cases brought by or against the state. Whether litigation involves the state or not, the same rules of substantive law apply.
- Procedural rules are meant to limit the extent of judicial intervention into administrative or executive autonomy. Hence, the tests of justiciability, standing, exhaustion of alternative remedies, and formal requirements of pleas all limit access to the courts and the ability of aggrieved citizens to obtain a remedy.
- Legislative provisions that strip the courts of jurisdiction in various situations (e.g., sections 10 and 16 of the Public Employees' Grievances Divan [Chambers] Act, section 4 of the Eviction from Public Premises Act, and section 3[3] of the Constitutional and Administrative Justice Act 1996) have greatly restricted the role of the courts.

The courts acquiesced to the wishes of the legislature and interpreted the wording of ousting statutes so as to support judicial abstention from interfering with these wishes.

Religion

By 1969, religion was already interwoven with politics and constitutional law. The political parties debating the character of a permanent constitution for the Sudan in 1967 could not agree on whether the country should be secular or Islamic. On May 7, 1969, the parties put the question to the Sudanese people in a referendum. Eighteen days later the military took power and pushed the question aside for several years. Following political reconciliation between the military regime and its opponents in 1977, the debate over Islamicization resurfaced. Five years later the regime surprised everyone by introducing what the regime considered Islamic laws. Since that time, the interrelationship of law, religion, and the state has posed questions that are integral to an understanding of the legal and human rights situation in the Sudan. Two of the most interposing questions are whether human rights are compatible with Islamic law and whether the attack on Sudan's record of violating human rights is actually an attack on Islamic law. The clarification of this issue is crucial to the acceptance of international human rights standards by the average Sudanese Muslim.

With regard to the compatibility or incompatibility of an Islamic system of governance with multiparty democracy, the respect for minority rights, equality before the law, and a set of rights and obligations based on citizenship, it is my personal view that the behavior and orientation of any system of governance is determined not by the system of moral or religious beliefs its perpetrators would like to indoctrinate or associate themselves with. Rather, they are determined largely by contingent political and economic measures that a regime takes on a daily basis in order to consolidate its position and that of its followers. The present military regime in the Sudan would like to deflect criticism of its poor human rights record on a supposed Western animosity to Islam the regime claims itself to represent. The regime considerably succeeded in marketing this propaganda, albeit naively. The reason is that criticism of the Sudan human rights record is not always focused on praxis of violation of human rights but sometimes slips into incompatibility of the ethos of Islam with Western notions of human rights. The latter is not a fact in issue. What is at issue is whether or not the supposed Islamic system of governance in reign was installed by the people through free and fair elections. If not, then it is usurpation of power at the expense of civil and political rights which becomes a fact in issue of the first instance.

The 1998 constitution emphasizes a role of the state in the religious life of the country in the following terms:

- The state shall strenuously seek to elevate society toward religiousness (Article 12);
- The state shall endeavor through law to promote society toward virtuous morals (Article 16);
- People working for the state and in public life shall envisage the dedication of their work for the worship of God, and shall maintain religious motivation and give due regard to such a spirit in plans, laws, policies, and official business in the political, economic, social, and cultural fields (Article 18);
- Islamic law and the consensus of the nation, by referendum, constitution, and custom shall be the sources of legislation, and no legislation in contravention with these fundamentals shall be made, however, the legislation shall be guided by the nation's public opinion, the learned opinion of scholars and thinkers, and then by the decision of those in charge of public affairs (Article 65).
- The state shall strive for the elimination of religious, partisan, and sectarian fanaticism (Article 6).

The endowment of the state with a religious role is problematic. It legitimates theocracy thus enabling those in control of state power to suppress others in the name of religion. Religion becomes in effect relegated to the rank of a political ideology to be used to legitimize tyranny even when such tyranny is applied to further the economic and political interest of the ruling classes. Likewise the compatibility of this role with a doctrine of equality before the law without discrimination on the basis of religion is questionable. It is true that Articles 12, 16, and 18 do not specify any particular religion. However Article 65 is explicit on the emphasis of Islamic religion. Furthermore, discrimination in the selection for public office may not in the light of these articles be unconstitutional if committed against a nonpracticing believer, a pagan, or an atheist.

Summary

The constitutional and legal framework is a legacy which the postcolonial state in the Sudan could not develop to the better. Of the twentieth century, Sudan spent eighty-nine years under authoritarian rule, whether of the colonial governor general or the postcolonial military dictatorship. Two contrasting patterns of authoritarian legitimacy and democratic legality found expression in respective constitutions. Although outlived, the democratic experience bred a culture of constitutionalism that has proved resilient. Sudan has failed to develop the inherited legal framework to the better. It is the repressive features of the law that have actually been building up in the postcolonial era. The protective role is neglected and underdeveloped. Sudan, notwithstanding vast diversities and pervasive discrimination, has not to date enacted antidiscrimination laws.

Legal Institutions

The Judiciary

The Sudanese judiciary is modeled on a common law justice system. This section examines the institutional independence of the judiciary. Operational independence dictated by factors other than those examined here is dealt with in the section on the socioeconomic context.

The Self-Government Statute of 1953 and the Transitional Constitutions of 1956 and 1964 required that the administration of justice be performed by a separate and independent judiciary. From the outset, the Sudanese judiciary has consisted of two divisions—the civil division and the *shari'a* division. The latter comprises courts only endowed with jurisdiction over family law matters for Muslims. The civil court division is the conventional judiciary, endowed with jurisdiction to look into all civil and criminal cases in addition to family law matters for non-Muslims. The head of the *shari'a* courts is a Grand Kadi usually educated and trained in the Islamic law tradition, features of which are explained below. The head of the civil court system is a chief justice often educated and trained in the common law tradition.

The training of judges in the two divisions differs in practice and orientation. The principles and rules of procedure and evidence applied by the *shari'a* courts consist of Islamic rules of evidence and Islamic law of procedure, whereas civil courts apply rules and principles of the English common law tradition.

Judges of the *shari'a* division are educated in the *shari'a* division of the University of Khartoum School of Law, Islamic schools of law in other universities, and at Egyptian Azhar University. Judges in the civil division are educated in the mainstream division of the University of Khartoum School of Law. The curriculum of this division at the law school comprises all the common law subjects taught at English universities.

Traditionally, *shari'a* court judges could not adjudicate on matters of civil law. However, civil law judges treated matters of *shari'a* as laws of which they can take judicial notice without having to refer to a *shari'a* judge. The borderline between the two divisions has sometimes become blurred in favor of one or the other system. For example, in the beginning of the 1970s, a period dominated by the political left, the government granted the civil law courts jurisdiction over personal law issues involving Muslims. The change was opposed by orthodox Muslim judges and scholars and the regime abandoned it in favor of a return to the old division.

From 1983 on, there has been more shifting toward the dominance of the *shari'a* division. Following a political move toward Islamicization of laws and the administration of justice, an ever increasing number of *shari'a* division judges have been transferred to the civil law division. At all levels of the judicial hierarchy, *shari'a* division judges now occupy a significant number of seats on the civil bench. Recruitment policy is likewise now biased toward graduates of Islamic schools of law (examples are Omdurman Islamic University, the Quran University, Africa International University, and a few newly established *shari'a* law faculties). Application of Islamic substantive and procedural law now permeates all branches of the law and the entire legal system and is no longer confined to family law matters. This shift has changed the orientation of the judiciary. The system of precedents, once the cornerstone of the common law tradition, has lost much of its authority. The principles of evidence, procedure, professional responsibility, and formalism associated with the common law and the liberal tradition of legality are fading away. Islamic jurisprudence is not yet fully developed to provide immediate answers to these and other day-to-day issues in the administration of justice. To fill the gap the judges are allowed to apply their own perception of the Islamic point of view of the law to each particular case in priority to application of judicial precedents.[44]

The Sudanese judiciary was, until 1969, quite independent. Under the Self-Government Statute of 1953 and the Transitional Constitutions of 1956 and 1964, the procedures for the appointment, remuneration, and retirement of judges all insulated the judiciary from outside interference. Since 1969, however, the governments have created institutional constraints that have adversely affected the judiciary's independence. Under the Numeiri regime, not only was the judiciary purged and forced to bend to the will of the authoritarian government, but also the legislature passed laws that gave the president new powers in the appointment and removal of judges. These laws remained in effect throughout the reign of the regime. The current regime introduced similar laws, again limiting the authority of the judiciary. This is explained below.

Accountability to the Executive

Since 1973, judges have been accountable to the president for the optimal performance of their duties.[45] This meant that the president could initiate removal of a judge on the pretext of dissatisfaction with performance. Under the Judiciary Act of 1983, the president may appoint any judge to any judicial position, notwithstanding any law or rule to the contrary (section 29[2]).

Under the Judiciary Act, the president may decide that any judge of the Supreme Court, the president of the court of appeal, or the chief justice of the Sudan be tried by a disciplinary board (section 48). Judges may be dismissed on the ground of interest of service (sections 63–67). A judge may likewise be terminated at any time on the ground of "public interest," in accordance with the Public Service Pensions Act of 1992 (section 18[1][c]). A judge may also be dismissed in the interest of the service under the Public Service Act of 1991 (section 52[1]). It is the president who makes the decision of dismissal on these grounds. The president is not bound to explain how the "interest of service" or "public interest" is construed nor does the law define any of these phrases.

When the Constitutional Decree 2 of 1989 was in effect, a judge could be dismissed for no reason whatsoever (Article 2[6]). The decree empowered the president to dismiss any employee, and judges were actually dismissed on the basis of this decree. Although the decree was repealed in June 1998, the laws embodying the power to dismiss on ground of public interest or interest of the service are still in effect.

Special Courts

The mandate of the judiciary as guardian of civil rights and liberties of citizens and interpreter of the rule of law has been drastically curtailed. The limits on the courts' role in guaranteeing rights have been imposed in several ways. The first is by stripping the courts of the jurisdiction to hear certain types of cases, as discussed above. Additionally, the various governments have established systems of special courts, parallel to the judiciary, endowed with jurisdiction over matters that have been wrenched from the jurisdiction of ordinary courts. Following the 1975 amendment of the 1973 constitution, the government established a myriad of special courts, including, among others, state security courts for trial of offenders against state security law, public order courts for trial of offenders against public morality and public peace laws, and prompt justice courts for the administration of the hastily introduced self-proclaimed *shari'a* laws in 1983. The common denominator is always deprivation of the right to fair trial. Other than during the period of democracy from 1986 to 1989, special courts have remained an important aspect of the justice system in the Sudan.

On July 8, 1989, the new military regime passed the Constitution of Private Courts Act. This act empowers the president of the Command Council, military governors, and the governor of Khartoum to establish private courts consisting of three military officers or other competent and trustworthy persons (section 2).

These private courts have jurisdiction to try offenses under the Emergency Regulation of 1989 and several other specific laws. The act also left the door open for the president of the Command Council to endow the private courts with jurisdiction over other offenses. Private courts have the authority to impose prison sentences or any other type of penalty. The private courts may pass death sentences, which must be confirmed by the president of the Command Council. Sentences ranging from ten years to life imprisonment and the death sentence may be handed down subject to no restriction. Private courts have few procedural requirements, irrespective of the gravity of the offense and the severity of the potential punishment. Appeals of private court decisions are filed with a special court of appeal, also constituted by order of the president of the Command Council. The same act that allowed for the establishment of private courts also increased the potential punishment for some offenses over which the private courts have jurisdiction. Under the act, offenses covered by the Hashish and Opium Act of 1924, the amended Goods Control Act of 1989, and the amended Exchange Control Act of 1989 became capital crimes.

The Bar Association

In 1935, the colonial government passed a statute recognizing the role of lawyers and establishing their professional responsibilities and ethical standards.[47] Since then, the Sudanese Bar Association has gained prominence professionally, socially, and politically. The bar was always a leader in the struggle for civil and political rights, and members of the bar frequently volunteered to defend people accused of political crimes and other victims of oppression. Gaining prominence in 1959, this role of the bar continued in the freedom of expression cases involving section 105 of the Sudan Penal Code and Article 5(2) of the 1956 constitution during the 1960s.[48] Involvement of members of the dissolved bar in the defense of victims of violations continued under the present regime mainly pioneered by the Alliance for the Restoration of Democracy Lawyers. This is a dissident lawyers' organization parallel to the state-sponsored Sudan Lawyers Union.

As the reputation of the bar grew, so did the authoritarian regimes' hostility to it. For the time being, the Bar Association is not formally in existence. The military regime disbanded it, along with all other associations and trade unions, in 1989.[49]

The Socioeconomic Context

Even when institutional guarantees do exist to protect human rights, these are not enough. In day-to-day practice, institutional boundaries are often overstepped. This does not necessarily mean that statutory guarantees are not good enough. Even if Western style statutory guarantees of judicial independence are replicated in the Sudan this will not by itself produce similar results as in the West. Transplantation of legal frameworks does not by itself produce effective institutions in the host environment. It all depends on the stage of economic and social development which actually constitutes the substance of law (that is, law in action or living law) as opposed to the form. Furthermore, from the past experience of the Sudan, it appears that the facade of constitutional and legal protections often just obscures the illegal, and usually deniable, practices of maltreatment, oppression, torture, and inhumanity at the level of praxis. This discrepancy between the form of law and the law in action is not necessarily the product of bad law. Rather it is indicative of the limits of law to police an environment whose social and economic conditions are not conducive to that effect. Hence the specific social and economic factors discussed below are in one way or another all related to underdevelopment.

Ethnic and Cultural Diversities

Diversity is not by itself a negative factor. But in conditions of underdevelopment it could be. Vast regional economic inequalities have fueled centrifugal tendencies of regionalism and secessionism. These have in turn invited retaliation by the state to forcefully cement a subjectively value-judged national unity. The civil war in the Sudan, an outcome of deeply rooted economic and cultural grievances, continues to be the single biggest factor responsible for mass violations of human rights. It is civilians in the war zone who directly bear the brunt. The ramification of the war is felt all over the country, with mass displaced communities barely sheltered and nourished. The resources consumed by the war inflict even more damage on the country and its ability to secure decent standards of living and services. The war has retarded constitutional development and undermined the chances of democracy.

Democratic Constitutional Guarantees

The democratic constitutional guarantees may provide less protection than they promise. The political fragility and vulnerability of democratic governments have often put them on the defensive. In their fear of a military takeover or the social and economic paralysis of general strikes and demonstrations that might precipitate such a takeover, democratically elected governments in the Sudan have, on occasion, violated the constitution and disregarded the rule of law. For example, the Emergency Regulation of 1989, currently in effect, was initially enacted in 1987 by the democratically elected government. Likewise, it was a democratic government that widened the executive power to dismiss public employees. In 1987, the democratically elected government introduced the Termination of Service in the Public Interest Regulation, thereby increasing the executive's authority to dismiss public employees arbitrarily.

The influence of politics on the law is far-reaching, pervasive, and corrupting. The law is wielded by military regimes to suppress the forces of democracy and by democratic regimes to suppress those who lead and support the authoritarian regimes. The rule of law is, in effect, sacrificed under all regimes. This tendency is illustrated by events that followed the April 1985 uprising that overthrew the Numeiri regime. Earlier, Numeiri's regime had enacted the Indemnity Act of 1977, legislation intended to immunize the regime's supporters from prosecution or civil litigation for any act done by them in their official capacity.

When the drafters of the 1985 Transitional Constitution decided to try the army officers who had staged the coup back in 1969, they simply amended the Indemnity Act of 1977 in the new constitution. The amendment allowed the trial of persons who had occupied positions on the Command Council of the junta. The drafters of the constitution made the amendment retroactive to August 17, 1978. When the accused petitioned the Supreme Court to declare the amendment, and thus the trial, unconstitutional, their petition was dismissed on the ground that the 1985 Transitional Constitution deprived defendants of the right to challenge the retroactivity of laws. The courts then saw their role as to secure constitutionality of laws. Constitutionality of the constitution is seen as beyond judicial mandate. This is of course a self-imposed restraint the judiciary in the Sudan has learned to exercise.

Aware of the dominant role of politics, the judiciary has had to take a realistic and pragmatic approach of bowing to political pressure, in order to secure its very existence. This succumbing to pressure could be due to awareness on the part of the judiciary of the limits of law. But the pressure on individual judges should not be underestimated either. After all judges have family responsibilities and need to earn a living. The instinct of survival is much stronger than the drive toward justice. In situations when there had to be a choice between losing the job or losing judicial autonomy the majority chose the latter. In 1966, the High Court and the Council of Ministers came into direct confrontation over whether the court could nullify legislation that it found to be unconstitutional. The crisis culminated in the resignation of the chief justice on May 17, 1967. Nobody else walked out. In 1983 the judges did not walk out upon the trial and execution of the late Mahmoud M. Taha even though the trial and execution were later to be described by the judiciary as unconstitutional.

In the years that followed, the Sudanese courts chose not to risk taking firm positions for what they saw as just and equitable. The events of 1966 and 1967 were the anomalous prelude to decades of judicial docility.

Social and Economic Context

The social and economic context within which legal institutions operate in the Sudan keeps the law from playing a meaningful role in improving the human rights situation. The social utility of the law is slim; the number of people whose lives are affected by the law, whether for better or worse, is limited. For the majority of rural people, legal institutions are nonexistent or inaccessible. More than civil and political rights, the rural population is in dire need of basic necessities—food, health care, education, fuel, shelter, and medicine. Lack of such necessities, itself a violation of economic and social rights, also militates against respect for the civil and political rights. Poverty and starvation coerce the poor into civil and political enslavement. The constitution and the law are concerned mainly with civil and political rights. The beneficiaries of this type of rights are the privileged few who have conquered poverty and look forward to win civil and political rights. To be meaningful to the population, discussions of human rights must be more than just discourse on the black-letter law. Much needs to be done to adapt the human rights discourse to the endemic circumstances in the Sudan. An issue of immediate clarity is that economic and social rights should come to the forefront.

Notes

1. Fatima Babiker Mahmoud, *The Sudanese Bourgeoisie: A Vanguard of Development?* (London: Zed Press, 1984), p. 27.

2. Fouad Ajami, *The Arab Predicament* (Cambridge: Cambridge University Press, 1982), p. 62; Martin E. Marty and R. Scott Appleby, *Fundamentalisms Observed: The Fundamentalism Project*, vol. 1 (Chicago: University of Chicago Press, 1991), p. 347.

3. Hassan al-Turabi, January 2001, "Why Did NIF Not Sign the Charter for the Defense of Democracy in the Late 1980s?" January 2001, Khartoum, pamphlet in Arabic.

4. Anglo-Egyptian Agreement of 1899, Articles 3 and 4.

5. Anglo-Egyptian Agreement of 1899, Article 9.

6. Magisterial and Police Powers Ordinance, 1905, *Sudan Gazette*, no. 73. 1/3/1953.

7. *Laws of the Sudan*, vol. 1 (3rd ed.), supp. to *Sudan Gazette*, 21/3/1953.

8. Sudan Transitional Constitution (Amendment) 1964, Inaugural Sentence, special supplement to *Sudan Gazette* 30/10/1964.

9. Turabi, "Why Did NIF Not Sign the Charter?"

10. *Khalid Hassan Abbas and Others v. Sudan Government* (1986) *Sudan Law Journal and Reports* (hereafter *SLJR*) 135.

11. Siddig Abdel Bagi Hussein, "Women and Employment Law in the Sudan," in *Women, Law and Development*, ed. Balghis Badri and Siddig Abdel Bagi Hussein (Warwick, UK: University of Warwick, 1993), 193, mimeograph.

12. Paragraph 7 of "Guidelines on Selection," the Central Recruitment Board, 1981, reads: "no person shall be appointed in any post in the public service unless he or she is holder of a security clearance certificate from the State Security Department."

13. Constitutional Decree no. 1, Articles 2 and 3.

14. Constitutional Decree no. 2 (6).

15. Amended Constitutional Decree, no. 2, Articles 1–6.

16. Emergency Regulation of 1989, section 39.

17. Emergency and Protection of Public Safety Act 1/1998, supp. 1 to *Sudan Gazette*, no. 1631, 15/1/1998.

18. Emergency and Protection of Public Safety Regulation of 1998, Statutory Instrument no. 1/1998, supp. to *Sudan Gazette* no. 1631, 15/1/1998.

19. *Laws of the Sudan*, vol. 3 (4th–5th ed.), vol. 6 (6th ed.), supp. to *Sudan Gazette*, 29/8/1939.

20. 1975 Amendment to the Permanent Constitution of the Sudan of 1973, Articles 2 and 2(a).

21. Constitution of the Republic of the Sudan of 1998, Article 108.

22. *Ebrahim Yousif Habbani and Others v. President* cc/cs/1/2000.

23. Report of the Special Rapporteur, Gaspar Biro, submitted in accordance with the Commission on Human Rights Resolution 1993/60, UN Document E/CN.4/1994/48 1 Feburary, 1994.

24. *Building Authority of Khartoum v. Evangellos Evangellides* (1958) *SLJR* 16.

25. See Transitional Constitution of 1964, Article 64; Transitional Constitution of 1985, Article 53.

26. Amendment of November 22, 1965, to the Transitional Constitution of 1964.

27. *Joseph Garang and Others v. Supreme Commission and Others* (1968) *SLJR* 1.

28. Kotaro Tanaka, *Journal of the International Commission of Jurists* 11 no. 2 (1973), para. 1, as quoted in (1968) *SLJR* 11 per HCJ Salah Eddin Hassan.

29. *Asma Mahmoud Mohamed Taha and Another v. Sudan Government* (1986) *SLJR* 163.

30. *Unity Bank Employees' Trade Union v. Registrar of Trade Unions* (1987) *SLJR* 299.

31. Concerning Freedom of Association and Protection of the Right to Organize, ILO Convention no. 87, July 4, 1950. Not signed by the Sudan.

32. *Mahgoub Bureir Mohamed Nour v. Sudan Government* (1989) *SLJR* 27.

33. *Council of Ministers v. Hashim El Muatasim* (1991) *SLJR* 125, *Minister of Transport and Communication v. El Sir Mohamed Ali* (1990) *SLJR* 139, *Council of Ministers v. Mohamed Ahmed Abul Azzaeim* sc/cv.rv/31/91, *Abdel Rasoul Musa and Others v. Sudan Government* (1988) *SLJR* 45, and *Izzeddin Hamid v. Council of Ministers*, sc/cv.rv/39/91. In all cases the dismissal that gave rise to the application for judicial review took place before June 30, 1989.

34. *Eastern Khartoum Tenants v. Sudan Government* (1978) *SLJR* 117.

35. *Omer Ahmed Mohamed and Others v. Governor of Khartoum and Another* (1992) *SLJR* 322. The latent reason for the decision was that the chief justice issued Circular No. 3/1989 on 9/11/1989 directing that no application for judicial review of decisions made under the Eviction of Public Premises Aact of 1969 shall be allowed because the Trasitional Constitution of 1985 articles incorporating the right to litigation had been suspended together with the 1985 constitution.

36. President of the PSAB, speech to Elquwat El Musslaha Newspaper, no. 1076, August 7, 1989.

37. Chief Justice Circular No. 2/1993.

38. Lawyers Committee for Human Rights, *Defense of Rights: Attacks on Lawyers and Judges in 1991* (New York: Lawyers Committee for Human Rights, 1992), pp. 132–36.

39. *Laws of the Sudan,* vol. 3 (4th–5th ed.), vol. 6 (6th ed.), supp. to *Sudan Gazette* 29/8/1939.

40. Defense of the Sudan (Amendment) Act 1974.

41. Defense of Sudan Act of 1939, sections 3 and 4.

42. Turabi, "Why Did NIF Not Sign the Charter?"

43. The 1989 regulation was subsequently replaced by the Emergency Declaration of November 12, 1999.

44. Civil Transactions (Amendment) Act 1990 and 1993 sections 559 (6) and (7).

45. Sources of the Law Act of 1983, section 2.

46. Permanent Constitution of the Sudan of 1973, Article 187.

47. Advocates Ordinance 1935, Laws of the Sudan 1939, Title xxi subtitle 6, 15/9/1953.

48. *SLJR* (1961) 80 (1966) 99.

49. See Constitutional Decree 2 of 1989, Article 3.

Chapter 11
Uganda
The Long and Uncertain Road to Democracy

Livingstone Sewanyana and Taaka Awori

While human rights performance in Uganda has arguably improved since the 1970s and 1980s, human rights abuses still abound. Police routinely beat and mistreat suspects. Hundreds languish in inhuman conditions in prisons while the court system drags through a backlog of cases. Women are subject to violence in the home and have little hope of redress in the legal system. Children in northern and western Uganda are abducted from their homes and forced to fight as rebels against their government.

This chapter analyzes the reality and prospects of the legal protection of human rights in Uganda through an examination of the constitutional and legal framework for the protection of human rights; the judiciary and legal profession; the status of nongovernmental human rights organizations and other NGOs; and the political, social, and economic context.

The analysis reveals that, notwithstanding a number of shortcomings, the constitutional and legal framework essentially provides for the vindication of human rights. In this sense, therefore, the prognosis for the legal protection of human rights in Uganda is good. The constitutional and legal framework, however, operates within a context, and, unfortunately, the current political, social, and economic context has limited the potential benefits of this legal framework. This context has thus undermined the potential power of the constitution and the law in the protection of human rights.

We conclude with a set of policy recommendations and practical strategies which attempt to capitalize on the positive elements of the constitutional order, while, at the same time, addressing the challenges. These recommendations are provided from a practical point of view and include ideas for litigation, training, and networking among individuals, groups, and organizations engaged in the legal protection of human rights in Africa. We hope that these recommendations will provide a means by which the legal system, along with other sectors of the society, can become a vital and powerful tool in the protection and promotion of human rights.

Uganda's Historical Background, Demographic Profile, and Economic Situation

In October 1962, Uganda gained independence after half a century of British colonial rule. Before colonization, this region was governed by diverse ethnic groups, some of which had been organized into powerful kingdoms. Given this history, the new nation attempted to balance interests and manage conflicts between these various groups. However, the cracks in the system soon became apparent. On January 25, 1964, the First Battalion of the army mutinied, refusing to obey orders and demanding pay raises. Even though the mutiny was soon suppressed with British assistance, no effort was made by the political leadership to redefine the role of the military.[1] This had disastrous consequences for the growth of constitutionalism and the rule of law, as history would soon prove.

In 1966, after a four year power struggle, Prime Minister Milton Obote drove the president of Uganda and the kabaka (equivalent to king) of Buganda, Sir Edward Mutesa II, out of his palace and into exile. The 1962 constitution, which had been established at independence, was abrogated and eventually replaced by an Interim Constitution, which was in turn replaced by the 1967 constitution. During the next few years, Milton Obote sought to consolidate his power by banning political activity and relying heavily on the armed forces, the General Service Unit, and, after 1968, the Special Force to settle political issues.[2] A state of emergency which had existed in only one part of the country since Obote took power was later extended to the rest of the country.

On January 25, 1971, a coup d'état abruptly removed Milton Obote from power and replaced him with Major General Idi Amin Dada. During the following nine years, all representative civilian institutions were abolished or subordinated to the will of Amin. Suspected political opponents were detained, tortured, and sometimes publicly executed. Under Amin's rule, terror and gross human rights abuses became the order of the day. Stories about detainees who were buried alive or forced to kill other detainees were common.[3] The summary expulsion of close to 90,000 Asians from Uganda was further testimony to Amin's reign of terror.

In 1979, Amin threatened to attack Tanzania and capture a region of that country called "the Kagera Salient" that he claimed belonged to Uganda.[4] Amin's threats precipitated an invasion by the Tanzania People's Defense Forces and Ugandan exile forces. From 1980 until 1986, Uganda was ruled by, in succession, Yusuf Lule, Godfrey Binaisa, Paulo Muwanga, Milton Obote, Tito Okello, and, eventually, Yoweri Museveni. Yoweri Museveni, through the National Resistance Movement (NRM), attempted to show that he and his government had brought a fundamental change to politics in Uganda and not a mere changing of the guard. Consequently, they promised democratic elections for the presidency and Parliament, elections which were finally held in 1996. In the year previous to that, a new constitution was promulgated after extensive consultation with the Ugandan people. Uganda had begun its long and arduous path to democracy.

Uganda has a population of approximately 20 million people, with women constituting 50.9 percent of the population. From 1980 to 1991, the population grew from 12 million to 16 million, an average annual growth rate of 2.7 percent. Though this is a relatively high growth rate, it is lower than the rate seen between 1969 and 1980. There has been speculation that the decrease in the growth rate in the 1980s was most likely influenced by the socioeconomic decline and the internal conflicts in Uganda during that period. Like many African countries, Uganda's population is largely rural; an estimated 90 percent of the population live in rural areas. Over 60 percent of Ugandans live below the poverty line. English is the official language, though most Ugandans speak only indigenous languages from the Bantu, Nilotic, and Nilo-Hamitic language families.

In the 1997 *Human Development Report* by the United Nations Development Program, Uganda was described as having "two faces" because of the sharp paradox which characterizes the country's profile.[5] One face of Uganda is its stellar economic performance over the past decade. In 1987, the government embarked on the Economic Recovery Program, which involved the promotion of prudent fiscal and monetary management, the improvement of incentives to the private sector, liberalization of the economy, reformation of the regulatory framework, and development of human capital through investment in education and health.[6] In addition to creating an environment conducive to private sector investment as a means of promoting economic growth, the government began a process of privatizing parastatals, liberalizing control over foreign exchange and encouraging private participation in the development of the country's infrastructure.

To a large extent the Economic Recovery Program achieved its main objectives. Through tight monetary and fiscal policies, the annual inflation rate fell and is currently in the single digits, trade has been liberalized, and the exchange rate for the local currency, the Ugandan shilling, has stabilized.[7] Government revenue collection has also improved. The resulting macroeconomic stability has led to increased investment rates and economic growth.

The other face of Uganda, however, is one of pervasive poverty and underdevelopment. Herein lies the paradox. The economy has been growing at an average annual rate of 6.5 percent since 1986, but over 50 percent of the population still lived in poverty in 1995.[8]

The persistence of civil strife in some areas of northern and western Uganda is often cited as the reason these parts of the country lag behind other regions in economic development. The AIDS pandemic in Uganda has also contributed to the pervasive poverty as it drains the productive sector. Conservative estimates indicate that 1.7 million people have died or been afflicted with AIDS.

Compounding the legacy of civil strife, instability, and AIDS is Uganda's large debt. Uganda's external debt burden stands at U.S.$3.59 billion.[9] The government spends U.S.$150 million annually in debt service, which is more than three times the amount spent on education and seven times the spending for health. The structural adjustment programs, which have been part of the government's economic recovery program, have exacerbated the poverty of the most vulnerable in society. Thus, while the country's economic performance is certainly commendable, there has been little attention given to improving the lives and economic position of most Ugandans.

Constitutional and Legal Framework for the Protection of Human Rights

Background and Status of the 1995 Constitution

Uganda's constitutional and legal framework is largely governed by its current constitution. The roots of this constitution can be traced back to December 21, 1988, when the National Resistance Council enacted Statute No. 5 of 1988. This statute established the Uganda Constitutional Commission and gave it the responsibility of developing a new constitution.[10] Previous to this, Uganda had had two constitutions, both of which had served more to centralize power in the hands of the executive than to place power in the hands of the people.

The Constitutional Commission's mandate was to consult the people and make proposals for a popular and lasting constitution based on a national consensus.[11] In fulfilling this mandate, the commission received over 25,000 submissions from the general population on what they wanted to see in the constitution. From these submissions, the commission drafted a constitution that sought to:

1. guarantee the national independence, territorial integrity, and sovereignty of Uganda;
2. establish a free and democratic system of government that would

guarantee the fundamental rights and freedoms of the people of Uganda;

3. create viable political institutions that would ensure maximum consensus and orderly succession of government;
4. recognize and demarcate divisions of responsibility among state organs of the executive, the legislature, and the judiciary, and create viable checks and balances between them;
5. endeavor to develop a democratic, free, and fair electoral system that would ensure people's representation in the legislature;
6. establish and uphold the principle of public accountability of the holders of public offices and political posts; and
7. guarantee the independence of the judiciary.

This draft constitution was debated by a Constituent Assembly during 1994 and 1995 and, on September 22, 1995, the new constitution was adopted and enacted. The 1995 constitution occupies a status of supremacy with respect to other laws in the country. This status is set out explicitly in Article 2 of the constitution, which provides that:

(1) This Constitution is the supreme law of Uganda and shall have binding force on all authorities and persons throughout Uganda.
(2) If any law or any custom is inconsistent with any of the provisions of this Constitution, the Constitution shall prevail, and that other law or custom shall, to the extent of the inconsistency, be void.

While far from perfect, the new constitution represents progress from the earlier constitutions and presents hope for the development of constitutionalism in Uganda.

Overview of the Constitutional Provisions Relating to the Protection of Human Rights

The 1995 constitution has specific provisions addressing the issue of human rights both in the preamble as part of the National Objectives and Directive Principles of State Policy and in the body of the constitution as a specific chapter dedicated to Fundamental and Other Human Rights.

Human Rights in the Preamble to the Constitution

The National Objectives and Directive Principles of State Policy are a set of objectives set forth in the preamble of the constitution which are supposed to guide all organs of the state or nonstate actors in applying or interpreting the constitution or any other law. The National Objectives are also expected to be used as guiding principles in making and implementing any policy decisions. The first article in the National Objectives provides that the president shall report to Parliament and the nation at least once a year on all steps taken to ensure the realization of these policy objectives and principles.

With respect to human rights, the National Objectives provide that:

1. The state shall guarantee and respect institutions that are charged by the state with responsibility for protecting and promoting human rights (for example, the Human Rights Commission) by providing them with sufficient resources;
2. The state shall guarantee and respect the independence of NGOs that protect and promote human rights;
3. The state shall ensure gender balance and fair representation of marginalized groups;
4. The state shall ensure the protection of the aged;
5. The state shall provide adequate resources for the various organs of government;
6. The state shall give priority to the right to development;
7. The state shall recognize the rights of persons with disabilities;
8. The state shall promote free and compulsory basic education; and
9. The state shall take all practical measures to ensure the provision of basic medical services.

The presence of these rights in the preamble would not, by itself, ensure their justiciability. Fortunately, many of these rights are also set forth in the body of the constitution where their justiciability is more certain. Nonetheless, the inclusion of human rights as part of clearly stated government policy is a powerful tool in holding the state accountable for its actions or omissions with respect to human rights.

Human Rights in the Body of the Constitution

The body of the Ugandan constitution is arranged into nineteen chapters. The fourth chapter is dedicated to the protection and promotion of fundamental and other human rights and freedoms. The constitution provides that certain of the twenty enumerated rights are nonderogable. These rights include: (1) freedom from torture, cruel, inhuman, or degrading treatment or punishment; (2) freedom from slavery or servitude; (3) the right to a fair hearing; and (4) the right to an order of habeas corpus. The constitution, however, allows for a limitation of the other rights by an act of Parliament during a state of emergency if such measures are deemed (by Parliament) reasonably justifiable (in "the public interest") for dealing with the emergency.

The constitution also provides that if a person is detained under an emergency law: (1) the detainee should be notified within twenty-four hours of the grounds upon which he or she is detained; (2) the spouse or next-of-kin should be notified and allowed access to the person within seventy-two hours after commencement of the detention; (3) details of the detention should be made public in the media no more than thirty days after its commencement. There is thus an attempt in the 1995 constitution to limit both the circumstances in which the government may derogate from its human rights obligations, and the rights that it can violate in an emergency situation.

The constitution provides that the courts shall enforce the respect for fundamental rights in that any person whose rights have been violated may apply to the court for redress, which may include compensation. It also provides that any person or organization may bring a complaint about the violation of another person's or group's human rights, thereby opening the door for public interest litigation. There is thus no issue of standing to require that the petitioner be the person who suffered the injury. In addition to the courts, the constitution provides for the creation of a Human Rights Commission with powers to investigate and, in the event of a violation, require payment of compensation, obtain release of a detained person, or use any other legal remedy.

Undoubtedly, the constitution's chapter on fundamental rights and freedoms represents significant progress in the constitutional protection of human rights in Uganda. There is the recognition of a broad range of civil and political rights and to some extent of social and cultural rights, such as the right to education and the right to a clean and healthy environment. Unfortunately, the other important economic, social, and cultural rights, such as the right to development and the right to basic medical services, while recognized in the preamble, remain nonjusticiable due to their absence in the body of the constitution. More importantly, however, Chapter 4 establishes the legal framework for the protection of human rights by clearly delineating the rights protected by entrusting the courts with the power to provide a remedy when a violation occurs, and by permitting individuals and organizations to bring a cause of action on behalf of someone else.

Record of Ratification and Reservation of International Treaties

Within the last decade, Uganda has ratified many of the international human rights treaties, including, among others, the African Charter on Human and Peoples' Rights, the OAU Convention on the Rights of Refugees, the International Covenant on Civil and Political Rights (ICCPR), the International Covenant on Economic, Social, and Cultural Rights (ICESCR), the Convention Against Torture and Other Cruel, Inhuman, or Degrading Treatment or Punishment (the "Torture Convention"), the International Convention on the Elimination of All Forms of Racial Discrimination (the "Race Convention"), the Convention on the Rights of the Child, the Convention on the Elimination of All Forms of Discrimination Against Women, and the Convention Relating to the Status of Refugees. Uganda, however, has not signed the Convention on the Prevention and Punishment of the Crime of Genocide, the Convention on the Non-Applicability of Statutory Limitations to War Crimes and Crimes Against Humanity, nor the Second Optional Protocol to ICCPR Aiming at the Abolition of the Death Penalty.

Even though Uganda has signed many of the international human rights treaties, it consistently fails to meet its reporting requirements under each treaty. For example, Uganda has never submitted the required reports for the African Charter, and four others are currently due: one report is due under the ICCPR, two are due under the ICESCR, three are due under the Torture Convention, and one is due under the Race Convention.

While it is commendable that the government has ratified so many human rights treaties, without periodic reporting it is difficult for them and others to assess their compliance under these conventions. This in turn raises questions as to how seriously the government takes its responsibilities under the international human rights treaties.

The Possibilities of Using International Human Rights Norms as Legal Protection in Domestic Litigation

One of the key questions arising out of the relationship between international human rights law and domestic law regards what are the most appropriate juridical means of achieving the aims and intentions of international law in state legal systems.[12] Under the civil law systems in Africa, treaties have direct application, subject only to their being reciprocally applied by the other parties to the treaty. On the other hand, in common law systems international treaties can only be applied domestically if they are specifically brought into the municipal legal system through enabling legislation. As a common law jurisdiction, Uganda falls into the latter category.

The requirement of enabling legislation for the domestic application of international treaties is set forth in the 1995 constitution. Article 123 provides that the president has the authority to make treaties, conventions, or agreements, and Parliament shall make laws to govern ratification of treaties, conventions, agreements, or other arrangements. More importantly, however, the constitution provides in Article 79(2) that:

"Except as provided in this Constitution, no person or body other than Parliament shall have power to make provisions having the force of law in Uganda except under authority conferred by an Act of Parliament."

The legal implication of this provision is that, even though an international human rights treaty has been signed by the executive, it does not affect private rights until Parliament has implemented enabling legislation. Thus in *R. v. Home Secretary, ex parte Brind*, Ralph Gibson stated:

An international treaty such as the Convention for the Protection of Human Rights and Fundamental Freedoms is made by the Executive. It does not directly affect the domestic laws of this country, which can be changed only by Parliament. It is not within the powers of the court, by application of a rule of statutory construction, to import [into] the laws of this country provisions of a treaty for direct application by the court. Only Parliament can do that. It would be a usurpation of the legislative power of Parliament for the court to do more than construe the legislation which Parliament passed in order to establish a meaning.[13]

While the 1995 constitutional provisions and common law principles render it difficult for the courts to directly apply international law in domestic litigation, there is no express prohibition on courts applying international human rights *norms* to interpret domestic laws in a manner that broadens, supports, and protects the respect for human rights. In fact, a strong argument could be made that the constitution would even support this use of human rights norms in its designation of the courts as the enforcer of human rights protection.[14]

Further support for this use of international norms is provided by the fact that in other common law jurisdictions, the use of human rights norms to bolster common law principles or domestic legislation in human rights cases is becoming more acceptable. As stated by a judge in one common law jurisdiction: "Often when common law judges are faced with ambiguities of legislation or uncertainty of the common law, it is appropriate and legitimate, in filling the gap to have regard to international human rights norms."[15] Thus, despite the constitutional requirement of enabling legislation for the direct application of international human rights treaties, support for the use of international human rights norms in interpreting domestic legislation can be found in the constitution and common law practice.

This section of this chapter seeks simply to describe the legal framework for the domestic application of international human rights norms. The reality of whether international human rights norms are actually used in domestic litigation in Uganda requires different analysis that is not provided here. The context in which this framework operates will be discussed below.

Provisions for the Investigation and the Prosecution of Torture, Crimes Against Humanity, and Grave Breaches of Humanitarian Law

In view of the frequent occurrence of torture, crimes against humanity, and grave breaches of humanitarian law in parts of Africa, such as Somalia, Rwanda, Liberia, and Nigeria, there has been increasing interest in determining whether the domestic legal systems in African countries have provisions for prosecuting these types of crimes. Of the three (torture, crimes against humanity, and grave breaches of humanitarian law), Ugandan law only explicitly provides for the prosecution of torture. Article 24 of the 1995 constitution provides that: "No person shall be subjected to any form of torture, cruel, inhuman or degrading treatment or punishment." In the event that someone has been subjected to torture, Article 50 of the same constitution entitles the victim to apply to a competent court for redress, which may include compensation. Uganda has also ratified the Convention Against Torture and Other Cruel, Inhuman, or Degrading Treatment or Punishment which provides that each state party shall ensure in its legal system that the victim of an act of torture obtains redress and has an enforceable right to fair and adequate compensation including the means for as full rehabilitation as possible.

Domestic law, however, has no specific provisions that provide for the prosecution of crimes against humanity and grave breaches of humanitarian law. Crimes against humanity can broadly be described as gross human rights violations committed, during times of war or peace, on a large scale or systematically against a civilian population.[16] Humanitarian law, which is codified in the four Geneva Conventions, provides a base level of protection to all persons during armed conflict. While the acts of murder and torture committed during the 1970s and 1980s could easily be considered crimes against humanity, and the atrocities currently being committed in northern and parts of western Uganda could be seen as grave breaches of humanitarian law, no attempt has been made in Uganda to develop domestic legislation under which the perpetrators of these crimes could be prosecuted.

Instead, with respect to the atrocities committed during the 1970s and 1980s, the government established a Commission of Inquiry for human rights violations committed between 1962 and 1986, pursuant to Legal Notice No. 5 of 1988. This commission sought to inquire into all aspects of violations of human rights, breaches of law, and excessive abuses of power committed against persons in Uganda by the government or its servants, agents, or agencies. Three key factors, however, seriously undermined the effectiveness of this commission.

First, the commission was severely underfunded. By 1992, four years after it was established, funding was down to 20 percent of its original levels, though the workload had not decreased. This resulted in serious delays in producing a report. The reporting delay was one of the major causes of the second factor in the commission's ineffectiveness: the failure to prosecute. Without the report, it was argued that prosecutions could not begin. Even after the report was issued in October of 1994, however, charges were still not brought against those people the commission found to be culpable.

The third factor concerned the stipulated period of review for the commission: 1962 to 1986. The year 1986 was presumably chosen by the government because this is when Museveni's NRM assumed power. The fact that the commission had to limit its inquiry into the atrocities of former regimes, even though atrocities clearly continued after 1986 while the NRM was consolidating its power, undermined its credibility in the eyes of many. Ultimately, the commission's investigations helped the country understand the causes and circumstances surrounding the period of political instability. However, the subsequent failure to prosecute those found guilty and the decision not to look into abuses committed by the regime in power left many feeling that justice had not been served.

Similarly, in dealing with grave breaches of humanitarian law, the government has not enacted domestic legislation to prosecute the responsible parties. For example, at this time in northern Uganda, the rebels of the Lords Resistance Army (LRA) abduct children to fight as rebels and also, in the case of young girls, to be used as sex slaves. LRA rebels cut off the lips and ears of civilians or brutally murder them with machetes. When caught, however, the rebels who committed these grave breaches of humanitarian law are not prosecuted under a special legislation to deal with these forms of crimes but, instead, are prosecuted under the broad crime of treason. This is unsatisfactory because treason is a political crime, which has often been abused in many countries to harass and intimidate political opponents of the regime in power. As such, a charge of treason does not address violations of humanitarian law by the LRA in northern Uganda.

In sum, the government needs to enact domestic legislation to deal with crimes against humanity, so that such crimes are actually prosecuted. Additionally, it needs to enact laws specifically outlawing grave breaches of humanitarian law, in order that these crimes be recognized and punished as what they are, rather than under the broad category of treason.

The Relationship Between Customary Law and Statutory Law

The legal system of Uganda is formed by a unique combination of laws and institutions of diverse origin which reflect the historical context in which the laws were introduced. As in other African countries, there is a plurality of laws consisting of enacted statute laws and common law principles derived from English law which are applied alongside customary laws.

Although it is almost entirely unwritten, customary law continues to provide a primary reference for the regulation of the lives of most Ugandans with respect to basic activities and relationships, including family life and property rights. Customary law also plays a more important role in local council courts ("LC courts," see next section) than in constitutionally established courts where it is subordinate to statutory law and common law principles.[17]

In applying customary law, the judiciary is limited by section 8(1) of the Judicature Act (II) of 1967, which provides that: "Nothing in this Act shall deprive the High Court of the right to observe or enforce the observance of, or shall deprive any person of the benefit of, any existing custom, which is not repugnant to natural justice, equity and good conscience and not incompatible either directly or by necessary implication with any written law."

In observance of this provision, the judiciary has devised certain tests to ascertain their suitability for enforcement. Such tests include the repugnancy doctrines of compatibility with natural justice, equity, and good conscience. It is interesting to note that customary law is subject to the repugnancy test before it may be applied, whereas the "received" English law (English statutes introduced during the colonial era to provide a necessary basis of administration) is only subject to adaptation to local conditions.[18]

Ultimately, however, because of the subsidiary role it has played in the determination of disputes in constitutionally established courts, customary law has not had a large impact on the *legal* protection of human rights in this particular forum. The subsidiary role it plays in these courts is very different, however, from the critical role it plays in regulating the lives of a majority of Ugandans in ways that are often very discriminatory, especially with respect to women. In this light, there is need for exploring ways of holding the state accountable for its failure to effectively combat discriminatory customary practices, such as female genital mutilation and the exclusion of women from holding and controlling land, from a human rights perspective.

The Judiciary and the Legal Profession

The Structure and Organization of the Judiciary

Structure

The 1995 constitution lays out the current structure and organization of the judiciary. The constitution creates four levels of courts. These include the Supreme Court at the top, the Court of Appeal below it, and the High Court below the Court of Appeal.

The Supreme Court, as in many countries, serves as the final court of appeal in Uganda. Below it the Court of Appeal serves two key functions:

as a court of appeal from judgments made at the High Court and as a Constitutional Court. In serving the latter function, the Court of Appeal/Constitutional Court determines any questions as to the interpretation of the constitution. The High Court has unlimited original criminal and civil jurisdiction and has exclusive jurisdiction as the court of first instance in cases involving capital punishment as the maximum sentence for the offense.

Below the High Court are the magistrates courts. The magistrates courts are organized into hierarchical levels that include the chief magistrates court, grades 1, 2, and 3, with grade 3 being the magistrates court of the lowest jurisdiction. The chief magistrates and magistrates grade 1 have professional legal qualifications as advocates, while the magistrates grade 2 and 3 are not professionally trained as lawyers but, instead, have completed a year of specialized training in law.

Article 142 of the constitution provides that judicial officers are appointed by the president, acting on the advice of the Judicial Service Commission. The approval of Parliament, however, is required for an appointment to be confirmed. The tenure of judicial officers is also governed by the constitution, which provides that an officer shall vacate the position upon reaching the age of seventy years in the case of the chief justice, the deputy chief justice, justices of the Supreme Court, and justices of the Court of Appeal, and sixty-five years in the case of the principal judge and judges of the High Court. Other than these age limitations, a judicial officer can only be removed from office for incompetence or misconduct.

In addition to the courts provided for in the constitution, Uganda has local council (LC) courts (discussed above). These courts were statutorily established in 1988 to adjudicate minor disputes at the village, parish, and subcounty levels. The LC courts have jurisdiction over civil cases arising from debts, contracts, or assault, up to a maximum value of Ush 5,000 (roughly equal to US$5), and over certain property cases arising from conversion, damage, or trespass without a maximum value. They also have jurisdiction over civil disputes governed by customary law concerning land, family matters, and customary bailment. Finally, they have jurisdiction over minor criminal infringements of by-laws made by the local government. Appeals from the LC courts go from the village court to the parish court, from there to the subcounty courts, from there to the chief magistrate's court, and eventually to the High Court.

Training

The training of judges is primarily organized through the Judicial Training Committee, which is appointed by the chief justice. In organizing the training of judges, the Training Committee is mandated to determine the training needs within the judiciary, plan periodic training courses which respond to these training needs, identify overseas institutions offering relevant training programs, select and approve judicial officers and other staff to go for training locally or internationally, and consider applications for departmental consent or sponsorships for individual officers to go for training. The Registrar for Research and Training is the officer in charge of the actual implementation of the programs, including the logistical arrangements.

In addition to the Judicial Training Committee, there is a Judicial Service Commission. This commission is mandated by Article 147(1)(c) of the Constitution of the Republic of Uganda "to prepare and implement programmes for the education of, and for the dissemination of information to judicial officers and the public about law and the administration of justice." From the wording of this provision, it appears that the Judicial Service Commission has some responsibility toward the training of the judiciary. To date, however, the commission does not appear to have played any major role in this regard. Despite the institutional mechanisms established to provide continued education and training for judicial officers, it would appear that only the lower cadre of judicial officers, namely the magistrates, systematically receive continued education or training. The judicial officers of the High Court, Court of Appeal, and Supreme Court appear to receive training only sporadically. In part this can be attributed to the difficulty in finding appropriate courses and appropriate trainers. The judges are loath to be trained by anyone they consider below their station and have been known to consider any recommendation of training as a questioning of their competence.

Independence of the Judiciary

Independence of the judiciary can be defined broadly as the belief of all judges that they are free to decide matters before them in accordance with their assessment of the facts and their understanding of the law, without any improper interference, inducement, or pressure, direct or indirect, from any quarter or for whatever reason.[19] This section, therefore, seeks only to examine how the constitutional framework establishes and either protects or undermines the independence of the judiciary, and not whether judicial independence actually exists in reality. Since the latter issue is so closely intertwined with the political environment, it is covered in more detail in the next section.

Recognizing the importance of judicial independence to the protection of human rights and the rule of law, the 1995 constitution instituted a number of safeguards to protect the judiciary from undue influence. Article 128 of the Ugandan constitution provides that: (1) "In the exercise of judicial power, the courts shall be independent and shall not be subject to the control or direction of any person or authority"; (2) no person shall interfere with the courts or judicial officers in the exercise of their judicial functions; (3) all organs and agencies of state shall accord to courts such assistance as may be required to ensure the effectiveness of the courts; (4) a person exercising judicial power shall not be liable to any action or suit for any act or omission by that person in the exercise of judicial power; (5) the administrative expenses of the judiciary, including salaries and allowances, shall be charged on the Consolidated Fund; (6) the judiciary shall be self-accounting and may deal directly with the ministry responsible for finance in relation to its finances; and (7) the salary, allowances, privileges, and so on of a judicial officer shall not be varied to his or her disadvantage.

One of the central foundations of independence of the judiciary lies within the manner in which judges are appointed and removed. When the executive has the sole power to appoint, the executive often interprets this as also having the sole power to remove, given the age-old (but intrinsically flawed) belief that "he who appoints, can remove."[20] Under the 1995 constitution, the chief justice, the deputy chief justice, the principle judge, and the justices of the Supreme Court, the Court of Appeals, and the High Court are appointed by the president acting on the advice of the Judicial Service Commission and with the approval of Parliament (Article 142[1]). The power to appoint judges, therefore, is in executive hands, but is tempered by the requirement that the legislature approve the choices.

The power to remove judges also rests in the hands of the executive. This power, however, is exercised without the oversight of Parliament that is provided in the appointment of judges. The instances in which the executive may remove a judicial officer are, however, extremely limited. The constitution provides that a judicial officer may be removed from office for *only* three reasons, other than mandatory retirement. These reasons are: (1) inability to perform the functions of his or her office arising from infirmity of body or mind; (2) misbehavior or misconduct; or (3) incompetence (Article 144[2]).

The investigation and determination as to whether any of the preceding conditions has occurred is made by a tribunal consisting of former judicial officers who are appointed by the president. Though the decision of whether a tribunal should investigate a judicial officer is not made by the president, it is made by those he appoints, namely members of the Judicial Service Commission or the cabinet.[21] It has been argued that this procedure is problematic not only because it is likely to be conducted in secret, but also because it is susceptible to manipulation and abuse. For example, it is possible to imagine a situation in which the president "presents a recommendation as coming from [the] Cabinet, when in fact, it has been self-initiated."[22] The other problem is that, other than their initial role in approving those the president has nominated for the cabinet and the Judicial Service Commission, Parliament has no oversight function in the process of removing judges. This is a serious weakness in the constitutional framework to preserve the independence of judges.

The other constitutional provisions that have the tendency to undermine the independence of the judiciary are those involving the office of the executive. Uganda's political history has poignantly demonstrated that the judiciary's difficulty in maintaining its independence has been caused by the excess of power concentrated in the executive's hands. Unfortunately, this excess of power in the hands of the executive is entrenched by the constitutional provisions that effectively put the president over Parliament and the judiciary. For example, Article 98 of the constitution provides that: "While holding office, the president shall not be liable to proceedings in any court." Given that circumstances may arise where it will be essential for the president to be subject to judicial process, this immunity elevates the executive unjustifiably above the judiciary. Article 98 of the constitution also provides that the president "shall take precedence over" all persons in Uganda. One commentator has described this provision as, "an obvious colonial relic that has led to the development of what some scholars have referred to as the 'Imperial Presidency'—a President who is above the law."[23] Again, provisions such as these only have the undesirable effect of strengthening the executive, often at the expense of the other branches of government and the notion of separation of powers.

In sum, while the 1995 constitution has taken some positive steps to preserve the independence of the judiciary through, for example, the procedures for appointing judges, it does not go far enough. Provisions still exist, such as those relating to the removal of judges and powers of the executive, that may ultimately undermine the very independence that the framers of the 1995 constitution sought to safeguard.

The Structure and Organization of the Legal Profession

The legal profession in Uganda is composed of lawyers working in private practice, the civil service, private corporations, public corporations, and NGOs. As in other developing countries, most of the lawyers are concentrated in urban areas. Most lawyers in Uganda are trained at the Faculty of Law in Makerere University where, after three years, they receive an LL.B. degree.

After obtaining the LL.B. degree (which normally takes three years), graduates attend the Law Development Center for another nine months to obtain a postgraduate diploma in legal practice. In addition to the traditional law school classes, the Faculty of Law offers a number of courses in human rights, but these courses are taken by choice, rather than being required of all students. Furthermore, selected students participate in a program run by the Human Rights and Peace Center at the university, in which they spend eight to ten weeks interning in a human rights NGO of their choice. All lawyers are required to belong to the Uganda Law Society, a statutorily created body that regulates the activities of lawyers in the country. In the past, institutional weaknesses and a hostile political environment prevented the Law Society from playing an active role in the protection of human rights in Uganda. Today, while the Law Society provides legal aid services through the Legal Aid Project (LAP), it, like the legal community generally, remains largely silent on sensitive human rights issues.[24] Though the life-threatening risks inherent in any human rights advocacy during the 1970s and 1980s undoubtedly had a negative effect on the legal community, these risks are much diminished today with the improvement in the country's human rights record. One would, thus, expect to see more of an active role played by lawyers, if the fear of reprisal was indeed the reason they were inactive in the human rights movement.

Two factors may help explain the legal community's passivity even in today's more open political environment. First, though much work has been done with respect to constitutional and legal reform in Uganda, the battle for human rights has not been primarily waged in the courts. Instead, education has been a major tool in protecting and promoting human rights in Uganda. The professional capacity of lawyers in this respect has not, therefore, been in great demand. Second, as in many parts of the world, the legal community in Uganda remains a largely bourgeois and conservative community that is not eager to disrupt the norms and rules that give it status in society. Thus, the few human rights cases which lawyers have actively litigated have been limited to protecting the interests of powerful elites who seem to be simply challenging the distribution of power among other elites and not fundamentally challenging the distribution of power and its impact on the protection of human rights. There is, therefore, a need for the legal community to redefine its historical role and take a more active part in the struggle for the protection of human rights.

Political, Social, and Economic Context

The Political Context

In order to understand the current practice and future prospects of the legal protection of human rights in Uganda, one must first understand the political context in which the legal provisions and institutional framework currently operate. This process of contextualizing the legal protection of human rights in Uganda's historical and political environment reveals two key factors that will be relevant in devising strategies to promote this approach to protecting human rights.

First, the civilian and military dictatorships ruling Uganda in the 1970s and 1980s drastically undermined the power and independence of the judiciary in a manner that is still being felt today. Strategies aimed at strengthening the institution and independence of the judiciary and inculcating a spirit of activism toward the protection of human rights among judiciary officers, therefore, are critical. Second, in Uganda there is an important relationship between democratic governance and the legal protection of human rights. The concrete steps taken in the last decade to build a functioning democracy portend well for the legal protection of human rights. Not only does democratic governance allow for the possibility of an independent judiciary to support the legal protection of human rights, but it also fosters an open atmosphere in which people are empowered and not so afraid to fight for their rights in the courts. Therefore, strategies to promote the legal protection of human rights should also support institutions and policies that further develop democratic governance in the country.

The Legacy of Executive Interference with the Judiciary

During the period of civilian and military dictatorships in the 1970s and 1980s, the legal protection of human rights was all but impossible, because, as described in the historical background, any perceived opposition, *legal* or otherwise, was dealt with in the severest manner possible. The authority and independence of the judiciary, the essential institution in the legal protection of human rights, were severely eroded during this period. The judiciary's loss of autonomy still limits its ability to act as the bulwark in defense of human rights because, during that dangerous period, the judiciary protected itself by deciding cases against individual liberty and for executive power. One particularly apt example of the judiciary's response to the assault on its independence is provided by Joe Oloka-Onyango in what he describes as "Matovu's ghost."[25]

In *Uganda v. Commissioner of Prisons, ex parte Matovu*, the High Court sought to examine the validity of a detention order issued under the 1966 constitution. Even though the court found that it had the jurisdiction to hear the case despite the fact that it involved a highly political question, the court declared that it lacked authority to rule on the validity of the constitution, because, "Courts, legislatures and the law derived their origins from the Constitution, and therefore the Constitution cannot derive its origin from them, because there can be no state without a Constitution."[26] In describing the court's decision, Oloka-Onyango argues that "the reluctance of the court to deal with the substance of the case was only in part related to the legal questions that were involved." He explains that the court was "responding to the objective reality of their existence within the particular political conditions prevailing at the time. . . . [I]n upholding the detention order issued against Matovu . . . the Court implicitly sanctioned government action in the infringement of individual liberties," a judicial decision that was to have lasting repercussions.[27] Thus, the court in this case justified the extraconstitutional abuse of power by the executive, as it did the extraconstitutional loss of it by the judiciary and the population.[28] This attitude toward the protection of individual liberties still haunts the judiciary as the following two cases demonstrate.

The first of these cases involves three journalists and their embarrassment of a foreign president. This case is illustrative of the persistent, though reduced, interference by the current executive in the affairs of the judiciary, and the judiciary's frequent capitulation to the executive, at the expense of individual liberties. The case of the journalists began on January 29, 1990, when Abdi Hassan, a BBC stringer, Festo Ebongu of the government-owned *New Vision,* and Alfred Okware of the *News Desk* magazine attended a State House press conference given by the visiting president of Zambia at the time, Kenneth Kaunda. During this conference, President Kaunda was asked certain allegedly "embarrassing" questions, presumably by these three journalists. The questions concerned Zambia's relations with the apartheid regime in South Africa, President Kaunda's long stay in power, and the alleged involvement of his son in a murder. Because of these questions, the journalists were arrested and charged under section 51 of the Penal Code.[29]

The charges against Festo Ebongu and Alfred Okware were dismissed by one of the chief magistrates in Kampala, Hensley Okalebo, on the grounds that the questions they put to President Kaunda did not degrade, revile, or expose him to hatred or contempt, nor did they disturb the peace and friendship between Uganda and Zambia. Despite this dismissal, the two were rearrested as they left the court and were only released on bond several days later. In order, apparently, to discourage the independence and impartiality that he displayed, Okalebo was quickly transferred to the nondescript municipality of Mukono, approximately twenty kilometers from Kampala. In a highly irregular move, the state brought in the chief magistrate from Masaka, Edward Bamwite, who denied bail to the third journalist, Abdi Hassan on highly spurious, if not actually discriminatory, grounds.[30] While these transfers were effected by the judiciary, the authors believe them to have been done with undercover influence from the executive. Fortunately, on appeal, the High Court and later the Court of Appeal dismissed the charges against this journalist on the same grounds on which Magistrate Okalebo had earlier dismissed the case against Festo Ebongu and Alfred Okware.[31] As stated previously, this case demonstrates the negative effects that executive influence on the judiciary can have and the willing-ness of some members of the judiciary to capitulate to that influence to the detriment of human rights.

The second case involves the use of a colonial relic, the sedition statute. In a decision that one commentator has described as "more executive than the executive itself,"[32] the chief magistrate of Buganda Road Court in Kam-pala convicted Haruna Kanaabi, editor of the *Shariat* newsletter, of sedition pursuant to sections 41(1)(a) and 42(1)(c) of the Penal Code, and for publishing false news pursuant to section 50(1) of the same code. He was sentenced to five months imprisonment and fined USh 49,500 for the first offense and fined USh 1,200,000 or one year's imprisonment for the sec-ond offense.

In the allegedly seditious material, Kanaabi had sarcastically stated that Rwanda was a district of Uganda, that Rwandan president Pasteur Bizi-mungu was the central government representative of the Ugandan district of Rwanda established in 1994, and that President Museveni had gone to solicit votes for the then impending presidential elections. This sarcasm was not appreciated by the chief magistrate. She stated: "A look at the arti-cle in question reveals the use of highly sarcastic language. . . . Another person reading it can easily get the impression that such words have the in-tention to arouse the sentiments of Ugandans who view the presence of Banyarwanda in this country with disaffection."[33]

While the magistrate recognized that Article 29 of the 1995 constitution protects freedom of expression, she stated that Article 43(2) of the consti-tution allows for the limitation of certain rights as long as the limits set by the government are not more restrictive than what is "demonstrably justifi-able in a free and democratic society." Rather than deciding whether the statute in question, or the government's action in this particular case, had imposed limits on the freedom of expression rights of Haruna Kanaabi be-yond that which is demonstrably justifiable in a free and democratic soci-ety, the judge evaded the issue. She stated:

This court is not a Constitutional Court. It therefore lacks the capacity to interpret the provisions of the Constitution beyond the literal meaning. As such, I am of the view that where a state having regard to its supreme law keeps on its statute books a law that makes it an offence to do a certain act and hence limit the enjoyment of a specified freedom, this Court shall accept that restriction as lawful and shall go ahead to punish any transgression of the same according to the existing law until such a time as the state deems fit to lift such restriction after realizing that such re-striction violates a certain right.[34]

If a student of law believed that the judiciary could be counted on as the protector of constitutional rights, the magistrate's decision would have quickly shattered all such illusions. Essentially, she left it to the executive,[35] in many cases the very person who violates human rights, to protect human rights. The Kanaabi case, while proving the persistence of *Matovu*'s ghost, also demonstrates the judiciary's conservatism, its preference for a positivist approach to the law, and its reluctance to breathe life into the human rights provisions set forth in the constitution and the international human rights covenants to which Uganda is a party.

Because the legal protection of human rights is largely dependent on an effective and functioning judicial system, the understanding of how this system actually operates in a given political environment is critical. The previously cited cases demonstrate that historically the political context has weakened the judiciary's independence and capacity to protect individual liberties. While current executive incursions on judicial independence have decreased since the 1970s and 1980s, they have by no means ceased to exist, as the two cases discussed above reveal. Whether seen as apparent judicial abdication of responsibilities or as a consequence of interference by the executive, this is a reality and challenge that must be addressed in the struggle for the legal protection of human rights.

Democratic Governance and the Legal Protection of Human Rights

The good news is that, despite such challenges, there is already improvement and still more room for hope. As already stated, in Uganda, democratic governance (or the semblance thereof) has improved the chances for the legal protection of human rights. During the past decade, Uganda has taken bold strides toward the creation of democratic governance and the rule of law. In 1995, a new constitution was promulgated after extensive and widespread consultation with a large section of the population. In 1996, Uganda had what has been called its first democratic presidential and legislative elections. The introduction of more democratic institutions has undoubtedly encouraged many to be more assertive about their rights in a situation where previously the risks had been high. The creation of a more democratic atmosphere has also, to a limited degree, encouraged judicial officers to assert their independence and impartiality.

It should be noted, however, that while Uganda is slightly more democratic than it was before, certain categories of rights, namely economic and social rights, continue to be violated, as is made evident by the paradox in the Ugandan economy, described above. The paradox is that despite Uganda's stellar economic performances, Ugandan people remain among the poorest in the region and, indeed, in the entire world. The legal protection of these social and economic rights is particularly difficult not only because the government slavishly follows the structural adjustment policies developed by the IMF and the World Bank, but also because the rights have been rendered nonjusticiable by their omission from the body of the constitution.

Accordingly, while the slow emergence of democratic structures portends well for the legal protection of human rights, this only applies to civil and political rights.

The Social Context

In order to understand the current practices and future prospects of the respect for human rights in Uganda, we must also consider three important factors related to the social context in which these practices and prospects take place. These factors are the perception by the majority of the populace of the formal judicial system as inaccessible, corrupt, and irrelevant to their lives, the inaccessibility and insensitivity of the judicial system and the institutions supporting that system to the needs of women, and the preference by a large section of the population for customary laws and LC courts.

Inaccessible, Corrupt, and Irrelevant

The perception of many Ugandans that the formal justice system is inaccessible, corrupt, and ultimately irrelevant can largely be attributed to the historical role and manner in which the courts have operated. The perception of inaccessibility is derived largely from the costs of defending rights in the courts, the distance to the courts, the unfamiliarity with technical and confusing procedures, and the use of an unfamiliar language. In many ways the formal judicial system has remained an alien, disempowering institution for the average Ugandan.

Although an estimated 90 percent of Ugandans live in the rural areas, many of the courts are located in urban areas, particularly in the capital city or the central towns or municipalities of each district. Given the poor transportation infrastructure and the absence of affordable public transportation to these urban centers, the courts' physical location becomes a hindrance to their use by the average Ugandan in the rural areas. Unfortunately, even when people can get to the courts, the atmosphere is far from encouraging.

First, the filing fees and the cost of hiring a lawyer are prohibitively high for many. While Article 28(3) of the 1995 constitution provides for legal representation at the expense of the state as part of the right to a free trial, this requirement only applies to persons charged with crimes that carry a sentence of death or life imprisonment. This category should be broadened to provide counsel for defendants who cannot afford lawyers' fees in all criminal cases, regardless of the magnitude of the sentence.

Second, the atmosphere of the courts makes many Ugandans feel out of place. In Uganda today, the judges and lawyers in the higher courts still don white wigs and flowing black gowns, as they did during the colonial era. This continued adherence to customs that were imported from a colonial power before independence raises suspicions in the minds of average Ugandans that the judicial system is there to serve other people's interests. Additionally, the procedural rules, which are technical and perplexing even to many lawyers, render the system more alien. For the majority of Ugandans, the rules are confusing and, therefore, disempowering. Finally, the use of English in the courts further compounds the sense of mistrust and suspicion. Unless they have had some education, many Ugandans do not understand English, much less the legal terms used by the judges, magistrates, and lawyers during hearings.

Besides contending with the reality that the courts are inaccessible to many Ugandans, any strategy to promote the legal protection of human rights must also contend with the general perception that the courts are corrupt. This perception, which is broader than simply the idea that members of the judicial system are "on the take" financially, can largely be attributed to the previously described historical context in which judicial power was exercised. Ugandans will not quickly forget how the judiciary was used to consolidate power in the hands of a few at the expense of the majority, nor can they ignore the fact that the judiciary does not always act independently. This sense that the judiciary is there to serve the interests primarily of the political elite is combined with the idea that the judiciary will serve the interests of the well-off elite. In other words, particularly at the lower levels of court, with the right amount of money, a file might get conveniently lost or a judgment might be favorably issued.

Ultimately, the combination of inaccessibility and perceived corruptibility of the formal judicial system has rendered the system largely irrelevant to Ugandans with respect to dispute resolution or the protection of human rights. Because most Ugandans do not necessarily see the judicial system as a system that discharges "justice and fairness," they would not think to protect their human rights through legal channels. There is thus a need to address the physical accessibility, the cost, and the sense of disempowerment and injustice associated with the formal justice system if the legal protection of human rights is to be promoted effectively.

Inaccessible and Insensitive to the Needs of Women

As in many other African countries, Uganda's gender profile demonstrates widening gender disparities; there is a dichotomy between women and men regarding access to productive resources, poverty levels, education, employment opportunities, and participation in the political process. Indeed, though women make up 70 percent of the total agricultural labor force and 70–80 percent of the food production labor force, only 7 percent of women own land.[36] These gender disparities are a reflection of cultural practices and attitudes that subordinate women. The formal legal provisions and institutional framework that make up the formal judicial system and administration of justice are not immune from these discriminatory attitudes. The result has been that women, more than ever, have come to expect less from the judicial system in terms of the protection of their rights. Alternatively, one can see this as growing disparity between the expectations of men and women that the judicial system will protect their rights.

Women's access to the formal institutions of the judiciary is even more limited than men's. Women constitute the majority of the country's poor, and, thus, they are disproportionately affected by the high costs and fees required by the court and lawyers. Furthermore, given that women also form the majority of the country's uneducated and illiterate population, the language and procedures of the formal judicial system are even more alien to them than to Ugandan men. To compound this problem, all the formal institutions of the justice system are male dominated. Women constitute only 41 percent of all state attorneys, 17 percent of High Court judges, about 7 percent of chief magistrates, 22 percent of grade 1 magistrates, and 12 percent of the police force.

Once in court, women often face discrimination and gender bias from the judges and magistrates. These judges and magistrates are imbued with societal values regarding the status of women, and it is not unusual for them to apply these values, even though such application results in a violation of the woman's rights. Unless redressed, this state of affairs would be a failure of the law of Uganda in protecting women's rights in general. Women must also contend with blatantly discriminatory laws which are applied even though they clearly violate the provisions in the constitution that provide for equality under the law.[37]

The result has been that women have tended to take recourse in the LC courts, which are comparatively cheaper, less formal, and easily accessible. Even this recourse, however, has not been free of discrimination. Access to these local courts is sometimes denied because of the cultural and patriarchal hegemony of husbands or male relatives.[38] For example, the cultural patriarchal hegemony in LC Courts is reflected in such practices as requiring women to sit on the floor or being denied sufficient opportunities to present their case, especially when perceived to be contrary to the wishes of husbands and male relatives. Also, these courts mainly enforce customary law which has intrinsic gender biases that discriminate against women. Finally, members of these courts are mainly men from within the community but without any knowledge of the law, who, therefore, tend to make partial and uninformed decisions.

Strategies to make the judiciary more effective with respect to the protection of human rights should ensure that the system is one that responds to the needs of all people. Because women have been particularly ill-served by the formal justice system, when formulating such strategies, special attention should be paid to the needs of women.

Preference for Customary Law and Local Council Courts

One of the most important features of the LC courts for ordinary Ugandans is their accessibility with respect to geographical proximity, reduced monetary costs, familiar (peer) "judges," understandable language, and lack of convoluted and confusing legal technicalities.[39] Accordingly, when disputes arise, particularly with respect to land, Ugandans in rural areas turn to these courts in the hope of obtaining some type of "popular justice." It has been found, however, that while the LC courts are a popular innovation in the administration of justice, the fact that they apply and administer laws that are essentially elitist and discriminatory (especially against women) means that they can also be problematic from a human rights point of view.

It has also been found that LC courts regularly exceed their jurisdiction, often at the behest of the litigants.[40] Without proper training and expertise, the decisions proffered by LC courts in handling matters beyond their jurisdiction can result in serious violations of one of the concerned parties' rights. For example, it is not uncommon for LC courts to be asked to adjudicate cases involving defilement (statutory rape). Even though defilement is a capital offense that can only be tried by the High Court, the LC courts sometimes settle such disputes by fining the offending party a stated number of chickens or goats. Given that these courts are more relevant to the average Ugandan than the higher judicial courts, they also need to be targeted in the legal protection of human rights. Those sitting on these courts need to be sensitized on human rights norms and how to apply customary law in a manner that does not violate human rights.

The Economic Context

Like many other institutions in the country, the judiciary suffered greatly from the political turmoil and civil strife which beset Uganda from 1972 onward. Essentially, the period of the 1970s and 1980s saw the looting and almost total destruction of the judicial system, and it is still struggling to recover. During the period of destruction, the judicial system survived on small or nonexistent salaries. The inadequacy of salaries has had a serious impact on the judiciary's effectiveness. The skills and staffing of the judiciary leave a lot to be desired. Until recently, for example, it was difficult to fill judicial vacancies because of the more attractive pay and conditions in the private sector.

There has also been a hesitancy to invest too much in the training of support staff because the staff do not actually belong to the judiciary but to the Public Service Commission. They can thus be moved around at the whim of the Public Service Commission. In the courts, support staff are in short supply, the equipment is outdated, consisting mainly of stencils and manual typewriters, and there is a lack of easily available documentation on the laws of Uganda.

The other institutions involved in the administration of justice, the Directorate of Public Prosecutions (DPP), the police, and the prisons, have also been affected by the destruction of the 1970s and 1980s. The police are undertrained and underpaid, there are few state attorneys in the DPP's office, there is lack of transport especially for prisons, and the salaries for the police and prison officers are ridiculously low. All these difficulties inevitably result in extraordinary delays in handling cases. This, in turn, affects people's faith in the legal system, making them more reluctant to bring cases. People also cease to see the courts as a place in which they can seek a quick remedy when a right has been violated. Accordingly, the delays in judicial proceedings render the system inefficient and unattractive for victims.

The Status and Role of Human Rights Organizations and Other NGOs

In the last decade, civil society in Uganda has grown beyond all expectations. Within civil society, nongovernmental organizations (NGOs) and community-based organization (CBOs) have been particularly active. These organizations have been involved in a wide range of activities, from broad human rights promotion to development activities on both the national and local, grassroots level. In order to operate, NGOs must register with the NGO Board, a statutorily created national body, while CBOs must register with the district authorities. In Article 5 of the National Objectives and Directive Principles of State Policy in the 1995 constitution, it is provided that: "The state shall guarantee and respect the independence of nongovernmental organizations which protect and promote human rights." While many NGOs appreciate the need to have some government oversight, many find the registration requirements excessively bureaucratic and cumbersome. It has also been argued that the registration requirements have been used by the government to prevent organizations it dislikes from operating legally by unduly delaying their registration process.

Despite the fact that many organizations are actively involved in the protection of civil, political, economic, and social rights, only a few actually call themselves human rights NGOs. This is because, as in many parts of the world, those working in various communities to provide basic needs such as water and health facilities have not begun to see their work through a human rights framework. Accordingly, these NGOs and CBOs are more likely to see themselves as development organizations rather than as human rights NGOs.

Those that do consider themselves to be human rights NGOs vary according to the rights they seek to protect. Some work generally on civil and political rights and others focus on specific groups of rights such as the rights of children and the rights of women. Though all these organizations work on human rights, the level of activism varies according to the issue involved. Those working on women's rights and children's rights, for example, have been extremely successful in getting their issues onto the national agenda and in pushing through reforms and policy changes where necessary. While part of their success can be attributed to the personalities that have championed these causes, to a larger degree their success can be attributed to the fact that their agendas appear to be generally perceived, for the time being at least, as politically "less threatening" to the government. The situation seems to be different for NGOs working on other human rights issues, as they are constantly under the threat of having their activities characterized by the current political regime as subversive and politically motivated. There has thus been some degree of self-censorship by these NGOs to avoid such labeling by the government. This has in turn affected their level of activism.

Given the scarcity of local funding, many national NGOs have had to rely on funding from international donors to finance their activities.[41] Essentially, without donor funding and technical assistance, activities and operations would cease. The dependency on donor funding has had two negative consequences. First, NGOs have had to, for the most part, follow the agendas of the donors, regardless of whether these agendas actually respond to the priorities of the local population. For example, NGOs working on human rights generally tend to focus on civil and political rights to an almost total exclusion of economic, social, and cultural rights. Second, the NGOs have had difficulties generating local constituencies. Since the principal funding is from the donors, accountability is to these same donors. This dynamic is not lost on local communities who, consequently, do not feel a sense of ownership with regard to the projects, even when they are the beneficiaries. While some organizations are attempting to break the cycle of dependency, the relative youth of many of the organizations and the absence of indigenous donors makes this difficult.

In the past, the relationships between the Ugandan human rights NGOs and the international human rights NGOs have also served to further detach local NGOs from the communities they intend to serve. The international human rights NGOs tend to use their wealth of experience and better access to vast resources to prescribe an agenda that often does not reflect the needs of the community they claim to serve. This is slowly changing, however, as the international NGOs recognize the critical role played by the local NGOs in protecting and promoting human rights and are attempting to develop the capacities of these local NGOs to better respond to the needs of their communities.

Despite these challenges, the future prospects for local human rights NGOs in Uganda are good. There is more collaboration and cooperation between NGOs both within the cities and between regions. Local NGOs include Action for Development (ACFODE) which focuses on the empowerment of women, the Slum Aid Project that addresses social/health issues, and DENIVA, a national umbrella organization that works to increase exchange of information among NGOs. The ability of these and other organizations to protect human rights in a manner that is responsive to the needs of a local constituency, however, could be severely stunted unless real measures are taken to address the problem of donor funding. Local NGOs are currently more responsive to the needs of their donors than those local communities. When local NGOs become more dependent on local funding, they will become more accountable to these local communities.

Conclusions and Recommendations

Conclusions

There has been a manifold improvement in the human rights performance of Uganda in the last decade. This improvement does not mean, however, that the human rights record today is perfect. Human rights violations still abound, and these violations must either be prevented or investigated with the purpose of providing redress to the victims. This chapter has been concerned with and explored the possibilities of the *legal* protection of human rights in Uganda.

As stated at the beginning of this chapter, the choice and focus on the legal approach was not meant to suggest this was the best or the only means of protecting and promoting human rights. Indeed, as long as human rights abuses continue, there is a need for diverse and multidisciplinary strategies to address the situation. Nevertheless, in the wake of the growing trend on the African continent to develop new constitutions, an understanding of the possibilities of protecting human rights under these new constitutions is particularly appropriate and timely.

The analysis of Uganda's 1995 constitution reveals that, notwithstanding a few shortcomings, the constitutional and legal framework essentially provides for the legal vindication of human rights against violations. The constitution has a fairly comprehensive bill of rights, it mandates the courts to provide redress in the event of violations, and it allows organizations or individuals to sue on behalf of victims. The ratification by Uganda of many of the international human rights instruments and the requirement that customary law be applied only when it conforms to principles of fairness and justice lend further credence to the idea that the legal framework, at face value, provides an effective avenue for the protection and promotion of human rights. At least in this sense, the prospects for the *legal* protection of human rights in Uganda are good.

The constitutional and legal framework, however, operates within a context. To date, unfortunately, the current political, social, and economic context has prevented the potential benefits and opportunities from being realized. For example, because judges have been reluctant to use international human rights norms in their decisions, the potential benefit of using such standards to bolster national legislation has been lost. Moreover, because the executive has sought to interfere in matters affecting the judiciary, judges have failed to take advantage of the provisions protecting the independence of the judiciary in the constitution. Because of cultural values subordinating women, women have been unable to avail themselves of the provisions in the constitution providing for equality. We could give even more examples, but the essential message is that often the value provided by the constitutional and legal framework is minimized when this framework is put into its context. This means that any strategy to deploy the law in the vindication of human rights must take advantage of the opportunities offered by the constitutional framework and develop means to address the challenges that arise, given the context in which the law operates.

Having said this, the following recommendations have been designed to do essentially what has been prescribed: capitalize on the positive elements of the constitutional framework while addressing to the extent possible the challenges.

Recommendations

This section attempts to include only those recommendations that are practical and attainable. Accordingly, many problems that have been cited in this chapter have not been addressed. The hope, however, is that by starting to work on the smaller, tangible issues that can feasibly be addressed, eventually the capacity to manage the larger issues will be increased and/or the negative impact of these larger issues will be diminished.

Strengthen the Capacity for Legal Protection of Human Rights

The capacity of local NGOs to conduct public interest litigation should be strengthened. The more these NGOs are able to mount credible, well-prepared cases, the harder it will be for the government to credibly label them as subversive. Other African human rights NGOs which have had experience in public interest litigation and international human rights NGOs could assist local human rights networks in improving the methods and means to conduct public interest litigation.

Development organizations need to be trained to see their work within a human rights framework. Many development organizations in Uganda have yet to perceive the basic needs they provide through a human rights framework. Although the Constitution of Uganda guarantees economic, social, and cultural rights, NGOs are still not adopting a human rights approach to these entitlements. If these organizations could begin to see these needs as rights, they would be better able to avail themselves of the powerful tool of the law in securing these rights. Through networking with the general human rights NGOs, these development organizations can encourage the human rights organizations to move past the traditional civil and political rights agenda into economic and social rights that are at times more relevant to the communities they all claim to serve. The human rights networks together with the Uganda Human Rights Commission, which was set up in November 1996 and is fully functioning, could provide the necessary training.

The LC courts should be provided with basic human rights training. A majority of Ugandans are not comfortable with using the constitutionally established court system and prefer instead to use the LC courts. For a number of reasons, these attitudes will not change overnight. Consequently, as long as the LC courts are going to be used by a significant portion of the population, they should be provided with basic human rights training, particularly with respect to the human rights of women. Many might not even be aware of what rights are protected in the constitution and the international human rights treaties to which Uganda is a signatory. With this sort of training, the LC courts will be encouraged to incorporate these human rights norms in their decisions, thereby diminishing the chances that they will issue judgments that clearly violate rights protected in the constitution. The training can be conducted by local human rights NGOs working in conjunction with the Ministry of Local Government, the Judiciary and district authorities.

Judges and magistrates in the traditional courts should be provided with human rights training. Often judges and magistrates are reluctant to use human rights norms because they are not familiar with them or do not fully understand their scope. There is thus a need to familiarize both the judges and the magistrates with the human rights provisions in the constitution and the international human rights instruments to which Uganda is a signatory. Human rights NGOs should work with the Judicial Training Committee to ensure that this training is provided.

Increase the Effectiveness of and Access to the Legal System
by All Sections of the Population

Initiatives should address the barriers to women's access to the legal system and the discrimination embedded in the justice system and legal traditions. As in many other countries on the African continent, women constitute the majority of the victims of human rights violations. In Uganda, women are subject to violence or the threat thereof, they are effectively denied the right to own land, the right to participate in the decisions affecting their lives, and, in the case girls, the right to formal education. The legal system, however, has failed miserably in addressing these violations. Cultural values discouraging women from using the legal system, discriminatory laws, and attitudes in the legal system all contribute to this injustice. Uganda must, therefore, create an initiative to understand and address the issue of women and the justice system. This initiative must not only seek to fully understand cultural attitudes and how they affect women's use of the legal system to vindicate their rights, but should also take concrete measures to address the identified issues. This initiative should be a collaborative effort between human rights NGOs and the Ministry of Gender and Community Development, which is concerned with improving the welfare of women, youth, and the disabled.

The government should give substantial funds to legal aid providers in order to increase the access to the legal system for persons who cannot afford lawyers' fees. Given the level of poverty in Uganda, many individuals cannot afford the cost of having a lawyer. This is a serious barrier to their access to the legal system. The current legal aid providers, however, are overwhelmed by the number of clients they have to serve on a limited budget. The government should, therefore, provide funding to existing legal aid providers to enable them to better serve the increasing number of persons requiring such aid.

Lawyers and human rights organizations should use more participatory methods in handling human rights cases. All over the world, the tendency is for lawyers to act like they are the sole repository of knowledge and wisdom. Because they possess technical knowledge not possessed by most people, it is understandable that lawyers should develop such an attitude. However, such an attitude disempowers clients and alienates them further from the justice system. While it is not suggested that lawyers give their clients a thorough training in all the intricacies of the law, a concerted effort should be made to ensure that clients are given all the necessary information to make informed decisions regarding their rights and are briefed on the consequences of their actions at all times. Similarly, there should be a commitment to avoid using clients as a means for publicity or legal victory. Rather, the clients and their rights should at all times be a priority.

Sharing Information and Networking

Human rights decisions from other common law jurisdictions, particularly from elsewhere in Africa, should be widely circulated. The failure to cite relevant human rights decisions from other common law jurisdictions to fill gaps in national law and jurisprudence can partly be attributed to ignorance about these judgments on the part of the judiciary, the lawyers litigating the cases, and the human rights NGOs. Mechanisms to widely distribute publications on human rights cases in a cost-effective manner, such as those compiled by the International Centre for the Legal Protection of Human Rights (Interights), based in London, should be devised. Access to these cases would enable judges, magistrates, lawyers, and human rights NGOs to better understand the scope of the rights and the manner in which their protection can be articulated and could ultimately be used as support for decisions protecting human rights. This should in turn be used to create a similar database of human rights cases decided in Uganda to be shared with other countries.

Networking between lawyers on human rights issues should be encouraged. Through the work of various law societies, networking in the East African region has been quite good. Networking on human rights issues, however, needs to be increased. Since lawyers in Uganda have not necessarily been in the forefront of the human rights struggle, they could learn a lot from lawyers from other African countries who have been more active. Such networking should involve the sharing of experiences and methods in which challenges were faced and overcome.

Networking to provide mutual protection needs to be encouraged. Since one of the reasons for the reluctance to conduct litigation on sensitive human rights issues is the possible negative response from the authorities, systems need to be put in place whereby members of the human rights community in Uganda and the region can support each other in any eventuality. Often such support only comes from northern human rights NGOs; it would help, however, to also have support from similarly situated human rights NGOs on the continent.

Litigation and Alternative Means of Seeking Remedies

Human rights NGOs should conduct more public interest litigation. Though some concrete steps have been taken to change this situation (for example, the legal resources project of the Foundation for Human Rights Initiative, of which one of the authors is director), currently none of the Ugandan human rights organizations are conducting public interest litigation on constitutional rights. There is, however, a dire need for public interest litigation on carefully chosen issues affecting the rights of people at the grassroots level. Thus far, the few cases that have been brought before the Constitutional Court to date, have been brought by powerful elites, who are seeking through the courts to protect their own interests. This confirms the perception among the general population that the judicial system is there only to serve the interests of the well-off and political elite. In order to restore the population's faith in the judicial system, therefore, it is important that the system is also used to protect their rights. While litigation through legal aid serves this purpose to a limited extent, it does not often have the impact that public interest litigation would have.

The Uganda Human Rights Commission should be used when redress or remedies are needed quickly. The delay in obtaining redress from the traditional court systems can be critical in preventing some victims from using the legal system. In these instances, the Human Rights Commission, which has the power to investigate, order the release of a detainee, or provide a remedy when a violation has occurred, should be used. In this manner, the law is still being used to vindicate the right, but the forum is different.

The Independence of the Judiciary

The human rights community should actively monitor the independence of the judiciary and take a stand when it is threatened. The perception that the judiciary is not independent has led to cynicism about the judicial system. This cynicism has, in turn, been detrimental to judicial independence, because the few judges who have stood up to executive pressure and interference have not been given the necessary support from the community. This support, especially from the human rights community, could work to prevent further executive interference, as the executive becomes aware that people are watching and are willing to take a stand on the issue. This is particularly true under the current government, because it works hard to maintain a good public image and to distinguish itself from its predecessors.

Legislative Advocacy

All discriminatory laws and statutes that violate the human rights provisions of the constitution should be eliminated. Though the constitution provides that all statutes that contravene its provisions should be declared null and void, these statutes remain on the law books and they still continue to be used by judges and magistrates. This seriously undermines the human rights protections offered by the constitution and should, therefore, be addressed by legislative advocacy.

The human rights community should lobby Parliament to develop legislation for the prosecution of crimes against humanity and grave breaches of humanitarian law. The failure to prosecute all those found guilty of committing atrocities by the omission of inquiry into human rights violations of the 1970s and 1980s has seriously undermined Ugandans' belief that those who commit such horror against them will be brought to justice. Prosecution of those who masterminded and willingly committed the atrocities in the north under legislation for grave breaches of humanitarian law rather than under the broad umbrella of treason would be an important recognition of the horrors committed against the civilian population, rather than simply an acknowledgment of their stand against the government.[42] Ugandans must, more than most, recognize the importance of human rights. They have been tortured, raped, beaten, and brutally murdered. The population cannot but appreciate the respect for human rights and the rule of law. One could not ask for a better environment in which to struggle for the legal protection of human rights. Nevertheless, the people of Uganda are cynical. They want to see some results before they believe the current constitutional order and that the legal system that upholds it can actually protect their rights. Herein lies the challenge which we have no choice but to overcome, because the cost, as Ugandans know only too well, might be too high.

Notes

1. Uganda Constitutional Commission, *The Report of the Constitutional Commission: Analysis and Recommendations* (Kampala: Constitutional Commission, 1993), p. 51.

2. J. Tumusiime, *Uganda Thirty Years, 1962–1992* (Kampala: Fountain Publishers, 1993), p. 35. The General Service Unit and Special Force was a paramilitary force outside the legally established security apparatus created to spy on those organizations of state and people thought to be antiestablishment.

3. Ibid.

4. Phares Mutibwa, *Uganda Since Independence* (Kampala: Fountain Publishers, 1992), p. 98.

5. United Nations Development Program (UNDP), *Uganda: A Human Development Report 1997* (Kampala: UNDP, 1997), p.1.

6. See Bonnie Keller, *Uganda: Country Gender Profile* (Stockholm: Swedish International Development Cooperation, 1996); J. B. Mugaju, *An Analytical Review of Uganda's Decade of Reforms: 1986–1996* (Kampala: Fountain Publishers, 1996).

7. Keller, *Uganda: Country Gender Profile*, p. 49.

8. Ibid.

9. *Uganda Debt Network Newsletter*, March 16, 1998, p. 5.

10. See *Uganda Constitutional Commission Report.*

11. Ibid., p. 1.

12. Muhammad Haleem, "The Domestic Application of International Human Rights Norms," in *Developing Human Rights Jurisprudence* (London: Commonwealth Secretariat, 1988), p. 101.

13. *R. v. Home Secretary ex parte Brind*, 1 AC 696, 726 (1991), cited in G. P. Tumwine-Mukubwa, "International Human Rights Norms in the Domestic Arena," *East African Journal of Peace and Human Rights* 3 (1996), pp. 39–40.

14. Article 50(1) of the 1995 constitution provides that, "Any person, who claims that a fundamental or other right or freedom guaranteed under this Constitution has been infringed or threatened, is entitled to apply to a competent court for redress which may include compensation."

15. M. D. Kirby, "The Role of the Judge in Advancing Human Rights by Reference to International Human Rights Norms," 62 *Australian Law Journal* 514 (1988).

16. Steven R. Ratner and Jason S. Abrams, *Accountability for Human Rights Atrocities in International Law* (Oxford: Clarendon Press, 1997), pp. 45–67.

17. This is because, under the current legal framework, the constitution is the supreme law of the land followed by statutory law and common law principles and then by customary law. See Article 2(1) of the 1995 Constitution and Section 3(2) of the Judicature Act (II) of 1967.

18. B. J. Odoki, *An Introduction to Judicial Conduct and Practice*, 3rd ed. (Kampala: Law Development Centre, 1990), pp. 149–50.

19. Adama Dieng, "The Independence of the Judiciary and Rule of Law," in *The Judiciary in Transition*, vol. 3, ed. Mona Rishmawi (Geneva: Centre for the Independence of Judges and Lawyers, 1994), p. 53.

20. Joe Oloka-Onyango. "Judicial Power and Constitutionalism in Uganda." In *Uganda, Studies in Living Conditions, Popular Movements and Constitutionalism*, ed. Mahmood Mamdani and Joe Oloka-Onyango (Vienna: JEP Book Series, 1994), p. 502.

21. Article 144(4) of the 1995 Constitution. Both members of the cabinet and the Judicial Service Commission are appointed by the president subject to the approval of Parliament. See Articles 113 (1) and 146(2) of the 1995 constitution.

22. Oloka-Onyango, "Judicial Power," p. 502.

23. Ibid.

24. See the example provided in Oloka-Onyango, "Judicial Power," 503, of the case in the United States concerning President Nixon's refusal to hand over the Watergate tapes. In *U.S. v. Nixon*, the Supreme Court ordered him to do so stating, "Neither the doctrine of separation of powers nor the need for confidentiality of high level communication, without more, can sustain an absolute, unqualified, presidential privilege of immunity from judicial process under all circumstances."

25. This statement does not apply to the female members of the legal community who have been at the forefront of the struggle for women's human rights through the very active and dynamic Ugandan Chapter of the International Federation of Women Lawyers (FIDA).

26. Oloka-Onyango, "Judicial Power," pp. 482–493.

27. *Uganda v. Commissioner of Prisons, ex parte Matovu* (1966) EA 514 at 540.

28. Oloka-Onyango, "Judicial Power," p 483.

29. Ibid., p. 489.

30. "Truth from Below," *Censorship Report*, London, Article 19, October 1991, pp. 63–64. Section 51 of the Penal Code provides that: "Any person who without such justification as would suffice in the case of defamation of a private person, publishes anything intended to be read, or any sign or visible representation tending to degrade, revile or expose to hatred or contempt any foreign prince, potentate, ambassador or other foreign dignitary with intent to disturb peace and friendship between Uganda and the country to which such prince, potentate, ambassador or dignitary belongs, is guilty of a misdemeanor."

31. The magistrate brought in specifically to hear the case denied Abdi Hassan bail on the grounds that Abdi was of Somali origin and because, living in a rented accommodation, he lacked a permanent place of abode. See Oloka-Onyango, "Judicial Power," p. 495.

32. See *Attacks on Justice—The Harassment and Persecution of Judges and Lawyers* (*June 1990–May 1991*) (Geneva: Centre for the Independence of Judges and Lawyers of the International Commission of Jurists, 1991), p. 123.

33. Joe Oloka-Onyango, "Kanaabi: Freedom on Trial," *New Vision,* December 27, 1995, p. 11.

34. *Uganda v. Haruna Kanaabi*, Criminal Case No. U977/95, 12.

35. Ibid.

36. It is true that the legislature has the duty to amend the law, but in a country where the executive determines the trend of events and has the discretion to propose legislation, which we argue is the case in Uganda, it would be reasonable to conclude that the matter is in effect left to the executive in this case.

37. UNDP, *Human Development Report,* p. 4.

38. Ibid.

39. See, for example, *Wakanyira v. Wakanyira,* Divorce Cause No. 31 of 1995, in which the magistrate applied section 5 of the Divorce Act, chapter 215, stating that a man seeking divorce on the basis of adultery need only prove this ground to obtain the divorce, whereas a woman seeking a divorce on the basis of adultery must prove the adultery and another ground, such as cruelty or desertion.

40. John-Jean Barya and Joe Oloka-Onyango. *Popular Justice and Resistance Committee Courts in Uganda* (Kampala: New Vision, 1994), p. 8.

41. Ibid., p. 7.

42. Ibid.

43. This is not so much the case for grassroots CBOs, who have smaller operations that can be financed locally.

44. We say "willingly committed" because all too often those arrested in the northern conflict and held for treason are children who were abducted and forced to fight as rebels. The irony is that when these children risk death by surrendering to the government forces they stand a chance of being labeled abductees and not being prosecuted. But, if they do not surrender and are captured, then they are called rebels, regardless of whether they in fact consented to fight in the war.

Contributors

Abdullahi A. An-Naʿim is Charles Howard Candler Professor of Law at Emory Law School, Atlanta.

Meaza Ashenafi is executive director, Ethiopian Women Lawyers Association (EWLA), Addis Ababa, Ethiopia.

Taaka Awori is assistant social development adviser, British Department for International Development (DFID), Kampala, Uganda.

Nana K. A. Busia, Jr., is director of West Africa Programs, International Alert, London.

Bibiane Mbaye Gahamanyi is program officer (in charge of civil society and policy advocacy in the framework of ACP-EU Cooperation), Enda Tiers Monde, Dakar, Senegal.

Siddig Hussein is assistant law professor, Faculty of Law, University of Khartoum, Sudan.

Ibrahima Kane is legal officer for Africa, Interights, London.

Luis Mondlane is associate member of the Centro de Estudos Africanos, Universidade Eduardo Mondlane (Center for African Studies), Maputo, Mozambique.

Abdelaziz Nouaydi is professor of international law and constitutional law, University Mohamed V, Rabat, founding member of Moroccan Human Rights Organization, and currently adviser to the Prime Minister of Morocco.

Chinonye Edmund Obiagwu is national coordinator for the Legal Defense and Assistance Project (LEDAP), Lagos, Nigeria.

Chidi Anselm Odinkalu is senior legal officer for Africa, Liberty and Security, for Interights, London.

Lucrecia Seafield is program officer for the European Union Foundation for Human Rights in South Africa, Pretoria.

Livingstone Sewanyana is executive director, Foundation for Human Rights Initiative (FHRI), Kampala, Uganda.

Index